Praise for Allan Fergus

"*Golf in Scotland* is an excellent guide to the Scottish links, their hills, and many other amenities of the Scottish game."— **Michael Murphy**, author of *Golf in the Kingdom* and *The Kingdom of Shivas Irons*

"Allan Ferguson has paved the way . . . . Take an iron or two out of your bag and carry this book instead."—**Michael Bamberger**, author of *To the Linksland*

"If you're inclined to travel to . . . Scottish courses, your best guide is Allan McAllister Ferguson's *Golf in Scotland*."—**Lorne Rubenstein**, Toronto *Globe and Mail*, author of *A Season in Dornoch*

"Laced with history and local lore as well as the nitty-gritty of modern golf travel, *Golf in Scotland* may prove an indispensable guide for the wise golf traveler."—**James Dodson**, author of *The Dewsweepers, Final Rounds*, and *A Golfer's Life*

"Allan Ferguson has written such an extraordinarily useful guide to golf in Scotland that I wish he would tackle other areas too: plumbing, tax planning, car repair, holiday decorating, anything."— **David Owen**, author of *My Usual Game*

"Valuable insider information . . . the book gives the skinny on planning a trip to the Auld Sod."—***Golf Magazine***

"The best inside track on how to do golf in Scotland." —**Michael Tobert**, author of *Pilgrims in the Rough: St. Andrews Beyond the 19th Hole*

"Two essentials for your golf holiday in Scotland—a knockdown shot into the wind and Allan Ferguson's book, *Golf in Scotland*. The best and most comprehensive guide available."—**Graeme Lennie**, *Head Professional, Crail Golfing Society, Fife, Scotland*

"There's simply no substitute for 'on-the-ground' knowledge and, when it comes to golf trips to Scotland—in knowing where to play, where to stay, and how much you ought to pay—there's no substitute for Allan Ferguson's *Golf in Scotland*."
—**Curtis Gillespie**, author *of Playing Through: A Year of Life and Links Along the Scottish Coast*

"A must for those headed for the old country."
—**Tom Kensler**, The Denver *Post*

"Allan McAllister Ferguson won't make many friends in the tour guide industry . . . but he'll compensate for that with a big boost in popularity with the individual traveler."—**Jeff Barr**, *Golfweek*

"*Golf in Scotland* has to be THE guide for visitors to the Home of Golf."
—**Donald Ford**, author of *A Photographic Celebration of The Open Championship Venues, 1860-2010*

And the Travelers Write

"Allan is the Rick Steves of Scottish golf."—**Doug Cruce**, Williamston MI

"We just returned from Scotland. The information and advice provided in *Golf in Scotland* was a great help and made the planning almost as enjoyable as the actual trip."—**Bob Patterson**, Kingwood TX

"I read your book from cover to cover several times. All the tips and recommendations you made were on target."
—**Bradford Hathaway**, Newburyport MA

"I have made twenty trips to Scotland over the past fifteen years and I found your book to be absolutely the most informative book on the subject."—**Dennis Tosh**, Oxford MS

"Kudos to your book, which convinced me I could go it alone in the planning process."—**Roger Thornton**, Simpsonville SC

"My son and I just returned from our golf trip to Scotland and it was GREAT! Your book was priceless. Everything went exactly as you said it would."
—**Todd Early**, Acworth GA

"A note of thanks for your outstanding book . . . . Was able to book eight players on both St. Andrews and Muirfield with your advice."—**Josh Weller**, Greenland NH

"Just returned from a 12-day trip to Scotland arranged completely through your book and cannot thank you enough. My golfing buddy and I had the time of our lives." —**Stephen Friend,** Redondo Beach CA

"Allow us to get in line to sing your praises. We stumbled upon your book as we started to plan a trip to Scotland for our 50th birthdays. We easily saved over $2,000 each. " —**David Heim,** Chesapeake VA, and **Tim Hogan,** Orlando FL

"Your advice was invaluable and your course descriptions were uncannily accurate. Thanks to you I ended up looking like a genius." —**David Wells,** Big Canoe GA

"You are awesome. This book is going to make my second trip to Scotland more likely and more affordable."—**Bob Dammon**, Sewickley PA

"*Golf in Scotland* saved us a great deal of time, money, and aggravation. We truly can't thank you enough."—**Jennifer Gordon**, Vancouver BC, Canada

"Your tip about Open competitions was a true gem. I've since told my friends about it and they can't believe it."
—**Ward Thomas**, W Boylston MA

"Thanks for writing your book and sharing your wisdom."
—**Joe Burns**, Easton MD

GOLF IN SCOTLAND:

A Travel-Planning Guide

with

Profiles of 74 Great Courses

by

Allan McAllister Ferguson

Fourth Edition

WFPublishing
a division of WF Enterprises, Inc.
Denver • Colorado

First edition June 2001
First edition, second printing February 2002
Second edition April 2003
Third edition July 2005
Revised third edition January 2009
Fourth edition February 2012

Published by:
WFPublishing
a division of WF Enterprises, Inc.
1743 S. Marion St.
Denver CO 80210 USA
303-722-3441; 800-835-6692 (toll free in USA)
fax: 303-722-3441
Email: aferguson@fergusongolf.com
Web: http://www.fergusongolf.com

Library of Congress Control Number 2012900534

Cover photograph by Donald Ford - 18th hole, Carnoustie
Cover design by NZGraphics; graphics by Rust Graphics and VANGO Graphics
Photographs in text by Allan Ferguson and Rick Nedell
Index by Lisa Rosenburg
Printed in the USA by Sheridan Books

ISBN 978-0-9710326-4-4

Dedicated to the memory of Kenn Rust,
who was not able to see this project through to completion.

Allan McAllister Ferguson
President, Ferguson Golf
Denver CO USA
February 2012

TABLE OF CONTENTS

Preface to the Fourth Edition

THIS BOOK STEMS FROM my work as a travel planner. That includes the accumulated experience from some twenty trips I've made to Scotland since 1998 and from trips made by clients of Ferguson Golf.

The premise here is simple: *Most first-time golf travelers to Scotland need a helping hand; they don't need to have their hands held.* If you picked up this book because the title intrigued you, you are already halfway toward booking your trip directly and saving hundreds, even thousands, of dollars. With this book you truly can do it yourself without doing it alone.

Getting to Scotland is easy. The challenges come at the end of the plane ride. This is not just a book about Scottish golf. It's a book about *smart traveling* and, specifically, how to plan a trip on your own and thus avoid the overpriced package tours sold by tour operators. It's a book about how to get comfortable with the idea of doing it on your own and, consequently, not only saving a lot of money, but having a superior trip as well. *Golf in Scotland* is pitched at the North American market, but golfers everywhere, even in the UK, can benefit from the my perspective and attention to detail.

Organization of the book

In the "Prologue," I make and rest my case for avoiding the tour operators. In truth, this is the heart of the book. If you accept my premise that you don't need a tour operator, then you can read on with an open mind. Honestly, with this book, a computer, and a telephone, there is no reason to even consider using a tour operator. Why? Because there are no good deals among the package tours to Scotland.

In Part I, I have tried to bring all the crucial issues that most people face up to the front of the book. We start with Frequently-Asked-Questions (FAQs) followed by chapters on "Key Issues and Decisions," "When to Go," and "Where to Go." Together, these chapters serve as a rough guide to the rest of the book.

Part II takes up the nitty-gritty of trip planning. Chapter One deals with the four elements common to every golf trip: *air travel, vehicle rental, tee times,* and *lodging.* Careful study of this chapter will pay big dividends. Chapter Two is devoted to St. Andrews and the Old Course simply because, "Everyone Wants to Go—and Why Not?". Featured here are eight ways to get a tee time on the Old Course. Chapter Three is loaded with travel tips and more information to smooth and enrich your journey.

In Part III we come to the critical detail—the main course, if you will, or rather *seventy-four courses,* fully described and profiled so that any golfer can write, send a fax, call, or email to get a tee time. Everything you need to know is here: *addresses - phone numbers - websites - key contacts - visitor policies - prices and deposit requirements.*

I want to direct your special attention to page 146 where you will find an index listing all the courses in this book in price order, from most expensive to least expensive. Predictable courses everyone knows hug the high rungs of the list. Looking farther along the list—from Blairgowrie on down—a full forty of the seventy-four courses described here peg their green fees at £60 or less (under $100). For those who want to make a golf trip to Scotland but who cannot afford to shell out $2,000 to $3,000 on green fees, I urge you to work off the bottom of the list among those under £60. When you do that, not only will you spend less than $1,000 on golf for a seven to ten-day trip but, trust me, you will have a more "down home" experience, you'll meet more Scots, and, in the end, you will have as good a trip as those partaking of the high-priced spreads.

Along with the objective data in "The Directory of Courses," you'll find my subjective evaluations of the courses. This is where I try to answer the question, "Why should I want to play this course?". It is also where you'll find my recommendations on lodging, food, and nongolf attractions in and around the major golf venues. Photos, graphics, sidebars, and travel tips dot "The Directory of Courses" and other sections as well.

Appendices include a list of useful internet sites (now more than 200) and a bibliography. Together, these can help you learn more about Scotland and Scottish golf—a rewarding journey for all who love golf and the land of its origin.

Even with all the information between these covers, if you still think you'd like to engage a travel planner, you can learn more about how I work by visiting my website ***www.fergusongolf.com***. Whether through this book or in person, I want you to experience a golf trip to Scotland that is *more fun, more rewarding*, and *less expensive* than anything offered in a pre-packaged tour.

Yours for great golf (and travel) in Scotland,

Allan McAllister Ferguson
President, Ferguson Golf
Denver CO USA
February 2012

Prices and the Exchange Rate

All prices are current to either 2011 or 2012. Throughout, I have used an exchange rate of £1 = $1.75. Based on recent history, this could lead to overestimating costs by a modest amount. That's ok. Better to be high than low.

Notes on exchange-rate history and the cost of golf in Scotland

For several years, between 2006-08, golfers were groaning under the weight of an exchange rate averaging £1 = $1.90. Then, with international economic upheaval unleashed in 2008, came a "flight to the dollar." During 2008, the dollar strengthened (or the pound crashed) from £1 =$1.97 to £1 = $1.48. Voila! Rather suddenly a trip to the Home of Golf was discounted by about twenty-five percent. In other words, the economy may have been bad in the USA, but things looked a lot worse in the UK and Europe.

Over the past three years, 2009-11, the dust has settled a bit and the exchange rate has fairly steadily averaged £1 = $1.60, a close approximation of where it stood in the early years of the first decade. Thus, I have struck upon £1 = $1.75 as a mean number between the prevailing averages of those years, 2006-11, and a pretty good number for an even longer period.

Regarding the high cost of golf in Scotland, the real culprit—apart from overpriced tours and short-sighted golf course committees—is *inflation* in the travel sector of the economy. High oil prices have pushed up air and petrol prices. Lodging rates have increased. And food prices have gone through the roof in the UK. Why it costs twice as much to brew a cup of coffee or a glass of beer in the UK as opposed to the USA or just about any other place in the world, I have yet to figure out.

Telephone/Fax Calling Procedures

All UK telephone and fax numbers in this book are formatted this way: 01334-466-666 (main telephone number for the St. Andrews Links Management). To call that number, do this:

From the United States: Dial 011 (international long distance), then 44 (country code), then the number in Scotland without the leading "0" (i.e., 011-44-1334-466-666).

In Scotland: Use the leading "0" and dial the rest of the number from anywhere in the country (i.e., 01334-466-666). For a local call, use the last six digits.

PROLOGUE:

NOW MORE THAN EVER—AVOID THE TOURS!

OVER THE PAST DECADE, one important change in golf travel has occurred: With the full flowering of the internet and the development of reviewing sites like ***www.TripAdvisor.com***, now, more than ever, it's not just advisable to avoid the tours—it's easy.

Virtually all courses have their own websites and many feature online booking. Most quality lodgings have their own websites. Marketing associations promoting quality lodging abound. Everyone uses email, so you don't even need a phone if you don't want to make international telephone calls. In short, ***any golfer with (1) a little time, (2) a computer or a telephone, and (3) this book can plan a great golf trip to Scotland and save hundreds or thousands of dollars by avoiding the tour operators.***

No doubt, there may be some good deals in the golf travel industry to some places in the world, but, when it comes to Scotland, good deals in package tours simply do not exist. Here's the truth and the most important concept for you to absorb from this book: *Tour operators typically mark up Scottish golf trips by fifty percent to more than one hundred percent from retail.* I tell you this from the perspective of more than ten years of trip planning and analysis of dozens of "package tours" offered by operators in the industry.

Deception is the daily bread of tour operators. They practice deception in two ways: (1) they imply that their "buying power" allows them to deliver travel services to you, the customer, at wholesale prices; and (2) they imply that you will benefit immeasurably from their "local knowledge" or "expertise." Not to put too fine a point on it, that is pure malarkey.

Generally, tour operators are buying services at retail and re-selling them to travelers for as much as *two times retail*. The truth is (1) with few exceptions, golf courses in Scotland don't give significant discounts; (2) rental car agencies in Scotland don't give significant discounts; and (3) only the most expensive hotels (e.g., Turnberry, Gleneagles, the Old Course Hotel, Fairmont St. Andrews) extend discounts or pay commissions to tour operators (note the incentive to put customers in the most expensive hotels).

As for "expertise," this is either inconsequential or highly overrated. Going to Scotland is not exactly like making a trek to a third-world country. The paths are well-worn. Itineraries are available on the internet. For advice, lodging hosts are as good or better than tour operators. Basically, there are no wrong answers. In other words, it doesn't make much difference whether you stay at the Castlemount B & B, the Dunvegan Hotel, or Rusacks in St. Andrews; at Sandhill B & B, the South Beach Hotel, or the Marine in Troon. You're going to have a good experience at any of these places and they are all within a quarter-mile of a championship golf course. The only important difference is price and that is easily determined with a few phone calls or a simple internet search. No—what you are really buying from a tour operator is an expensive bag tag, an even more expensive advertisement in a slick golf publication, and a retired guy in a green coat to meet you at the airport.

Going to Scotland is not exactly like making a trek to a third-world country. The paths are well-worn.

My mission is to help golfers traveling to Scotland get value for their hard-earned money and, more important, have a memorable, human experience. If the tour operators don't like me, that's ok. Ideally, I want you to return home with the feeling that you discovered Scotland, Scottish golf, and the Scottish people—not just the "rota courses," a few expensive hotels, and the concierges. Ideally, I want you to return to Scotland as soon as possible and, to achieve that, I want to show you how to make *two trips for the price most people pay for one trip.*

The purpose of this book is to give you, the golfer, all the information you need to plan a good trip at any price level. I am not opposed to someone spending a bundle of money if that's what they want to do. I have my point of view—skewed to the middle-of-the road in terms of price and toward Scotland's by-ways and golf courses off the beaten path. But all the information is here, whether the trip orientation is budget, middle-of-the-road, or high-end; "rota" or "hidden gem."

Regardless of your budget, if I can show you that buying a package tour from an operator is the worst possible way to go, then you would be open to other possibilities—correct? Then let's begin.

Benchmark costs for your trip

First, let's establish benchmark costs for your trip so that you can easily assess the real cost of a tour offering. Following are *per-person* costs circa 2011-12 for a group of four golfers on a fairly typical, moderately-priced, seven-night/six-course itinerary. For longer trips, take the daily average and multiply times the appropriate number of days.

Transportation - If you rent a vehicle from the right place (see Part II, Chapter One), you will pay about **$240** for a minibus with automatic transmission.

Lodging - Just about everywhere in Scotland, £45 to £55 ($75 to $95) will buy you a good night's sleep *and* breakfast at a three-star hotel or a four-star

B & B. In St. Andrews you'll pay more for a hotel but not necessarily for a B & B or guest house. Assuming the upper end of this range, budget **$675** for lodging. It could be less. Obviously, it could be a lot more, but then we wouldn't be dealing with a moderately-priced trip.

Golf - Assume a mix of expensive and mid-priced courses: *Prestwick* and *Western Gailes* in Ayrshire; *North Berwick West Links* and *Gullane #1* in East Lothian; and *St. Andrews' New Course* and *Kingsbarns* in Fife. Cost: **$1,230.** If you were to play St. Andrews' Old Course, that would add about $260 not included in this calculation.

TOTAL = $2,145 ÷ 7 days = $306 per day

If you see a "budget" or "moderate" trip similar to this priced between $3,000 and $3,500 ($425 to $525 per day), you will know that the margin built into the trip is about $900 to $1,400 *per golfer*—or a gross profit of $3,600 to $5,600 for four golfers. It's no wonder there's such a glut of tour operators! That kind of profit is hard to resist.

Following are descriptions of two trips that came to me in 2010 for travel in 2011 *after* the golfers had received proposals from major tour operators (who, kindly, shall go un-named). Keep in mind, every package is comprised of three elements: green fees, lodging, and transportation.

CASE STUDY #1 - This proposal came from a company that was selling a "guaranteed tee time" on St. Andrews' Old Course on behalf of a guest house that had been granted that time by the Links Trust management. In other words, the tour operator had purchased the tee time from the guest house at a premium (with the guarantee of a minimum stay of three or more nights), added another premium for Old Course play, then went looking for a buyer (read about this method of getting on the Old Course on page 108). Here was the proposal:

- *seven nights lodging* - double occupancy for four nights in St. Andrews in a 3-star guest house and three nights in Troon in a 3-star hotel
- *six rounds of golf* (St. Andrews Old and Jubilee, Carnoustie, Turnberry Ailsa, Royal Troon Old and Portland)
- *self-drive minibus* with automatic transmission

For this package, the quote was **$4,595 for the golfers** and **$1,550 for the nongolfer** (this trip included a nongolfing spouse).

If one were to book all the elements of this trip directly, including an advance reservation on St. Andrews' Old Course, the **real cost of this trip would be about $1,800.** Thus, the premium and profit extracted from the unsuspecting buyer on this trip would be about $2,800 *per golfer*; and the hapless nongolfer would be paying $1,550 for seven nights' lodging and her share of a minibus—all of which could be booked directly for about $790.

Admittedly, a premium is in here for Old Course play. So, how much is that worth? I did this trip, including my planning fee and *three additional top-drawer courses* (Kingsbarns, Western Gailes, and Prestwick) for **$2,740 for the golfers** and **$988 for the nongolfer**. And, yes, that included a "guaranteed tee time" on St. Andrews' Old Course. How did I do that?

- First, I applied for and received a "trade time" through the Old Course Experience for play on the Old Course and St. Andrews' Castle Course. There was a premium to pay, but not nearly so injurious as the tour operators' premium (read about this method of securing an Old Course tee time in Part II, Chapter Two, page 107).
- Next, I bought a "sunset" time at the Turnberry Hotel—a prepaid late afternoon time discounted from the regular green fee (see Part I, Chapter Four, page 38 for more detail).

Everything else remained the same, though I substituted a four-star B & B for the three-star B & b. Then we added three additional courses at a cost of about $700. In sum, *for about $2,000 per person, this group could have done the same trip that the tour operator was going to sell to them for $4,595*. As it was, they played more golf and had marginally better lodging for about $2,000 per person less than the tour operator's price!! I add the exclamation marks simply to say that this is one of the most egregious "ripoffs" I've seen in my years of analyzing trips offered by the operators.

CASE STUDY #2 - This was another trip with an Old Course time procured from a St. Andrews hotel—this time an expensive place located on The Scores not far from the first tee of the Old Course. That's fine, but what kind of price do we pay for location? This group was seriously golf-intensive with little interest in fancy digs. Yet the tour operator insisted on putting them up in four-star luxury accommodations throughout the trip. Here were the elements:

- *eleven nights lodging* - double occupancy at the Highgrove House in Troon, the Marine Hotel in North Berwick, and the St. Andrews Golf Hotel in St. Andrews.
- *fifteen rounds of golf* (including several 36-hole days)
- *self-drive transportation* in a minivan with automatic transmission.

For this trip, the tour operator quoted **$5,495** per golfer. Compared to the incidence of highway robbery cited in Case Study #1, this is a much more reasonably-priced trip with better accommodations and a lot more golf. Nevertheless, I thought it was too much to pay for the guarantee of an Old Course tee time. With some modifications, I did essentially the same trip for about **$3,000.** How was that possible?

- First, I persuaded these guys to drop two days in East Lothian in favor of two more days in St. Andrews.
- Second, with 5-6 nights in both Troon and St. Andrews, this opened up the possibility of self-catering. We rented a four-star flat in Troon and a five-star flat in St. Andrews. Instantly, their lodging cost dropped from about $1,500 to about $600.
- Third, with more nights in St. Andrews, they agreed to ballot for Old Course play instead of buying an advance reservation through a hotel (they were successful).
- Fourth, in Ayrshire we bought a combination ticket (The "Gailes Experience") for Dundonald, Western Gailes, and Glasgow Gailes, saving about $150.
- Fifth, since they were seriously overbooked, I persuaded them to cut three courses and put more flexibility into their schedule with an open day for movement of courses to accommodate play on St. Andrews' Old Course.

With these changes this group had a more flexible, focused trip with excellent lodging, while achieving their main goal of playing the Old Course at St. Andrews. Having spent $3,000 instead of $5,500, they also were much more likely to consider this a first trip of many instead of their "trip of a lifetime."

Obviously, the cost savings in both these cases were enough to buy a round-trip airline ticket for every traveler. I could repeat examples like these *ad nauseum*—but you get the idea. To use another Latin phrase, it's *caveat emptor* ("buyer beware"). If you don't have information, you can't fight the tour operators. Some present their services accurately; most do not. *Not one of them will tell you their cost basis*; it's all obscured in a "package price." You have to dig up the details yourself. Once you've done that, you'll be in a position to bargain with them. More likely, once you've done that you'll be in a position to do it yourself and, in the process, create a trip that is *more fun, more rewarding,* and *less expensive* than anything offered by a tour operator.

More Notes and Some Personal Observations

International golf travelers tend to be a highly-educated, professional bunch—teachers, business executives, CPAs, attorneys, doctors, et. al. These are people who, in their professional and family lives, are knowledgeable and careful about financial matters. Thus, it never ceases to amaze me how so many of them will turn over their expensive travel decisions to a tour operator without doing the homework necessary to know whether the product they are buying is reasonably priced. Most of the time these are people who have done a considerable amount of golf travel on their own, at least in North America. And, yet, when it comes to making a golf trip to Scotland, they lose confidence and think they have to hire an "expert."

At the same time, I understand the process. I know what happens when people start considering a golf trip to Scotland. So often these are "bonding" experiences—among old friends and/or current golf partners; between father and son; between husband and wife. With growing anticipation, the trip to Scotland starts to take on an aura of glamour and, frankly, undue importance. This is what I call the "Trip of a Lifetime" syndrome. You can't afford to screw up that "Trip of a Lifetime."

Now the search for an expert begins. You browse the internet. You go to the back of major golf magazines to find advertisements for the various companies that offer tours. Or you call your favorite travel agent who has brochures from those same companies. You send off for some brochures or use the internet to download information. Most likely you talk to a few buddies who have made a trip to Scotland and you start to get all kinds of earnest advice ("Oh, you've *got* to play Kingsbarns").

At some point, you get around to making a decision. All the trips seem expensive. But, of course, this is your *trip of a lifetime*. It may be the one and only trip you'll ever make to the Home of Golf. So you don't want any mistakes. You've heard so many stories about how difficult it is to get on Scottish courses. You've heard the hotels and food are awful. All of sudden you feel like you need help.

I know. I've "been there, done that." The first time I went to Scotland, I used an operator. With three friends from high school days, I had a great time. The agency did a good job for us. I asked for a tour a bit off the beaten path and they gave it to us. No complaints.

But here's the problem with this scenario (and every other operator-planned trip): When you get to Scotland you will see the room rates at your hotel posted in a public place. When you go to the golf course you'll see the green fees posted. And you know from previous experience the approximate cost of a rental vehicle. When you start adding up these numbers, you don't have to be a CPA to figure out who just made a nice big profit on your *trip of a lifetime.* You know what you paid (an "all-inclusive" package price). Now you know what you *could* have paid. Subtract the latter from the former and you have *operator profit.*

Was it worth the money? Only the buyer can answer that question. I'm not against fair profit. But I think most people who go through this experience end up feeling fleeced. On that trip with my high-school friends, I fell in love with Scotland, but, as I learned more, I became disgusted with the game tour operators play with the golf public.

What's the root of the decision-making problem? As usual, the answer is a lack of information. Even though information is available and increasingly easy to get, most people don't have the time or inclination to do the necessary research. And, even if they do, admittedly, the accumulated research can be pretty confusing. Consequently, many intelligent people end up buying overpriced golf trips to Scotland. They simply give up and turn their travel decisions over to an "expert."

I fell in love with Scotland, but, as I learned more, I became disgusted with the game tour operators play with the golf public.

I want to change that situation. I want to make *you* the expert. Ideally, I want you to take the approach that you are going to make *two trips for the price most people pay for one trip*. I guarantee, when you adopt that attitude, you'll feel the pressure coming off. You'll no longer feel like you have to "do it all" in one trip. All those rota courses may not seem quite so important. And the Old Course may even assume its proper perspective—one of many great courses to be played on more than one trip.

Getting there is half the fun

Apart from the dollars-and-cents side of travel, there's something more important—and that's what you gain from the process of creating a trip. When you create a trip, or at least participate in the creation of a trip, it becomes an educational, learning experience. And, with an interesting and culturally-rich country like Scotland to study, you can only become wiser and better for having made the effort. Sure, it takes an investment of time and energy. But the result is worth it. That's why the first three items I send to my clients are (1) a detailed map of Scotland; (2) a questionnaire designed to elicit their thoughts about travel in Scotland; and (3) a copy of this book. I want my clients to be involved in their trip because I know the more deeply they are involved the more the trip will become *their* trip rather than the trip I designed for them. Anticipation of the event is just as important as the event. Or, as one of my clients reported, "Reading all this material is like foreplay. We just can't wait to go." Remember: getting there is, indeed, half the fun.

Knowledge is power

After reading this book, even if a person chooses to engage a tour operator, I hope that he or she at least will have enough information to take a *bargaining* approach with an operator. Knowledge is power. If you know how to determine the real cost of a trip, you will have a powerful bargaining chip in your hand. You don't need to accept the "list price" of an operator's tour. Treat it just as you would treat the list price of a piece of real estate or a new car. If an operator wants your business, you'll be able to negotiate a discount from the list price.

Distinguishing between travel agents and tour operators

My quarrel is not with travel agents. They are information brokers who sell the packages assembled by tour operators. My quarrel is with the tour operators who sell the romance of golf in Scotland without regard for fair profit or for the democratic spirit of the game. This targeted and clever selling of Scottish golf primarily to affluent consumers has had many unfortunate effects. Primary among them is that some of the finest golf courses in the world have been turned into ghettos for the rich—overpriced, overplayed, and now off limits to most visitors (including Scots) of average income. What's more, places like Gleneagles, Castle Stuart, Kingsbarns, Muirfield, Royal Troon, and Turnberry, with their exorbitant green fees, have ensured that most visitors, if they choose to play those courses at all, will play only once and never come back. For most golfers, these truly will be once-in-a-lifetime experiences, and that is unfortunate for the clubs, the hotels, and the golfers alike. It's a lose-lose-lose proposition.

Some of the finest golf courses in the world have been turned into ghettos for the rich—overpriced, overplayed, and now off limits to most visitors (including Scots) of average income.

Where the price increases will stop no one knows. Scottish courses can only raise prices so far before they push people away to other, more affordable locations. One could argue that has already happened. Golf tourism to Scotland has declined significantly since 2000. Evidence indicates that some have begun to "see the light." Management committees at top-shelf clubs like Cruden Bay, Crail, and Lundin Links have held the line on prices in recent years and now are relatively good bargains compared to the courses mentioned in the preceding paragraph.

Now that we've dealt with the tour operators, let's get on with the important business of planning a great trip and saving big bucks.

PART I

THE BIG PICTURE

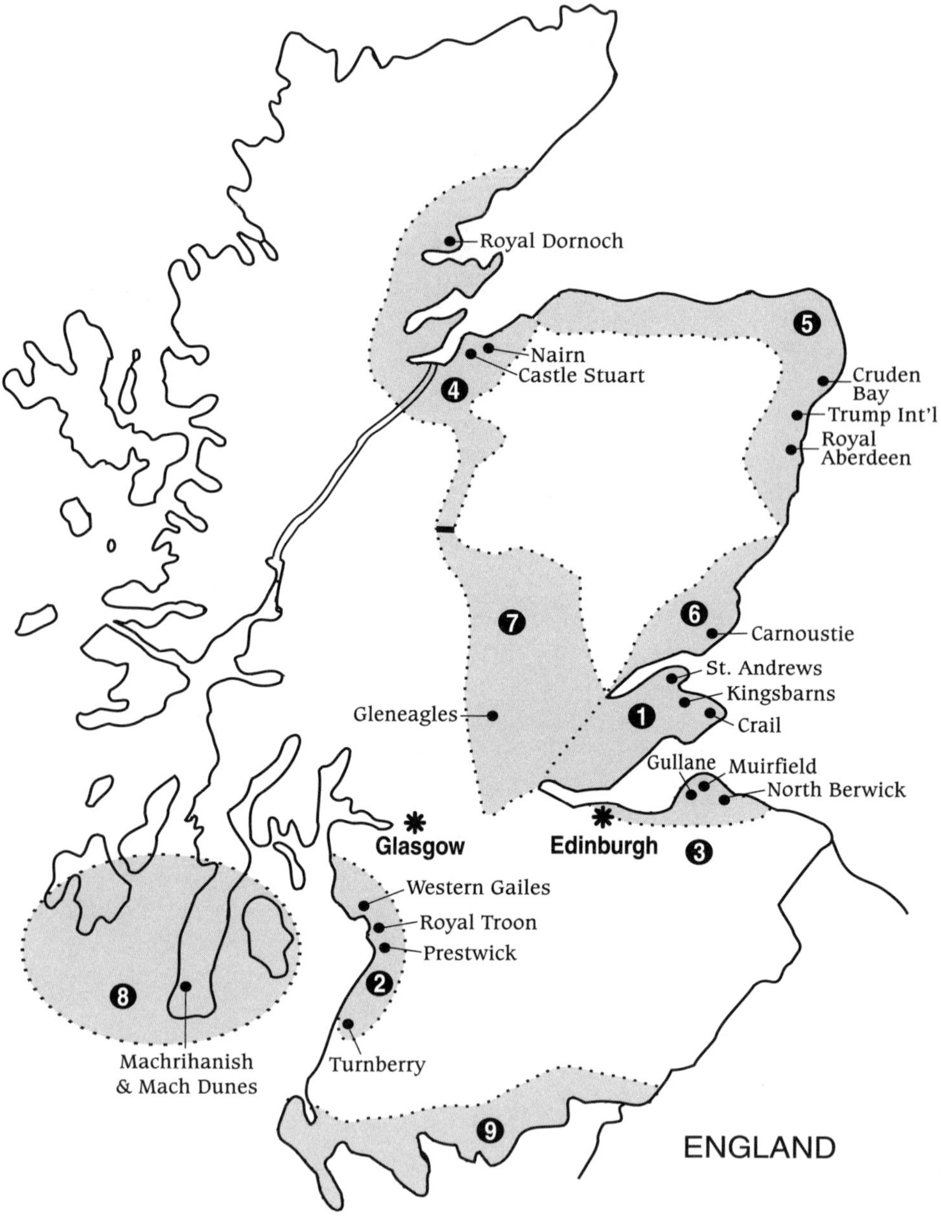

Nine Golf Regions and Twenty of Scotland's Most Popular Courses

CHAPTER ONE

How to Use This Book Most Effectively and Frequently-Asked Questions (FAQs)

THIS BOOK IS ORGANIZED as logically as I am capable of organizing it. But it's not a novel meant to be read from front to back. It's a guidebook with lots of information more or less valuable to the reader depending upon one's level of experience and interest. Accordingly, you'll be jumping back and forth, dipping in and out. The following is intended to help you do that most effectively. I've also included here some of the most frequently-asked questions I've received over more than ten years of trip planning. Together, this chapter and the next chapter on Issues and Decisions should help you dive into the rest of the book.

First, let's get oriented . . .

The map on the facing page locates twenty high-priority golf courses in nine regions where most travelers go to play golf in Scotland. This is important stuff. Often, I find people know about Cruden Bay, Royal Dornoch, Troon, Turnberry, St. Andrews, Carnoustie, Muirfield, et al., but they don't know where those courses are. Study this map carefully and then study the more detailed map and indices starting on page 143 in "The Directory of Courses." These maps will give you the lay of the land and help you think about putting an itinerary together.

. . . and get familiar with the regional names

The next important bit of orientation is a fair understanding of Scotland's regions, so that when you see a reference to "Fife" or "Ayrshire" you know where that is. The seventy-four courses included in this book all fall within nine regions indicated by the shaded areas. All but one are coastal. The highlighted numbers in black circles reflect my sense of golfer priorities—i.e., Fife (St. Andrews) first, the South last, and everywhere else in between. In priority order, they are:

1 - Fife
2 - Ayrshire
3 - East Lothian
4 - Dornoch/Inverness (Ross-shire)
5 - Northeast/North Coast (Aberdeenshire/Morayshire)
6 - Angus
7 - Perthshire/Central
8 - Arran/Kintyre/Islay
9 - South (Dumfries/Galloway)

Then, answer the question, "How important is St. Andrews' Old Course to your trip?"

If the Old Course is your major objective, go straight to page 104 to learn about the advance reservation process and other options for landing a tee time on the Old Course. Your assessment of this issue will affect how you deal with the rest of your trip—when you go, where you go, and when you can start booking the other parts of your trip.

If the Old Course is of secondary or no particular importance to your trip, the odds are you are not making a first trip to Scotland. Whether or not that's the case, you can go on to . . .

Read Part 1, Chapter Two, "Key Issues and Decisions"

You should have a clear fix on all the questions raised there. Obviously, you can't make bookings if you don't know how many people are traveling, when you are going, where you are going, etc. References to the rest of the book in this chapter should help you think about those issues and decisions.

Pin down your travel dates with the help of Part I, Chapter Three, "When to Go"

For some, travel dates are fixed and that's that. For others with date flexibility, information in this chapter can help you identify the best travel time for your particular group. For example, if St. Andrews' Old Course is a "must play," it might be wise to avoid August and September when the course is either at peak demand or closed to visitors. That's not to say you can't get on the course at all during those months, but the fact is the odds are not as good as in other months.

Next, consider the thirteen itineraries outlined in Part I, Chapter Four, "Where to Go"

One or more of these itineraries is likely to be just about right for your party. With a tweak here or there, you will end up with a well-designed trip that is more fun, more rewarding, and less expensive than anything offered in a tour package. They're all good. As I often say, "No wrong answers, just decisions to make."

Get familiar with "The Directory of Courses"

Having read "The Four Elements of a Golf Trip" (Part II, Chapter One), you should be ready to start booking. The Directory of Courses is where you'll find all the detail you need—visitor policies, prices, deposit or prepayment requirements, and phone numbers. This is also where you'll find my recommendations on lodging and nongolf attractions in and around the major golf towns and regions. For example, if you want my recommendations for lodging in Nairn, you'll find that kind of detail in the directory entry for Nairn Golf Club.

Finally, use the Index and Appendix C

A guidebook without a good index is practically useless. This book has a good one. Use it. If you want my recommendation on caddies and tipping, look it up. If you want some lodging ideas in the Dornoch/Tain area or the location of the nearest whisky distillery, look it up. It's all there in the index.

Appendix C is a compendium of some 200 websites. About two-thirds of those are lodging sites; the other third will direct you to information about travel in Scotland and the United Kingdom.

FAQs

When is the best time to go to Scotland?

If this is a question about weather, the answer is between mid-April and mid-October; the weather can be wonderful or miserable any time. If this is a question about course availability on the top-drawer courses, the answer is just about anytime if you've made reservations far enough in advance. If you haven't done that, mid-April through May and late September through late October will give you the best options. The first half of July, before the Open Championship, is a bit of a quiet "window" in the summer. For more detail, see Part I, Chapter Three, "When to Go."

How do I get a "guaranteed tee time" on the Old Course?

(1) Apply for an advance reservation on the first Wednesday of September preceding intended year of play; (2) if you cannot do that or miss the date, apply on the first Wednesday in January of the year of play; (3) ask a tour operator if you can purchase a "trade time" without any hotel requirements; (4) ask a tour operator if they have any times available through members of the St. Andrews Hotel and Guest House Association; (5) as a last resort, buy a time from The Old Course Experience. For more detail on this and the next two questions, see Part II, Chapter Two, from page 104 and see ***www.standrews.org.uk***.

How does the daily ballot (the "lottery") work at St. Andrews?

Submit a request by 2 p.m. *two days prior* to desired date of play (i.,e. Monday for Wednesday, Tuesday for Thursday, etc.). Ballot results are announced the same day after 4 p.m. There is no ballot on Friday because the Old Course is closed on Sunday.

Can I get a tee time through the Old Course Hotel?

The Old Course Hotel is not affiliated with the St. Andrews courses or their management. However, as one of the major hotels in St. Andrews (and like other members of the St. Andrews Hotel and Guest House Association), the hotel is granted some tee times to package and re-sell to the public. The current number of tee times is twenty and these are sold by the hotel under the rubric, "Suite

Golf" (see ***www.oldcoursehotel.co.uk***). The hotel is also a participant in The Old Course Experience (for more information, see page 108).

How much do caddies cost?

Depending upon the course, between £30 and £45. Some courses have "trainees"—usually young folks who might cost in the range of £15-30.

How much should I tip a caddie?

St. Andrews and Kingsbarns have written guidelines to remove the guesswork from this thorny issue. I quote from Kingsbarns: £5-10 "adequate service," £10-15 "exceeded expectations." St. Andrews adds, "If you feel the service has been exceptional the gratuity may exceed this."

What's the dress code? Can I wear shorts?

The dress code is "smart casual." Shorts are allowed almost everywhere but not a good idea anywhere. The weather is changeable and generally cool. The gorse is prickly and the rough is thick. In short, shorts are not very practical. Some clubs are specific about wearing shorts only with long "knee socks." Anklets are frowned upon and can become cause for an enforced trip to the changing room at some clubs. One more thing: if you're wearing a hat, upon entering the clubhouse, take it off. For more detail, see page 119.

To play the Ailsa course, do I have to stay at the Turnberry Hotel?

No—but it's not that simple. Turnberry is a resort (rather than a private club) so they have lots of tee times. Hotel residents have preference for the tee times. Historically, non-residents could book only two weeks prior to date of play. In 2010 the hotel started selling discounted high-season "sunset" times starting at 5 p.m. and bookable any time on a prepaid basis. The best advice is to check with the hotel for current policies and special deals that come and go. See ***www.turnberry.co.uk***. If you *must* have an assured tee time at Turnberry and you are not interested in a sunset time (or sunset times are no longer available), then you should stay at the hotel—and your lodging cost will increase dramatically.

I've never stayed in a B & B. Are they nice? Or are they too fancy?

Bed and breakfast and guest houses are the preferred lodgings of most Europeans. Unlike in North America, where scarce B & Bs are often sought out for special occasions like honeymoons and anniversaries, these small businesses are ubiquitous in the UK and offer great value with a homey touch. In my experience a four-star B & B or guest house in Scotland is equal to and, more often, *better* than accommodation in a more expensive hotel. They almost always have more unique character and connection to the local folks. For more detail, see pages 84-90.

Can I rent an apartment or house?

Yes. The Brits call this "self-catering." Any group based in one place for the greater part of a week or on a stay-and-play trip, should consider renting. Self-catering properties offer the greatest "value for money"—more room, more amenities for less = smart travel. Most properties are rented from Saturday to Saturday. Those rented by the day normally require a minimum three or four-night stay. For more detail and a list of self-catering websites, see pages 85-6.

I need to use my computer. Where can I connect?

Pretty much anywhere—that is, odds are more than good that your lodging will have free wi-fi. Apart from that, seek the nearest hot spot at a library or an internet coffee shop or pub.

What about phones? Will mine work? Should I rent one?

Most people have some kind of mobile phone (or "communication device"). When traveling internationally, they are great until you use them. Then, more often than not, you start bouncing signals around the world, chalking up expensive minutes on both domestic and international calls. If you have a phone with a sim card ("subscriber identity module"), the cheapest phone solution is to buy a new "sim" card from a UK carrier. In my experience, the carrier with the best coverage in Scotland is O^2. Avoid Virgin. Don't rent a phone from an online company. A better idea is to simply buy an inexpensive phone. You won't pay more than about $40-50 and a new phone often is sold with a package of "free" minutes. Phones, sim cards, and "top-up" cards are widely available at phone and electronics stores, stationeries, pharmacies, and even vending machines at the airport.

The Phones 4 U store on Market Street in St. Andrews. Just one of many outlets to serve your communication needs.

Should I ship my clubs to Scotland?

Only if golf is *part* of a longer trip involving no golf. Otherwise, the incidence of permanently lost or stolen clubs in transit is extremely low. Airlines must deliver delayed clubs and they are on the hook for lost goods (check carrier and international regulations). If your airline doesn't cover full value (most do not), travel insurance is cheaper than the cost of shipping. If you don't want to risk the loss of precious clubs, consider renting (for more detail, see page 118).

Should I purchase UK currency before leaving home?

If it makes you feel comfortable having some UK cash in your pocket upon arrival, go ahead. But it's not really necessary. From the moment you step off the plane, ATMs are ubiquitous. Just make sure you have some cash in your bank account and your credit card company knows you are traveling and making expenditures in a foreign country.

Can I combine a trip to Scotland and Ireland?

Of course you can but, unless you have two weeks or more, I do not recommend it. In my view, a typical seven to ten-day trip combining Scotland and Ireland doesn't do justice to either country—either the golf courses or the cultures. Logistics become more complicated and transportation costs increase accordingly. You end up spending too much time getting to and from and through airports.

I'm going to be in St. Andrews and Troon and I want to visit a whisky distillery. Where are the nearest ones?

Scotland's most famous single-malt distilleries are up north in and around the Spey Valley and out west on the isle of Islay. Golfers staying in the central belt are rather limited to Auchentoshan in Glasgow, Famous Grouse (Glenturret single malt) and Tullibardine near Crieff, and Glenkinchie at Pencaitland (East Lothian). For more detail, see pages 127-29.

How do I get a refund of the Value-Added Tax? Can I get a VAT refund on hotel and golf expenses?

The Value-Added Tax is applied to and included in the price of all goods and services. Best guideline: you can claim a refund on goods that can be carried out of the country. Thus, on a pleasure trip you *cannot* claim a refund on products or services consumed in the country. A sweater, yes; a round of golf, no. Retailer participation in the "VAT Retail Export Scheme" is voluntary. Check with the retailer before you buy. Get a formal VAT receipt. Collect your refund either directly from the retailer or submit your claim to a customs official in the international departures area of your departing airport. Is it worth the hassle? Unless you are on a business trip or have bought a trunkload of cashmere sweaters, I'm not sure.

How far is it to St. Andrews from Edinburgh? Glasgow?

Drive time from Edinburgh to St. Andrews is one hour. From Glasgow airport to St. Andrews, about two hours. Thus, Edinburgh and Glasgow are one hour apart. Caveat: these are urban areas, so it depends upon time of day. Avoid "rush hour" traffic through Glasgow at all cost. For more drive time information, see page 122.

I don't want to drive on the left side of the road. Can I use public transportation?

Major train routes follow the east and southwest coasts where many of Scotland's top-drawer links courses are located. So, the answer is a qualified "yes." Combined with local resources (i.e., taxis) for transport, this is entirely feasible—particularly when one is based in St. Andrews, Troon, or North Berwick/Gullane where you are literally surrounded by quality golf courses. If you are planning to move around a lot, a combination of expense and the idea of schlepping golf clubs on and off a train or bus should dissuade you. See page 125 for a map of Scotland's major train routes.

The Carnoustie train station is no more than one-quarter mile from the championship golf course. Major train routes follow the east and southwest coasts where many of Scotland's links courses are located.

What is the author's favorite course?

St. Andrews Old Course is in a class by itself. Other than that, I don't have one. They are all wonderful in their own way—just like our kids.

You should be ready now to "drill down" a little further, addressing two key issues and eight decisions before starting to book your trip.

CHAPTER TWO

Overview of Key Issues and Decisions

Issue #1 - The "Trip of a Lifetime" or one of several?

THIS IS THE MOST IMPORTANT issue I will raise in this chapter. My orientation should be clear: I want you to go to Scotland as often as possible. The biggest mistake golfers make when they start thinking about a trip to Scotland is buying into the tour operators' romantic notion that this is a "once-in-a-lifetime" event. Once you accept that marketing ploy, cost consciousness disappears. You are ready to spend whatever it takes to have that "once-in-a-lifetime" experience.

Now, think about it. It's really not that hard to get to Scotland. Strong competition on air routes in and out of the UK keeps prices fairly reasonable. Travel during "shoulder season" can further reduce the cost of air transport.

If at all possible, let's ditch that idea that this is going to be the "Trip of a Lifetime." Instead, take the approach that this is going to be the first of several trips to enjoy golf as it was meant to be played in a welcoming country of unsurpassed beauty, hospitality, and character.

Let's be specific: say you've heard about and want to play the following courses—the Old Course, Castle, and the New Course at St. Andrews, Kingsbarns, Muirfield, Gullane #1, North Berwick, Royal Troon, Prestwick, Turnberry Ailsa, Western Gailes, Machrihanish, Gleneagles, Royal Dornoch, Castle Stuart, Nairn, Cruden Bay, Trump International, Royal Aberdeen, and Carnoustie. That's twenty courses—all worth playing. But how do you do that in seven to ten days? You don't.

My mission is to show you how to make two trips for the price most people pay for one trip. This is far better than buying into the "Trip of a Lifetime" trap.

Now, consider how much easier it becomes when you break that once-in-a-lifetime trip into two or three parts. Suddenly you feel the pressure release. You can relax. Now you can play all those courses, mix in a few "hidden gems," and get to know Scotland in a way few golf tourists do.

As I often tell my clients, "You're going to fall in love with golf in Scotland and you're going to want to go back." My mission is to show you how to make two trips for the price most people pay for one trip. This is far better than buying into the "Trip of a Lifetime" trap.

Issue #2 - How important is St. Andrews' Old Course? If it is the top priority, do you have an advance reservation?

Virtually every first-timer to Scotland wants to play the Old Course. That's understandable. If the Old Course is at the top of your priority list, it will have its effect on overall trip planning. In particular, it will affect when you can go. It may also affect how long you stay in St. Andrews and, thus, how much time you can give to other parts of the country. These issues are explored in the next chapter ("When to Go"), and in Part II, Chapter Two (from page 104, "Eight Ways to Get a Tee Time on the Old Course").

Most important, this issue relates directly to Issue #1 above. If you're making the Trip of a Lifetime and you don't have an advance reservation on the Old Course, that one course becomes a controlling factor in trip planning. Everything revolves around the Old Course. You could end up paying way more than necessary for a course that really isn't that difficult to book.

If one takes the view that this is the first of several trips to Scotland, the Old Course takes on a different kind of importance. It may still be "first among equals," but it becomes less obsessively controlling. It becomes one of many courses to be played—if not on this first trip, then on a second, third, or fourth trip. And it *will* be played, perhaps many times. This is a much different perspective than the once-in-a-lifetime approach to golf in Scotland.

Decision #1 - When to go

For most, the short answer is mid-April to mid-October. A longer answer is in Part I, Chapter Three. Here are the basics:

- The weather can be great or miserable any time. Odds are best for warm weather from May through August, but that doesn't mean much, so go whenever you can.
- April-May and September-October flank the busiest travel months and, thus, are generally preferable in terms of lodging availability, tee times, prices, and crowds. But even that is relative because May and September are among the busiest months of prime golf season. I think the April-May period is better than September-October for four reasons: (1) those months are closer to the summer solstice so you get more hours of daylight for golf; (2) spring is beautiful and the yellow flower of the gorse is in bloom on the golf courses; (3) people in the travel industry are fresher (like spring) and tend to give better service; and because . . .
- (4) *St. Andrews is a nightmare in September*. There's an RAF base at nearby Leuchars and their annual Air Show comes early in the month. Then there's the fall meeting of the Royal and Ancient; the Queen Victoria Cup; various golf club events; the beginning

of the fall term at St. Andrews University; and the Alfred Dunhill Links Championship in late September/early October. September in St. Andrews has become so busy that advance reservations are not taken on the Old Course during the month. Best to stay away unless you have a specific reason to attend one of the September events and book well ahead.

- June in St. Andrews is better than September, but graduation at St. Andrews University and various tournaments complicate the calendar. Consult the St. Andrews website for course closure dates *(**www.standrews.org.uk**)*.
- July is the best summer month for play at St. Andrews except when the Open Championship is scheduled there.
- Traditionally, August is the most intense vacation month of the year for Europeans. The Edinburgh International Festival draws tens of thousands of people from all over the world and, inevitably, some of that slops over to the golf regions. In general, plan and book well ahead and, with respect to Edinburgh, be prepared for high prices and either make the festival part of your itinerary or avoid the city.

That's the broad outline. And this does not even touch the most unpredictable, yet frequent, source of scheduling conflicts—i.e, the myriad member "medal days" and tournaments at the various golf clubs. All the more reason to make more than one trip to Scotland because odds are good that your itinerary planning will be complicated by one or more of these conflicts.

Decision #2 - How to get there

Air travel is the first subject treated in Part II, Chapter One. Here's my advice boiled down: (1) from one of several North American cities, fly either directly or with one stop to Glasgow or Edinburgh; (2) if you must fly through London or choose to fly through London (particularly Heathrow Airport), leave plenty of time to make your connection to Scotland. Why?—because even if you *can* make a connection within an hour or two, your golf clubs probably won't unless you are traveling straight through on British Airways.

Another alternative to London: Delta, USAirways, and British Midland offer flights from several American cities to Manchester, England, and, from there, on to various Scottish cities. Those who choose Northwest/KLM or Air France normally connect in Amsterdam or Paris. In my view, these continental connections are not much better than flying through London. They just prolong the agony of transatlantic flight.

Decision #3 - Where to go

The longest chapter in this book (Part I, Chapter Four), featuring thirteen itineraries, is dedicated to this subject. If you are a first-timer, the likely answer is that you will probably want to include St. Andrews on your itinerary. And why not?—it's the Mecca of international golf and several of my suggested itineraries focus on St. Andrews.

Apart from St. Andrews, I strongly encourage a look at the Highlands even if it's only a wee taste of the north with a drive up to Pitlochry, the "Gateway to the Highlands." Why? Because if the traveler never gets outside the belt of population around and between Glasgow and Edinburgh (home to about three million people), Scotland will seem much like every other urbanized, overcrowded place in the world. Only when the traveler gets north of Stirling and Perth does the countryside open up and grab at the heartstrings with eye-popping photo ops and calendar moments. To experience even a small slice of this "other Scotland" most likely will guarantee a return to this lovely land. It is for this reason that, among the thirteen itineraries in Chapter Four, I am partial to Itinerary #4. This itinerary combines a touch of the rural Highlands with the more heavily populated stretch from Carnoustie and Dundee down to St. Andrews. It does assume a tradeoff—that is, it postpones the high-priority Ayrshire coast (Troon, Prestwick, Turnberry, etc.) to another trip.

For the second or third-timer—well, Scotland is your oyster and anything goes. Personally, I am inclined to head straight for the Highlands and Islands where I know I'll spend less money, play what I think are the most interesting golf courses, enjoy the grandest scenery, and see more sheep than people (Itinerary #s 5, 6, 7, and 12). Not to give short shrift to the south of Scotland, I would add that I am rather partial also to Itinerary #8 tumbling along the River Tweed and traversing the rolling green hills of Dumfries-Galloway. Any one of these itineraries will fill to overflowing both your photo album and your memory bank.

Decision #4 - Whether to use a tour operator, a travel planner, or self-plan

This may seem the toughest decision to make but, contrary to conventional wisdom, it is not. You'll learn the most if you plan your own trip. If you don't have the time or patience for that, the next best choice is to hire a travel planner for a reasonable hourly rate or a flat fee (I know where you can find a good one!). The last choice should be a tour operator.

> ***Any intelligent person with some internet savvy, a telephone, and little time can plan and execute a great golf trip to Scotland.***

Unfortunately, the opposite order prevails. Most golfers think they need to buy the "expertise" of a tour operator who "knows the territory." Poppycock. Any intelligent person with basic internet savvy, a telephone, and a little time can plan and execute a great golf trip to Scotland. Many of the trips organized by tour operators are presented on their websites. Take a look at some of them. See what you like. Steal a few ideas. If you have this book, you'll have all the phone numbers you need to make bookings. As a matter of fact, if you read this book you'll know more than most of the tour operators, themselves. As for the time investment in trip planning—true, I may be able to do it all more efficiently and with more background knowledge. But planning the typical seven-to-ten-day trip is not that hard. Scotland is not a third-world country. How far wrong can you go?—especially if you are following the beaten path.

Decision #5 - The size of your golf party

Size does matter. In fact, the size of the golf party has a more profound effect on the character of a trip than any other single factor. And, on this subject, opinion and experience are all over the board.

For obvious reasons, the most common number in a golf party is four. Students of group dynamics would probably say this number not only makes sense on the golf course but everywhere else as well. Four fit nicely into a minibus. Lodging is simplified because a group of four can stay just about anywhere either in double occupancy or four singles.

Once past the most common configuration, the factors to consider get more interesting:

- *Two or three golfers* have more flexibility than four. Many golf clubs are partial to threes and twos and even reserve a block of time for "two-ball play" (e.g., Prestwick, Royal Dornoch, and many others). Twos or threes play faster than fours and Scots like that. Twos and threes also have a better chance of picking up a local resident or club member to fill out a tee time and, thus, meet more Scots with added benefits—i.e., a playing partner with intimate knowledge of the course being played (no need to pay a caddie) and maybe even a post-round invitation to the members' private dining room. In St. Andrews, twos and threes can more readily hook up with a local resident and enter the "local ballot" for play on the Old Course (for more detail, see page 106).

- *A single golfer* can enjoy all the flexibility and opportunities enjoyed by twos and threes *except* the ability to make an advance reservation at some golf clubs, particularly at the high-profile courses that are priorities for most visiting golfers (e.g., Muirfield and St. Andrews' Old Course). Most golf clubs will make a reservation for a singleton, but they don't do it with great enthusiasm. Often you'll be told, "Just turn up and we'll get you a game." On the other hand, given some patience and flexibility, a single golfer doesn't really need advance reservations. Though accepting this advice may take a leap of faith, the best advice for single golfers is to simply get on a plane to Scotland, jump in a rental vehicle, and go play golf wherever and whenever the spirit moves with a phone call ahead to pave the way. For those who prefer a little more structure, see my detailed discussion of this subject in Part II, Chapter One, pages 78-80.

- For *eight or more* golfers the social aspect of a trip becomes a more dominant factor. This is likely to be a group of guys, gals, or couples who play regularly together at the same club or otherwise have some social relationship. They are much more likely than a smaller group to engage a chauffeured bus or van ("coach" is the common term). They almost certainly will be more programmed and less flexible in terms of tee times, travel, lodging, and eating arrangements than a smaller group. For example, a group of eight or more is likely to lodge in a relatively expensive full-service hotel because, by law, a B & B may not house more than six guests. Logistically, if a group of eight chooses to self-drive, two vehicles will be required. In sum: what I am describing here is the likelihood of a relatively expensive trip. Contrary to the laws of "volume purchasing," it's fair to postulate a new law of golf travel: The larger the group, the more expensive the trip. That's not to say a large group will not have budget options or even volume discounts in some places, but, too often, when a group gets as big as eight to twelve or more, the planning is headed toward the resort track in the hands of a tour operator rather than a budget-conscious individual.
- A group of *twelve or more* probably will be traveling in something resembling a Greyhound bus, lodging in large hotels, and marching in lockstep to the dinner table. At some point, small-group dynamics become large-group dynamics and, in my experience, in any group of twelve human beings, there's always at least one horse's behind. Personally, I just wouldn't go there. But, to each his own; no wrong answers here—only different strokes for different folks.

Decision #6: "Stay and play" or move around?

The appeal of stay-and-play is in getting intimately acquainted with an area while maximizing the golf and minimizing packing and unpacking. If St. Andrews' Old Course is a high priority and a group does not have an advance reservation, then a stay-and-play approach in or near St. Andrews is the way to go. There could also be significant cost savings associated with renting on a week-long stay. The appeal of moving around may lie in playing more "name courses" and, more important, in becoming broadly acquainted with an appealing country and its people. A sensible middle ground on a seven to ten-day trip is to limit the moving around to two or three areas of the country. See Part I, Chapter Four, "Where to Go," for my discussion of this interesting subject.

Decision #7 - To drive or be driven

This subject has two facets: (1) objective cost issues; and (2) subjective risk tolerance. In terms of pure cost, here are the basics:

- It's a little unusual for a group of four or fewer to hire a driver, but it can be done. The cost ratio of a chauffeured versus self-drive trip will be about 3:1.
- Groups of eight are more likely to consider a coach and driver. Compared to self-driving, the cost ratio will be about 2:1.
- Groups larger than eight are most likely to prefer a chauffeured trip. Parity is reached at about twelve golfers. Beyond twelve, a coach and driver are actually less expensive than the self-drive option.

Regardless of the size of a group, in my view a chauffeured coach is the right decision in only four situations: (1) when there is a lot of ground to be covered and a lot of partying to be done; (2) when a group is comprised of golfers and nongolfers and the nongolfers want to enjoy guided sightseeing; (3) when members of a group are either too young or too old to hire a rental vehicle; (4) when all members of a group are absolutely petrified at the thought of driving on the left side of the road.

This last point, of course, leads to the subjective facet of this decision. There's no question that driving on the left side requires some adjustment and practice for North Americans. There is heightened risk involved. Personally, I have never found this to be a serious problem. I rather enjoy the change and the challenge. At the same time, I realize that some people are not comfortable with the heightened risk or simply do not want to experience the stress of adjusting to left-side driving. This is understandable and every traveler needs to assess the subjective part of this equation for themselves.

Finally, if a trip is organized around a stay-and-play theme with minimal transportation requirements, it rarely makes sense to hire a coach and pay a driver for sitting around twiddling his or her thumbs all day. If you don't want to self-drive, you'll save a lot of money by hiring "local transportation" (i.e., taxi service) for airport transfers and shuttling to and from the golf courses. For more on this subject, see page 71.

Decision: #8 - How much to spend

The cost of a trip is largely dependent upon two factors: (1) where you stay and (2) where you play. The next largest cost center can easily become caddies; if one is used for every round of golf, a caddy can add $70-$100 per round. The rest of the cost of a trip depends upon how expensively you eat and drink and how many souvenir sweaters you buy.

The Trip of a Lifetime: In terms of cost, working from the most expensive downward, let's take a close look at a "once-in-a-lifetime" trip that many golfers, in fact, take or would like to take.

- Eight nights lodging including one night at Turnberry Hotel.
- Ten rounds of golf: Turnberry, Prestwick, Royal Troon Old Course & Portland, Carnoustie, St. Andrews' Old Course & New Course (two-course policy), Kingsbarns, and Muirfield (two-round day ticket).
- Transportation - automatic minivan.

Where you stay: Ferguson's Golden Mean: you can lodge comfortably in Scotland for an average of £45-55 per person per night double occupancy. To assure a tee time at Turnberry, one should stay at the hotel. Total lodging cost on this trip with one night at Turnberry: $815-935. For lodging detail, see Part II, Chapter One, from page 84.

Ferguson's Golden Mean: you can lodge comfortably in Scotland for . . . £45-55 per person per night.

Where you play: Regardless of where you stay, any trip featuring golf at the courses listed above will be expensive. I call this "running the table" (on the Open rota courses). The cost, high season circa 2012: $2,205 for ten rounds of golf.

Transportation: Per-person cost for four sharing an eight-day rental of an automatic minivan: $280

TOTAL land package: $3,300 to $3,420

Obviously, one can spend a lot more than this depending upon where you stay. But the golf and transportation cost components are fixed. My point: anyone can have a "Trip of a Lifetime" to Scotland, playing all the most expensive courses, for about $3,300 rather than the $5,000 or more that tour operators typically pry out of unsuspecting victims.

The implied corollary here is that, *when one starts making less expensive substitutions for the top-drawer golf courses, trip costs can drop dramatically.* Again, I'll be specific: Let's say we substitute (1) Crail for Kingsbarns; (2) North Berwick for Muirfield; and (3) Western Gailes for Royal Troon. The lodging part of the equation remains the same, but the golf cost drops to about $1,600 and the total cost to between $2,700 and $2,815. You are no longer making a "Trip of a Lifetime," but you are spending less money and, in my view, not making much of a sacrifice in terms of the overall golf experience.

To re-cap, then, here are the main issues:

- Issue #1 - The "Trip of a Lifetime" or one of several?
- Issue #2 - How important is St. Andrews' Old Course to your trip and, if it is the top priority, do you have an advance reservation?

And here are the key decisions:

- Decision #1 - When to go (Part I, Chapter Three)
- Decision #2 - How to get there (Part II, Chapter One - Air Travel)
- Decision #3 - Where to go (Part I, Chapter Four)
- Decision #4 - Whether to use a tour operator, a travel planner, or self-plan
- Decision #5 - Size of the golf party
- Decision #6 - Stay and play or move around (Part I, Chapter Four)
- Decision #7 - To drive or be driven (Part II, Chapter One - Vehicle Rental)
- Decision #8 - How much to spend

Before getting to the nitty-gritty of trip planning in Part II, the next two chapters focus on "When to Go" and "Where to Go."

CHAPTER THREE

When To Go

THE MOST FREQUENTLY-ASKED QUESTION I get is, "What's the best time to go to Scotland?" One answer is, "Whenever you can." Scotland can accommodate any time of year. You might be surprised to learn that most golf courses in the various coastal "micro-climates" are open throughout the winter. What that means, of course, is that while it may be cold there's not much snow.

As a practical matter, most people want to be as warm as possible and enjoy the longest days of the year. This means going sometime during the six months from mid-April through mid-October. Family, school, and job considerations often limit travel options to the summer months of June, July, and August. Now we move toward a definition of high season for Scottish golf tourism. To be most precise, the busiest months of the year are: (1) July and August; (2) May, June and September; (3) April and October about equal. Most innkeepers and many golf courses consider May through September the high season. Thus, lodging and golf bargains often can be had during the "shoulder months" of April and October. Many B & Bs and guest houses close their doors for five months from November 1 to March 31.

Generalizations about the weather

Implicit in the question, "What's the best time to go to Scotland?" is another question: "What can I expect from the weather?". The only remotely intelligent answer to that question is, "You can expect the weather to be *unpredictable.*" I've been so cold in Scotland in June that I had to go shopping for gloves and a wool sweater. On the other hand, I've played golf in seventy-degree weather in May and October.

"What can I expect from the weather?" The only remotely intelligent answer to that question is, "You can expect the weather to be unpredictable."

So, if unpredictability is the key word, what generalizations can one make? For golfers, three generalizations are important:

- *The west coast is wetter than the east coast.* For example, though no more than sixty miles apart, Glasgow gets almost twice as much rain as Edinburgh during September and October. The ratio narrows during other months.

- *The west coast is warmer than the east coast.* All along Scotland's west coast, from south to north, you'll find semi-tropical plants growing in open air gardens during the summer. To my knowledge, nothing like that exists on Scotland's east coast. Why? Because the Gulf Stream waters wash the west coast. On the east coast, despite justifiable pride in their "micro-climates," they can get brutally cold winds off the North Sea at any time of year—and no one, not even the Scottish tourist board, can deny it.

- *An island climate is characterized by rapidly changing weather.* A typical Scottish day may bring sunshine, clouds, mist, rain, wind, and calm. This is why you are advised to *dress in layers*. Don't be surprised if, during a round of golf, you go from short-sleeved golf shirt to sweater to rain jacket to full rain suit before returning to sweater and golf shirt.

Temperature

The chart below shows average high and low Fahrenheit temperatures in Edinburgh for twelve months. As a measure, Edinburgh is as good as any. Temperatures don't vary much from north to south. For example, the average high temperature during January is precisely the same in the Orkney Islands and Inverness as it is in Edinburgh. East (Edinburgh) to west (Glasgow), on average, the west coast might be a degree or two colder in winter and a degree or two warmer in summer.

Extremes are rare—it doesn't get very cold and it doesn't get very hot.

This chart illustrates a fundamental point: *extremes are rare*—it doesn't get very cold and it doesn't get very hot. During the peak tourist season, May through September, daily high temperatures typically range between 55° and 75° Fahrenheit. For golfers, this is wonderful weather—soft, cool air and no oppressive, humid heat to beat you down and sap your strength (as in many parts of the United States and, for that matter, the rest of the world). The United Kingdom, indeed, is blessed with a climate congenial to golf. Here are the details:

Edinburgh - High and Low Temperatures - Monthly Averages

Jan	43	May	58	Sept	61
	34		43		49
Feb	43	June	63	Oct	54
	34		49		45
Mar	47	July	65	Nov	49
	36		52		40
Apr	52	Aug	65	Dec	45
	40		52		36

A further note on temperature: The UK, like most countries in the world, uses the Celsius (metric) temperature scale. Math majors may love the complicated formula for converting Celsius to Fahrenheit, but it's not necessary. Keep it simple. Most May-September temperatures will be between 10° and 20° C. Just remember:

10° C = 50° F   15° C = 60° F   20° C = 70° F

Before I get caught up short by the math majors, I know these are not precise numbers. They are close. With the weather, close is good enough.

Rainfall

You must bring good rain gear to Scotland. On the west coast from Oban on up, from August through April, it's wet a lot of the time—from six to ten inches a month. Fortunately, there aren't many golf courses in that part of the country.

For golfers, the lowest rainfall is around Edinburgh—on average, about two to three inches of rain during each of the summer months. That's not bad, especially when it comes in the form of a soft Scottish mist that hangs about all day and doesn't really get in the way of play. On the other hand, it can come in sheets and buckets and stay all day. Fortunately, those days are relatively rare and there's always a castle or museum or pub nearby where one can seek shelter. Most often, the sky will be intermittently cloudy and, out of the clouds, might come a quick burst of showers followed by warm sunshine. Who knows? Take everything said here (and everywhere else) with a grain of salt and remember this wee Scots limerick:

Whether it rains or whether it shines,
Whether it's chilly or hot,
You must weather the weather,
Whatever the weather,
Whether you like it or not.

The point is, there's *no* point in being concerned about the weather. Just go on your trip and take what comes. And be prepared!

While all commentary about weather in Scotland may begin and end with the word, "unpredictable," the basic truth is that you should expect rain. That's what makes Scotland blossom into a breathtaking land of green and yellow and lavender. That's what creates her mountain rivulets and trickling burns and flowing rivers. Warm rains are the stuff of elephantine leaves and semi-tropical plants on the west coast, of heather on the hills in the Highlands, and of springy turf and silky-smooth greens in all parts of the country. Whatever the weather, you'll enjoy Scotland for her beauty in sunshine or in shadow, in mist or in pouring rain.

Daylight hours

Scotland is one of the northernmost countries in the world, on latitude with Hudson Bay in Canada, Norway, and the southern reaches of Siberia. Consequently, in the months around the summer solstice (mid-June) the nights are short and the days are long. In May, June, and July you can play golf until 9 or 10 p.m. Twilight is long and lovely. This subject arises when my clients say, "I want to play early in the morning," and I say, "You can't get on that golf course early in the morning. The only available time is after lunch—and, by the way, you can play until ten o'clock at night."

Whatever the weather, you'll enjoy Scotland for her beauty in sunshine or in shadow, in mist or in pouring rain.

The tradeoff for the long days of May, June, and July are the short days of early spring and fall. Earth's time machine moves more rapidly in these northern climes. Starting September 1, daylight hours shrink at a rate of about forty-five minutes every two weeks. Thus, sunset in Glasgow on September 1 is at 7:11 p.m.; by October 15 it's at 5:17 p.m.; by the end of October sunset is at 4:40 p.m. (for detail, see "Appendix D").

The case for April and October

If your heart's desire is to play the Old Course and you want to get the best rates at hotels, the best months to be in Scotland are April and October. It's not unusual to find hotel rates cut dramatically after October 1 or certainly by October 15. In St. Andrews, most of the major hotels offer attractive package deals after play for the Alfred Dunhill Links Championship concludes in early October. And the golf courses can be surprisingly free of traffic. Personal testimony: On a Wednesday in late April recently, I was one of three singles playing on world-famous Cruden Bay. The same story at Brora—just me, the sheep, and few other lone wolves.

A special attraction of spring and fall travel is the beauty of the countryside. In the spring, daffodils line many of the highways and byways and fields of oilseed rape offer up a dazzling yellow display of welcome to Earth's new year. In the fall, an equally-appealing palette of autumnal browns and golds spreads over fields of newly-mown and gathered hay.

But tradeoffs are part of the bargain. In the spring, golf greens are not likely to be in "top nick." Course maintenance is conducted at that time, just as it is at most golf courses. In the fall, the heather is past its prime, gardens have lost their luster, and most nongolf attractions have either closed or adopted drastically shortened hours. In both spring and fall, daylight hours are shorter and one must risk the possibility of enduringly cold, nasty weather. For all the benefits, I think it's a good gamble and, if pressed on the point, I would choose April over October.

Calendar highlights

By month, following are additional factors that might influence your decision on when to go.

May-June

- May and June are visually stunning. Spring has sprung and bright yellow flowers on the gorse are in full bloom. The gorse will cost you strokes on the golf course, but at least you'll enjoy the view. In May you'll be a bit ahead of the summer tourist curve.

July

- Late in the month (third and fourth weeks), if the British Open and/or Senior Open are in Scotland, you'll have to plan well ahead—that is, plan ahead to make your reservations near the Open venue or plan on being somewhere else. Here are the announced venues for the Open Championship: 2012 Royal Lytham & St. Annes; 2013 Muirfield; 2014 Royal Liverpool; 2015 St. Andrews. The Senior Open will be staged at Turnberry in 2012 and at Royal Birkdale in England in 2013.

August

- Like May, August is a visual stunner with heather in bloom, casting its lavender glow over the countryside. The Highlands are especially beautiful.
- August is the busiest month because (a) that's when Europeans take their traditional summer holiday; and (b) the Edinburgh International Festival draws thousands of tourists from around the world. In other words, you are fighting for space not only with tourists from North America but with the Brits and every other nationality within striking distance of Scotland. Reservations must be made well in advance to lodge in Edinburgh and are recommended for most parts of the Highlands. Multi-night stays may be required, especially at weekends.
- Plan to arrive around the third week of the month when UK schools resume. You'll see a discernible drop in the level of tourist activity, particularly in the Highlands.

September

- Don't assume this is a quiet month. It's the most popular month for "empty nesters" and others avoiding the summer tourist crush. In St. Andrews, in addition to all the golf events (see below), September also sees the Leuchars Air Show and matriculation at St. Andrews University. It's a zoo. The only time to be in St. Andrews for play on the Old Course is early or late in the month.

The Old Course and your travel plans

For many golfers, playing the Old Course at St. Andrews is the "bottom line" of a trip to Scotland. Whether applying for an advance reservation or angling for your best shot in the daily ballot, you can't play the Old Course if it's not open to the public. Therefore, travel dates must be picked carefully. You will want to avoid or anticipate:

- *May - first full week:* Spring meetings of the Royal and Ancient Golf Club and the New Golf Club.
- *June:* St. Rule Trophy; St. Andrews Links Trophy; Rotary International Golf Tournament; graduation at St. Andrews University. Book lodging early or plan on staying somewhere outside the town.
- *First three weeks of July when St. Andrews hosts the British Open.* The course is closed late June and re-opens on the first Tuesday after the Open.
- *August - throughout the month:* The Royal and Ancient Golf Club is granted one to two-hour blocks of tee times most mornings *and* afternoons, thus decreasing the supply of tee times by as much as fifteen to twenty slots in a period of peak demand. This should not be considered a "stopper" for August travel, but it is advisable to allow a little more time for the ballot to work in your favor.
- *September - second and third weeks:* Queen Victoria Jubilee Vase Tournament; Bing Crosby Tournament; Royal & Ancient autumn meeting; Alfred Dunhill Links Championship late in the month and/or into early October. No advance reservations are offered during the entire month of September.
- *Early November through March:* To preserve the turf at the hallowed links during harsh winter months, golfers are issued a piece of Astroturf for playing shots from the fairways. Most visiting golfers are not interested in playing the Old Course in that way, in effect eliminating five months from consideration.

The above notes on Old Course busy dates and closings are for general guidance only. *For a complete calendar of events, consult* ***www.standrews.org.uk***. On the home page, find "Busy Dates" on the drop-down menu under the heading, "Playing Golf." For a wider discussion of the Old Course in your travel plans, see Part II, Chapter Two.

Now that we have some ideas about when to go, let's turn to the most important issue: *where* to go.

NOTES

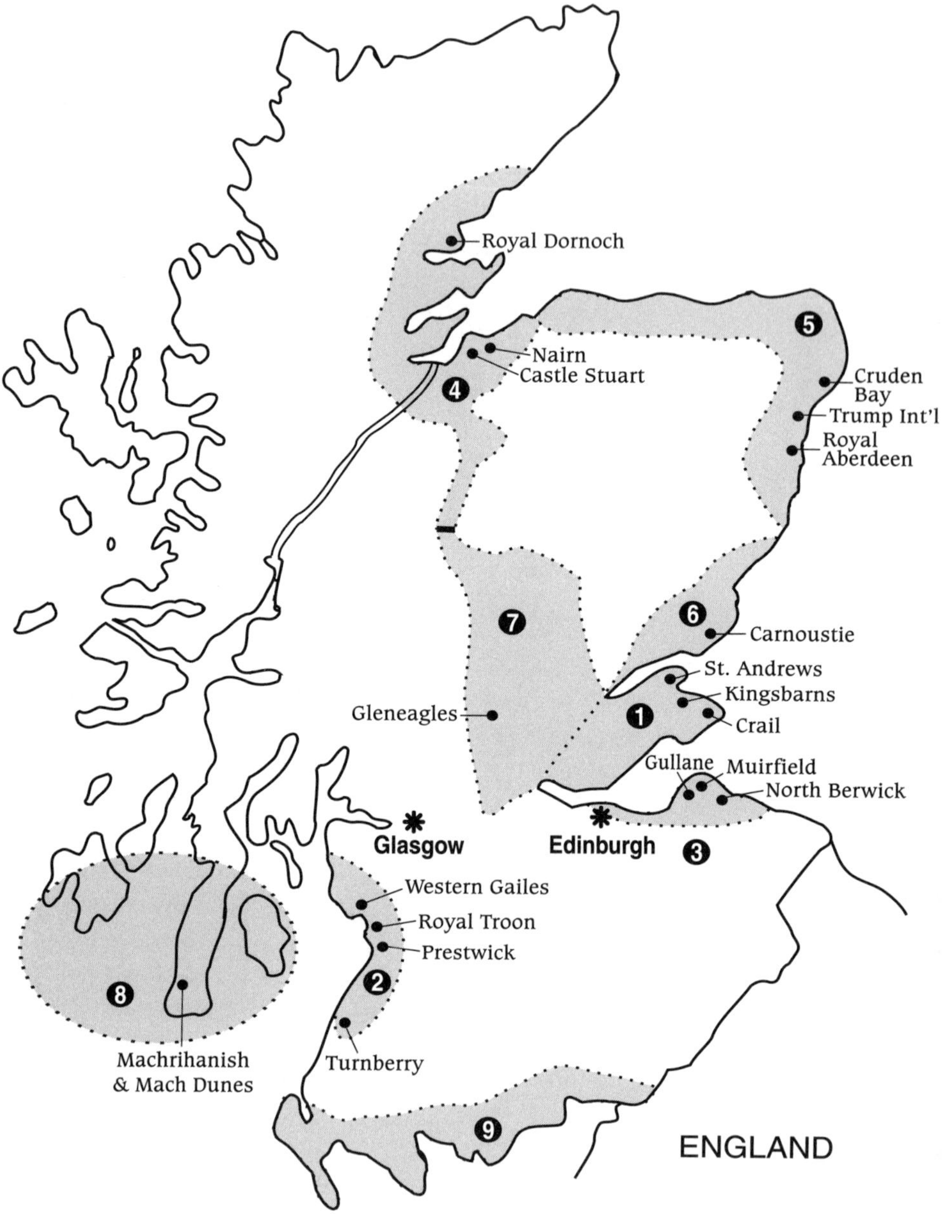

Nine Golf Regions and Twenty of Scotland's Most Popular Courses

CHAPTER FOUR

Where to Go

WHERE YOU GO DEPENDS upon three main factors—your priorities, the length of your trip, and, most likely, how many times you've been to Scotland. If you're a first-timer, you're probably not going to choose the Kintyre Peninsula over St. Andrews. On the other hand, if you've visited St. Andrews and played the Old Course, you may be quite keen to make the pilgrimage to Machrihanish on remote Kintyre.

Recalling now the map we saw on page 2, re-printed here on the facing page, think of my nine golf regions as "bases" for your trip. Virtually all the courses most visitors want to play are within these nine regions.

On a typical seven to ten-day trip I recommend limiting yourself to two or, at most, three bases. Beyond ten days, the number of bases can increase as the length of a trip increases.

On a two or three-base trip, this means three or four nights in each locale. With that much time, you'll feel more like you're "at home." You can get unpacked and stay unpacked. You can get to know your lodging hosts. You can get to know the streets and shops, the restaurants and the corner bartender. You can make forays out to the countryside or into the nearest city. Most important, you can spend your time playing golf instead of packing up, driving for several hours, then finding your next place to bunk down. The last thing you want to do on a golf trip is get into the tourist trap: "If this is Tuesday, it must be Carnoustie."

Some tour operators sell a seven-day package touting the world-famous courses at Troon, Dornoch, Cruden Bay, Carnoustie, and St. Andrews. That kind of routing is absurd—five bases in seven days, covering about 800 miles, requiring you to spend most of your free time in a car or bus (burning expensive petrol) and leaving no time to "savor the clubhouse," not to mention the countryside. This is not the right way to tour Scotland.

Likewise, some golfers will fly into and out of the airport at Machrihanish in one day just to say they've played that great course. But, in doing that, they miss the best part of the Machrihanish experience—the process of *getting there* by sea or land and, once there, exploring the wild and remote reaches of the Kintyre Peninsula. The golfer who flies in and out of Kintyre in one day will never know the thrill of driving down a single-track to Southend where, on a clear day, you can see all the way to Ireland; or of stopping at the Dunaverty

My playing partners at Dunaverty on the wild, sparsely-settled Kintyre peninsula.

Golf Club for a quick round on a course that will take you back to the nineteenth century as a reminder of the way golf used to be played. At unattended Dunaverty you'll drop your fee in an "honesty box" before leaving the first tee. You'll probably "play through" several bovine hazards as well. That's the kind of experience a traveler can savor long after the buzz of a championship course is forgotten. But it's not an experience a *hurried* traveler will ever have. No matter where you go, this is the single most important piece of advice I can give: *Don't hurry. Slow down and savor the clubhouse* (the golf equivalent of "smelling the roses").

The next important piece of advice: *book the golf before dealing with the lodging.* The pieces of the golf puzzle must fit. You can always find a place to stay. For example, in Ayrshire, Royal Troon takes visitors only on Monday, Tuesday, and Thursday. Western Gailes takes visitors on Monday, Wednesday, Friday, and small windows of time on the weekend. Prestwick will take visitors about any time during the week except Thursday afternoon. If you've been planning on playing Troon on a Wednesday and doubling up Western Gailes and Prestwick on a Thursday, all of a sudden it's "back to the drawing board." In Part III, "The Directory of Courses," these policy details are noted in the course entries in the data area under the heading *Visitor Policies*. For information on the booking process, see Part II, Chapter One, from page 76.

No matter where you go, this is the single most important piece of advice I can give: Don't hurry. Slow down and savor the clubhouse (the golf equivalent of "smelling the roses").

A few notes on the most popular combinations of bases

Without question, and understandably, the most popular combinations of bases come from Regions 1 (Fife), 2 (Ayrshire), and 3 (East Lothian) with a side-trip up to Carnoustie in Region 6. Fully seventy-five percent of the trips I plan cover two or more of these areas with St. Andrews, Carnoustie, Troon, and Gullane/North Berwick the focal points.

It's a lot of ground to cover, but all four of these areas can be visited on a ten or eleven-day trip. With all the planets aligned, a "trip of a lifetime" for many golfers might end up looking a lot like Trip 1 among the itineraries that follow this introduction. That's a trip featuring all of Scotland's past and present venues for the Open Championship. For this trip, tour operators typically charge something in the range of $5,000 and up. It can be done for a lot less but, even if camped out in a pup tent, the golf, alone, will cost about $1,800 because these are among Scotland's most expensive courses.

My aim in Trip 1 is to provide a good estimate of the time and money required to execute such a "dream trip." Obviously, if one has less than eleven days to travel or is not inclined to spend so much money, then you can cut and trim to suit the circumstances. In any case, most first-time travelers to Scotland want to at least have a go at some combination of St. Andrews Old, Muirfield, Carnoustie, Troon, and Turnberry. Bookings at Carnoustie, Troon, and Turnberry are relatively easy to manage. Muirfield and St. Andrews require some special attention.

Muirfield and St. Andrews

Muirfield takes visitors only on Tuesday and Thursday. Thus, tee times are severely limited. Starting at 8:30 a.m., Muirfield offers eighteen morning times (nine each off the first and tenth tees). Afternoon play is optional at additional cost and is restricted to "foursomes" ("alternate shot"). An online booking system was installed at Muirfield in 2005. It operates on a lead time of twelve to fourteen months (e.g., February for April of the following year). It took a few years for golfers to catch on to the online system, but now high-season times from May through September tend to sell out fairly quickly. April and October are typically slower to fill up. The booking pattern varies, so it's always worth checking at ***www.muirfield.org.uk***. And, since their booking window is so wide, it's also always worth going onto Muirfield's "waitlist." Cancellations do occur. However, if you are told that bookings at Muirfield must be made up to two years in advance, don't believe it. It's not true.

In the case of St. Andrews, booking policies put in place in 2005 by the Links Trust suggest an optimum planning window of eight to twelve months for securing an advance reservation on the Old Course. Reservation requests are accepted beginning the first Wednesday in September for the ensuing year. Unlike at Muirfield, however, if a golfer is not prepared to submit a request for an advance reservation at the optimum time, there are lots of other ways to "skin the cat" and these are explored in Part II, Chapter Two, under the heading "Eight Ways to Get a Tee Time on the Old Course." As I've said elsewhere, the importance and place of St. Andrews in a trip—whether the Old Course is pre-booked or a group is entering St. Andrews' daily ballot—will affect the shape of every itinerary.

If you are told that bookings at Muirfield must be made up to two years in advance, don't believe it. It's not true.

With the exception of these two special cases at Muirfield and St. Andrews, I want to stress that *golf tourists to Scotland do not need to book tee times eight*

Golf tourists to Scotland do not need to book tee times eight to fifteen months ahead of their travel dates. That is a myth promulgated by tour operators.

to fifteen months ahead of their travel dates. That is a myth promulgated by tour operators. In fact, at most courses, it is not possible to book any earlier than the last quarter of the year before the intended year of play because the club "diaries" are not open. The only thing the clubs will do is accept a letter of request and put it in a file for future action. In other words, don't worry, be happy. Your golf party can go pretty much anywhere, anytime it wants and, in most cases, could be booking tee times a few months, a few weeks, or a few days ahead of play. For more on booking tee times, see Part II, Chapter One, from page 76.

Stay and Play

One-base, one-week golf trips are becoming increasingly common in Scotland. Regional tourism councils, independent promotional groups, and some enterprising hotels are making the pitch to "stay and play," often accompanied by package deals that reduce costs at participating venues.

As one can see on the map and in the Geographic Index at the beginning of "The Directory of Courses" (page 143), each golf region offers a wealth of courses when a decision is made to stay and play. Even in Regions 8 and 9 where I have included only a few courses, rest assured, many more can be found.

Two further benefits of the stay-and-play approach: First, you can almost always negotiate a multi-night discount at a B & B or hotel. The magic number is usually three or more nights, but most places don't have a specific policy or, if they do, they don't announce it, so it's best to be direct and ask for the discount. Second, a stay-and-play approach can bring even greater savings and convenience through "self-catering." As we have seen, this is the British term for what Americans call "rentals." Generally, self-catering units are priced by the week and assume a Saturday-through-Saturday stay. Rentals can save a group a lot of money but, more important, they offer the comforts of home, including a fully-equipped kitchen. For some, that is appealing. For others, that's what they are trying to escape. The point is, this approach to golf travel is far different than the whirlwind approach offered by most tour operators. For more detail on

"Self-catering" on a stay-and-play trip means more quality and character for less money—in this case, a 5-star renovated farm stable for half the cost of a 4-star hotel.

self-catering, see Part II, Chapter One, pages 85-6. With that much introduction, let's take a look at several of the most popular stay-and-play choices.

St. Andrews and Fife—the obvious first choice

If St. Andrews' Old Course is the first priority of a trip, and if a group is without an advance reservation, the most sensible thing to do is simply go to St. Andrews and stay for the duration. St. Andrews is a pleasant and interesting place to be for a week. With or without an Old Course reservation, on a seven-night stay you could play two great courses a day in Fife and still leave others unplayed. And, even though St. Andrews is tucked away in a corner of the Kingdom of Fife, it is well located for making day trips to punctuate your stay. Dundee and Carnoustie are just half an hour to forty minutes away. Perth and Gleneagles are about one hour's drive time. And St. Andrews is near a rail line that whisks you into Edinburgh in about one hour. This is a "no-brainer" for anyone who wants to stay put for a week.

Ayrshire

Just as in Fife, anyone based in Ayrshire (Region #2) at Troon, Prestwick, or Ayr is surrounded by great golf courses literally lining the coast from Irvine through Gailes and Troon/Prestwick to the south end of Ayr. Farther south, about forty minutes from Troon, the courses at Turnberry punctuate "The Gold Coast." of Scottish golf. The exciting and constantly renewing city center at Glasgow (Scotland's largest) is easily reached via a train line visible from all the golf courses. In fact, the train line is precisely what brought golf to Scotland's southwest coast in the nineteenth century.

East Lothian and Edinburgh

From a base in the Gullane/North Berwick area (Region #3), golfers can reach at least twenty golf courses without driving more than twenty miles. The bonus is East Lothian's proximity to Edinburgh, one of Europe's most engaging cities. From the neo-classic symmetry of Edinburgh's New Town to the unruly crooks and bends of her medieval Old Town, this is the city to see when in Scotland. So, why not stay in Edinburgh and travel out to the golf courses? Some people do that, but I don't recommend it for two reasons: (1) as in any large city, lodging in Edinburgh is generally expensive; and (2) to put it mildly, driving in Edinburgh

My Edinburgh lodging advice: stay outside in the golf areas and take the train into the city.

is a challenge and parking is even harder. My preference is to stay in the small towns of the golf territory and take the train into the city. The trip from North Berwick to Edinburgh's city center takes just thirty-one minutes. From Drem, near Gullane, it's even less.

Dundee-Carnoustie-Arbroath-Montrose

While less glamorous than Fife, the coastal towns between Dundee and Montrose in Angus (Region #6) are perfect for a week or two of stay-and-play golf up and down the east coast. A base anywhere along here not only puts St. Andrews within easy reach but, with a little more effort, brings the courses around Aberdeen into play. Drive time from Montrose to Royal Aberdeen, for example, is no more than about one hour. Cruden Bay is half an hour farther on. Lodging options are plentiful along the short span between Dundee (Scotland's fourth largest city) and Carnoustie. Montrose, a town of about 12,000, has its own charm, perched as it is on a harbor and inland salt water basin. Most important, this base puts the golfer smack dab in the middle of the great courses in and around Carnoustie, including the underappreciated tracks at Barry (Panmure), Monifieth, Letham Grange, and Dundee (Downfield). Montrose boasts Scotland's fifth oldest golf club.

Way up north

In the Inverness/Dornoch area (Region #4) I am partial to Nairn as a stay-and-play base. Inverness is fine too, but I like the pace and accessibility of a smaller town. Despite its small size, Nairn offers all the lodging and culinary characteristics of a much larger town. Nairn boasts two championship golf courses of its own and is within a few miles of Castle Stuart to the west. Grantown-on-Spey in the heart of the Spey Valley is twenty-five miles due south. The golf courses in the Dornoch area (Royal Dornoch, Tain, Golspie, and Brora) are within one hour to one and one-half hours drive time. All that golf, plus loads of nongolf attractions, give plenty of reason to stay and play way up north.

Bearing in mind these factors and all those raised in the preceding chapters, on the following pages are thirteen itineraries designed to appeal to every golfer from the first-timer to the veteran traveler to Scotland. The first eight itineraries cover all the golf regions of Scotland. The next five are stay-and-play trips. Six of the itineraries cost less than $2,000. None of them costs more than about $3,000.

Introduction to the Itineraries

THIRTEEN ITINERARIES MAY SEEM like overkill. It is not. Each itinerary is unique, but there is overlap as well. For example, the first three trips all involve the major courses of Scotland that most visitors want to play at least once, including two courses at St. Andrews plus Carnoustie. One of the first three itineraries is likely to be pitch perfect for a high percentage of golfers making their first trip to the Auld Sod.

Itineraries 4-8 take us farther afield and may be most attractive to those who have already played Scotland's major courses in Ayrshire, Fife, and East Lothian. Or they could appeal to those who like their golf off the beaten path.

All these first eight trips involve movement through two or three of the regions identified on the map on page 28. They are planned as *ten-day trips*—eight days on the ground plus two travel days.

The first eight itineraries are followed by five stay-and-play trips that involve little driving. The stay-and-play trips are *nine-day trips*—seven nights with two travel days—and all feature rented lodging that typically rents from one Saturday to the next. Of course one can stay in a hotel, guest house, or B & B. But for a week-long stay in one place, the best value for money is in "self-catering."

Assumptions common to all trips

• All cost estimates use rates applicable in 2012 and an exchange rate of £1 = $1.75. Green fees assume high-season travel between May and September.

• Links courses near the sea are featured.

• With the exceptions of Trips 6 and 12, air travel is either through Glasgow or Edinburgh. Let price be your guide. All things equal, if your trip is on the east side of Scotland (e.g., East Lothian and Fife), it makes most sense to use the Edinburgh airport. If your trip is on the west side of country, Glasgow is the logical choice. If your trip is on both sides, you may want to use both Glasgow and Edinburgh. But it really doesn't matter that much. Glasgow and Edinburgh are only one hour apart. Your flight departure time and place most affects where you lodge the night before departure. If you are on the east side of the country the day before departure from Glasgow, I recommend getting back to a Glasgow airport hotel that evening. And vice versa—if on the west side, return to Edinburgh. Finally, if your trip is entirely in the north (Trips 6 and 12), the airports at Aberdeen and Inverness are options.

• To add more golf to an itinerary, consult Index 1, pages 144-45.

• I've chosen major courses well-known to most golfers. With few exceptions, they are all expensive. To reduce the cost of a trip, after consulting Index 1, see Index 2, "Courses by Price," on page 146. Substitute a less expensive course for a more expensive course (e.g., substitute Crail or Leven Links for Kingsbarns or Carnoustie in Trip 4).

• To lengthen a trip, splice portions of trips together (e.g., add Ayrshire courses to Trip 8 to make a full two-week trip). Combine any of the stay-and-play trips to make a trip of two weeks or more.

Assumptions applied to Trips 1-8 (the "moving" trips)

• Golf is scheduled every day, including day of arrival. That means eight rounds of golf. Where Royal Troon or Cruden Bay are on an itinerary, I have indicated "optional round at no added cost" because green fees at those clubs include optional play on the Portland course in the case of Royal Troon and all-day play at Cruden Bay on either the main course or the nine-hole St. Olaf course.

• Lodging cost on Trips 1-8 is pegged at £55 per person per night x 8 nights = £440 x 1.75 exchange rate = $770. This figure is for *double occupancy* in a B & B or guest house and includes breakfast. But it's also an *average*. In other words, you can pay less than £55 many places and if you book as a single, on average, you won't pay much more than £55. That depends upon whether a lodging has any rooms specifically designed for single occupancy. For more on this subject, see my discussion on pages 87-8.

• Transportation cost ($280 per person) assumes four golfers driving themselves in a minibus with *automatic* transmission. If you have fewer golfers, you can rent a smaller, less expensive vehicle, but you won't spend significantly less per-person and you might spend more. Hiring a full-time coach and driver will add more cost until you get to a group of twelve (see page 70 for my discussion of this topic).

Assumptions applied to Trips 9-13 (the stay-and-play trips)

• Transportation assumptions are the same as above except that with one less day involved, the cost is reduced by about $30 per person per day. *However*, note that on stay-and-play trips involving little driving, it may be possible to cut transportation cost as much as twenty-five percent by hiring a taxi company for airport transfers and shuttle service to and from golf courses. To illustrate this cost-saver, in Trip 13, "The Baker's Cookie," I have made this assumption.

• Lodging assumes self-catering (renting) in a flat or house for seven nights, typically Saturday through Saturday (but not always).

Trip 1 - The Trip of a Lifetime: Scotland's Open Courses, Past and Present

The Courses (8 rounds + 1 optional round at no added cost)

Prestwick - Royal Troon Old Course (Portland optional at no added cost) - Turnberry Ailsa - Muirfield (optional afternoon round) - Musselburgh Links - St. Andrews Castle - St. Andrews Old Course - Carnoustie

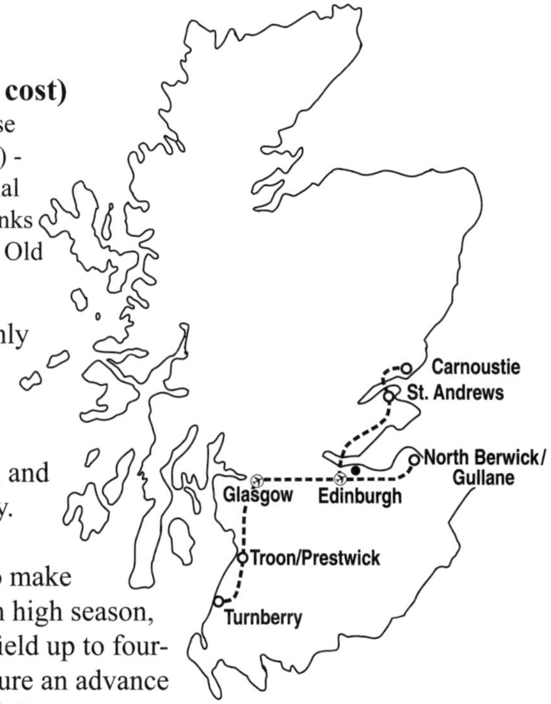

Comment: For that one-and-only trip to Scotland, this is the dream trip most people want to take. It requires foresight, long-range commitment, a little luck, and a considerable amount of money. Every Open course in Scotland, past and present, is included. To make this itinerary work, especially in high season, you must be able to book Muirfield up to fourteen months in advance and secure an advance reservation on St. Andrews' Old Course.

Ideal Routing

Day 1 - (Sat) depart
Day 2 - (Sun) arrive at Glasgow airport - lodging for *3 nights* in Troon/Prestwick; play **Prestwick Old Course**
Day 3 - (Mon) play **Royal Troon Old Course** - optional play on **Royal Troon Portland** at no added cost
Day 4 - (Tues) play **Turnberry Ailsa**
Day 5 - (Wed) a.m. - to East Lothian lodging in North Berwick/Gullane for *1 or 2 nights depending upon Old Course tee time on Friday.* p.m. - play **Musselburgh Links**
Day 6 - (Thurs) play **Muirfield** (once or twice); to St. Andrews lodging for *3 or 4 nights*
Day 7 - (Fri) play **St. Andrews Old Course**
Day 8 - (Sat) play **St. Andrews Castle Course**
Day 9 - (Sun) play **Carnoustie**
Day 10 - (Mon) depart from either Edinburgh or Glasgow, preferably Edinburgh; if Glasgow, then return to an airport hotel on Sunday evening

How to Do It - Notes

• Book *Muirfield* up to fourteen months prior to departure (e.g., April 2012 for June 2013, June 2013 for August 2014, etc.). See ***www.muirfield.org.uk*** for more information. Booking at Muirfield can be made on-line. Prepayment is required soon after booking. Visitors are accepted only on Tuesdays and Thursdays. Times between May and September go fast. Lunch and afternoon round are optional.

• Apply for an advance reservation for St. Andrews Old Course on the first Wednesday in September of the year prior to play (*except September* when no advance reservations are offered). See ***www.standrews.org.uk*** for an application form and complete instructions. No advance reservations are made on Saturdays. The Old Course is closed on Sundays. To be virtually assured of success in the advance-reservation process, it is best to (a) indicate availability for the widest possible range of dates; (b) apply for a time in April or October. For eight ways to book the Old Course, see my discussion beginning on page 104.

• In recent years, the typical wait to hear from St Andrews management has been about six weeks (mid-October). If you know you will make this trip *with or without an advance reservation on the Old Course*, make the rest of your key bookings as the courses open their "diaries" for the coming year. Carnoustie typically opens in August. Troon and Prestwick come along later. Turnberry is a special case (see FAQs below). Musselburgh can be booked closer to your travel date—even while you're traveling within a day or two of Day 5.

• If you will *not* make this trip without an advance reservation on St. Andrews' Old Course, then *don't* make a prepaid booking at Muirfield prior to hearing from St. Andrews. The downside of that decision: by the time you resolve your Old Course time, tee times at Muirfield may be gone. If you can live with that, fine. There are other great courses to play near Muirfield.

More Notes

• Even if a course has not opened its diary for the next year, you can request a spot on their waitlist. This can be a particularly useful strategy for high-season times at Royal Troon where demand is high and visitor times are limited. Weekend times at Carnoustie also are limited and deserve some early attention.

• Day 8 - The St. Andrews Castle Course is on this itinerary because, unlike the other courses at St. Andrews, it can be advance-booked on Saturday.

• The Turnberry time assumes purchase of a "sunset" tee time (after 5 p.m.) available in advance on a prepaid basis. A regular non-resident tee time may be purchased only two weeks prior to play.

• At Musselburgh Links, hickories can be rented.

• The optional afternoon round at Muirfield is played as "foursomes" (alternate shot) and costs an additional £60 ($105) circa 2012. For costing (below), the assumption here is one regular round with a morning tee time.

FAQs

• *What if Muirfield is booked by the time we get our advance reservation at the Old Course?* Go onto their waitlist; due to the long lead time for booking, cancellations do occur at Muirfield. If that doesn't work, book one of the other championship courses in East Lothian—Gullane #1, North Berwick West Links, Dunbar. You'll still have a great trip.

• *I'd like to see Edinburgh. Should we stay there?* My choice is always to stay in the golf towns and use the train to get into the city. From North Berwick or from Drem, near Gullane, you can be in "centre city" in about thirty minutes.

• *Do I have to stay at the Turnberry Hotel to play the golf course?* No—but it's not that simple. Turnberry is a resort course so they have lots of tee times. Hotel residents have preference for the tee times. Non-residents can book only two weeks prior to date of play (I always have been successful in booking in this way). In 2010 the hotel started selling discounted "sunset" times starting at 5 p.m. in high season and bookable any time on a prepaid basis. The best advice is to check with the hotel for current policies and special deals that come and go. See ***www.turnberry.co.uk***. If you must have an assured tee time at Turnberry and you are not interested in a sunset time (or sunset times are no longer available), then you should stay at the hotel—and your lodging cost will increase dramatically.

Estimated Cost

Golf - £1,037 x $1.75 = $1,815
Lodging - $770
Transportation - $280
TOTAL - $2,865

Trip 2 - The Historic Homes of Golf: East Lothian and Fife

The Courses

Musselburgh Links - Dunbar - Gullane #1 - Muirfield - North Berwick West Links - St. Andrews Old Course - St. Andrews second course (New, Jubilee) - Carnoustie - Crail

Comment: The great attraction of this trip is its combination of historic linksland with minimal driving plus easy access to Edinburgh. In addition to the great Open courses featured here, Dunbar, North Berwick West Links, and Gullane #1 are used as qualifying courses when the Open Championship is held at Muirfield. At Musselburgh Links we are playing on some of the oldest ground in golf; it's a gentle 9-hole start where hickories can be rented to remind us of the early days of golf. Ancient rock walls at North Berwick and Dunbar add to the antique flavor of this itinerary. In Fife and Angus we're playing on Scotland's most celebrated Open venues at St. Andrews and Carnoustie. With records stretching back to 1786, the Crail Golfing Society is certifiably the seventh oldest golf club in the world. Its present course on the Balcomie Links at Fife Ness was laid out by Tom Morris in 1895. Visit Edinburgh by train from North Berwick or Drem in East Lothian or from Leuchars in Fife.

Ideal Routing

Day 1 - (Sat) depart
Day 2 - (Sun) arrive at Edinburgh airport; to North Berwick/Gullane lodging for *3 nights*; play **Musselburgh Links**
Day 3 - (Mon) play **North Berwick West Links**
Day 4 - (Tues) play **Muirfield**
Day 5 - (Wed) play **Dunbar**; to St. Andrews lodging for *5 nights*
Day 6 - (Thurs) play **St. Andrews Old Course**
Day 7 - (Fri) play **St. Andrews second course (New, Jubilee)**
Day 8 - (Sat) play **Balcomie Links at Crail**
Day 9 - (Sun) play **Carnoustie**
Day 10 - (Mon) depart from Edinburgh

How to Do It - Notes

• Book Muirfield up to fourteen months prior to departure (see Trip 1 for summary detail). The assumption here is one regular round. An optional afternoon round at Muirfield is played as "foursomes" (alternate shot) and costs an additional £60 ($105) circa 2012.

• Secure an advance reservation for the St. Andrews courses (see Trip 1 for summary detail).

• After those missions are accomplished, book the rest of the trip starting with Carnoustie because that may be the other most difficult time (weekend) to book. Both Crail and Carnoustie accept visitors on the weekend, though only in the afternoon at Carnoustie.

• With a five-night stay in St. Andrews, it could be financially advantageous to rent a flat even if having to pay for a six or seven-night stay. Ideally, one would find a flat that rents by the day (typically for a minimum three or four-night stay). A number of these exist in and around St. Andrews (see page 102 for contact information).

Estimated Cost

Golf - £777 x $1.75 = $1,360
Lodging - $770
Transportation - $280
TOTAL - $2,410

Trip 3 - Southwest to East: Ayrshire and Fife

The Courses (8 rounds + optional round at no added cost)

Prestwick - Royal Troon - Turnberry Ailsa - Western Gailes - St. Andrews Old - St. Andrews New - Carnoustie - Kingsbarns

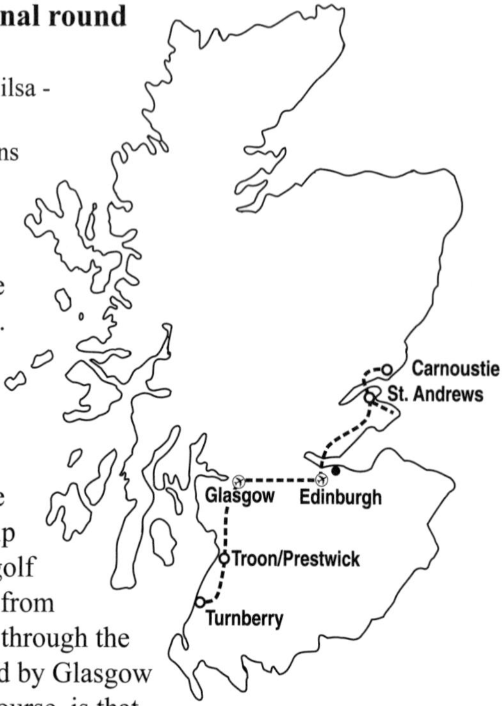

Comment: This is probably the most popular golf trip to Scotland, especially for first-timers (of course it's also one of the most expensive). It's not quite the "Trip of a Lifetime" (Trip 1), but it's close. Only the historic Open courses of East Lothian are left out. Western Gailes and Kingsbarns are more than adequate substitutions. This trip introduces Scotland's two leading golf coasts and, in the process, gets one from one side of the country to the other through the central belt of population dominated by Glasgow and Edinburgh. The downside, of course, is that it doesn't get you *out* of that populous region; but Troon and St. Andrews are both small to middlin'-size towns and, for those who like cities, Scotland's two largest can be reached easily by train from Prestwick/Troon and from Leuchars near St. Andrews.

Ideal Routing

Day 1 - (Sat) Depart
Day 2 - (Sun) arrive; to Troon/Prestwick lodging for *3 nights*; play **Prestwick**
Day 3 - (Mon) play **Turnberry Ailsa**
Day 4 - (Tues) play **Royal Troon Old Course** (optional round on **Royal Troon Portland** at no added cost)
Day 5 - (Wed) play **Western Gailes**; to St. Andrews lodging for *4 or 5 nights*
Day 6 - (Thurs) play **St. Andrews New** or **Old**
Day 7 - (Fri) play **St. Andrews New** or **Old**
Day 8 - (Sat) play **Kingsbarns**
Day 9 - (Sun) play **Carnoustie**
Day 10 - (Mon) depart

How to Do It - Notes

• Secure an advance reservation for the St. Andrews courses (see Trip 1 for summary detail).

• If you need to do this trip in reverse, starting in St. Andrews, I would depart on Friday, then play Kingsbarns on Saturday and Carnoustie on Sunday. That would put the St. Andrews courses on Monday/Tuesday, Western Gailes on Wednesday, Troon on Thursday, Prestwick on Friday, and Turnberry on Saturday. (Where there's a will, there's a way. Sometimes you have to play jigsaw-puzzle with course availability.)

• Assuming you have an advance reservation on St. Andrews' Old Course as indicated on the itinerary, and since this trip starts on the southwest coast and ends on the east coast, the most efficient arrival point is Glasgow with departure from Edinburgh. Let price be your guide. Arrival at Edinburgh adds one hour of drive time to Troon/Prestwick. If departing from Glasgow, return to an airport hotel the night before departure.

• Book the Carnoustie weekend time as soon as your St. Andrews time is secured. As a high-priority course, Carnoustie is scheduled on Sunday when St. Andrews' Old Course is closed.

• The Turnberry booking assumes purchase of a "sunset" tee time available in advance on a prepaid basis. A regular non-resident tee time may be purchased only two weeks prior to play (see Trip 1 for more detail). If you stay at the hotel and pay the resident green fee for a regular tee time add about $500 to the estimated cost.

• Visitors can play at Royal Troon on Monday, Tuesday, and Thursday.

• Visitors can play at Western Gailes on Monday, Wednesday, Friday, and in short blocks of time on Saturday and Sunday. Lunch is included with the green fee on weekdays only.

Estimated Cost

Golf - £1,105 x $1.75 = $1,934
Lodging - $770
Transportation - $280
TOTAL - $2,984

Trip 4 - A Taste of Scotland: Perthshire to Angus to Fife

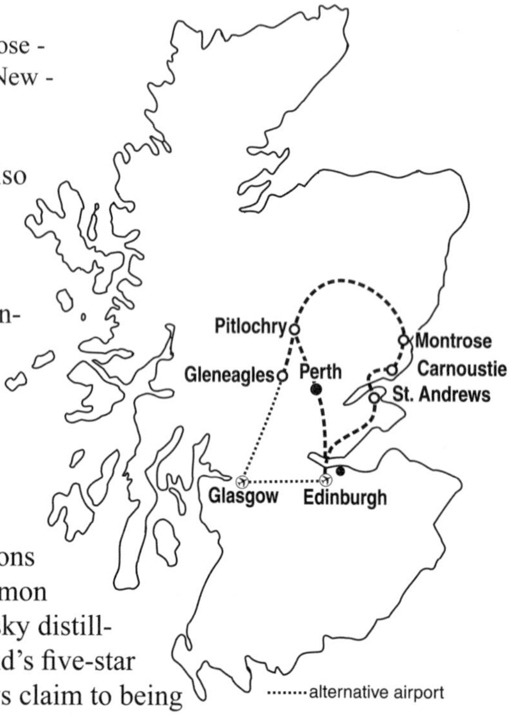

The Courses

Gleneagles Kings - Pitlochry - Montrose - Panmure - Carnoustie - St. Andrews New - St. Andrews Old - Crail

Comment: The title of this trip also could be, "The Spice of Life," for variety is featured here. This is a wonderful trip affording a look at small towns and large towns, mountain terrain and farm land, inland golf and seaside golf. At the geographic center of the country, Pitlochry bills itself Scotland's "Gateway to the Highlands." It's also one of Scotland's prettiest towns with lots of nongolf attractions including a repertory theater, a salmon run, mountain hikes, and two whisky distilleries. Gleneagles is one of Scotland's five-star international resorts. Montrose lays claim to being Scotland's fifth oldest golf club, and Panmure adjacent to Carnoustie almost qualifies as a "hidden gem." Carnoustie needs no introduction. Crail and St. Andrews New are turn-of-the-century Tom Morris creations that complete the package with the Old Course. This is essentially the first trip I took to Scotland and, if you follow my path, you will understand why I fell in love with the land, the people, and golf in this beautiful country.

Ideal Routing

Day 1 - (Fri) depart
Day 2 - (Sat) arrive either Edinburgh or Glasgow; to Pitlochry lodging for *2 nights*; play **Pitlochry**
Day 3 - (Sun) play **Gleneagles Kings Course**
Day 4 - (Mon) drive to Montrose; play **Montrose;** to Carnoustie lodging for *2 nights*
Day 5 - (Tues) play **Panmure**
Day 6 - (Wed) play **Carnoustie**; to St. Andrews lodging for *3 or 4 nights*
Day 7 - (Thurs) play **St. Andrews New**
Day 8 - (Fri) play **St. Andrews Old Course**
Day 9 - (Sat) play **Balcomie Links at Crail**
Day 10 - (Sun) depart

How to Do It - Notes

• Though an advance reservation at St. Andrews is always desirable, in this case it is not critical. Without a reservation on the Old Course, I would put Crail on Thursday and then ballot for Old Course play for three days and re-book Crail if necessary. With three days to ballot, success is virtually assured except perhaps in August.

• Day 3 - At Gleneagles, the Queens and PGA Centenary courses are also good choices. Buggies are available without restriction on the PGA Centenary.

• Day 4 - To experience one of Scotland's most scenic drives, take the A924 out of Pitlochry, then follow the A93 along the River Dee to its junction with the A957 a few miles east of Banchory. The A957 leads on to the A90 motorway that will take you quickly down to Montrose. Allow four hours drive time.

• Day 5 - Panmure is adjacent to Carnoustie. For additional golf, Monifieth is adjacent to Panmure. Carnoustie's Burnside course is also a good choice.

• Day 9 - If departing from Glasgow, return to an airport hotel.

Estimated Cost

Golf - £699 x $1.75 = $1,223
Lodging - $770
Transportation - $280
TOTAL - $2,273

Trip 5 - North and East: Inverness/Dornoch and Fife

The Courses

Nairn - Brora - Royal Dornoch - Castle Stuart - Kingsbarns - St. Andrews New or Jubilee - St. Andrews Old Course - Carnoustie

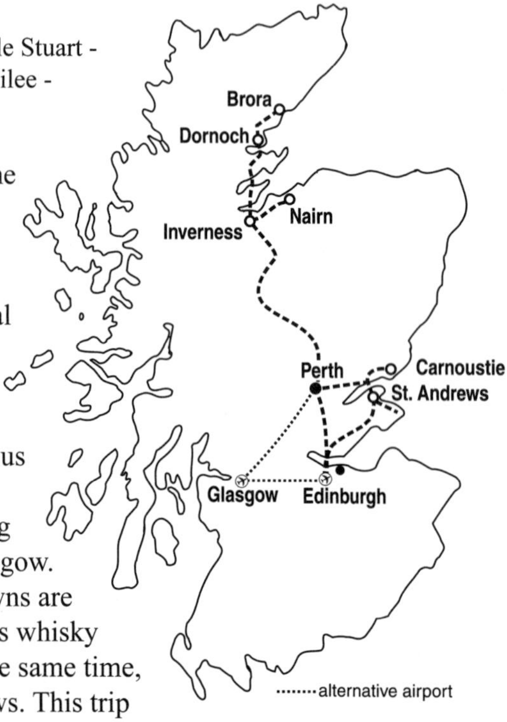

Comment: I expect this to become an increasingly popular trip as Castle Stuart continues its rise to the top ranks of UK golf courses. The northern combination of Royal Dornoch, Nairn, and Castle Stuart is as good as any other three courses in the country. The great attraction of this trip is that it gets us up along the spine (the A9) of the Highlands, away from the madding crowd around Edinburgh and Glasgow. The scenery is spectacular, the towns are attractive, the air is bracing, there's whisky galore, and the golf is grand. At the same time, the trip includes golf at St. Andrews. This trip could be done for something closer to $2,000 by substituting Tain for Castle Stuart and Crail and Lundin Links (or others in Fife) for expensive Kingsbarns and Carnoustie.

Ideal Routing

Day 1 - (Sat) Depart

Day 2 - (Sun) arrive either Glasgow or Edinburgh; to Nairn or Dornoch lodging for *3 nights*; play **Nairn** (option: play Nairn en route to Dornoch lodging)

Day 3 - (Mon) play **Brora**

Day 4 - (Tues) play **Royal Dornoch**

Day 5 - (Wed) a.m. play **Castle Stuart**; p.m. to St. Andrews lodging for *4 or 5 nights*

Day 6 - (Thurs) play **St. Andrews New, Jubilee,** or **Old**

Day 7 - (Fri) play **St. Andrews New, Jubilee,** or **Old**

Day 8 - (Sat) play **Kingsbarns**

Day 9 - (Sun) play **Carnoustie**

Day 10 - (Mon) depart

How to Do It - Notes

• Apply for an advance reservation at St. Andrews (see Trip 1 for summary detail).

• Book the Carnoustie weekend time as soon as possible after your St. Andrews time is secured. Carnoustie is scheduled here on Sunday when St. Andrews' Old Course is closed.

• Lodging in the north could be in Nairn, Inverness, or the Dornoch/Tain area. Drive time between Inverness/Nairn and Dornoch/Tain is about one hour, so some driving is required no matter where the lodging. I am partial to Nairn as a base. It's a small, walkable town with lots of lodging and food options, and it's close to the Spey Valley, the Whisky Trail, and other attractions around Inverness.

• In addition to all the distilleries in and around the Spey Valley, there are distilleries at Tain (Glenmorangie) and Brora (Clynelish) and also en route on the A9 at Pitlochry and Dalwhinnie.

• This trip could be done in reverse, thus reducing drive time on day of arrival. As in Trip 4, if that were done, I would back everything up one day—i.e., (1) depart on Friday; return on the following Sunday; (2) play Kingsbarns and Carnoustie on the first weekend; (3) play Castle Stuart on Saturday before returning to an airport hotel prior to departure.

• Day 9 - If in St. Andrews and departing from Glasgow on Day 10, return to airport hotel.

Estimated Cost

Golf - £907 x $1.75 = $1,587
Lodging - $770
Transportation - $280
TOTAL - $2,637

Trip 6 - North by Northeast: Aberdeenshire and the Moray Coast

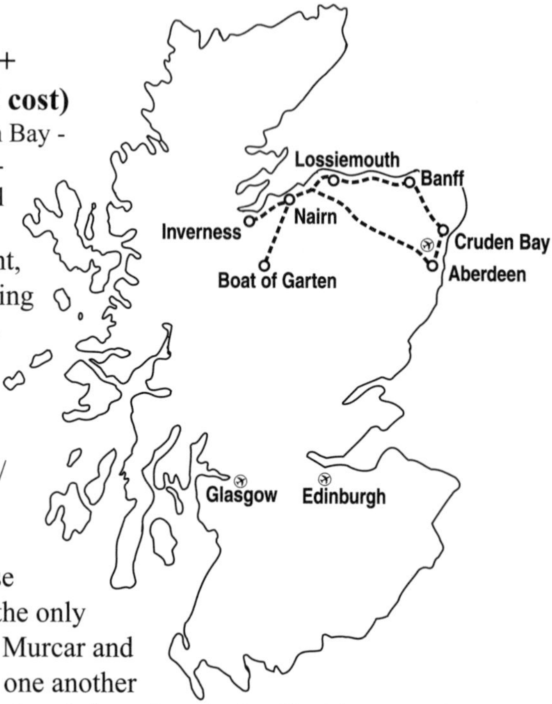

The Courses (eight rounds + optional round at no added cost)

Murcar - Royal Aberdeen - Cruden Bay - Castle Stuart - Moray Old - Nairn - Boat of Garten - Duff House Royal

Comment: This is a magnificent, tightly-drawn "loop" trip featuring Scotland's most dramatic duneland in Aberdeenshire, the best links golf on the Morayshire coast (east of Inverness), and two of Scotland's best parkland/heathland courses—Boat of Garten in the Spey Valley and Alister MacKenzie's Duff House Royal at Banff. Duff House is the only MacKenzie course in Scotland. Murcar and Royal Aberdeen are adjacent to one another on similar duneland and Cruden Bay is in a class by itself with eccentric blind shots and rumpled land in an incomparable seaside setting. Nongolf attractions of this itinerary include the Castle Trail, the Whisky Trail, and historic places like Culloden and Fort George near Inverness. To extend this trip, add several of the courses in the Dornoch area from Trip 12.

Ideal Routing

Day 1 - (Tues) Depart
Day 2 - (Wed) arrive; to Aberdeen area lodging for *3 nights;* play **Murcar**
Day 3 - (Thurs) play **Royal Aberdeen**
Day 4 - (Friday) play **Cruden Bay** (optional additional round at no added cost)
Day 5 - (Sat) a.m. to Nairn lodging for *4 nights*; p.m. play **Castle Stuart**
Day 6 - (Sun) play **Old Moray**
Day 7 - (Mon) play **Nairn**
Day 8 - (Tues) day in Spey Valley; play **Boat of Garten**
Day 9 - (Wed) en route to Aberdeen airport hotel, play **Duff House Royal**
Day 10 - (Thurs) depart

How to Do It - Notes

• Routing can be in/out of either Inverness or Aberdeen. The assumption here is Aberdeen.

• The days indicated work best with the suggested routing, but other days can work and might even be necessary if the routing is reversed because visitor play at courses in Aberdeenshire is severely limited on weekends. Royal Aberdeen takes visitors only after 3:30 p.m. on the weekend; two rounds at Cruden Bay probably would not be possible;

• Cruden Bay's current policy is all-day-play for one price. Thus, assuming weekday play, "optional round at no added cost."

• Day 6 - Moray Old is on Sunday here because that is the "quiet" day when low-flying jets are *not* flying in and out of the nearby Royal Air Force base at Lossiemouth.

• Day 9 - Duff House Royal is a logical stop on the return to Aberdeen. If returning to Glasgow or Edinburgh from Nairn, Duff House Royal should be swapped with Castle Stuart. Duff House will take visitors on Saturday after 11 a.m.

• To avoid Aberdeen traffic, my preferred lodging for this trip is north of Aberdeen, in or around Ellon or Newburgh mid-way between Aberdeen and Cruden Bay, or at Cruden Bay (see page 235 for more information).

• The new Trump International could be an expensive substitute for Murcar.

Estimated Cost

Golf - £652 x 1.75 = $1,141
Lodging - $770
Transportation - $280
TOTAL $2,191

Trip 7 - Ayrshire to Arran to Kintyre

The Courses (9 rounds + optional round at no added cost)

Prestwick - Royal Troon Old Course (optional round on Portland at no added cost) - Western Gailes - Shiskine (2x) – Machrihanish (2x) – Machrihanish Dunes (2x)

Comment: Mile for mile, course for course, this is my favorite trip in Scotland because it combines the great Open courses of the southwest with the most unusual of courses on Arran and Kintyre. It's the only trip where I unreservedly recommend multiple rounds on several courses for two reasons: (1) these are among Scotland's most eccentric courses with a host of blind shots and design characteristics that are so classic as to have become iconic to generations of golfers and course designers; and (2) with ferry crossings and slow-go driving, some special effort is required to get to Arran and Kintyre; therefore, it makes sense to linger over both the golf and the travel. To extend this excursion into Scotland's wild places, take a ferry to Islay for play on the famous Machrie course.

Ideal Routing

Day 1 - (Sat) depart
Day 2 - (Sun) arrive Glasgow; to Troon/Prestwick lodging for *3 nights*; play **Prestwick**
Day 3 - (Mon) lunch and golf at **Western Gailes**
Day 4 - (Tues) play **Royal Troon Old Course** (optional round on **Portland** at no added cost)
Day 5 - (Wed) a.m. to Arran lodging for *1 night* via car ferry from Ardrossan to Brodick; play **Shiskine**
Day 6 - (Thurs) a.m. play **Shiskine** again; p.m. to Kintyre lodging for *3 nights*; play **Machrihanish**
Day 7 - (Fri) play **Machrihanish** again
Day 8 - (Sat) play **Machrihanish Dunes**
Day 9 - (Sun) a.m. play **Machrihanish Dunes** again; p.m. return to lodging for *1 night* at Glasgow airport
Day 10 - (Mon) depart

How to Do It - Notes

• The best air route for this trip is in/out of Glasgow, about forty minutes from Troon/Prestwick. If Edinburgh is used, add one hour of drive time on both ends of the trip.

• Day 2 - Prestwick costs a little more on the weekend, but it's a great way to start a trip back in time.

• Day 3 - The green fee at Western Gailes includes lunch.

• Day 4 - Book Royal Troon as early as you practically can. Visitor times there are limited and tend to go fairly fast. Troon takes visitors only on Monday, Tuesday, and Thursday.

• Day 5 - Call Caledonian MacBrayne (08705-650-000) to book your crossings. The Ardrossan-Brodick crossing can be booked in advance. The Lochranza-Claonig crossing from Arran to Kintyre *cannot* be booked in advance; for that you show up at the ferry dock on the north end of Arran. The crossing takes about thirty minutes.

• Day 6 - Shiskine is a 12-hole wonder that cannot be missed—the highlight of this trip.

• At Machrihanish, be sure to check for promotional deals on the cottages and golf at Machrihanish Dunes. They are in "marketing mode" and often have offers that cannot be refused.

• Day 9 - Returning to Glasgow airport: you can make the long, scenic drive (about 3.5 hours to Glasgow) up and around Loch Fyne on the A83 or you can re-trace your route on the Cal-Mac ferries. The ferry costs a little more but involves less stress; the time commitment is about the same.

Estimated Cost

Golf - £763 x 1.75 = $1,335
Lodging - $770
Transportation - $280
TOTAL - $2,385

Trip 8 - The Southern Swing

The Courses

North Berwick - Glen GC - Dunbar - Roxburghe - Powfoot - Southerness - Stranraer - Portpatrick

Comment: We start with ground well-trod in East Lothian, but then head off to the "Borders" and Dumfries/Galloway regions of Scotland to experience a part of the country few golf tourists visit. That's unfortunate because this region is Scotland's "Lake District" without the crowds or high prices. Roxburghe, a Dave Thomas course, is among the best of Scotland's inland courses, and Southerness, a true "hidden gem," ranks among Scotland's ten best. Unique local layouts at Powfoot, Portpatrick, and Stranraer round out the excursion before heading back to Glasgow. For anyone on a second or third golf trip to Scotland, I strongly recommend this itinerary as a way to experience both the familiar and the relatively undiscovered. The nongolf aspects of this trip are significant, for this is a land of castles, abbeys, Sir Walter Scott, and Robert Burns; and remnants of historic Hadrian's Wall span the island a few miles across the border in England. A fair amount of driving is involved, but it's a scenic sojourn through pastoral landscapes.

Ideal Routing

Day 1 - (Thurs) depart
Day 2 - (Fri) arrive Edinburgh; to Gullane/North Berwick lodging for *3 nights*; play **North Berwick West Links**
Day 3 - (Sat) play **Glen GC**
Day 4 - (Sun) play **Dunbar**
Day 5 - (Mon) drive to Kelso; play **Roxburghe**; to Dumfries lodging for *2 nights*
Day 6 - (Tues) play **Powfoot**
Day 7 - (Wed) a.m. play **Southerness**; p.m. to Stranraer lodging for *2 nights*
Day 8 - (Thurs) play **Stranraer** or **Portpatrick**
Day 9 - (Fri) play **Portpatrick** or **Stranraer** and return to lodging for *1 night* at Glasgow airport
Day 10 - (Sat) depart

How to Do It - Notes

• Air routing - Ideally, into Edinburgh and out of Glasgow but, again, it doesn't make much difference. Let price be your guide.

• The assumption here is that the golf tourist on this trip has played all the major courses in Scotland and is now ready to branch out. Thus Muirfield in East Lothian is skipped. Some may prefer to add Muirfield into the mix; if so, the routing might be reversed or the days changed because Muirfield takes visitors only on Tuesday and Thursday.

• Day 2 - In the spirit of this trip, if North Berwick's West Links and Gullane #1 have been played on previous trips, play Craigielaw, Luffness New, Kilspindie, or one of the other courses at Gullane.

• Days 3 & 4 - Glen GC and Dunbar allow visitor weekend play with some restrictions and prices only slightly higher than weekday rates.

• Day 5 - En route to Kelso, Sir Walter Scott's country estate, Abbotsford, is a worthwhile stop a few miles west of Melrose.

• Due to its relative isolation from the main golf regions of Scotland, Roxburghe is not included among the seventy-four courses in this guidebook. Mark it up as a true "hidden gem." It's a Dave Thomas course—one of the best and most challenging of Scotland's inland courses.

• To extend this trip, finish up with several courses in Ayrshire (see Trip 10 for ideas).

Estimated Cost

Golf - £429 x 1.75 = $750
Lodging - $770
Transportation - $280
TOTAL - $1,800

Trip 9 - Stay and Play in St. Andrews

The Courses

St. Andrews Old - St. Andrews second course (New/Jubilee/Castle) - Carnoustie - Kingsbarns - Crail - Lundin Links - Elie

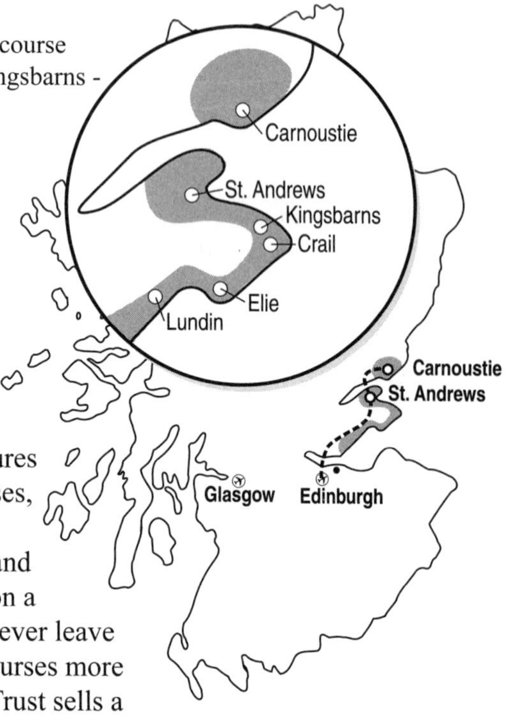

Comment: Unquestionably, the most popular of Scotland's "stay and play" venues—and increasingly so as travel costs increase and golfers discover the merits of "self-catering." St. Andrews has a magic all its own; after all, it's the "Home of Golf" for a reason—or, rather, many reasons. This trip features a combination of St. Andrews courses, the classic courses of Fife at Crail, Lundin, and Elie, plus Kingsbarns and Carnoustie. A variant on this trip: on a one-week stay, one could literally never leave St. Andrews by playing the local courses more than once. The St. Andrews Links Trust sells a seven-day pass for unlimited play on all municipal courses except the Old Course (see page 83 for information on St. Andrews' three and seven-day passes).

The Lineup

Day 1 - (Fri) Depart
Day 2 - (Sat) arrive; to St. Andrews lodging for *7 nights*; play **Kingsbarns**
Day 3 - (Sun) play **Carnoustie**
Day 4 - (Mon) play **Crail**
Day 5 - (Tues) play **Lundin Links**
Day 6 - (Wed) play **Elie**
Day 7 - (Thurs) play **St. Andrews second course (New, Jubilee, Castle, Eden)**
Day 8 - (Fri) play **St. Andrews Old Course** (if no advance reservation on Old Course, leave open for re-scheduling of courses to accommodate play on the Old Course by daily ballot).
Day 9 - (Sat) depart

How to Do It - Notes

• The preferred air route for this trip is in and out of Edinburgh.

• When self-catering, don't wait to book lodging until after your tee times are booked. If you've made a commitment to the idea of "stay and play," the secondary issue is "where to play." You'll have many choices. Most self-catering properties rent from Saturday to Saturday (not all). See page 86 for best websites and page 102 for sites specific to St. Andrews.

• Apply for an advance reservation at St. Andrews. If you don't get it, don't worry. You'll be able to enter the daily ballot for Old Course play every day. When you are successful, you can re-schedule or cancel a previously- booked course.

• Add about $90 if you choose the Castle Course as your second course in the advance reservation process at St. Andrews.

• This is a good trip to make when play on St. Andrews' Old Course is a high priority but you do not have a reservation. With all week to enter the daily ballot it would be highly unusual if you were not successful.

• Without a reservation on the Old Course, one or more of the St. Andrews courses can be booked while you are in town. No need to pre-book; if you do that, you'll have to pay in advance.

• To reduce the cost of this itinerary, substitute one of Fife's classic turn-of-the-century courses for expensive Kingsbarns and/or Carnoustie. Try Leven Links, Scotscraig, or Ladybank.

• Transportation cost can be cut by about twenty-five percent by using local transportation (i.e., taxi companies) for transfers to and from the airport and to golf courses outside St. Andrews.

• Transportation cost can be cut further by using train/bus service from Edinburgh airport to St. Andrews.

• Edinburgh is easily accessible by train from nearby Leuchars.

Estimated Cost

Golf - £747 x 1.75 = $1,307
Lodging - $440
Transportation - $245 or less
TOTAL - $1,992

Trip 10 - Stay and Play in Ayrshire

The Courses (7 courses + optional round at no added cost)

Dundonald - Western Gailes - Glasgow Gailes - Royal Troon Old Course (and Portland at no added cost) - Prestwick - Kilmarnock Barassie - Irvine Bogside

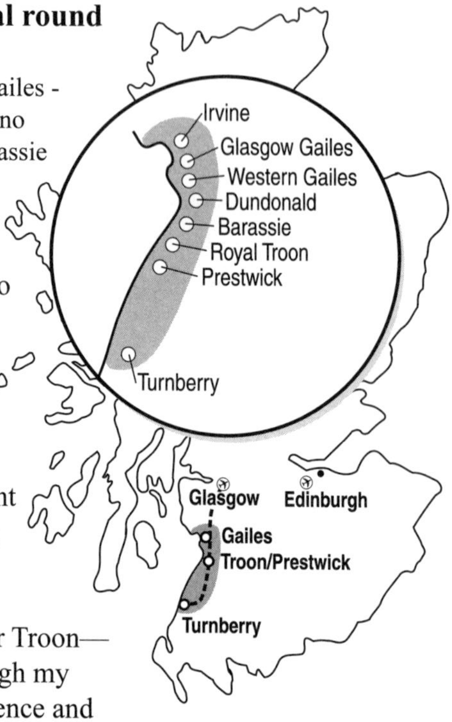

Comment: All these courses are situated along a strip of coastal land no more than ten miles long, surpassing even St. Andrews and Fife for Scotland's densest concentration of great golf courses. Thus, "stay and play" could not be easier. This combination of courses includes the past and present Open courses at Troon and Prestwick; the others have been used as qualifier courses when the Open is at Troon or Turnberry. Lodge in Ayr, Prestwick, or Troon—it doesn't make much difference, though my preference is for the small-town ambience and atmospheric harbor at Troon. Excellent restaurants dot the area and train service along the coast provides easy access to Glasgow. Adding to the density of Ayrshire golf, Troon has three good municipal courses—the Lochgreen, Darley, and Fullerton (the Lochgreen an unusual par 74).

The Lineup

Day 1 - (Fri) Depart
Day 2 - (Sat) arrive Glasgow; to Ayrshire lodging for *7 nights*; play **Dundonald**
Day 3 - (Sun) play **Prestwick**
Day 4 - (Mon) play **Western Gailes**
Day 5 - (Tues) play **Glasgow Gailes**
Day 6 - (Wed) play **Kilmarnock Barassie**
Day 7 - (Thurs) play **Royal Troon Old Course** (optional round on **Portland** at no added cost)
Day 8 - (Fri) play **Irvine Bogside**
Day 9 - (Sat) depart Glasgow airport

How to Do It - Notes

• The best air route for this trip is in and out of Glasgow, about forty minutes from Troon/Prestwick. If Edinburgh is used, plan on returning to the airport the evening of Day 8.

• Self-catering flats and cottages are not so abundant in Ayrshire as in some other regions, but there is a selection. Do some digging on the websites (see page 86) and ask for recommendations at the golf courses. If none of that works, ask for a weekly rate at one of the many B & Bs and guest houses in the Ayr/Troon/Prestwick area.

• Day 2 - Dundonald was designed by Kyle Phillips of Kingsbarns fame. As a daily-fee course, it is scheduled on Saturday here.

• Day 3 - Prestwick, Western Gailes, Glasgow Gailes, Irvine, and Kilmarnock all take a limited number of visitors on Sunday. Book as early as possible.

• During the week, Western Gailes takes visitors on Monday, Wednesday, and Friday.

• Royal Troon takes visitors only on Monday, Tuesday, and Thursday.

• The golf cost here assumes purchase of a "Gailes Experience" pass for Dundonald, Western Gailes, and Glasgow Gailes. Tee times are available all week at Dundonald and Glasgow Gailes; only afternoons on Monday, Wednesday, and Friday at Western Gailes. To book, consult the websites of the participating courses (see "The Directory of Courses").

• To reduce the cost of this trip, substitute West Kilbride or Bellisle for one or two of the more expensive courses . . .

• On the other hand, some may want to add Turnberry into the mix here. See Trip 1 or the "Directory of Courses" for booking detail. Turnberry is about thirty-five minutes south of Troon/Prestwick.

Estimated Cost

Golf - £607 x 1.75 = $1,062
Lodging - $440
Transportation - $245 or less
TOTAL - $1,747

Trip 11 - Stay and Play in North Berwick/Gullane

The Courses

Musselburgh Links - Glen GC - Muirfield - Luffness New - North Berwick West Links - Dunbar - Gullane #1

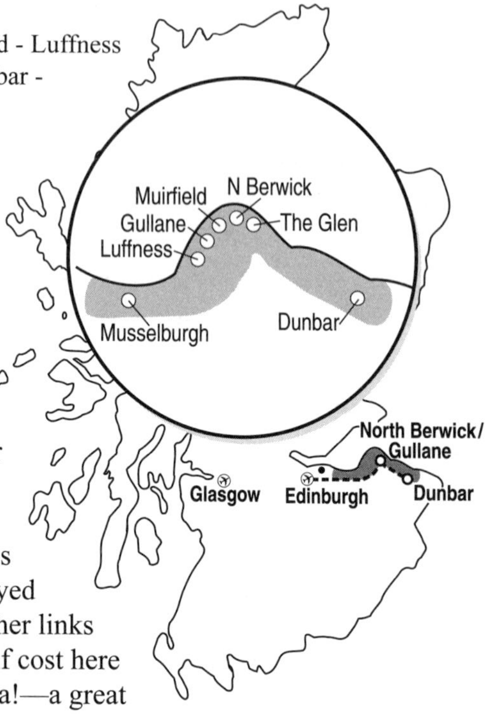

Comment: This entire trip happens within forty miles of the Edinburgh airport. Muirfield, Gullane #1, and Luffness New are all within walking distance of Gullane's main street. North Berwick's West Links and East Links (Glen GC) are on opposite ends of the small town. That is to say, whether self-driving or using local transportation for airport transfers and shuttling to a few golf courses, the transportation cost on this trip is minimal. If you've already played Muirfield and want to substitute another links course for that expensive one, the golf cost here easily could be lowered to $750. Voila!—a great golf trip for little more than $1400. And the golf is, indeed, great. After starting with golf's oldest ground at Musselburgh Links, East Lothian offers some of Scotland's most scenic seaside venues at Gullane #1, North Berwick (both Glen Golf Club and West Links), and Dunbar. Luffness New is a Tom Morris classic and Muirfield, of course, is Muirfield. Easy access to Edinburgh on the train is the cherry on the top of this golf treat.

The Lineup

Day 1 - (Fri) Depart
Day 2 - (Sat) arrive; to Gullane or North Berwick lodging for *7 nights*; play **Musselburgh Links**
Day 3 - (Sun) play **Glen GC**
Day 4 - (Mon) play **Luffness New**
Day 5 - (Tues) play **Muirfield**
Day 6 - (Wed) play **Dunbar**
Day 7 - (Thurs) play **Gullane #1**
Day 8 - (Fri) play **North Berwick West Links**
Day 9 - (Sat) depart from Edinburgh airport

How to Do It - Notes

• Apply for an advance reservation at Muirfield on Tuesday or Thursday up to fourteen months in advance. If the trip is organized too late to make a tee time at Muirfield, substitute one of the other courses in the area—e.g., Craigielaw, Longniddry, or one of the other courses at Gullane.

• My lodging preference is North Berwick. It's a bigger village than Gullane; there are more lodging options; the sea is more present; and there are more restaurant options. But it doesn't make much difference; they are sister towns only seven miles apart.

• Edinburgh is easily accessible by train from North Berwick or from Drem near Gullane.

Estimated Cost

Golf - £575 x 1.75 = $1,006
Lodging - $440
Transportation - $245 or less
TOTAL - $1,691

Trip 12 - Stay and Play in Inverness/Nairn

The Courses

Boat of Garten - Castle Stuart - Inverness GC - Moray Old - Nairn - Nairn Dunbar - Spey Valley GC

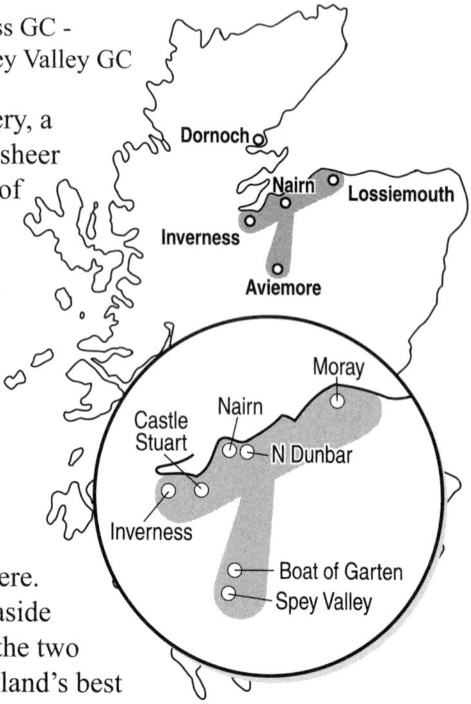

Comment: For course quality, scenery, a high ranking on our Fun-Meter, and sheer value, for my money this is the best of the stay-and-play choices.

The Highlands are special and the golf is first-rate. Many visitors, after having played Scotland's major lowland courses, simply go straight to the Highlands to stay for the duration of whatever time they have to give to Scotland. With history and hiking, castles and whisky, car touring and golf on your doorstep, all the best Scotland has to offer is here.

This trip combines four excellent seaside courses—Moray, Castle Stuart, and the two courses at Nairn—with three of Scotland's best inland courses—two in the Spey Valley and one at Inverness. It's easy enough to slip Royal Dornoch into this itinerary but, if one wants to play several of the courses in the Dornoch area, I recommend re-locating rather than making the drive from Nairn to Dornoch multiple times (about three hours round trip). In other words, do it once but not three times from a self-catering base. The best idea is to extend the trip either in the direction of Dornoch or to Cruden Bay and Royal Aberdeen on the northeast coast.

The Lineup

Day 1 - (Fri) Depart
Day 2 - (Sat) arrive Inverness; lodging for *7 nights* in Inverness or Nairn; play **Nairn Dunbar**
Day 3 - (Sun) play **Moray Old**
Day 4 - (Mon) play **Nairn**
Day 5 - (Tues) play **Boat of Garten**
Day 6 - (Wed) play **Inverness GC**
Day 7 - (Thurs) play **Spey Valley Golf Club**
Day 8 - (Fri) if a.m. play **Castle Stuart**
Day 9 - (Sat) depart

How to Do It - Notes

• If the price is right, an air route into Inverness is ideal. If arriving at Glasgow or Edinburgh, drive time to Inverness is about 3.5 hours.

• Self-catering properties abound throughout the region. Inverness offers the most choices but, as noted elsewhere, I am partial to Nairn as a base. It's a small, walkable town on the sea, with lots of lodging and food options, and it's close to the Spey Valley, the Whisky Trail, and other attractions in and around Inverness.

• For more links golf, substitute Fortrose & Rosemarkie or one of the courses at Hopeman or Lossiemouth east of Nairn for one or more of the inland courses.

• To further reduce the cost of this trip, substitute any of the courses in the area for expensive Castle Stuart.

• One of Scotland's best nine-hole layouts is located at Carrbridge, four miles from Boat of Garten.

Estimated Cost

Golf - £516 x 1.75 = $903
Lodging - $440
Transportation - $245
TOTAL - $1,588

Trip 13 - The Baker's Cookie: Budget Stay and Play in St. Andrews

The Courses

Crail - Leven Links - Lundin Links - Elie - Ladybank - St. Andrews New - Scotscraig

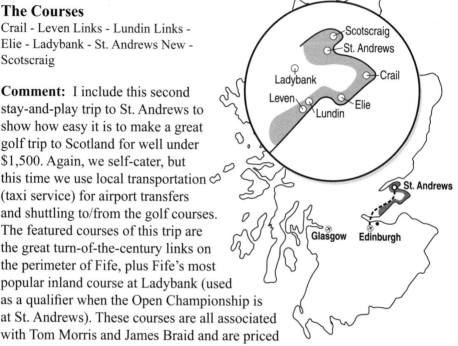

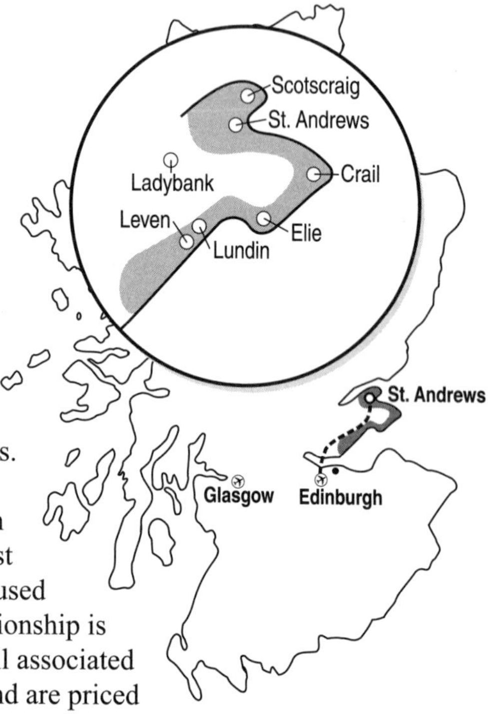

Comment: I include this second stay-and-play trip to St. Andrews to show how easy it is to make a great golf trip to Scotland for well under $1,500. Again, we self-cater, but this time we use local transportation (taxi service) for airport transfers and shuttling to/from the golf courses. The featured courses of this trip are the great turn-of-the-century links on the perimeter of Fife, plus Fife's most popular inland course at Ladybank (used as a qualifier when the Open Championship is at St. Andrews). These courses are all associated with Tom Morris and James Braid and are priced generally between £60-80. The high-priced spreads at Kingsbarns and Carnoustie are skipped. This could be an itinerary for a second or third visit to Scotland, but it could just as well be a trip for anyone on a tight budget or anyone who plans to enter St. Andrews' daily ballot for Old Course play. In the latter case, this lineup of courses minimizes financial damage if a tee time must be canceled to accommodate play on the Old Course. Excepting the New Course, they require no more than a fifty percent deposit.

The Lineup

Day 1 - (Fri) Depart
Day 2 - (Sat) arrive; to St. Andrews lodging for *7 nights*; play **Crail**
Day 3 - (Sun) play **Scotscraig**
Day 4 - (Mon) play **Leven Links**
Day 5 - (Tues) play **Lundin Links**
Day 6 - (Wed) play **Elie**
Day 7 - (Thurs) play **Ladybank**
Day 8 - (Fri) play **St. Andrews New** (book while in town).
Day 9 - (Sat) depart

How to Do It - Notes

• Preferred air route on this trip: in and out of Edinburgh.

• Pick your dates and book your lodging as soon as possible. The golf courses generally have many tee times for visitors and can be booked after lodging is secured. See page 102 for self-catering websites specific to St. Andrews.

• Mid-July through mid-August, Elie limits visitor play to after 3 p.m. During that time you may want to substitute another St. Andrews course for Elie or choose another course in Fife (see page 144 in "The Directory of Courses").

• If booked in advance, St. Andrews courses must be prepaid. The New Course is on Friday here with the implication that it will be booked during the week of your stay (or you will play the Old Course instead). In other words, rather than book the St. Andrews courses in advance, the best strategy is to book those courses when you are there.

• If balloting for Old Course play, Day 8 could be left open to accommodate re-scheduling of courses. If the Old Course is played instead of the New, add about $125 to the total cost.

• Transportation cost can be cut by using local transportation (i.e., taxi companies) for transfers to and from the airport and to golf courses outside St. Andrews. Here, I am estimating a saving of about fifteen percent.

• Edinburgh is easily accessible by train from nearby Leuchars.

• Courses for more golf under £80: Crail Craighead; St. Andrews Eden or Jubilee; 9-hole courses at Anstruther, Lundin, and Ceres (Kingarrock GC).

Estimated Cost

Golf - £428 x 1.75 = $749
Lodging - $440
Transportation - $210
TOTAL - $1,399

PART II

THE NITTY GRITTY

CHAPTER ONE

The Four Elements of a Golf Trip: Air Travel, Vehicle Rental, Tee Times, Lodging

Air Travel

THESE DAYS EVERYONE has their own approach to purchasing airline tickets. Some people use their trusty travel agent. Others prefer to call an airline straight away. Many book on the internet. Some people use frequent-flyer miles. Others use miles accumulated through credit-card purchases.

Given all these options—and the ever-changing dynamics of the airline industry—a book like this is not the place to look for specific information on prices and airline policies. What I *can* do is give you some advice, partly specific to current conditions, but generally based on the bigger picture that comes from years of experience.

Frankly, it bothers me a bit when clients plan a trip to Scotland only to delay buying their airline tickets until they can get "the best deal." To put this phenomenon in perspective: some people will blithely spend something like $500 for golf and one night at the Turnberry Hotel but put off buying an airline ticket with the hope of saving $100! My best advice on that subject is to buy your ticket whenever ready so that you can at least get the best available seat. Rates between North America and the UK do not change much between May and October.

Following are two more pieces of advice to guide your air arrangements. Both these items are based on an important principle: *it's no fun for a golfer to be in Scotland without golf clubs.* Barring a traffic accident, the worst thing that can happen on your trip is for you to arrive at your destination while your clubs are in London, Paris, Frankfurt, or Amsterdam—not for just a few hours but for a few days. If you are on a five or six-day trip and you don't get your clubs until the third or fourth day, you are going to be a decidedly "unhappy camper." Unfortunately, it happens. Why? The main reason is spelled H-e-a-t-h-r-o-w. This is another subject on which I've become an expert through personal experience.

Most visitors to the United Kingdom arrive via London Heathrow because most major cities in the U.S. are served by routes to London, and often the cheapest flights are to that second largest city on planet Earth. The airport at Heathrow is huge. It's a city within a city. Literally thousands of people are "processed" through Heathrow every hour. Given the size of the airport and the crush of humanity there, it is logistically challenging to get oversize luggage (i.e., golf clubs) through the Heathrow maze in less than two hours, *unless you are booked on the same airline throughout your trip.*

British Airways (BA) and British Midland International (BMI) are the main domestic carriers from London to airports in Scotland. For flyers on BA, logistical problems at Heathrow were mitigated in March 2008 with the opening of Terminal 5—used exclusively by BA. All customs, luggage handling, and connecting flights on BA are in that terminal. This arrangement has reduced the incidence of lost and delayed luggage.

The problem is, if your connecting flight is on BMI or if you are using any other airline for service into Britain, you will be shuttled through a labyrinth of Heathrow's back streets between the International Arrivals terminal, passport control, and the Domestic Departures terminal. If your domestic connection is on British Airways, you will be making the long trek out to Terminal 5. All this leads to my first piece of advice:

- *At London Heathrow Airport, unless you are flying solely on British Airways through Terminal 5, leave at least* ***three hours*** *between arrival time and your connecting flight to Scotland.*

Having allowed enough time for you *and your luggage* to make a connection, if your bags still do not arrive in Scotland when you do, you will need to go the "Baggage Claims" office where, bleary-eyed from lack of sleep, you will fill out claim forms and your patience will be taxed to the limit. Most often your luggage will arrive on the next flight and will be forwarded at the airline's expense to your first lodging address.

Ironically enough, *if you choose an international flight with a connection to Scotland, there is clear advantage to connecting through London rather than through a city outside the UK.* The reason: on weekdays BA and BMI run flights from London to Glasgow and Edinburgh about every two hours. Thus, your luggage most often will be delayed for only that length of time. From cities outside the UK, with fewer flights each day, the wait likely will be eight to ten hours at best and, more likely, at least a day.

All this rather depressing discussion of connecting points and delayed or lost luggage leads to my second and best piece of advice:

- *Fly nonstop to Glasgow or Edinburgh if you can.*

When you fly directly into Glasgow or Edinburgh you'll arrive at a relatively peaceful, pleasant place, without the "cattle car" environment of major airports. More important, you'll have an umbilical link with your golf clubs and clothes that were put on the plane at your point of departure. At this writing, daily nonstops to Glasgow and Edinburgh originate from the U.S. at Newark (Continental/United Airlines), New York (Delta), and Philadelphia (USAirways). Delta and USAirways fly only to Glasgow. In high season, Continental flies to both Edinburgh and Glasgow, thus providing the best coverage and arrival/departure flexibility. *Check with the airlines for the most current information.* All these options have in common the least amount of time in the air and at the airports and the best assurance that the golfer will not be separated from his or her clubs.

One-stop options

Another way to get to Glasgow or Edinburgh without going through London is on Aer Lingus via Dublin, Ireland. From Dublin, Aer Lingus has daily flights to Glasgow and Edinburgh. Still another idea is to fly through Manchester, England, on one of several carriers. From Manchester, one can connect to Glasgow, Edinburgh, Aberdeen, or Inverness.

For my money, the best choice among the one-stops is on Icelandair to Glasgow through Reykjavik from Boston, Denver, Washington DC (Dulles), Orlando (Sanford), Minneapolis, New York (JFK), Toronto, or Halifax. The layover at Reykjavik is only about one hour, so it's nearly as good as a direct flight and it's fun to see the moonscape terrain of Iceland from the air. Currently, Icelandair does not fly to Edinburgh.

Following is telephone and website information for the airlines mentioned above (and more). The country code for Ireland (Ryanair) is 353. easyJet is in England (44). For international calls, dial 011, then the country code, then the rest of the number.

Aer Lingus	800-474-7424	***aerlingus.com***
Air Canada	888-247-2262	***aircanada.com***
American Airlines	800-443-7300	***aa.com***
British Airways	800-247-9297	***ba.com***
British Midland	800-788-0555	***flybmi.com***
Continental Airlines	800-525-0280	***continental.com***
Delta Airlines	800-241-4141	***delta.com***
easyJet	870-600-0000 (int'l)	***easyjet.com***
Icelandair	800-223-5500	***icelandair.com***
Ryanair	871-246-0000 (int'l)	***ryanair.com***
United Airlines	800-241-6522	***united.com***
USAirways	800-428-4322	***usairways.com***

For toll-free numbers to other airlines, see ***www.inter800.com***. Finally, to find out how to talk to a real person, by-passing the infuriating numeric "option tree" used by the airlines (and it seems every other business these days), the most blessed website I have found in recent years is ***www.dialahuman.com***. Try it; you'll love it.

Vehicle Rental

Chauffeur-driven versus self-drive trips

THIS IS AN IMPORTANT ISSUE often most influenced by group size. The larger the group (8-12+ golfers/nongolfers), the more likely you are to use a coach and driver. The accent is upon togetherness, socializing, and getting a big group safely through a trip. Cost is not much of a factor because per-person cost diminishes as the number of travelers increases. Per-person cost in a group of twelve will not be much different than per-person cost for four on a self-drive trip.

For groups of four to eight, the issue is a tougher call. For eight, the cost differential is about 2:1. A group of eight on a self-drive trip will spend about $40 per person per day on two minibuses. The same individuals on a chauffeur-driven trip will spend about $70-80+. The ratio for a group of four will be more like 3:1. Clearly, self-driving is the most economical way to travel.

The rest of the decision is qualitative. Your choice will affect the kind of trip you have. Personally, I like to drive; I want to see Scotland "where the rubber meets the road." I like the freedom to come and go when and where I want. A group of eight, requiring two vehicles on a self-drive trip, gains the flexibility to go more than one direction for either golf or nongolf activities. In sum, this approach provides more individual freedom and less "group think." On the other hand, group think is fun too and chauffeuring takes the adventure out of driving on the left side of the road, negotiating roundabouts, and interpreting foreign traffic signs. And, if you have a personable and compatible driver, you can make a friend for life and receive the undoubted benefit of the driver's local knowledge.

Chauffeured transportation has lots of appeal, but for a group of eight golfers it's about twice as expensive as a self-drive trip.

If you choose the chauffeuring option, make sure your coach company is bonded, insured, and has a PCV license (passenger carry vehicle). Look for company-owned Mercedes and Volkswagen coaches as signs of customized quality. Choose a small, family-run business where you will receive personal attention and the best price. I've made a point of uncovering some in various parts of the country. Here are a few:

- *Capercaillie Travel,* Coaltown of Wemyss (nr Kirkcaldy), contact George Brand (01592-653-678; ***www.capercaillietravel.com***)

- *J.K.R. Luxury Coaches,* Strathhaven (nr Glasgow), contact Joe Russell (01357-521-553; ***www.jkrtravel.co.uk***)
- *McLaren Travel*, Troon, contact Roy Anderson (07885-852-885; ***www.mclaren-travel.co.uk***)
- *Rowan Travel*, Dundee, contact Steve Mackie (01382-320-376; ***www.rowantravel.co.uk***)
- *St. Andrews Executive Travel*, St. Andrews (01334-470-080; ***www.saxtravel.co.uk***)
- *Tour Drive Ltd.,* Gullane, contact Mike Scott, (01620-844-855; ***www.tour-drive.com***)
- *Williamson Travel*, Nairn, contact George Williamson (01667-453-322; ***www.williamsontravel.co.uk***)

Most important: If your trip is concentrated in one or two regions (e.g., Ayrshire, Fife, or East Lothian), then choose a transport company based in the area of highest concentration. Why?—because the driver should be able to return home most evenings so that you don't have to pay overnight expenses. That difference should show up in a quote received from your transport company. If it doesn't, ask about it.

"Local transportation"—an alternative to 24/7 coach service

For those on a stay-and-play trip within striking distance of one of Scotland's major airports (Glasgow, Edinburgh, Aberdeen, Inverness), consider using "local transportation" (i.e., taxi service) for transfers to and from the airport, golf courses, and nongolf attractions. There are way too many of these companies to list here. The best way to find them is to look in the online town or regional directories listed in Appendix C (page 277). *The cost of this option tends to be about the same as self-driving.* No need to be tied to a single company or driver, though that is a possibility. Service is engaged when and where it is needed. While staying in St. Andrews, Troon, or Gullane, for example, it makes absolutely no sense to be paying a driver 24/7 when you can walk to the golf course you are playing that day.

Self-drive rental

If the choice is a self-drive trip, reserve your vehicle as early as possible. There's no reason to wait. If cancellation is necessary, any deposits or prepayments made are normally fully refundable with sufficient notice. Penalties are not assessed for changes in pickup/dropoff plans.

This is a major expense that can cause way too much brain damage and cost way too much money. Call any of the name brands in the business. After you tell them you want to rent a vehicle in, say, Glasgow, the first question they ask is, "For what dates?". Then the fun begins: "Automatic or manual?" "Do you want loss damage waiver insurance?" "Zero liability insurance?" "Will that be one way or return?" "You want to add another driver?—that will be another $15 per day." "Oh, by the way, our price doesn't include a local airport surcharge of £17 and a daily road tax. Those are locally collected."

Go through this song and dance with three different companies and you could be pulling your hair out. It makes dealing with the airlines seem simple. By the time you get to the bottom line—with all the "add-ons" and surcharges not included in the base price—you can end up with an expensive rental and a giant headache.

Self-drive: the best independents

In previous editions of this book I have recommended the Arnold Clark company (***www.arnoldclarkrental.co.uk***) as the best choice among the various rental car companies. Nothing has changed. Arnold Clark is Scotland's largest auto dealer with Scotland's largest fleet of vehicles with automatic transmission. Arnold Clark is not a "brand" in the North American market, but just about everyone in the UK knows the company as the major player in the Scottish market. Here is contact information for Arnold Clark:

Arnold Clark 0845-602-1895 (from USA 011-44-845-602-1895)

In the spirit of full disclosure, let it be known that Ferguson Golf is a booking representative for the Arnold Clark company. We have preferred rates with them and we book vehicles for golfers during normal business hours at 800-835-6692. Even if I had no business relationship with Arnold Clark, I would recommend the company as preferable to any of the "brand name" dealers most people go to for a rental car. The reasons are legion:

• First, Arnold Clark caters to the American golf market with automatic transmission in every class, particularly among the SUVs and minibuses that most golf parties need.

• Second, their prices typically beat the brand names.

• Third, all charges are included in a quoted price and are uniformly quoted in pounds sterling. Rates include the value-added tax (20%), airport access fee, road tax, basic insurance (theft, collision), and unlimited mileage. No surprises. In contrast, the brand names nickel-and-dime you with a confusing laundry list of add-ons—some quoted in pounds and some quoted in US dollars.

• Fourth, you won't pay a "premium location" airport tax (typically about £20) because they are off-site agencies with locations near Scotland's major airports.

• Fifth, fees for extra drivers, additional insurance, and one-way drops are lower than the exorbitant fees charged by the brand names.

• Sixth, with twenty-three locations in Scotland, Arnold Clark has good local coverage in case of breakdown or other emergency.

TRAVEL TIP
Ferguson Golf has preferred rates with the Arnold Clark company. To book a vehicle in the USA, call 800-835-6692.

Sixt, a German-based car rental company and one of Europe's largest, is also always worth checking. They have a good selection of automatic vehicles. For an online quote, see ***www.sixt.co.uk***. Their phone numbers at the Glasgow and Edinburgh airports are 0844-499-3399 and 0131-333-0020 respectively.

The brand names

If you want to test my advice on this subject, if you are a loyal Hertz or Avis customer, or you really *want* to shop the brand names, following are suggestions on how to proceed:

• *Check the internet first, but call to follow up with the question, "Is this the best you can do?".*

• *Always check more than one source.* Why? Your first pass establishes a price benchmark. From there you can do some bargaining. If you ask them, rental car companies will usually match the price of a competitor. Most of them have a "beat-rate" supervisor—someone with authority to make a deal. Your goal is to ratchet the price downward as far as it will go—or at least to get add-ons subtracted or reduced. Remember, it never hurts to ask. Ask for a lower price. Ask for a free upgrade. Ask for a specific car. Ask them to eliminate the fee for an additional driver. If you don't ask, you won't get.

Ideal for four golfers—a minibus with automatic transmission.

• *Invoke your affiliations.* Be sure to ask about any discounts you might secure by virtue of associations, memberships, employment, etc. These might include AARP, AAA, frequent flyer memberships, government or corporate affiliation. But don't ask for the discounted rate until *after* you've received a quote for a "base rate." Most often the reply will be, "That is our lowest rate," but the response might be, "I can reduce that rate by five percent." If you ask for the discounted rate first, you'll never know whether you were quoted a base rate that got called a "discounted rate."

Who to call? At Scottish airports you'll find the usual cast of characters—Alamo, Avis, Budget, Hertz, National—plus a European agency, Europcar.

AutoEurope is a broker for some of them (a varying list depending upon location), allowing for some one-stop shopping. Here are toll-free telephone numbers for the major car rental companies:

Alamo	800-522-9696
AutoEurope	800-223-5555
Avis	800-331-1212
Budget	800-472-3325
Dollar	800-800-4000
Enterprise	800-325-8007
EuropCar	877-940-6900
Hertz	800-654-3131
National	888-868-6204
Thrifty	800-847-4389

With all the mergers and acquisitions that have occurred in the car-rental industry (e.g., Enterprise-Alamo-National), one might think shopping would be simplified. That's not necessarily the case. All the companies, merged or not, operate independently with their own fleets and price structures.

On the following page is a worksheet to help you track car agency data with the objective of comparing "apples to apples." Good luck.

Frequently-asked questions

Do I need an international driver's license to rent a car in Scotland? No. You need a valid driver's license and your passport.

What is the age limit for drivers? Depending upon car size and individual company policy, minimum ages vary from 21 to 25. At the upper end, the age limits vary from 71 to 75. Arnold Clark does not have an upper age limit but requires a medical certificate from drivers over 75.

What should I do if I have an accident or mechanical breakdown? Your rental car company will provide full instructions and contact numbers.

Is a minivan big enough for four golfers? The typical European minivan is better for three golfers or two golfers and two nongolfers. For four golfers I recommend the next step up in size—a VW Caravelle or Mercedes Vito *minibus.*

Should I buy the deductible ("excess") insurance? Check with your insurance agent to determine whether the deductible is covered by your personal auto insurance. Major credit card companies normally cover the deductible if their card is used to book and pay for the rental.

What is an "estate" vehicle? That's the British term for station wagon.

RENTAL VEHICLE WORKSHEET

Company ____

Phone Number ____

Airport: On-site ___________ Off-site _____________

Confirmation # ______________________________________

Date of Inquiry ____________________ Clerk ID _____________________

Vehicle Size: subcompact, compact, mid-size sedan, large sedan, station wagon, minivan, minibus

Pickup Date: _______________________ Approx Time ______________

Return Date: _______________________ Approx Time ______________

\# Days __________

Automatic Transmission ________ Manual Transmission ____________

_________ Basic Rate (typically includes 20% VAT, unlimited mileage, fire/third party insurance)

_________ Discounted Basic Rate - Notes ______________________________

_________ ADD Location (airport) Surcharge

_________ ADD Road Tax _______ per day x _________ days

_________ ADD Additional Driver(s) ___________ per driver per day x _________ driver(s) x _________days OR flat fee ___________

_________ ADD Collision Damage Waiver (CDW) _________ per day x ________ days

_________ ADD One-way Dropoff

_________ ADD other insurance (e.g., theft, reduced or zero liability)

_________ ADD GPS mobile unit __________per day x __________days

_________**TOTAL** x $1.75 if quoted in pounds sterling = **$**__________

NOTES:

Tee Times

Contacting the clubs

BEFORE CHEAP LONG-DISTANCE phone service, fax machines, and email, the common way to make a reservation at a Scottish course was by written request accompanied by a formal "letter of introduction" from a club professional. That is emphatically *not* the case today. The Scots are polite and somewhat more formal than Americans, but they are modern people, quite good at extracting money from tourists as efficiently as possible rather than by "snail mail."

Thus, the quickest, most effective way to reserve a tee time at most courses is to make a telephone call. If you do that from the west coast of North America, it means getting up pretty early. The time differential is eight hours, so you'll need to make calls before 8 a.m. and not later than 9 a.m. Most offices at the well-traveled courses are open until at least 4 p.m. or 5 p.m. At the lesser-known clubs you may find the secretary's hours sporadic or confined to the morning hours. If that's the case, then you'll probably be communicating by fax or email. Here are the time differentials in the United States:

- Pacific Time - 8 hrs. - call before 8 a.m.
- Mountain Time - 7 hrs. - call before 9 a.m.
- Central Time - 6 hrs. - call before 10 a.m.
- Eastern Time - 5 hrs. - call before 11 a.m.

I recommend, first, a look at a club's website and, then, a phone call because you can get answers most quickly that way and a phone call gives you maximum flexibility to confirm details regarding alternative available times, visitor restrictions, deposits, club rental, caddie hire, directions, etc. Sometimes you can get a feel for the ambience of a club just by talking with people on the phone. This is also a good time to request lodging recommendations. If you have trouble reaching someone with authority to book a time, then send an email or a fax and wait for a reply.

When making a tee time you'll most often talk, not with a club secretary, but with a booking secretary—like one of the friendly and efficient ladies at Crail Golfing Society.

Most often you will *not* talk with the secretary of a club but, rather. with an office assistant. Usually at least two communications will be necessary—the first to formally request a time, then a second to confirm group composition and payment details by fax or email. If it can all be done with one phone call, so much the better.

The efficiency of fax machines and email

Admittedly, fax machines and email cost less than phone calls, and there's a certain satisfaction gained from firing off a half-dozen communiqués to Scotland at 10 p.m., then waking up the next morning to find that most of your trip was booked overnight while you were sleeping! It's an efficient way to start the process even if some follow-up work is necessary. If you like this approach, below is a sample letter for you to adapt in making a booking inquiry. All detail necessary to customize this letter for individual courses is in Part III, "The Directory of Courses."

SAMPLE - ADVANCE RESERVATION REQUEST LETTER

Date

ATT: Alistair MacDonald, Secretary, Lundin Golf Club
RE: Visitor inquiry - advance reservation

Dear Mr. MacDonald:

This is to inquire whether Lundin Golf Club can accommodate four visiting golfers, preferably with a morning tee time, on __DATE__.
If so, following is information for confirming an advance reservation and making the required deposit.

LEAD GOLFER: A Ferguson, hdp 10, Wellshire GC, Denver CO
CREDIT CARD: MC 0000-0000-0000-0000 Exp 09/14 3-digit code 999
OTHER GOLFERS: Donald Rex, hdp 13, City Park GC, Denver CO; Robert Thompson, hdp 12, Overland Park GC, Denver CO; Donald Bruning, hdp 15, The Dunes GC, Thornton CO.

THANK YOU in advance for your assistance with this request.

Allan Ferguson
1743 S. Marion St.
Denver CO 80210
ph/fax: 303-722-3441
aferguson@fergusongolf.com

Online booking

The most visible online booking service developed over the past decade has been ***www.teetimescotland.com***. Though based in the UK, it is woefully incomplete and inaccurate. The problem is, "Garbage in, garbage out." The booking services are dependent upon the clubs for supplying up-to-date information and that is not always done. The clubs are mostly interested in selling their "off-peak" times through these kinds of businesses, so tee time selection is inferior. Also, many golf clubs have set up online booking systems of their own in recent years and do not participate with the booking services. These are current and accurate and could not be easier. The trend is in this direction.

In either case, at most high-profile golf clubs, an online system simply cannot substitute for a telephone call and a personal conversation with a booking assistant. It is in that conversation that you can glean information about local events, club events, lodging tips, etc. So, why book online when you could be on the phone talking to someone at a club? The value of personal contact cannot be underestimated.

Important information for single golfers

Often a client will say to me, "I've heard that a single golfer can't make a tee time in Scotland." This is a myth. On the contrary, the single golfer has distinct advantages in making tee times.

The only important exceptions to this rule are at Muirfield, St. Andrews, and Carnoustie. Muirfield books only fours; advance reservations for singles at St. Andrews are severely limited; Carnoustie limits single advance booking to three days before play unless they have booked a group of three that you can join. Otherwise, a single can make an advance booking at virtually all other courses, including Royal Troon, Prestwick, Royal Dornoch, Western Gailes, North Berwick, Gullane #1, and Kingsbarns. Understanding this subject is both interesting and instructive because it relates to the Scottish attitude toward golf and course management.

For two reasons Scots will not routinely "fill a foursome" the way course managers do in the United States. First, they are more interested in the pace of play than they are in filling a course to capacity. They tend to favor twos and threes as much as fours, and many courses actually reserve early and late hours for the two-ball matches often preferred by club members. The Scots would rather get a dozen two-ball matches around in three hours than six or seven four-ball groups in four-plus hours. A five-hour round is out of the question.

Second, if two or three golfers have made a tee time during visitor hours, the Scots won't automatically put other golfers with that group until they ask permission of the booked golfers. In other words, you don't have to play golf with someone you don't know unless you agree to do so. What a novel idea!—enough to make an American club pro cringe. This is a broad generalization. The most heavily-played courses *will* pair singles and twos with other golfers.

In the pairing procedure, a single golfer looking for a game may be asked for his or her handicap. Why? Because, for the enjoyment of all, the Scots normally won't put a total duffer out with a scratch golfer. Another novel idea American course managers could well emulate.

So, what does all this mean for the single golfer? Well, it's good news. First, it means that at most courses you'll find lots of "holes" in the schedule of tee times—lots of places for a single golfer to slide into a game with two or three other players. Second, it means most often you'll be playing with golfers of comparable ability. The process can lead to hooking up with compatible singletons during your stay in Scotland.

Since my wife is a nongolfer, I have considerable experience as a single golfer in Scotland. Here's my approach:

• If a course is on my "must-play" list, I'll pre-book it and let the booking secretary know that I would be glad to have others join me.

• I'll leave most days unbooked—thus avoiding prepayments and deposits and, at the same time, creating maximum flexibility for golf or nongolf activities depending upon weather, mood, etc. Then I'll have a list of "optional" courses for play and start phoning through the list in priority order until I find a tee time that works best for our schedule.

• Normally, I'll call a course the day before I want to play and ask to speak to the secretary, the booking assistant, or, most likely, the professional. I'll explain that I'm there as a single golfer and would be interested in a game with a club member if that can be arranged. Sometimes I'm successful with that approach to play with an "insider," sometimes I'm not—but rarely do I encounter a course that is fully booked.

Single golfers—get proactive!

The greatest plus for a single golfer in Scotland is the opportunity to meet other travelers, locals, and club members. From these encounters a great range of positive, serendipitous consequences can follow. To facilitate those opportunities, especially at the courses lightly traveled by visitors, the golfer must be proactive. Apart from the opportunities involved, there is a simple matter of sociability. Without taking some initiative, a single golfer could end up playing a lot of rounds alone. For some, this is not a concern. Others really don't enjoy the game without company on the course. If you are among the latter, I strongly advise a call to the professional shop a day or two in advance of play to make it clear that you would like to "join or be joined" with other golfers. To be even more proactive about it, another idea is to contact the *club secretary* a few weeks in advance of play and ask him or her to post a message on the members' bulletin board. To make it easy and ready to post, send the note by fax on a half-sheet of paper. The note might read something like this:

Single Visiting Golfer Seeks Playing Partner

I'm a single golfer from the USA who would enjoy meeting one or more club members for a round of golf.

My tee time - **Monday, 20 August, 10:30 a.m.**

If you would like to join in a round of friendly international competition, please contact me. I'll be pleased to hear from you.

Allan Ferguson
1743 S. Marion St.
Denver CO 80210
aferguson@fergusongolf.com
303-722-3441 (ph/fax)
handicap - 10

Step-by-step booking advice

Using Part I, Chapter Four, "Where to Go", and Part III, "The Directory of Courses," pick the courses you want to play and determine their visitor policies. Then take the following three-step approach:

• *Arrange your courses in priority order.* Start provisional booking from the top down—from "must-play" to "optional." Certain courses on your ideal itinerary are likely to be "linchpin" courses—ones that either allow the rest of the schedule to work logistically or are at or near the top of a must-play list. For example, if Royal Troon is on your must-play list, it's usually a good idea to schedule the Ayrshire coast early in the week because Troon accepts visitors only on Mondays, Tuesdays, and Thursdays. Your odds of booking are best if you have the flexibility to play either Monday or Tuesday rather than only on Thursday.

• *Schedule "daily fee," public, and resort courses on the weekends.* At most private clubs (i.e., most golf courses in Scotland), visitor access on weekends is restricted. Maximum flexibility to play when you want to play on Saturdays and Sundays can be achieved by booking the daily fee, public, and resort courses on those days. Examples of these are: Kingsbarns, The Duke's Course, and the courses at Fairmont St. Andrews in Fife (Region #1); the courses at Gleneagles in Perthshire (Region #7); Turnberry and Belleisle in Ayrshire (Region #2). In St. Andrews, the Old Course is closed on Sunday; the other courses are open.

• *Unless you are self-catering, secure all your tee times before you make arrangements for lodging.* As Robert Burns wrote, "The best-laid plans of mice and men gang aft agley" (often go awry). All the pieces of the tee-time puzzle must fit before you start booking accommodations. You could have a well-laid plan only to find out that two of the courses on your must-play list are closed to visitor play on the days you want to be there. What to do? Well, at that point, you either change your priorities or start rearranging the itinerary to accommodate your must-play courses.

Open competitions

Open competitions are nearly as old as golf in Scotland and, if the moment is right, these offer the best and cheapest ways to get beneath the surface of Scottish golf and enjoy the game at the club level. Single golfers, particularly, are well advised to seek out these events. Typically one-day affairs, open competitions take place practically every day at some club, somewhere in Scotland, from April through October. Events are organized for all levels of ability in every imaginable format—scratch, handicapped stroke play, seniors, mixed doubles, senior mixed doubles, Stableford, four-ball, foursomes (alternate stroke), etc., etc. The best part: the entry fee at these events, even at the most expensive courses, is rarely more than £10 to £20. If one can find an open event at a relatively expensive course (like just about every course in this book), savings can be huge. Moreover, visiting golfers get to meet and play with golfers from the UK and often from other countries as well.

The best source of information on these open competitions is *The Wee Yellow Book of Amateur Golf Events in Scotland (WYB) WYB* is now published in both print and electronic format. Registration for the online version is free at ***www.weeyellowbook.com***.

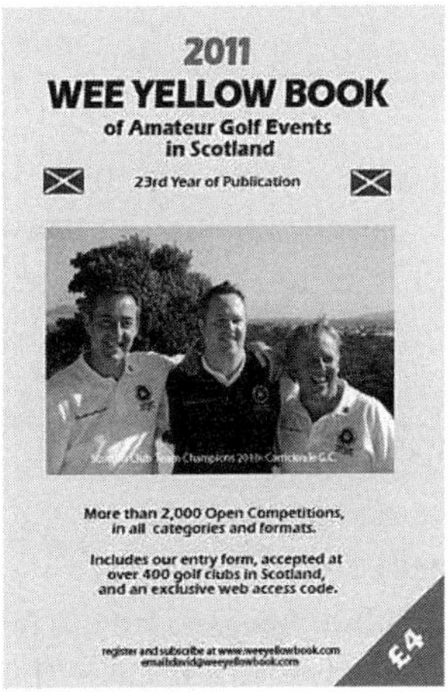

The Wee Yellow Book—Scotland's passport to open competitions for amateur golfers.

Scottish golf clubs fix their competition dates during the last quarter of every year for the ensuing year. *WYB* compiles and publishes that information by the end of January. Events are organized by date, category, and region.

The Scottish Golf Union (***www.scottishgolf.org***) also compiles information on open club competitions. There's a good search function on their website, but it's not easy to find. On the Home Page, in a column on the right side of the page, click on a box labeled "Open Competitions." You can also get there by following Home>Play the Game>SGU Golf Central, then finding the box labeled "Open Competitions."

Apply early; open club events tend to fill up quickly. Late January into early February is the time to start looking if you can. On the other hand, most of the events occur at more or less the same time every year. With some online searching or an old copy of *WYB,* one can get a jump on the competition by contacting a club earlier than January or February.

Another way to get information on open competitions is to simply visit the websites of clubs in the vicinity of your travels. Though not all clubs list their competition dates, most do so under page headings like "open events," "calendar," or "fixtures."

Since 2001 when I started writing about open competitions, readers have written to me to relate interesting stories featuring great savings. Here's one from a single golfer: With July travel dates known well in advance—based first in North Berwick, then in Inverness—my reader began looking in January for club events that fit his schedule. He found one-day "gents opens" at Royal Musselburgh, Montrose, Inverness, and Boat of Garten. He called the club secretaries who waived prepayment requirements. Each of the events cost £15 (total £60) compared to regular green fees at the time of £146—a saving of £86 or about $150. More important, he had the satisfying experience of playing competitive golf with Scots on their own turf and, to top it off, he won low-net honors at Boat of Garten and walked away with a £55 gift certificate good at any member club of the Scottish Golf Union!

Even though many open events fill up well in advance, I have stumbled into several of these while traveling without advance reservations. In other words, if one is looking for a game, it never hurts to make a telephone inquiry or drop in on a club. Frequently the answer will be, "Come on ahead. Weel find room fer yae."

Regional Packages and Promotions

Some golf courses in various regions of Scotland wisely have combined forces to promote themselves with package prices. There must be at least twenty of these regional programs—most of little interest to the visiting golfer. On the other hand, following are several of considerable interest in the most heavily-traveled regions:

- *Ayrshire Open Qualifier Discount Card* - Play on Prestwick St. Nicholas, Kilmarnock Barrasie, and Irvine Bogside with optional play on the new Dundonald Links at additional cost. The program is administered by Wilkinson Golf; order by phone or by mail. For more information, see ***www.wilkinsongolf.com*** or call 01383-629-940. For residents of the U.S., Wilkinson Golf has a toll free number: 1-800-868-1106.

- *The Gailes Experience* - Involves Western Gailes, Glasgow Gailes, and Dundonald—all within spitting distance of one another—at an irresistible package price. Play at Glasgow Gailes and Dundonald is unrestricted; Western can be played only in the afternoon on Monday, Wednesday, or Friday. Administered at Western Gailes; email ***enquiries@westerngailes.com*** or call 01294-311-649.

- *Carnoustie Country Dream Ticket* - Includes three excellent Open qualifiers (Monifieth, Montrose, and Panmure) and the Open venue itself—the championship course at Carnoustie. These are the best golf courses in Angus—a perfect combo on a three or four-day stay in or around Carnoustie. The program is administered by Scotia Travel. For more information see ***www.carnoustiecountry.com*** or call 0141-305-5050.

- *Carnoustie Country Classic* - A four-day event in early May featuring Stableford net competition for amateur golfers of all stripes (handicap maximums - men, 24; women, 36). The accent is on sociability. This is the same group of courses involved in the Carnoustie Country Dream Ticket. A good bargain at a great spot on the calendar to combine with play in and around St. Andrews. For more information see ***www.carnoustiecountry.com*** or contact the secretary at Monifieth Golf Club (01382-532-767 or ***secretary@monifiethlinks.com***).

- *St. Andrews Links Trust three and seven-day Passes* - For unlimited play on all the courses at St. Andrews except the Old Course. Not sold in advance; passes are available at the clubhouses and from the starters and can be used over a period of seven and fourteen days respectively. Great to have on an extended stay in St. Andrews. For more information, call 01334-466-666 or see ***www.standrews.org.uk***. On the Home page, from the drop-down menu under "Playing Golf," select "Green Fees."

Frequently-asked questions

Do I have to prepay green fees? That depends upon the course. Some require full prepayment; most require a deposit ranging from a token (e.g., five or ten percent) to a substantial amount (fifty percent); some require no advance payment at all. For details see the deposit entries in "The Directory of Courses."

Can I use my credit card to book a tee time? With few exceptions, yes. Just make sure it's MasterCard or VISA; American Express won't get you far in Scotland, especially at the golf courses.

Can I use a different credit card from each member of my group for deposits? The clubs prefer to deal with a "lead golfer." It would then be up to the lead golfer to get reimbursed by the other golfers.

What information do I need to provide? A lead golfer's name, number of golfers, contact information, and credit card details. St. Andrews management will ask for all golfers' names, handicap indices, and home clubs (where indices are kept).

I see that the golf clubs prohibit "trainers." What does that mean? That's the British term for "tennis shoes."

Lodging

SCOTLAND HAS A GREATER range and quantity of accommodations per capita than any place in the world. The country is dotted with literally thousands of modest bed-and-breakfast operations while boasting palatial international resorts among the finest in the world. In between are unique and attractive small hotels and country houses, as well as "purpose-built" hotels and an increasing number of standardized, American-style hotel chains. Tourism is big business in Scotland.

Most of these accommodations are graded and cataloged annually by VisitScotland (formerly the Scottish Tourist Board) in two publications available in any good bookstore or Tourist Information Office in Scotland. These are: *Where to Stay: Bed and Breakfast (year)* and *Where to Stay: Hotels and Guest Houses (year).* VisitScotland also publishes volumes on camping and "self-catering" (rental) accommodations. These publications are hard to obtain in North America but, fortunately, all the information is available online at ***www.visitscotland.com***.

The VisitScotland publications are not guidebooks. They are comprehensive listings of all member establishments. Guidebooks, by definition, are selective, though I find the most popular of the general guidebooks (*Fodor's, Frommer's, Lonely Planet*) unsatisfactory when it comes to accommodations. Specialized publications are better. But here's another idea: when you call your courses to make tee times, ask the secretary or booking assistant about accommodations in your price range. Usually they'll give you good recommendations and you'll be getting those recommendations from a local source.

Internet searching

Most hotels, guest houses, and B & Bs have their own websites. Certainly that is the trend. But many guest houses and B&Bs gain access to the web via one or another promotional group. Primary among these is the tourist board's ***www.visitscotland.com***. Less comprehensive but well organized is

www.smoothhound.co.uk. Others are the Automobile Association's site, ***www.theaa.com***, and ***www.aboutscotland.com***, the most selective of the services. Together, these provide a thorough overview of lodging options in all price categories. See "Appendix C" for more listings of promotional services.

B & Bs, guest houses, and hotels

The distinction between B & Bs and guest houses in Scotland may elude foreigners but, essentially, the difference is that a B & B is smaller than a guest house. By law, a B & B may accommodate no more than six lodgers. A guest house will have at least four rooms (usually more than four). In times past, there was a further distinction: many guest houses offered an evening meal. Today, some still do—but not many. With few exceptions, an evening meal is not an option at a B & B. Virtually all hotels—even small hotels (up to twenty rooms)— have a liquor license and a dining room/bar for lunches and evening meals. Hotel bars and dining rooms often are gathering places for locals. Most hotels have a sitting room or lounge—usually a feature also of guest houses and B & Bs. All establishments serve a traditional "Scottish Breakfast." These days you'll also have healthier fruit and cereal options (see page 123, for a sample breakfast menu).

B & Bs and guest houses offer best value for money and hosts who "know the territory." Here, golfers are greeted at The Glebe House in North Berwick.

Self-catering

This is the British term for what Americans call "rentals." Just as with conventional lodging choices, comfort levels and vintages run the gamut from basic to luxurious and from contemporary to refurbished rustic. Many self-catering units are transformed farm cottages and croft houses in rural locations. Others are modern apartment units in towns and cities or are "purpose-built" specifically as income-producing properties on private land. *Most self-catering units assume a full week stay from arrival on Saturday through departure on a following Saturday morning,* but that is not always the case, especially during the "shoulder" months of April and October. Prices vary by season, but one can generally be assured of getting a lot more value for a lot less money compared to conventional accommodations.

Any golf party on a stay-and-play trip of at least a week should consider self-catering. Self-catering creates the option of eating in or eating out, thus reducing food and drink expenditures. If the big Scottish breakfast does not appeal, a self-caterer has more control over breakfast options. In short, a rental unit offers the comforts of home, including a fully-equipped kitchen. For some, that is appealing. For others, that's what they are trying to escape.

To give you a clearer idea of what a self-catering unit offers, on a trip a few years ago I made the following partial inventory of kitchen and living room amenities at a self-catering farmhouse in Aberdeenshire:

Self-Catering Inventory

Kitchen: stove, toaster, microwave, cutlery, two sets of dishes, refrigerator, paper towels, pitchers, coffee maker, cutting boards, bread bin, sugar, cooking oil, vinegar, salt, pepper, spices, flour, thermos, coffee pot, drinking glasses, wine glasses, apron, pots, pans, hotpads. *Living room:* fireplace, kindling, wood, easy chairs, sofa, sound system, television, stacks of tourism brochures and information, wall-maps of Scotland and the local area. *Other*: vacuum, grocery bags, broom, dust pan, iron, detergent, cleansers, washing machine and dryer.

Staying for a week or more?—This house for up to six people in St. Andrews costs about the same for one week as one *room in a 3-star hotel.*

Early booking is advisable with self-catering properties for several reasons: first, they are either booked or they're not and most bookings are for a full week; second, they are fewer in number than conventional choices; and, third, this is the preferred method of lodging for many Europeans. The good properties tend to get grabbed up early, particularly for dates in August and September when many Europeans like to travel.

The best websites for finding rental properties

Over the past decade, rental websites of international proportion have developed. The biggest players in the field are TripAdvisor's ***www.flipkey.com*** and HomeAway, Inc.'s ***www.homeaway.com***, plus two subsets of that database, Vacation Rentals by Owners (***www.vrbo.com***), and Owners Direct (***www.ownersdirect.com***). My spotchecks of these databases indicate reasonably good coverage of rentals in the golf towns of Scotland. More properties can be unearthed by checking websites specific to Scotland. The best of these are ***www.assc.co.uk***, the site of the Association of Scotland's Self-caterers, and ***www.visitscotland.com***. For websites specific to Fife and St. Andrews, see page 102.

The star system and pricing

VisitScotland grades all establishments on a five-star scale. Among hotels, five stars are reserved for "world-class" establishments—the Turnberrys and Gleneagles of the world. Four stars mean "excellent;" three stars connote "very good;" two stars indicate "good;" and one star—well, you don't want to go there.

Four stars are often found on country-house manors and mansions adapted to the hotel trade—in fact, you can look for those magic words, "Country House Hotel" and be pretty sure you're going to have an extraordinary lodging experience.

Members of VisitScotland participate in the association's star-based grading system. Normally, a four-star B & B is "can't miss" lodging

Three-star hotels are consistently good, frequently full of character, and most price-attractive to the majority of tourists. I've cited a dozen or so of this class in Part III, "The Directory of Courses" and in "Appendix C" as favorites of golfers. *Typically, a three-star hotel will be priced in a range of £45 to £55 ($75-95) per person per night.* From this benchmark, price extrapolations can be made downward and upward (i.e., two-star £30-40; four-star £60-£70+ per person per night).

Prices in each category vary dependent upon location. For example, Edinburgh is significantly more expensive than Inverness and the three-star hotels in St. Andrews are £10-20 more than the three-star norm. The best bargains will often be found at the two-star hotels, but you need to be careful in that group. These tend to be the smallest of hostelries and they can be either acceptable or too small to maintain a high standard.

Interestingly enough, while four and five-star hotels are pricey and few in number, you'll find lots of guest houses and B & Bs with these rankings. Typically, they are priced in the same range as the three-star hotels and, for my money, they offer the best value and best personal experiences for golfers and nongolfers alike. Compared to most hotels, these B & Bs offer more spacious lodging and the personal touch of hosts who "know the territory."

Making reservations

After consulting guidebooks, browsing the internet, and talking to folks at the clubs, you should be ready to contact your chosen hostelry. Again, I prefer the rapid response, flexibility, and personal contact afforded by a telephone call. Here's what to consider and ask about when you call:

• *Priced per person or per room?* The aggravating European tradition of pricing per person per night (pppn), hangs on in Scotland and is worth special comment. Single travelers or unrelated travelers sharing space will find lodging in Scotland a good bargain—remember, those £40 (more or less) are buying you a breakfast so big that you can easily skip lunch. On the other hand, even ordinary lodging quickly gets expensive for a family pairing in a room, because that money is all coming out of one bank account! This pricing tradition is slowly changing due to pressure from chains like Thistle, Holiday Inn, Travel Inn, and TraveLodge—all of whom offer space on a per-room basis. Be sure to ask whether quoted prices are *per person* or *per room.*

• *Single room or single supplemented room?* Even when traveling in a group, many people prefer to have their own single room. Some lodgings have rooms specifically designed for singles. Always ask. A single room will cost less than a "single supplemented" room where a single lodger is taking space designed for double occupancy. Typically this surcharge might increase the cost of a room from, say, £40 to £55, whereas the room would cost £80 double occupancy. In this hypothetical example, the "supplement" is £15.

• *Multi-night stay discount.* Many lodgings will grant a modest discount on stays of three nights or more. Some will offer that verbally or in writing but more often you have to ask.

• *Bed sizes; double or twin-bedded rooms.* Scots distinguish between *double* rooms and *twin-bedded* rooms. In their lexicon, a "double room" typically has one bed that may be a double (4'6"), a king (5'0"), or a super-king (6'0"). Except at Buckingham Palace, queens seem to have gotten lost in the shuffle. A "twin-bedded" room has two twin or single beds or a single and a double—ideal for same-sex golf parties. Some beds can be converted from one configuration to another (two "zip-and-link" singles equal a super-king). Among couples, if one person is a picky sleeper, the twin-bedded room may be preferable. In a similar vein, if you're used to space afforded by a king-size bed, a standard European double or even a "king" (equal to a five-foot queen in North America) might not be suitable.

• *Bath/shower facility.* Most people these days are partial to showers. Many lodgings of all descriptions have shower stalls only. Some B & Bs and guest houses do not have a shower in all rooms. Still others offer bathtub/shower combinations in which the shower is jerry-rigged over the bathtub. Be sure to ask about shower facilities if it is important to you. The main point: If the room is described as a "bathroom," it normally has a *bathtub*, most often with a shower installation; otherwise it will be described as a "shower room."

An alternative to booking accommodations yourself is to use the services of VisitScotland's Tourist Information Offices (TIs). For a small fee, these offices will make bookings for you at member hotels, guest houses, and B & Bs. This is a particularly useful service for those traveling without advance reservations, but it is a service available to anyone at any time.

One final note: I firmly believe the more money you spend on lodging the more you separate yourself from the ordinary people, the customs, the heart and soul of Scotland (or, for that matter, any other place). Taken to extreme, this philosophy might point towards flea-bag hotels and youth hostels. Of course, that's not what I mean. I mean simply that many accommodations are available in the mid-price range of £45 to £55 ($75 to $95 per person per night). That's why I don't recommend places like the Old Course Hotel or Rusacks in St. Andrews; the Carnoustie Golf Course Hotel; the Marine Hotel in North Berwick; or the Newton Hotel in Nairn. These places are popular with tour operators. But they are places where you're just another number—one of thousands of tourists (usually Americans) passing through their relatively impersonal doors every year.

The more money you spend on lodging the more you separate yourself from the ordinary people, the customs, the heart and soul of Scotland.

Scotland is one of the special places in the Anglo-American world where a traveler can still experience a tradition of B & Bs, guest houses, and small hotels of distinction, with unique character and highly personal service—a tradition all but extinct in the United States. That's the kind of tradition a savvy traveler will seek out rather than choose a hotel one might as easily find at Myrtle Beach, Palm Springs, or Dallas.

Frequently-asked questions

Do I need to make reservations? Most golfers want to have everything pinned down so, sure, get the reservations made. My basic advice here is to confirm the tee times first and then address the lodging. Certainly, it is feasible for a single golfer or a couple to freelance and take what comes. Even then, decisions may be dictated by time and place. If you want to stay on the Isle of Skye in August, for example, it would be foolish not to make a lodging reservation. Edinburgh in August is another time to make a reservation; that's when the International Festival draws huge crowds from around the world. On the other hand, most of the time, in a large town or city like Inverness, Aberdeen, Glasgow, or Edinburgh, a stop at the local Tourist Information Office will get you a room straightaway.

Do I have to stay at the Turnberry Hotel to play the Ailsa course? Technically, no. But it's a busy resort and residents have priority at the course. For non-residents, the drill involves calling for a tee time within two weeks of desired date of play. Personal testimony: I have never failed to get non-resident golfers onto the Ailsa, even in high season. No guarantees, but, to my mind, this approach sure beats paying for the hotel. Better yet, buy a prepaid "twilight time." For more information, see "The Directory of Courses - Turnberry Hotel."

Do I have to stay at the Carnoustie Golf Course Hotel to play the championship course at Carnoustie? No. For more information, see "The Directory of Courses - Carnoustie Golf Links."

Can I get an Old Course tee time through the Old Course Hotel at St. Andrews? As a member of the St. Andrews Hotel and Guest House Association, the Old Course Hotel receives an allocation of about twenty-five tee times annually. Check with hotel reservations regarding those times. Apart from that, the hotel has no relationship with the Links Trust that administers the golf courses in St. Andrews and, therefore, has no special access to tee times.

What does "en suite" mean? It's a highfalutin' term picked up from the French; it means a bath/shower and toilet are in the room. Even though virtually all hotel rooms in Scotland include toilet and bath/shower, the term hangs on from an earlier age when the "WC" was down the hall or around the corner. If a room is described "with private bath," it means the bathroom is *not* in the sleeping room but is nearby and is reserved for sole use by the occupant. Often these bedrooms have a wash basin in the room.

Should I take a hairdryer? You'll find them in most rooms, though they may be hidden in a dresser drawer. If there is none, ask at the desk. Nine out of ten times they'll have one for you. Bottom line: don't bother to pack one.

Do I need a converter to make my appliances work with UK electrical current? Depending upon age, probably not. Most modern devices, including laptop computers, are designed to adapt to either 120 V or 230 V current. However, you do need an *adaptor* for use with Britain's "13-amp," three-prong plugs. These are readily available at airport travel stores and many other sources. For more information, see ***www.kropla.com***, "electricity around the world."

Telephone/Fax Calling Procedures

From the United States:

Dial 011 (international long distance), then 44 (country code), then the number in Scotland without the leading "0" (i.e., 011-44-1334-466-666).

NOTES

CHAPTER TWO

St. Andrews Up Close: Everyone Wants to Go—and Why Not!

TRAVELING TO ST. ANDREWS carries with it an undeniable sense of drama. I think of it as a modern-day pilgrimage to Shangri-La or Oz. You know there's a shining city upon a hill awaiting, and you're pretty sure there's a pot of gold at the end of this rainbow. And, you're right. St. Andrews does not disappoint. It's everything one hopes for and maybe a little more.

From Edinburgh, you cross the Forth Bridge (nine miles from the Edinburgh airport) on the M90, leaving airports and cities and crowds far behind. Only a few minutes along, the A92 branches eastward off the M90 and then sharply northward into the Kingdom of Fife. Now, shedding another layer of modernity, the "dual carriageway" disappears near Glenrothes as you press on through rolling farmland past Freuchie and Ladybank to join the A91 just fifteen miles outside St. Andrews. Time elapsed: only about forty minutes to this point but so different as to be in some other time and place.

Getting here from Glasgow takes a little longer—about ninety minutes, first northward on the M80, then eastward along the length of the A91, skirting Stirling and the golden bluffs of the Ochil Hills, slowing at tiny farm villages, driving ever more deeply into the peaceful countryside of Fife. The tensions of travel ease and the drive begins to feel like a pilgrimage. You're on your way to the place where the game of golf was conceived, nurtured, and codified. You're ever so close to St. Andrews.

Now the A91 takes you straight through the bustling market center of Cupar, ten miles west of your destination. After clearing Cupar, a few miles along, you cross a flowing stream marked, "Eden." Could this place name be entirely coincidental?

Now, as the A91 slides gracefully to the southeast, you round a bend and there St. Andrews appears on high ground above the Fife countryside. You wind your way into town past university playing fields, take a left on Golf Place just past the second roundabout, and . . . there it is. In an instant all you've seen in books and on television is before your eyes. In one grand sweep you take it in: the vast, flat field encompassing the first and eighteenth fairways of the Old Course; the golden beach curving off into the distance; the intimidating first tee exposed for all to see; the mammoth eighteenth green ringed around by white fence and idling observers; the imposing Royal and Ancient clubhouse, looking as though it has stood since time immemorial.

The imposing Royal & Ancient clubhouse overlooking the first tee at St. Andrews' Old Course.

Now more details catch your eye: the British Golf Museum across the street behind the R & A; the starter house, the caddie pavilion and putting green bounded by more white fence; the Victorian stone buildings alongside the eighteenth fairway; Tom Morris's golf shop; Rusacks Hotel; the Old Course Hotel off in the distance near the seventeenth green. There's "Grannie Clark's Wynd" where people are walking and cars are driving right across the middle of the first and eighteenth fairways! And, beyond it, the Golfers' Bridge across Swilcan Burn.

Eventually you make your way down the West Sands Road to the car park and the Links Clubhouse where you find all the golfer's amenities for a stay in St. Andrews—information desk, changing rooms, pro shop, and the starter's office for the New Course and Jubilee. Maybe it's time for some refreshment in the handsome lounge, or a jaunt up to the rooftop observatory for a bird's-eye view over the linksland.

Finally, you've arrived at St. Andrews! Now it's time to find your lodging, get settled, and explore the Auld Grey Toon.

The lay of the land

St. Andrews, with a permanent population of about 22,000 including university students, is compactly laid out and entirely walkable. Six golf courses spread out in the shape of a giant fan on the flat, low ground to the west/northwest of town. Town buildings occupy high ground above the linksland and rocky cliffs that separate the West Sands (golf courses) from the East Sands about a mile away around a bend in the coastline.

Looking at a town plan of St. Andrews, the medieval character of the place is plain to see. Once the ecclesiastical center of Scotland, the heart of the old city was at the east end of town where the dramatic cathedral and cemetery grounds meet the coastline. Here, along Abbey Walk, Castle Street, and the Pends, one can trace the remains of old city walls leading to the ruins of a 13th-century castle—first the bishop's home—perched on a promontory above the rocky shore.

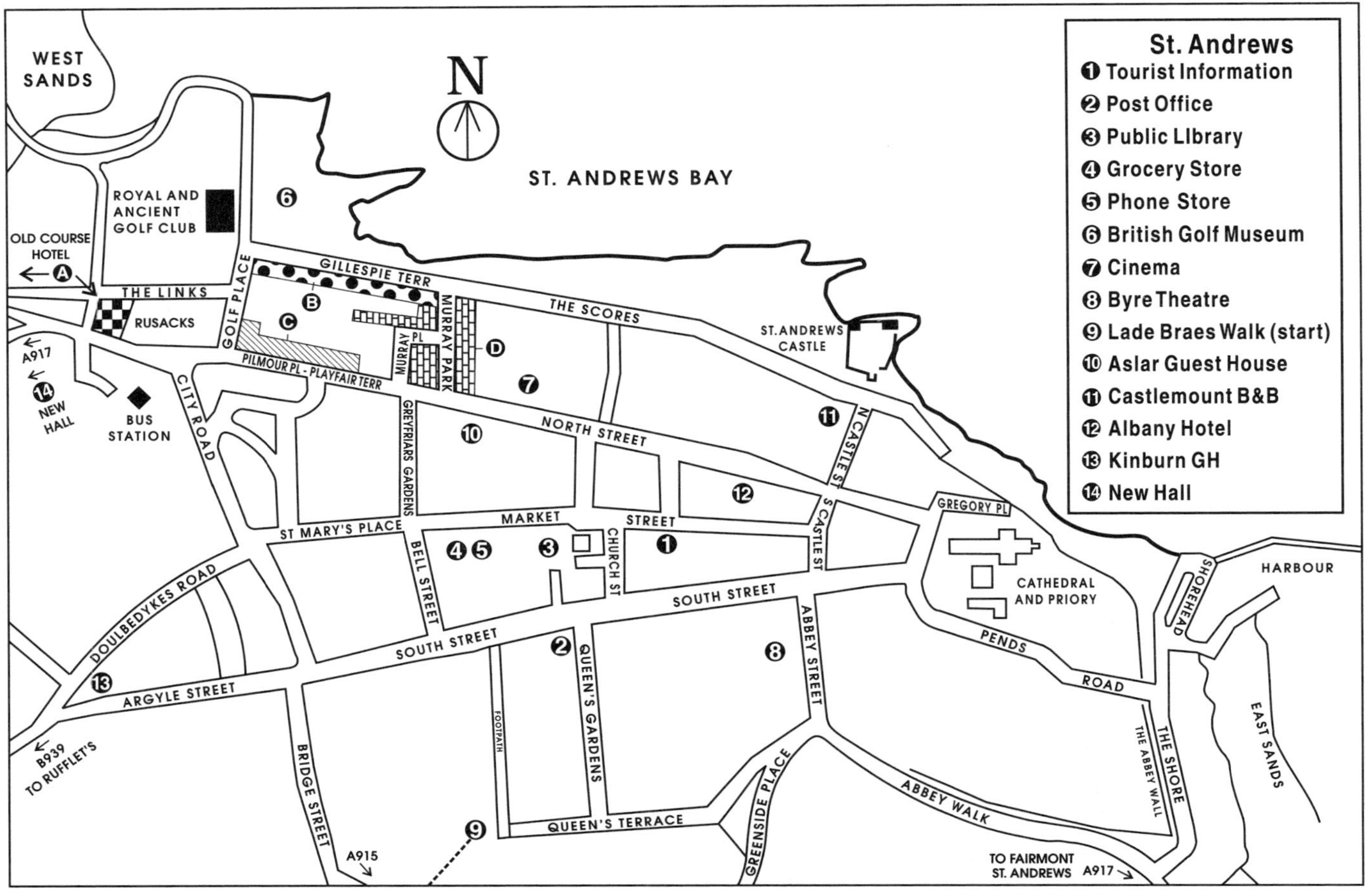

St. Andrews
1 Tourist Information
2 Post Office
3 Public LIbrary
4 Grocery Store
5 Phone Store
6 British Golf Museum
7 Cinema
8 Byre Theatre
9 Lade Braes Walk (start)
10 Aslar Guest House
11 Castlemount B&B
12 Albany Hotel
13 Kinburn GH
14 New Hall
WEST SANDS
ST. ANDREWS BAY
ROYAL AND ANCIENT GOLF CLUB
OLD COURSE HOTEL
THE LINKS
RUSACKS
GOLF PLACE
GILLESPIE TERR
THE SCORES
MURRAY PL
MURRAY PARK
PILMOUR PL - PLAYFAIR TERR
ST.ANDREWS CASTLE
A917
NEW HALL
BUS STATION
CITY ROAD
GREYFRIARS GARDENS
NORTH STREET
N CASTLE ST
GREGORY PL
MARKET STREET
ST MARY'S PLACE
S CASTLE ST
CHURCH ST
BELL STREET
SOUTH STREET
CATHEDRAL AND PRIORY
SHOREHEAD
HARBOUR
DOULBEDYKES ROAD
ARGYLE STREET
QUEEN'S GARDENS
ABBEY STREET
PENDS ROAD
FOOTPATH
THE ABBEY WALL
THE SHORE
EAST SANDS
B939 TO RUFFLET'S
BRIDGE STREET
QUEEN'S TERRACE
GREENSIDE PLACE
ABBEY WALK
A915
TO FAIRMONT ST. ANDREWS A917

Just as the town's golf courses fan out from the first tee of the Old Course, four streets fan out from the cathedral grounds to define the commercial and spiritual core of modern St. Andrews. Three of these streets—North Street, Market Street, and South Street—offer up a lot of traffic and most of St. Andrews' shops and restaurants, pubs and other public places. None is longer than about three-eighths of a mile. A fourth street, between North Street and the coast, is called "The Scores." This street leads directly and symbolically from the bishop's castle to the first tee of the Old Course and is remarkable for its peaceful contrast to the trio of commercial streets just mentioned. East of Murray Park, The Scores is a leafy one-lane track lined by ivy-covered walls and university buildings. Between Murray Park and the R & A clubhouse, The Scores becomes Gillespie Terrace where university buildings give way to a long block of offices and expensive ocean-front hotels and apartments.

At the east end of town you'll find the atmospheric remains of medieval St. Andrews as well as the graves of Tom Morris and Tom Morris, Jr.

Photo by Rick Nedell.

Marked on the map on the previous page, on Market Street and South Street, are several places of special interest to golfers and nongolfers alike. At 70 Market St., you'll find the Tourist Information Office ❶. Start here for information about "What's On" in Fife and St. Andrews during your stay. It's a well-stocked TI with excellent staff. Next is the post office ❷ inside the WH Smith Bookstore at 90-92 South Street where you can go to send postcards to your golf buddies back home (and, incidentally, exchange money and pick up a phone card). Other nearby practical destinations are the public library ❸, the Tesco food store ❹, and Phones 4 U ❺ near the corner of Market and Bell.

Looking for entertainment in St. Andrews? There's golf history at the British Golf Museum ❻ near the R & A clubhouse. Try a feature film at the local cinema ❼ or performing arts at the Byre Theatre ❽. But the best entertainment in St. Andrews is all around you—that is, in pounding the paved streets of this enchanting town. It's a place with ancient roots and, as author Michael Tobert advises, "Look up when you walk the streets of St. Andrews. That's where the history is. It's in the details of the buildings." And, finally, my favorites: for peaceful relief from the streets, there are the beaches and the shady walk along Lade Braes ❾ through quiet neighborhoods where the land falls off precipitously to the south of Queen's Terrace.

Lodging In and Around St. Andrews

AS ONE OF SCOTLAND'S MAJOR tourist destinations, St. Andrews is blessed with a wealth of lodging options in every price category. This section presents an overview of choices and websites for more information. To that end, I've organized my comments on St. Andrews lodging generally by proximity to the golf courses and, among the first four groups, generally by price. Proximity and price tend to coincide around the links so, rather than locate all the individual hotels on the map, I've indicated four main areas (A, B, C, D) of lodging choices near the links. All price estimates are quoted ***per person per night (pppn)*** *double occupancy* high season 2012 (exchange rate £1 = $1.75).

The crème de la crème (Area A)

In town that would be *The Old Course Hotel* (01334-468-001; ***www.oldcoursehotel.co.uk)*** and *Rusacks Hotel* (01334-474-321; ***www.macdonaldhotels.co.uk)***. *Rufflet's Country House Hotel* (01334-472-594; ***www.rufflets.co.uk)*** is about a mile and one-half west on Strathkiness Road. Three miles out of town in the other direction (on the A917) is the monumental *Fairmont St. Andrews* (01334-837-000; ***www.fairmont.com***). High-season prices for rooms in these places start at about £100 pppn ($175). From there they ascend rapidly and vary widely depending upon the season, size, and location within the hotel. My approach to these hotels is to enjoy their sumptuous public spaces but stay elsewhere.

"The Scores" (Gillespie Terrace) (Area B)

Eastward from the corner of Golf Place and Gillespie Terrace (the 18th green of the Old Course), four hotels offer million-dollar views from oceanfront windows at rates a cut or two below the *crème de la crème*. In order, from the corner to Murray Park, these are: The Scores Hotel, the St. Andrews Golf Hotel, the Hazelbank Hotel, and the Russell Hotel.

The Scores Hotel (01334-472-451; ***www.bestwestern.com***) has thirty rooms and a handsome pub called "Chariots"—so named to honor the feature film, "Chariots of Fire," filmed primarily on the West Sands of St. Andrews. On the cherry-wood walls of Chariots are hung photographs, sketches, and oil portraits of 127 famous Scots from several centuries and all walks of life. Expect to pay £90 to £110 pppn ($160 to $195). This is pricey for a three-star Best Western hotel, but the location is the best in town. An approved thirty-room expansion of The Scores soon will lift this hotel into the large hotel category, comparable in size to Rusacks.

A bit farther along, we come to the *St. Andrews Golf Hotel* (01334-472-

611; ***www.standrews-golf.co.uk***), the classiest (and most expensive) of these four. Once locally-owned, the hotel is now run by the Hotel du Vin chain, offering twenty-two rooms of varying size and price. In a basement space, students, townfolk, and visitors mingle at "Ma Bells"—best to avoid a room over the pub.

Near the corner of Gillespie Terrace and Murray Park, are the *Hazelbank Hotel* (01334-472-466; ***www.hazelbank.com)*** and the *Russell Hotel* (01334-473-447; ***www.russellhotelstandrews.co.uk***). Each is family-run and has ten rather average rooms costing £70 to £80 pppn ($125 to $145). The Russell has an attractive dining room and lounge popular with locals and visitors alike.

In every case here, we're talking location-location-location. I've quoted a range of prices because an ocean-view room costs more than an "inside" room and a suite costs more than a standard room. Also, most of these hotels offer discounts to tour operators—that is to say, there may be room to negotiate on price. The best idea: save these hotels for the shoulder season or off-season when rates are reduced.

North Street (Pilmour Place-Playfair Terrace) (Area C)

Eastward from the other corner of Golf Place are four more notable small hotels—the Dunvegan Hotel on the corner of Golf Place and Pilmour Place; the Ardgowan Hotel farther along on Playfair Terrace; plus Ogston's and Greyfriars up by Murray Park. These are small hotels run in the best Scottish tradition—popular gathering places with full bar and restaurant facilities. They frequently show up on mid-price tour packages and, given their popularity and small size, one should book well in advance. Prices are similar to those at the Hazelbank and Russell, though in a wider range. Expect to pay from £60 to £75 pppn ($105 to $130).

The *Dunvegan Hotel* (01334-473-105; ***www.dunvegan-hotel.com***) is St. Andrews' most famous small hotel. This is the place to go to see and be seen. In 2002 the hotel acquired three "Auchterlonie Suites" in the historic corner building across the street from the ten-room main hotel. Layered onto the hotel's popular golfers' lounge and Claret Jug Restaurant, these spacious rooms further increased the Dunvegan's appeal to small groups of golfers. The owners here are Jack and Sheena Willoughby. Jack is a transplanted

The Dunvegan Hotel on Golf Place—St. Andrews' most popular small hotel.

Texan (A & M) who first lived in Aberdeen where he was involved with North Sea oil exploration and drilling. When the opportunity came to buy the Dunvegan in 1994, he settled in St. Andrews and has since become a local institution and minor celebrity in international golf with hundreds of guests returning annually to enjoy his and Sheena's welcoming little inn.

Next along the street at #2 Playfair Terrace the *Ardgowan Hotel* (01334-472-970; ***www. ardgowanhotel.co.uk***) is a mainstream three-star hotel with prices starting at about £60 pppn ($105). Popular on many "budget" golf tours, the Ardgowan is the largest of these four hotels, having acquired additional space from the old Pilmour Hotel in 2011 and now counting thirty-three rooms. A few steps down from street level, the hotel operates "Playfair's" bar/restaurant.

At the corner of Murray Park and Pilmour, the thirteen-room *Ogstons* (01334-473-387; ***www.ogstonsonnorthstreet.com***) lends a touch of class to the middle of town. The menu in their small dining room ("Oak Rooms") is among the most extensive in town and of consistently good quality. The "Lizard Lounge" is down the stairs here. Nearby *Greyfriars* (01334-473-387; ***www.greyfriarshotel.com***) has twenty rooms of varying size and price. Its bar is pitched at the student population and the food service tends to reflect that demographic.

Note that these four hotels all are on North Street, St. Andrews' busy main drag, and their lifeblood is food and drink. It can be fun to be in the thick of things, but ask for a room on the interior, away from North Street, and as far from the pubs as possible.

The best value for money (and quietest place) on this stretch resides two doors down from the Dunvegan at *5 Pilmour Place* (01334-478-665; ***www.5pilmourplace.com***). It's a guest house rather than a hotel and one of St. Andrews' best. Six rooms starting at £75 pppn are superior to the average hotel room.

Murray Park and Murray Place (Area D)

Remarkably affordable lodging near the golf courses can be found on Murray Park and Murray Place. Guest houses and a few self-catering properties line these two Murrays. With only a couple of exceptions, all are graded four-star, typically priced from about £45 to £55 pppn ($75 to $95)—in other words, about half the cost of the hotels in this area and

Both sides of Murray Park are lined with guest houses and B & Bs.

TRAVEL TIP
Attention singletons! Several guest houses on the Murrays have small rooms specifically designed for singles and typically priced around £45. These include Cameron House, Glenderran GH, Montague GH, and Doune House.

every bit the bargain for a town as pricey as St. Andrews. All are within easy walking distance of the golf courses. Most of these establishments have their own website, but they also can be found on ***www.stayinstandrews.co.uk***. There are too many to mention, but among them are 6 Murray Park, Annandale Guest House, Arran House, Burness House, Cameron House, Craigmore Guest House, Doune House, Lorimer House, Montague Guest House, and Glenderran Guest House—all good choices for the savvy traveler.

On the fringe of this area, close enough to include here, are the *Aslar Guest House* ⑩ (01334-473-460; ***www.aslar.com***) and *Castlemount B & B* ⑪ (01334-475-579; ***www.castlemount.net***). Both are four-star properties impeccably furnished and efficiently managed by on-site owners with considerable style and flair. They are similarly priced, starting at about £50 pppn. The Aslar sits across from the cinema near the corner of Murray Park and North Street. Castlemount is on The Scores with a view to the castle. The Aslar's central location is a big plus; parking is more available around Castlemount.

Parking in the golf quadrangle

With the exception of several of the luxury hotels, what I've described to this point is lodging in the quadrangle of blocks directly east of the R & A clubhouse and the first tee of the Old Course. A major problem for all these establishments—thus, for *you* and, indeed, for all of St. Andrews—is parking. The medieval streets in the central part of this fair city are simply not designed to accommodate the modern automobile in anything like the numbers vying for space every day.

What to do? First, take whatever advice and help your lodging host can provide. Second, take whatever free space you can find and be glad you got it. Third, before getting into your car, think about the possibility of walking.

Alternatively, consider other accommodations where the parking challenge is less severe. To that end, following are suggestions in two more lodging groups—the first, in St. Andrews but outside the golf quadrangle; the second, literally outside of St. Andrews.

Other options in St. Andrews

In the small-hotel category is the *Albany Hotel* ⑫ on the cathedral end of North St. (ph 01334-477-737; ***www.thealbanystandrews.co.uk***). The Albany is comparable to the hotels in Group C above. It's a restored Georgian with twenty-two rooms—popular on mid-price golf tours and, though on busy North

St., just far enough away from town center to improve the parking odds. Cost: about £70 pppn ($125). With five singles over-priced at £97 pppn ($170), this is one choice for a small group looking for single occupancy. As with other hotels, don't accept the "rack rates;" they may be negotiable.

Farther afield—but not much because St. Andrews is not a big town—is *Kinburn Guest House* ⓭ on Double Dykes Rd. (ph 01334-474-711; ***www.kinburnguesthouse.co.uk***). Immaculate Kinburn can accommodate a group of eight or more in four twin-bedded rooms plus a two-room suite with private bath. One super-satisfied guest at Kinburn recently commented, "After thirty years of staying in B & Bs we have voted this the best B & B in Scotland." No question it's among the best in St. Andrews.

In a class by itself, summer housing is available in the University of St. Andrews' *New Hall* ⓮ (01334-463-000; ***www.discoverstandrews.com***). Perfectly acceptable lodging for the budget traveler, New Hall is not far from the Old Course and is three-star rated by VisitScotland. For that same budget traveler, excellent B & Bs in private homes scattered throughout the greater St. Andrews area are available at lowest rates (typically £40 to £50 for singles and £35 to £45 pppn doubles). Most belong to the St. Andrews Bed and Breakfast Association (***www.standrewsbandbs.com***).

Outside St. Andrews

There's a lot to be said for getting out of St. Andrews, whether a short distance or a twenty-minute drive to one of the picturesque fishing villages on the south coast of Fife. In "The Directory of Courses" I have cited lodging choices at Lundin Links (see *Lundin Golf Club*), and Crail (see *Crail Golfing Society*). To these I would add:

• *Balmashie Cottages* (01334-880-666; ***www.balmashie.co.uk***). A self-catering property with flexible booking (less than a week) in comfortably refurbished farm buildings on extensive grounds looking out to the sea over the Fairmont St. Andrews Kittocks Course. Three miles southeast of St. Andrews off the A917; ideal for families and golf groups of varying size.

• *Mansedale House* (01334-850-850; ***www.mansedalehouse.co.uk***). An elegant three-room b & b in Strathkinness village five miles west of St. Andrews on the B939.

• *Inn at Lathones* (01334-840-494; ***www.theinn.co.uk***). Great location five miles southwest of St. Andrews on the A915. A 400-year-old coaching inn with a popular restaurant; pricey but special.

• *The Old Station* (01334-880-505; ***www.theoldstation.co.uk***). Classy modern property in a quiet countryside location two miles southeast of St. Andrews off the A917 near Fairmont St. Andrews.

• *The Peat Inn* (01334-840-206; ***www.thepeatinn.com***). Mid-way between St. Andrews and Largo, eight luxurious suites and one of Scotland's top restaurants—for those on a splurge.

Self-catering in St. Andrews and Fife

To save serious money, self-catering is the way to go, especially in St. Andrews. St. Andrews is loaded with lots of good rental options for groups from two to eight or more. See pages 85-6 for my general discussion of this topic. In addition to the broad-based websites mentioned there, two rental companies of note specialize in properties in Fife. The *East Fife Letting Company (EFLC)* (01333-330-241; ***www.eastfifeletting.co.uk***) markets a handful of rentals in St. Andrews and has a strong stable of properties in the fishing villages on the south coast from Crail to Leven. *Kingask Country Cottages* (01334-472-011; ***www.kingask-cottages.co.uk***) plows the same Fife ground as EFLC and also rents properties in East Lothian.

As for individual properties, *Balmashie Cottages*, cited above, is especially good for groups larger than eight. One of the best properties in St. Andrews for up to eight golfers is at *6 Queens Gardens* (***www.standrewsvacationhome.com***). Five-star comfort in a golf-themed apartment on North Street in the heart of town can be enjoyed at *#2 Albany* (***www.albany-apartments.com***). Across from the Rusacks Hotel, among the most elegant of two-bedroom units in town, is Claire McLeary's *10 Links Crescent* (01334-828-862; ***www.linkscrescent.com***). At the quiet end of town, down by the castle, two superb three-bedroom units are offered at *Old Admiralty House* (01620-825-5770; ***www.oldadmiraltyhouse.com***). On the budget side of the ledger, The University of St. Andrews rents five-bedroom units in their *David Russell Apartments* (01334-463-000; ***www.discoverstandrews.com***). These are only a few of the many excellent rental properties in St. Andrews. A search of the self-catering websites will lead to big savings and quality accommodations for less money!

In sum, there's something for everyone in St. Andrews. You can pay a little or a lot. Demand is high, but competition is keen, and that works to the benefit of the tourist. Consider your preferences, then start digging and don't be afraid to do some negotiating, especially at the big hotels

The Golf Courses at St. Andrews

St. Andrews Links Trust

IN 1974 THE ST. ANDREWS Links Trust was established by an Act of Parliament to deal with the increasing numbers of visitors descending upon St. Andrews to play golf on the ancient links. The Trust was charged with maintaining the courses as *public* courses with assured access to all and with particular regard for the citizens of St. Andrews.

In carrying out their charge, the trustees have taken a variety of actions—some popular, some controversial. Surely the most popular was redesign of the Jubilee Course by Donald Steel in 1988-9, thus giving St. Andrews three championship-level courses side by side. Next, to accommodate beginning and high-handicap golfers, a new eighteen-hole course (Strathtyrum) and a nine-holer (Balcove) were opened in 1993. Additionally, a Golf Practice Center was carved out of the Eden Course (some say to the everlasting ruin of the little track adjacent to the Old Course). A large clubhouse was built in 1995 to accommodate visiting golfers ("unnecessary," grumbled the old-timers). A smaller clubhouse at the Eden was finished in 2000. In 2000-01 an extensive, expensive, and controversial irrigation system was installed on the Old Course. In 2003 the Trust announced plans for a seventh public course on ground situated two miles south off the A917 adjacent to the courses at Fairmont St. Andrews Hotel. Now completed and christened "The Castle Course," even this visionary venture has been hugely controversial. Many locals say the course was not necessary and was little more than an excuse to spend £10-12 million accumulated by the Links Trust.

To pay for all these changes, the St. Andrews Links Trust revised fee structures (constantly upward, of course), with special attention to visitors' wallets. In the mid-1970s a visitor could play the Old Course for about £5; by the mid-1980s the cost was £15; by the late 1990s, the fee reached £60. In 2001 the rate was pegged at £85. In 2003 it jumped to £105. In 2008-09 the green fee was £130. The £150 mark was reached in 2012. Has inflation increased 3,000 percent in forty years?—no. Is the Old Course thirty times better than it was forty years ago?—of course not. Is demand thirty times greater?—yes, probably so, and then some.

Devising a system responsive to visitor demand, while continuing to guarantee democratic, affordable access to the Old Course *and* some preference for local residents, required the wisdom of Solomon. The Trust's multipart answer was an advance reservation system, the now-famous daily ballot for visitors, and the local ballot for residents. Unfortunately, the committee created serious controversy in 1995 when it entered into a ten-year contract with a London-based entertainment agency to manage and sell about one thousand tee times annually to the public and to "the trade" (i.e., tour operators and travel agencies) *without* gaining control over the agency's pricing policies (see my discussion of *The Old Course Experience* below). This action introduced elitism and obscurity to the booking process at St. Andrews. The Prowse contract expired in 2005, but controversy has continued brewing while the Old Course Experience has continued operating on a year-to-year basis. Even though the Links Trust is run as a publicly-funded charitable trust established by an Act of Parliament, trustees have been less than forthcoming about their arrangements with the Prowse agency.

The net result of Links Trust history since 1974: lots of money for the Trust; a booking system that manages demand reasonably well, though not so democratically or cleanly as one would hope; a basketload of controversy over the years; and, at bottom, Europe's largest golf complex with 117 holes on seven courses. Thanks to the Links Trust, comprised over the years of individuals dedicated to golf at St. Andrews, there's something for everyone at The Home of Golf. That much is not debated. Detailed information about the courses at St. Andrews, links news, and management policies can be found at the Links Trust's excellent website, ***www.standrews.org.uk***.

Eight Ways to Get a Tee Time on the Old Course

WHEN I BEGIN EXPLORING itinerary options with a potential client, early in the conversation I ask one key question: *How important is the Old Course to your trip?* The answer to that question influences all aspects of trip planning. Before addressing that question, I want to provide some context for the discussion—namely, an explanation of how to get a tee time on the Old Course. You have *eight options:*

• ***Make an advance reservation.*** The current policy: Golfers seeking an advance reservation are asked to submit an application for play during the ensuing year beginning the *first Wednesday in September, at 10 a.m. Greenwich Mean Time (GMT).* Applicants contacting management before that date and time will be asked to reapply at the designated time. Application can be made by email at *reservations@standrews.org.uk*; by fax to 011-44-1334-477-036; or by mail to Reservations, Pilmour House, St. Andrews Links Trust, St. Andrews KY16 9SF. Obviously, those in queue on or soon after that first Wednesday in September will have the best odds of getting a tee time. Management promises to respond by the end of October to those requests made on the first Wednesday in September. If you've secured a time, you can proceed with planning the rest of your trip. If your bid has failed, you can weigh your other options.

This is a process more easily described than accomplished. Making an advance reservation at St. Andrews requires considerable forethought, as well as the freedom to make a date-specific commitment as much as thirteen months prior to play. Management requests information that may be a challenge to present. They want: (1) the name of a "lead golfer" to receive all correspondence and make payment; (2) names of all other golfers; (3) handicaps; (4) home courses; (5) a specific date of requested play (Monday through Friday; all play on Saturdays is by ballot); and (6) choice of a second course to play (an advance date on the Old Course requires play on another of the St. Andrews courses). This level of detail is required to help prevent speculative booking by tour operators. A minor modification might be made along the way (e.g., substitution of one player for another), but wholesale variations from the original request are not allowed and the lead golfer must remain the same. A single golfer may apply for an advance reservation; depending upon the month, from May to September ten to fifteen slots per month are allocated to singles. For more information on the advance-reservation process, see ***www.standrews.org.uk***. On the Home page, from the drop-down menu under "Playing Golf," click on "How to Book." A box at the top of that page shows a link to "Advanced Reservations" and at the bottom of the Advanced Reservations page are links to booking guidelines and application forms for singles and groups of up to eight golfers.

A goal of golfers the world over—that picture on Swilcan Bridge. It's not that hard to get on the Old Course.

In Part I, Chapter Three, I stressed the importance of checking the Old Course calendar for conflicts and closure dates, with the admonition that "You can't play the Old Course if it's not open." I reiterate that admonition. Check the Links Trust website and/or call the reservations office if you have any doubt about the availability of a date. On the website, from the the Home page, on the drop-down menu under "Playing Golf," click on "Busy Dates."

If you request a date when the Old Course is not available by advance reservation, you will be notified and asked to re-submit for another date. Due to conflicts with annually-scheduled tournaments and other special events, no advance reservations are made for September dates. The Old Course is closed on Sundays.

• ***Apply for re-opened dates in January.*** Naturally, with distribution of advance reservations, cancellations inevitably occur. Some people don't pay on time; some people ask for dates they can't keep; some people have business or family emergencies that force them to cancel travel plans; some people get sick; some people die. With any of these eventualities, openings occur. In recent years these openings have been offered beginning the first Wednesday in January. Before you give up on the goal of an advance reservation, give this a try. No waitlist is kept.

• ***Enter the daily visitor ballot***. On this subject I quote directly from the Links Trust website:

> Nearly half of the total number of tee times on the Old Course each year are allocated to the Daily Ballot to give people who have been unable to book in advance a chance of playing. Golfers should provide their names, home club and handicap details (24 for men and 36 for women) either by phone (1334-466-666) or at one of the clubhouses before 2 p.m. . . . The draw will be made shortly after that and the results posted by 4 p.m. each day. There must be at least two golfers in the group.

In January 2012, the Links Trust introduced the *48-hour ballot* (i.e., Saturday for Monday play; Sunday for Tuesday play, etc.) There is no ballot on Friday. Results are available online and at the clubhouses.

Chances vary according to the time of year, how busy the course is, and the weather. Daily odds are even or better in April and October; perhaps more like one in three during peak months May to September. August is the toughest month for balloting because (a) it's the peak of peak season and (b) the Royal and Ancient monopolizes some thirty time slots every day.

Let me stress: *This is the way most visitors to St. Andrews get a tee time on the Old Course.* Among all my clients without an advance reservation (most of them), rarely have I had someone come back from St. Andrews without having played the Old Course. How rarely?—roughly one in twenty-five. Those are pretty good odds. Again, the caveat: without a reservation you just have to give St. Andrews about three days to achieve that kind of success ratio through the ballot. To see results of the daily ballot, click on "Today's Ballot" in the box at the top right of the Home page of the St. Andrews website,

• ***Enter the daily local ballot.*** Each day, two hours of tee times are reserved for "local ticketholders." The pool of applicants in the local ballot is much smaller than in the visitor ballot. Thus, if you can get into the local pool, your odds of getting onto the Old Course improve. To enter the local ballot, you need to pair up with a resident of St. Andrews who will play a round of golf with you and who will enter your name or names in the ballot. How do you that? Maybe you already know someone who lives in St. Andrews or belongs to one of the golf clubs there. If not, when you get into town, start talking to people. Chat up the bartender, the shopkeeper, the waiter, or a university student. Most important, talk to your lodging host. He or she most assuredly will know a local resident who might be looking for a game. This method of getting on the Old Course is not "by the book" (except when you buy this book), but it's entirely legitimate. It's a great way for a single golfer to avoid the walk-on queue.

• ***Walk on.*** Singles may not enter the daily ballot. Though a few advance reservations are allotted to singles, joining the walk-on queue is the most common way single golfers get on the Old Course. Obviously, this is another option for groups of golfers willing to split up. Since many advance reservations and ballot applications are made for two or three golfers, each day the starter has a varying number of open slots. And, because many Scots play in twos and threes, this is also your best shot at playing with locals who know the course. With a first tee time of 6:30 a.m. in the summer, single golfers, often with coffee and continental breakfast in hand, start queuing up at the Old Course starter house at about 5:30 a.m. Alternative to the morning queue, one might check with the starter mid-to-late afternoon to inquire about the possibility of evening play. Inclement weather can bring the best opportunity for walk-on play. While a little rain won't stop visitors who have traveled thousands of miles to play the Old Course, locals, who can play any time, may prefer to sit out a rainy day.

> The cost of these first five methods of getting on the Old Course is the current green fee plus, in the case of advance reservation, another green fee on the Castle Course, New, Jubilee, Eden, or Strathtyrum. From here on, the options get considerably more expensive.

• ***Buy a "trade time."*** The Old Course Experience (OCE), a subsidiary of Keith Prowse Ltd., acts as the broker for about five hundred tee times sold to the "trade" (i.e., tour operators). This is one of the main sources of all those heavily-advertised "guaranteed tee times." Normally, tour operators then wrap the tee times into package tours and re-sell them to the public. During September and October, while waiting for word from the Links Trust regarding your application for an advance reservation, call a tour operator and ask them if they will apply for a "trade time" for you without any strings attached. Trade times are marked up about fifty percent by the OCE. The tour operator will lay on more markup, so the tee times may end up costing twice as much as regular green fees on the Old Course and a second course, but that probably will be better than getting roped into a trip fully planned by a tour operator. All Old Course times are date-specific. They are distributed on the same schedule as the advance times from the Links Trust. As long as you are willing to pay the ultimate price, there is no harm in applying for a trade time. If successful in the advance-reservation process, you can let the OCE time go; if unsuccessful, you have a "fallback" opportunity to play the Old Course while minimizing the financial impact.

• ***Buy a St. Andrews hotel or guest house package that includes an Old Course tee time.*** Each year members of the St. Andrews Hotel and Guest House Association (SAHGHA) are allocated something like 200 to 250 tee times for four golfers. Members of the association are listed and their establishments are described at ***www.stayinstandrews.co.uk.*** The largest, most prestigious hotels—Old Course Hotel, Rusacks, Rufflets—get the lion's share of the allocated times. Small hotels and guest houses get only a handful (no more than five or six). The allocation is made in the fall when other advance reservations are doled out. Tee times are date-specific and, like all advance reservations, require play on another of the St. Andrews courses.

Most of the hotel and guest house tee times go to longtime patrons—people who come back year after year to vacation in St. Andrews—or to favored tour operators who bring trade to the establishments. Nevertheless, this is an avenue worth pursuing and it is probably advisable to start with the large hotels first. In addition to a premium for the tee times, all will require a minimum stay of three or more nights and the hotels will require a fixed-price dinner or two for good measure.

There is no efficient way to reach the two dozen guest houses through a central office. As a practical matter, most of the guest houses market their tee times through tour operators; others deal directly with buyers. Ferreting all this out is a time-consuming matter of collecting phone numbers and/or email addresses and making inquiries indicating your available date or dates. Even if a guest house doesn't have a tee time for a specific date, they may be able to swap dates with another member of the association. This is a good way to get one of those "guaranteed tee times," but it requires the persistence of a bulldog.

• ***Buy "The Old Course Experience."*** Tour operators can be removed from the picture by dealing directly with the The Old Course Experience. Read all about it at ***www.oldcourse-experience.com.*** Currently, the Old Course Experience offers three, four, and five-night packages. Prices in April and May are slightly lower than those from June through October. Hotel participants in the program are The Old Course Hotel (most expensive), Fairmont St. Andrews, and Rusacks (least expensive). Here's what you get circa 2012 for the least expensive package on a three-night stay: (1) tee times on the Old Course; either the New, the Jubilee, or the Castle; and either Kingsbarns or Carnoustie; (2) three nights of double occupancy bed and breakfast; (3) three lunches in the Links Clubhouse; (4) one three-course dinner at the hotel; (5) a driving range pass. The lucky customer also gets a "souvenir group photograph taken on the first tee of the Old Course" and "return transfers from your hotel to the golf course" (about 200 yards from the back door at Rusacks to the first tee of the Old Course). The price for this "experience"?—a mere £1,900 or $3,230. By the way, that price is *per golfer* or about $13,000 for a foursome—and, remember, that's for the *least expensive package*! The four and five-night prices will really take your breath away.

The Old Course Experience—turning St. Andrews into a golf ghetto for the rich.

If a person could get a tee time on the Old Course by advance reservation or in the daily ballot, and assuming the choice of Carnoustie rather than Kingsbarns, the actual cost of the package described above would be about £880 or $1,500. In other words, the Old Course Experience is selling that high-season tee time on the *publicly-owned* Old Course for a premium of more than $1,700. And that, friends, is how Keith Prowse Ltd. is working to turn St. Andrews into a golf ghetto for the rich.

Is any golf course worth $1,700? I don't think so. In my view, there is only one remotely reasonable time to buy into the Old Course Experience and that would be when a golfer has a terminal illness and must play the Old Course before he or she dies. Otherwise, the world would be better off if all the money that goes to the Old Course Experience went instead to charity.

How important is the Old Course to your trip?

With some context in place, let's take another look at this question. For many people, playing the Old Course is the "bottom line" of a trip to Scotland. The guarantee has to be in place. Without it, they'd rather stay home. If you fall into that category, you have five options: (1) secure an advance reservation by application; (2) persuade a tour operator to sell you a "trade time;" (3) find a hotel or guest house with an Old Course tee time; (4) sign up for a tour package; or (5) buy the Old Course Experience. None of the other methods of getting on the Old Course carries a guarantee of success.

If you can plan far enough ahead to apply for an advance reservation and succeed, you are miles ahead of everyone else. But most people either don't know when they need to apply or they start planning too late. Every spring I get calls from people who say they want to go to Scotland in the summer and, of course, they *must* play the Old Course. Usually I'm successful in convincing them to stay-and-play in St. Andrews and put their trust in the daily ballot, but, in recalcitrant cases, these are times when I suggest consideration of The Old Course Experience rather than a package tour. With this approach, one can pay the Keith Prowse piper, while retaining the flexibility to plan the rest of a trip for a reasonable price—in effect, creating a "tour within a tour." But—Old Course Experience or a tour—it doesn't make much difference. Either way, it's expensive. When it comes to the Old Course, guarantees cost a lot of money—except by advance reservation.

Most often, golfers simply cannot or will not buy into the outrageously priced Old Course Experience. Yet the Old Course remains their primary objective. In this case, if the idea of a package tour also has been rejected, the options become: (1) the daily visitor ballot; (2) the daily local ballot; or (3) walking on as a single or duo. In the first two cases, I recommend an itinerary that keeps you within striking distance of St. Andrews so that the Old Course bell can be answered when it rings. This means a stay-and-play itinerary in Fife or a circumscribed itinerary combining, for example, Fife and Angus. Your objective is to ballot the Old Course for a full week, if necessary. Given that much time, your success in getting on the Old Course is virtually assured. Here's what I recommend to make this approach work most effectively and efficiently:

- Arrive in Scotland on Saturday; ballot the Old Course by 2 p.m. for Monday play (or have your lodging host do it for you). Check the ballot results after 4 p.m. If chosen for play on Monday, call your pre-booked Monday course to cancel or re-schedule the tee time.
- On Sunday, when the Old Course is closed, play an expensive priority course like Kingsbarns or Carnoustie.
- If not chosen in the ballot on Saturday, ballot again on Sunday for Tuesday play and continue that process throughout the week if necessary.
- For Monday through Friday play, book yourself at courses that require only a modest deposit. In Fife, these could include Crail, Lundin Links, Leven Links, Ladybank, and Scotscraig (see "The Directory of Courses" for details and more ideas). If cancellation becomes necessary, the monetary damage is minimized.
- Toward the end of the week, leave at least one day unbooked. If and when you need to move a course to accommodate play on the Old Course, you'll have this open space for re-scheduling. All the courses will gladly help with re-scheduling if they can. Another way to use an open slot is for play on St. Andrews' Castle Course, New

Course, or Jubilee. Though pre-booking these courses is an option, I don't recommend it because (a) 100 percent prepayment is required and (b) due to booking policies and frequent cancellations, it's normally easy to walk on at one of these courses during the week. I'd rather have the flexibility than the pre-booked time.

Fixation on the Old Course limits your ability to discover the rest of Scotland.

This approach to the Old Course, almost assuredly, will get you a tee time and, more important, an affordable trip focused on a small area of Scotland. Believe me, even if you don't get on the Old Course, you'll have a great trip and play a lot of good golf.

Closing words on the Old Course

This is my basic advice regarding the Old Course and Scottish golf: *To the extent that you can disenthrall yourself of the Old Course, you will have a greater range of itinerary options.* In other words, fixation on the Old Course limits your ability to discover the rest of Scotland.

To be more specific: *without an advance reservation* on the Old Course, it is not logically consistent to say that, in seven days, your main priority is to play the Old Course, but you also want to play Royal Troon, Prestwick, Turnberry, Carnoustie, and Royal Dornoch. If your main priority is to play the Old Course, then you must plan accordingly. That means staying in or near St. Andrews and minimizing schedule conflicts with other high-priority courses. But, with the Old Course in proper perspective, championship courses in various parts of the country can be scheduled.

So, what is "proper perspective"? Ideally, the Old Course should be treated as icing on the cake. If you get on, fine. If you don't, fine—maybe next time. I can understand those situations that truly are once-in-a-lifetime trips—a father and son's last opportunity to play golf together; an 80-year-old's birthday trip to the Old Country; a dying golfer's last wish. Those are special occasions that deserve extraordinary measures to get on the Old Course.

Golfers' Bridge across Swilcan Burn at the home hole on St. Andrews' Old Course—ideally, ONE of many great Scottish courses to play on more than one trip.

Photo by Rick Nedell

Otherwise, why take a once-in-a-lifetime approach to Scottish golf? If you like Scottish golf—and most likely you will—then you can go back time and time again. And, if you can afford to go once, surely you can afford to go twice—particularly if you've read this book and have avoided the tours. The entire case I've made to this point is that you can make two trips for the price most people pay for one trip. In that context, the Old Course takes on "proper perspective"—*one* of many great Scottish courses to be played on more than one trip.

Comment on the St. Andrews advance-reservation process

The St. Andrews Links Trust policies regarding advance reservations on the Old Course—particularly its contract with Keith Prowse Ltd. operating as The Old Course Experience—ought to be condemned as a national scandal.

Consider for a moment the inconveniences the Links management visits upon golfers the world over. First, reservations are not accepted until about six weeks *after* the Open Championship (late July) when visitors start to get interested in making a golf trip to Scotland. Then, not only do they make their best customers in North America get up in the middle of the night (or stay up) to submit an application at 10 a.m. Greenwich Mean Time on the first Wednesday in September, they make all those people wait another eight weeks for a reply. Links management says, in effect, "Oh, we have so many applications we have to do it that way." Well, they had about 1,800 applications (a record) in 2011—a volume that easily could be cleared in two weeks by three staff people processing eight applications an hour. After all, this *is* the twenty-first century and the necessary technology is available (if there's any doubt about that, the Links Trust perhaps could consult with their friends at Carnoustie or Muirfield or Royal Troon).

As a direct result of this inexcusable time lag, for anyone wanting to play the Old Course, travel planning is effectively put on hold until the end of October while potential customers wait for word from St. Andrews. This has a negative affect on everyone involved in Scottish tourism—from airlines, to rental car agencies, to tour operators, to hoteliers, and to other golf courses. In short, St. Andrews' policies not only harm Scottish golf tourism, they harm Scottish tourism in general. Moreover, the treatment golfers receive is a negative for both St. Andrews and Scotland. That's why it's a national issue.

Next we come to the ethical issues surrounding Keith Prowse Ltd. and The Old Course Experience. Despite operating as a charitable trust charged with protecting the interests of St. Andrews residents, the Links Trust in 1995 found a way to justify allowing private interests to profiteer from selling access to *publicly-owned* linksland. In other words, the Links Trust, in effect, sells the *same product* for two different prices—one for the general public and one for the those willing to pay a premiun. In curbstone language, that's called scalping. Without a logical leg to stand on, they've been defending themselves ever since 1995 with remarkable arrogance.

Writers Peter Finch and Dean Knuth explored the moral obtuseness of the Links managers in an incisive article published by *Golf Digest* in July 2005 under the title, "A Scalping in St. Andrews." Their article laid bare the serious divisions among San Andreans and the disdain so many locals have for Links management. Most tellingly, Alec Beveridge, the revered general manager of the Links Trust from 1984 to 1992 was quoted as saying, "I would have fought tooth and nail to stop the Links-Prowse contract." The late Sandy Rutherford, one of the principal architects of the Links Act of 1974, called the Links-Prowse arrangement "a farce." Finch and Knuth summed it up: "It's a bit like paying for 'scalped' tickets . . . the difference is, the scalping at St. Andrews is officially sanctioned."

Someday, somehow, I believe the Links Trust will change its ways. All the other major courses in Scotland—Carnoustie, Muirfield, Royal Troon, et. al—operate their booking systems on a first-come, first-served basis. Online booking is available. Everyone is treated equally—no operator discounts, no handouts to interest groups (including hotels and guest houses), no officially-sanctioned profiteering by outside sellers. Speculative buying is prevented just as it is now at St. Andrews—by requiring that the buyers be the people who show up to play.

New management came to St. Andrews in 2011. Hope springs eternal.

CHAPTER THREE

A Potpourri of Useful Information

General

• *General advice.* The single best website I have found for travel advice is ***www.independenttraveler.com.*** Before you leave, check it out.

• *Specific advice.* Apart from this book, the best source of excellent advice specific to golf in Scotland is at ***www.golfnook.com***. This accessible and literate website is the work of Mary-Alice and Richard Jafolla of Vero Beach, Florida. Veteran travelers to Scotland, Mary-Alice and Richard know value for money and will help get you off the beaten path. Another good one is ***www.theindependentgolfer.com***.

> **TRAVEL TIP**
> **For a well-organized compilation of travel tips, especially regarding air travel, see *www.cheapflights.com/travel-tips.***

• *Passport.* Don't forget it. You'll need it to get in and out of the UK. Also good to have with you when shopping.

• *Travel insurance.* Some people buy it; some don't. Deposits made on rental vehicles and hotels are normally refundable with adequate cancellation notice. Prepayments and deposits for golf are generally transferable but not refundable. The big factor here is air fare. Airline liability for lost or damaged golf clubs is inadequate. Check with your insurance agent and credit card carrier to determine coverage with those sources. The myriad travel insurance products can be screened online with a service like ***www.squaremouth.com.***

• *Checked luggage.* It's no use trying to give specific advice on this moving target. The only good advice: "Check with your carrier."

• *Varying weight restrictions.* Airline weight and size restrictions vary wildly for both regular and oversize checked luggage, not to mention carry-ons. By international agreement, airlines must honor the baggage weight limits from the country *where travel originated.* Generally, North American-based airlines have more liberal allowances than UK-based carriers. This issue can come into play when flying through Ireland (Aer Lingus) or London (connecting with British Midlands). Don't let them apply local restrictions to your international flight. For information, check ***www.golftravelguide.com***.

• *Carry-on luggage.* Unfortunately, luggage and golf clubs don't always arrive when you do. Just in case, pack your carry-on with all valuables, toiletries, and at least one change of clothes. You can rent or borrow clubs, but it's no fun shopping for essentials on your first day in Scotland.

• *Flight survival kit.* Earplugs, blindfold, water, thermos, breath mints, eyedrops, aspirin or equivalent, towelettes. With your toiletries kit packed in your carry-on, that toothbrushing can sure feel good midway over the Atlantic.

• *Lightweight and drip-dry.* This is old-hat advice, but, it's true, you'll have a better trip when you focus on what *not* to pack and then think about how to minimize the weight and maximize the efficiency of what you do pack. The best line of lightweight travel gear is at ***www.packinglight.net***. If you like the Rick Steves approach to travel, there's a good one-page packing list at ***www.ricksteves.com*** and the Steves group sells a variety of well-designed travel bags and accessories.

• *Jet lag.* Lots of advice out there about how to deal with jet lag. You'll probably arrive at your Scottish destination sometime late morning. Once you get to your hotel, here's what I recommend: get unpacked; lay down; take a nap, but set an alarm and *don't allow yourself to sleep for more than about 1-2 hours*; get up; exercise; have dinner; go to bed at a normal time. You should sleep well and be ready to play golf the next day. Some folks like to play golf on day of arrival—doesn't appeal to me, but I'm no spring chicken. A good compromise is a warmup round on one of Scotland's excellent nine-hole golf courses.

• *Money management for threes, fours, or more.* Designate a "treasurer" to manage a fund for cash payment of incidentals like lunch, a round of drinks at the 19th hole, etc. This eliminates check-splitting and hassling over minor expenses. When the "kitty" is empty, ante up a set amount per person and start over.

The iconic British phone kiosk is fast disappearing. Take a photo of one while you can.

• *Additional expenses.* How much will you spend above and beyond air fare and your "land package" (lodging, golf, rental car)? Here's a rule of thumb: add 1/3 to your air + land package. Example: $1200 air + $2600 land package = $3,800; add $1,250 more or less for food, petrol, additional golf expenses (trolleys, yardage books, caddies), and miscellaneous spending. How much "more or less"?—that depends on how much you drive, how expensively you eat, how many sweaters you buy, and, most important, how many caddies you hire.

• *Telephones.* If you have a mobile phone, check with your carrier to determine whether it can be adapted for use in the UK. I do not recommend renting a mobile phone from an internet company. The prices look good until you use the phone; then they hit you for super-expensive minutes. Same for "smart phones." Better to buy an inexpensive phone in the UK. Cell phones can be purchased at grocery superstores (Morrisons, Tesco, ASDA) and phone stores starting at about £30. British Telecom prepaid calling cards for domestic and international use on land lines and cellular technology are available at post offices in £5, £10, and £20 denominations. "Top-up" service on prepaid cell phones is available at many locations—phone stores, pharmacies, grocery stores, etc.

• *"Skype it."* Cut your communication cost to practically zero by becoming a user of VOIP (Voice Over Internet Protocol). The big players are Skype, Google Voice, Tango, and Line2. Software downloads are free. Experts advise to get a VOIP phone number, forward all calls to that number, then use your computer as a telephone.

• Use *Google Earth* to get the lay of the land before you arrive. The download is free at ***www.google.com***. Use the "street view" feature to check out your lodging site before making a commitment.

• *Provisions.* My first stop after leaving the rental-car agency is a Tesco, ASDA, or Morrisons superstore to get cash and stock up on fruit, vegetables, bottled water, and other liquid refreshments.

Golf—odds and ends

• *Become a temporary member of a St. Andrews Golf Club.* The New Club and the St. Andrews Golf Club—both located in stately buildings along the 18th fairway of the Old Course—offer visitors inexpensive temporary membership with full access to club facilities—lockers and showers, members bar and lounge, restaurant, snooker rooms. Cost varies depending upon length of membership, but no rate is more than £5 per day. This is a convenient and enjoyable way to meet locals, eat, and drink in St. Andrews. Food and drink prices are so low at the clubs, the membership cost can be quickly covered with lunch and a few pints. Arrangements should be made in advance of your arrival in St. Andrews. Contact the secretary at the club of your choice (01334-479-799; ***www.thestandrewsgolfclub.co.uk***; 01334-473-426; ***www.newclubstandrews.co.uk***).

Not a bad place to hang out! At minimal cost, visitors can enjoy full access to two of St. Andrews' private golf clubs situated along the 18th fairway of the Old Course.

• *Hickories anyone?* What better way to get into the spirit of golf in Scotland than playing a round with hickories. If near St. Andrews, it's easy to do at *Kingarrock Golf Club* just outside Ceres village about fifteen miles west of St. Andrews (01334-653-421; ***www.kingarrock.com***). At Kingarrock they'll set you up with five hickories, a replica of the Haskell ball as played circa 1898, and a "souped up" ball of the sort played by Bobby Jones in 1924. After the round, enjoy some shortbread, a glass of ginger beer, and maybe a wee dram of something stronger. The same kind of tender loving care is not offered at the *Old Links at Musselburgh* (***www.musselburgholdlinks.co.uk***), but that's another place where you can give a go to the hickories.

• *Shipping golf clubs.* It's expensive. Expect $250-350 one way. But is that too much to pay for peace of mind and protection for an expensive set of golf clubs?—only you can decide. Check with the usual suspects—FedEx, UPS, DHL. Internet-based services include ***www.sportsexpress.com***, ***www.theluggageclub.com***, and ***www.luggageforward.com***. If you follow my advice (avoid London; fly directly into Scotland), you probably won't need to be concerned about forwarding your clubs.

• *Renting golf clubs.* Given the cost of shipping and the airlines' rapacious add-on luggage fees, some golfers are opting to rent clubs. Most of the pro shops at the courses included in this guidebook rent quality equipment for prices ranging typically from £25-35. If playing a half-dozen rounds, that can add up pretty quickly—in which case, a longer-term rental with a single set of clubs makes better sense. To meet that need, *Golf Gear Hire* (0131-454-0131; ***www.golfgearhire.com***), was set up by Stuart Simpson. Located near the Edinburgh airport, a representative from Simpson's company will meet you or deliver top-of-the-line clubs upon your arrival in Scotland. Check the website for latest equipment and delivery rates.

• *Protecting your golf clubs.* If using a soft-side travel bag, turn the clubs upside down in your golf bag and tie them together with a bungee cord. Stuff the rain cover with towels and clothes to pad the exposed end of the golf bag.

• *"Left luggage"* This is the British term for short-term storage of luggage. This is something to consider if you carry golf clubs in a hard-shell case. I'll avoid the hard-shell versus soft-side carrier debate, but what do you do with all those hard-shell cases when you get to your destination? One solution is to leave them behind at Left Luggage. You'll find Left Luggage at all the major airports and train stations. Typical price: about £7.50 per day for oversize luggage.

• *Shoes.* My greatest space saver—simple black leather athletic shoes suitable for any occasion, including golf. I don't even pack golf shoes—just a pair of ribbed overshoes for waterproof covering. My shoes stay dry *and* clean. Actually, this is a fairly serious issue. It can take a couple of days for a pair of soaked golf shoes to dry out. In other words, if you take golf shoes, take two pair.

• *Water.* The Brits just don't believe in public water fountains. You won't find any on most of the golf courses either. Carry water. Ask for water in restaurants. Keep hydrated.

Clothing and dress—for golf and otherwise

• *Dress in layers and what to avoid.* The least useful article of apparel: a short-sleeve golf shirt, but take a couple anyway for summer wear and/or a bottom layer. Most often you'll be most comfortable in a long-sleeve, lightweight jersey of some kind. Then layer with variously-weighted sweaters, windbreakers, etc. Just as at home, "smart casual" is the watchword—no jeans, no cargo pants, no "trainers" (tennis shoes). Thanks to certain professional golfers, turtle-necked sweaters are fine these days.

This attire won't get these guys into the Royal & Ancient, but they'll get a good chuckle at the first tee.

• *Men - pack a jacket and tie and leave them in a corner of your vehicle.* The idea here is to be prepared for that moment when you meet a local club member and get invited into what is usually called the "members' dining room" or "members' lounge" where jacket and tie are mandatory. Entry into the Royal and Ancient in St. Andrews also requires a coat and tie; when in St. Andrews, be prepared to be invited for a visit. All courses have a less formal lounge/dining area for visitors and members. At most hotels you'll find the atmosphere quite relaxed.

• *Shorts.* In times past, "short pants" were associated with school-boy attire in the UK and adults simply didn't wear them. Gradually, that has changed. Shorts are showing up on the streets and at more golf courses (usually with long socks at the most prissy private clubs—no anklets allowed). Apart from all that, given the vagaries of weather and the sharp edges of gorse and rough, shorts are just not practical golf attire in Scotland. Best to wear long pants at the golf course and reserve the shorts for lounging, hiking, etc.

The laundry on Woodburn Terrace in St. Andrews. Drop off your clothes and pick them up later that day or the next day — cleaned and folded.

• *Laundry.* It always pays to travel light. The best way to do that is to take enough clothes for one week. On longer trips have your laundry done for you at a *laundry service*. These are not self-serve laundromats common in North America. Drop your clothes off and pick them up later that day or the next day—cleaned and folded. I've never paid more than £10 pounds for a load of wash. CAUTION: Do *not* have your laundry done by a hotel. You will pay an arm and a leg.

Following are laundry services in some of Scotland's golf centers:

Carnoustie - Perfect Laundry, 18 High Street, 01241-410-394
Inverness - New City Laundrette, 17 Young St., 01463-242-507
Nairn - Can-Do Cleaners, Harbour Rd, 01667-452-211
North Berwick - Kleaning Ark, 27 Quality St., 01620-894-790
Pitlochry - Laundrette & Dry Cleaners, 3 W. Moulin Rd., 01796-474-044
St. Andrews - Careform, 14B Woodburn Terrace, 01334-475-150
Johnson's Dry Cleaning, 153 South St., 01334-474-524
Tain (nr Dornoch) - Tain Dry Cleaners, 13 King St., 01862-894-443
Troon - Darley Laundrette, 149 Dundonald Rd., 01292-314-997
Troon Ironing Services, Barassie St nr Portland, 01292-318-935

Driving in Scotland

• *Fuel.* Make sure you know whether your vehicle uses diesel or regular fuel; the two cannot be mixed—well, they can be, but you won't like the result. Return your vehicle with a full tank.

• When your tank is low, *fill up* when you can. Scotland does not have a gas station on every other corner. It's easy to find yourself low on petrol and searching in vain for a petrol station.

• To prevent heart attacks, *prices at the pump* are quoted in litres. Four litres is a bit more than one U.S. gallon. The current price of a litre of unleaded petrol in Scotland is about £1.35. Multiply times four and you get a breath-taking £5.40 ($9.50) per gallon.

• *GPS software* for the UK is available from the manufacturers. Portable units are offered by car companies for a daily fee (typically £5-10). Main problem:

the shortest way is not always the best way in Scotland. On a circumscribed trip requiring little driving, a GPS could be more trouble than it's worth. On the other hand, some people swear by them.

• *Directions.* Take a compass with you. It can come in handy when hiking in the countryside, walking in a town or city with winding streets, or regaining your bearings while driving without a GPS.

Parking areas or "lay-bys" appear about every five miles on major highways

• Somewhere on the dash or visor, your rental car may have a reminder, "drive left" or "stay left." Use a sticky note or its equivalent and put another sign on the dash: "**look right**." Americans are so used to looking left before turning at intersections, it's a difficult habit to reverse. One lapse could be your last lapse. Obviously, it's best to look both ways, but *always* look right.

• The *light change sequence* from red to yellow to green at traffic lights is short. Do not try to scoot through an intersection on yellow.

• On multi-lane and major two-lane "A" highways, *parking areas* appear about every five miles and are marked by a square sign with a white "P" on a blue field. An advance-warning sign is normally positioned about one-quarter of a mile before the pulloff. These are one-lane sidings without services other than perhaps a trash bin. It's a good place to pull over and read a map rather than trying to drive and read a map at the same time.

Highway signs are big and bold and quite tourist-friendly.

• *Directional signs* are big and bold. On the major highways they feature white lettering on a green field. Signs with white lettering on a brown field announce tourist attractions. Secondary roads tend to retain old markers with black letters on a white field.

• To really enjoy driving in Scotland, get onto the *"B" roads* and the *"single tracks."* On the single tracks, the going is slow but, after you've adjusted to the pullover protocol for oncoming traffic, you'll enjoy the pace and see parts of the countryside that most tourists never see. The protocol? The driver closest to a passing place pulls over, flashes the lights, and lets the other other driver proceed.

• *Roundabouts* are designed to keep traffic moving. Those who live in the New England states know they work pretty well most of the time. You'll see few intersections controlled by traffic lights in Scotland. All traffic moves clockwise. Yield to to traffic on the right (remember, "Right is Might"). In two lanes leading to a roundabout, stay left if turning left. Use the right lane if turning right (you will circle three-quarters of the roundabout and signal a leftward exit). Either lane may exit straight ahead. Use your turn signals to let other drivers know what you are doing. How ingenious!

• *Prevent theft.* Always lock your vehicle. It's the only way to guarantee insurance coverage. More important, take your golf clubs out of the vehicle and store them in your lodging when not at a golf course. This is particularly important if you are driving a minibus or minivan bearing a rental-car agency sticker. These are great vehicles, but they are rolling advertisements announcing, "affluent golfers with expensive golf clubs within."

• *Drive times* are more important than distances. Here are the basics on popular point-to-point routes:

Edinburgh - North Berwick: 45"
Edinburgh - St. Andrews: 1 hr

Glasgow - Edinburgh: 1 hr
Glasgow - Troon: 45"
Glasgow - Turnberry: 1 hr, 15"
Glasgow - St. Andrews: 2 hrs
Glasgow - Inverness: 3 hrs, 30"
Glasgow - Aberdeen: 3 hrs

Inverness - Dornoch: 55"
Inverness - Aberdeen: 3+ hrs
Inverness - Machrihanish: 6+ hrs

St. Andrews - Carnoustie: 45"
St. Andrews - North Berwick: 2 hrs
St. Andrews - Gleneagles: 1 hr, 15"
St. Andrews - Troon: 2 hrs, 45"

Carnoustie - Aberdeen: 1 hr, 30"
Aberdeen - Cruden Bay: 35"
Cruden Bay - Inverness: 3 hrs
Aberdeen - St. Andrews: 2 hrs, 15"

Dornoch - Tain: 10"
Dornoch - Golspie: 15"
Dornoch - Brora: 25"

The breakfast buffet—cold "starters" before tackling a hot "full Scottish breakfast" of eggs, meat or fish, and potatoes.

Food

• *Breakfast.* Tour operators like to plug a "full Scottish breakfast" as a benefit of their tours. The fact is, breakfast is served almost everywhere and is included in the price of lodging. Some of the chain hotels offer breakfast at additional cost. What is included in a full Scottish breakfast and what other options are presented? Here's a sample menu from a typical B & B:

BREAKFAST MENU

Fruit Juices: orange, grapefruit, tomato, pineapple

Cereals: Cornflakes, Rice Krispies, Weetabix, Crunchy Nut Cornflakes, muesli, porridge

Full Cooked Breakfast: bacon, sausage, black pudding, lorne sausage, tomato, mushroom, scones, and fried egg OR choose from the following to create your own breakfast: bacon, sausage, lorne sausage, black pudding, tomato, mushroom, fried bread, fried potato, fried egg, scrambled egg, poached egg, boiled egg, grilled boneless kippers

Toast and Bread: white or wholemeal, croissants

Condiments: marmalade, jam, butter, Flora (margarine brand)

Beverages: tea, coffee, drinking chocolate

BREAKFAST IS SERVED 7 - 9:30 A.M. DAILY

Black pudding is "blood sausage"—a gift of dubious distinction from Germany. "Scones" are a uniquely Scottish treat made from potato and normally grilled or fried. At most establishments, the breakfast buffet table includes yogurt, fresh fruits, and a fruit compote, most often of grapefruit sections and/or prunes. Jokes can be made about rolling out the door to the golf course, but, truly, breakfast in the UK is a satisfying, civilized way to start the day.

• For *best values,* look for "Bar Meal" signs. Protocol: go to the bar to read the menu and place your order; pay at the bar; your food will be brought to you or your name will be called for pickup at the bar. Tipping? Ten percent is plenty.

• *Portions* are large and the Scots don't mind your sharing. An extra plate charge would be highly unusual. Money-saving advice: order two soups and one entree; share the entree and you'll have lunch or dinner for two for about $40.

• Virtually every golf course has an informal lounge with a respectable menu of soup, sandwiches and other fare at reasonable prices. The Scots have a way with soup. The soup's always on and almost always good and hot (very hot - watch out).

Nongolf activities/shopping and money

• Make a *Tourist Information Office (TI)* and/or bookstore one of your first stops. Good information is the key to a good trip. Maps, history books, golf guides, tourist site brochures, and specialized publications—all can enhance your travel experience.

• Good *hikes* can be found close by, no matter where you are. Look for "Forest Enterprise" signs; ask your lodging hosts or the nearest Tourist Information Office.

• If you and/or your travel companions—golfers or nongolfers—visit even a few major attractions run by the *National Trust for Scotland*, it can pay to buy a one-year membership in the Trust. Rates vary for individuals, families, and seniors. In the golf areas, famous sites include the exhibit hall and battlefield at Culloden, Brodie Castle, Culzean Castle, Falkland Palace, and Crathes Castle. See ***www.nts.org.uk***.

For the best in local information, make a Tourist Information (TI) Office one of your first stops.

• *Shop hours/VAT.* Most shops open at 9 a.m. and close by 6 p.m. You can reclaim the Value Added Tax (VAT) on goods carried out of the country (not on hotel or green fees). When you make relatively expensive purchases (e.g., £20 or more), ask for a Tax-Free Shopping Form. Shopkeepers administer this program—they either participate in the "scheme" or they don't. VAT reimbursement forms can be processed by mail or at your point of international departure. For more detail, ask for Customs and Excise Notice 704, *Traveller's Guide to the Retail Export Scheme*. Is it worth the hassle? If you spend a lot of money, it is. Otherwise, I'm not sure.

• *Credit cards* are accepted at most stores and restaurants. MasterCard or Visa preferred. American Express won't get you very far, especially at the golf courses. Purchasing on credit is the best way to track expenses. Most banks charge 1-3% on each transaction. Capital One currently does not levy a charge on international transactions.

American Express won't get you very far in Scotland, especially at the golf courses.

• *ATMs* seem to be on every other street corner. It's the quickest way to satisfy cash needs, though most banks charge for these transactions too. Check your bank's daily limit on withdrawals.

• *Exchange cash* at banks or at UK post offices at little or no cost. Avoid currency exchange services at airports, hotels, etc.

Scotland's Rail System

Occasionally I am asked, "Instead of driving, can I make a golf trip using public transportation?". The answer is a qualified "yes." By definition, links courses are near the sea and, not so coincidentally, Scotland's major rail lines traverse the east and southwest coasts where many of the country's top golf courses are located. In fact, rail companies were instrumental in developing resort destinations like Turnberry on the Ayrshire coast and Cruden Bay north of Aberdeen (a spur line now defunct).

Train-based transportation is particularly germane to a stay-and-play itinerary. Arriving at Glasgow International Airport, it's a simple matter to taxi to the Paisley train station for a 30-minute transfer to Troon or Prestwick. Likewise, from the Edinburgh airport, one can be in North Berwick or St. Andrews in about one hour. From there it's a matter of using local transportation (i.e., taxis) or your own two feet to get to and from the golf courses.

Noting the map that follows, we see that the major golf towns on the Ayrshire coast are all on a rail line. Indeed, the rail line is a boundary on most of the courses. Northward through the middle of Scotland, the rail line parallels the A9 highway and passes near or through Gleneagles (Auchterarder), Pitlochry, Kingussie, Newtonmore, Aviemore, and Inverness. The east coast line not only connects major golf centers but is one of the great scenic train rides in Britain. Speaking of scenic, the line from Inverness to Kyle of Lochalsh tops the charts, and the line from Fort William to Mallaig is a world-famous steamer that can drop the itinerate golfer at Arisaig near the door of Traigh Golf Club—Scotland's most arresting nine-hole track. For timetables and connections, see ***www.scotrail.co.uk***.

Moats and malts—castles and whisky

Castles and whisky distilleries—not necessarily in that order—are the attractions cited most frequently on the golfer's list of nongolf interests. One or two of each can add a nice finishing touch to any golf trip. In the case of castles, that's easily accomplished. Figuratively speaking, in Scotland there's a castle or ruined abbey around every other bend in the road. Whisky distilleries are fewer and farther between and, for that reason, I've included a map locating some distilleries on page 129.

Many of Scotland's most important, heavily-traveled, and oft-photographed castles lie outside my nine major golf areas. In the lowlands, these are the great castles at Edinburgh, Stirling (think William Wallace, Mel Gibson and *Braveheart*), and Doune (think *Monty Python*) a few miles north of Stirling. For anyone heading northward on the A9, these latter two are easily accessible. The west coast and islands of Scotland are dotted with romantic ruins including Eilean Donan, seat of power of the Macraes and Mackenzies; and the famous Urquhart Castle on Loch Ness. Balmoral Castle, the Highland home of Britain's royal family since Victoria's day, is just off the A93 in the Dee River valley near Braemar.

Glamis Castle near Carnoustie (childhood home of Elizabeth Bowes-Lyon, Great Britain's "Queen Mother").

Within my designated golf areas, following are one or more of the most compelling castle attractions in each area. More information can be sought from local Tourist Information offices. The best web page I have found on the subject is at ***www.electricscotland.com/history/castles/index.html***.

Region #1 (Fife) - Falkland Palace at Falkland; St. Andrews Castle.

Region #2 (Ayrshire) - Culzean Castle (18th century) a few miles north of Turnberry on the A719; Royal Dundonald a few miles northeast of Troon on the road to Kilmarnock (A759).

Region #3 (E Lothian) - Dirleton Castle at Dirleton village near Gullane; Tantallon Castle a few miles east of North Berwick on the A198.

Region #4 (Inverness/Dornoch) - Cawdor Castle between Inverness and Nairn (associated with Macbeth); Dunrobin Castle at Golspie (ancestral home of the Sutherlands); Inverness Castle in the middle of town; Brodie Castle a few miles east of Nairn.

Region #5 (Northeast) - Dunnottar Castle at Stonehaven (associated with Franco Zefferelli's *Hamlet*); Slains Castle at Cruden Bay (19th century - associated with *Dracula*).

Region #6 (Angus) - Glamis Castle near Carnoustie (childhood home of Elizabeth Bowes-Lyon, Great Britain's "Queen Mother") about eighteen miles north of Dundee.

Region #7 (Perthshire) - Blair Castle near Pitlochry; Scone Palace at Perth (where rests the Stone of Destiny and the throne of Scottish Kings).

Region #8 (Arran/Kintyre/Islay) - Brodick Castle at Brodick on the Isle of Arran.

Region #9 (South) - Castle Kennedy a few miles east of Stranraer; Caerlaverock Castle (14th century) eight miles southeast of Dumfries near Powfoot GC.

Visiting a distillery requires a little more effort. They aren't around every bend in the road except up north in the Spey River Valley and on Islay. Golfers concentrating on high-profile golf in Fife, Ayrshire, and East Lothian (Regions 1-3), are rather limited to Glenkinchie (#1 on the map), The Famous Grouse Experience at Crieff (#4) and Tullibardine (#3) near Gleneagles. Glenkinchie is located near the village of Pencaitland about ten miles south of Haddington, making it easily reachable from a base in Gullane or North Berwick. Like most distilleries these days, Glenkinchie is owned by a multinational beverage conglomerate (in this case, Diageo). Glenkinchie has a good visitor exhibit hall and tour. Famous Grouse is a hugely popular, moderately-priced blended whisky. The site of the Famous Grouse Experience is the formerly independent Glenturret Distillery, a maker of premium single-malt whiskies with claim to being Scotland's oldest distillery. Drive time to Crieff from St. Andrews or Carnoustie is about one hour, fifteen minutes, making it a manageable and enjoyable day trip perhaps combining golf at either Crieff or nearby Gleneagles. Tullibardine is at Blackford, a few miles west of Gleneagles.

Farther north along the A9 are two distilleries at Pitlochry (Edradour and Blair Atholl) and the Dalwhinnie Distillery (#7), another thirty miles north of Pitlochry. While within reasonable reach of the lowland golf areas, these more likely might serve as congenial rest-stops to or from the northern Highlands. Pitlochry is about halfway between Inverness and the airports at Glasgow and Edinburgh. Golfers following my Itinerary #4 ("A Taste of Scotland") may base in Pitlochry for a few days, in which case, Edradour is a particularly attractive choice, renowned as Scotland's smallest distillery (with weekly output of about 160 gallons). It sits in a pretty vale just off the A924 one mile east of Moulin village.

Now we come to "Speyside," one of the two areas where distilleries *are* around every other figurative bend in the road. Branching off the A9 thirty miles southeast of Inverness, the A95 winds through the sparkling Spey River Valley and is the main highway on the official "Whisky Trail"—a signposted circular route encompassing some fifty whisky distilleries. On the accompanying map, I have cited seven of the labels best-known to North Americans. An eighth, Glen Grant (at Rothes), is not exported across the Atlantic—this, because it is the best-selling whisky in Italy! Glen Grant is included because it's an especially attractive distillery with extensive garden and forest walks available to visitors. For those continuing up to the Dornoch/Tain area, Glenmorangie (#15 at Tain) is the logical choice. With a wide range of premium whiskies, Glenmorangie has been an aggressive marketer in the U.S. in recent years.

Dalwhinnie distillery, about thirty miles north of Pitlochry, is a popular stop en route to or from the northern Highlands.

Next in line are the famous whiskies of Islay. Those on the southeast side of the island around Port Ellen display the pungent, "peaty" qualities associated with Islay whiskies. The four distilleries toward the northeast end of the island produce a lighter, though still powerful, expression. There's another distillery (Isle of Jura) on neighboring Jura and, for those golfers on a trip including Arran and Kintyre, there are small, but interesting, distilleries at Lochranza (#23) and Campbeltown (#24, Springbank).

Connoisseurs of whisky tend to be as obsessed with their favorite subject as are wine-lovers and golfers! Not surprisingly, then, informative websites abound. Some of them are industry sponsored (e.g., ***www.scotch-whisky.org.uk***). To this eye, the most objectively informative website is ***www.dcs.ed.ac.uk***. Managed by John Butler of the University of Edinburgh, it is also "the web's oldest malt whisky site (1994)." Others are ***www.scotchwhisky.net*** and ***www.whisky.com***. The Islay Whisky Society has its own website at ***www.islaywhiskysociety.com*** and, of course, virtually all the distilleries have their own website.

One final note: During peak travel months, many distilleries are open to visitors for tours on weekends, but they are not operational. Also, during July or August, distilleries are "quiet" or "silent" (non-operational). This is the time when annually-scheduled maintenance is carried out and employees are given a chance to breathe some fresh summer air. To see an operational distillery, visit distilleries during the week and, in July or August, call your intended target to make sure it is not only open but operating.

Locations of Twenty-Four Whisky Distilleries

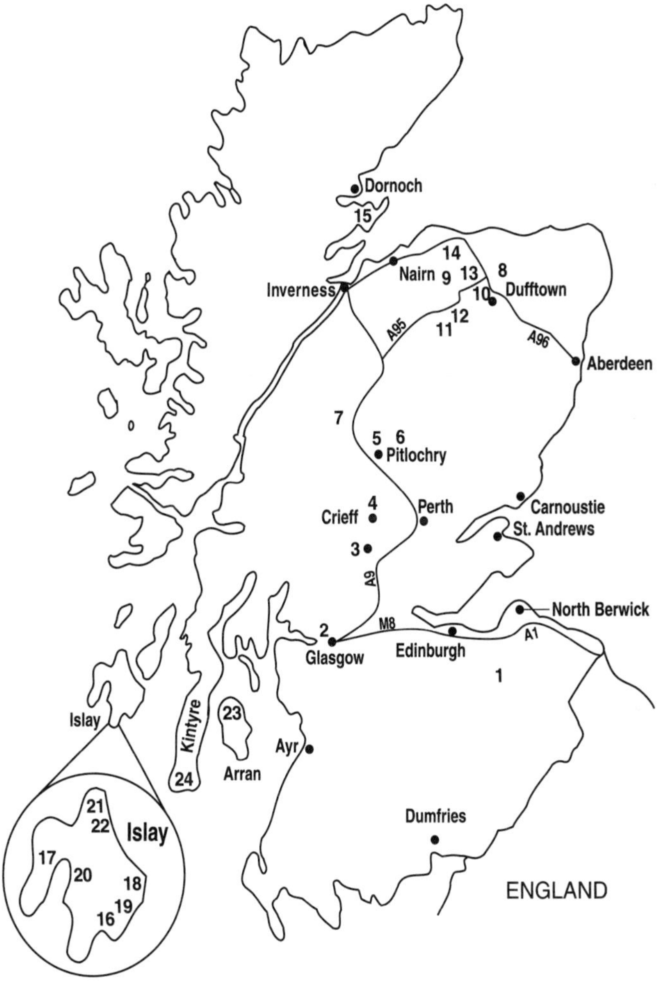

Lowlands and Southern Highlands
1. Glenkinchie
2. Auchentoshan
3. Tullibardine
4. Famous Grouse
5. Edradour
6. Blair Atholl
7. Dalwhinnie

Speyside
8. Strathisla
9. Glen Grant
10. Glenfiddich
11. Glenlivet
12. Glenfarclas
13. Macallan
14. Glen Moray

Northern Highlands
15. Glenmorangie

Islay
16. Laphroaig
17. Bruichladdich
18. Ardbeg
19. Lagavulin
20. Bowmore
21. Bunnahabhain
22. Caol Ila

Arran/Kintyre
23. Lochranza
24. Springbank

PART III

THE DIRECTORY

OF

COURSES

Preparing for Play in Scotland

MANY OF GOLF'S GREAT WRITERS, including Herbert Warren Wind and Bernard Darwin, have tried to define links golf—its unique qualities and history. Is it seaside golf?—yes. But is all seaside golf links golf?—clearly not. Is it always "out and back," like links in a string of sausages?—maybe in its purest form, but not always. If there are trees or an artificial lake on a course, is it a true links course? Questions like these propel discussion. Ultimately, the most interesting question is, "Is seaside golf in Scotland unique? Is it different than seaside golf in Florida, California, Spain, or Portugal?" Certainly, one can make the case that the environment is different—the air, the temperature, the precipitation—and these combine to make Scottish links golf qualitatively different than golf in other places. But then what about links golf in Ireland and England? Well, as you see, this topic can generate an essay or book—and it has.

In brief, links golf in Scotland has both locational and qualitative aspects. Locational: yes, near the sea—in purest form a relatively narrow strip of sandy, non-arable lowland between settled and/or arable land and the sea. The narrow characteristic of linksland led to the familiar out-and-back design of many Scottish courses, basically two fairways wide (e.g., Royal Dornoch, Nairn, Western Gailes, Brora, Cruden Bay).

But always narrow? No, exceptions abound. The key word in the previous paragraph is *low*land—lowland near the sea that, over centuries and eons, was subject to periodic inundation and continual sedimentary processes. Thus the land became sandy and non-arable—"waste land" fit mostly for grazing and, eventually, for golf. So, being seaside is not enough. Linksland might well extend some distance inland due to the character and geologic history of the land. And high ground near seaside, never subject to the ebbs and tides of sand and sea, may not be linksland at all (e.g., at Stranraer). The soil might be rich, giving rise to a great variety of plants, grasses and trees.

So, we come to the qualitative aspects: sandy soil that drains water and does not allow lakes to form; salt-water air and residues in the soil that prevent or retard the growth of trees; hardy grasses and plants capable of growing in sandy soil and salt air; dunes, hillocks, and depressions associated with the blowing and drifting of sand. The cumulative effect of these—along with those environmental aspects of mild temperatures, the likelihood of strong winds, and frequent rains—all add up to golf on a Scottish links course.

Four holes (10-13) inhabit this narrow strip of linksland at Cruden Bay.

Does it add up to golf unique in all the world? Now we approach the literary territory explored with such effect by Wind and Darwin, Peper and Campbell, Finegan and Bamberger. Fortunately, you can go to Scotland and form your own opinion.

Parkland and heathland courses

Often these descriptors are used interchangeably though, in fact, they describe different conditions. It's another sticky wicket: generally, parkland and heathland courses are inland, away from the sea—though not necessarily far inland (e.g., Belleisle, Royal Musselburgh). The defining differences between parkland and heathland have to do with (a) soil and (b) vegetation supported by the soil. Parkland soil is relatively rich and retentive of moisture, giving rise to a variety of deciduous trees, wild grasses, and even lakes—in short, the kind of land associated with pastures and woods. Heathland has more in common with linksland—sandy, peaty soil, quick to drain, and relatively poorer in nutrients, thus supporting scrubby heather and evergreens but not much more. The best clues are in the rough: grass on the parkland courses; heather on the heathland courses. Most inland courses fall clearly into one camp or the other. Ladybank and Glasgow Gailes are heathland courses through and through, just as there's no doubt about the parkland status of Inverness Golf Club and the courses at Gleneagles. Others, like Panmure and Golspie, have qualities of linksland, heathland, and parkland. In these cases, in "The Directory of Courses," I've indicated that a course is a "hybrid."

Handicap certificates

Virtually every course will indicate in its statement of visitor restrictions, "handicap certificate required." Some courses are more specific: "Handicap certificate required - men 24, ladies 36." The St. Andrews Links Trust is even more specific: "All golfers wishing to play over the Old Course must be in possession of a current, official handicap which should be presented to the Starter on the day of play and the maximum handicap is 24 for men, 36 for ladies . . . . **Proof of handicap must be in the form of a handicap card or handicap certificate, a letter of introduction from a golf club is no longer acceptable as proof of handicap"** (their bold emphasis).

Most courses rarely ask to see proof of handicap. On the other hand, certain courses like St. Andrews Old *require* that document and will check every time. Therefore, one should be prepared. Whether through a national association (USGA in the United States) or another handicapping service, registration is easy. See ***www.usga.org*** for more information on handicapping.

Buggies (golf carts)

Scots call them "buggies." Americans call them "carts." Whatever they're called, these machines constitute the most dramatic example of differing attitudes toward the game of golf.

In Scotland golf is still considered a *walking* game—a game encouraging quiet conversation with companions while taking a healthful stroll through natural terrain. I am not romanticizing anything here. This is the hallmark of golf in Scotland. Therefore, by and large, buggies are available only to those with a physical or medical condition that makes walking eighteen holes difficult, if not impossible. Where buggies are available for "general hire," they are expensive—typically £25 to £35 ($45-60). The message is, "It's one thing to need a buggy, but if you really don't need one, but still want one, we're going to make you pay for it—big time!".

This attitude contrasts sharply with the prevailing attitude at most golf courses in the United States where, under the influence of real estate developers, greedy professionals, and sheer laziness, "cart golf" has replaced golf as it has been played for centuries. This is the single biggest difference in the golf experience that visitors to Scotland will see and, of course, it has had its ultimate effect on course design. In Scotland, even at new courses that offer buggies for general hire (e.g., Kittocks at Fairmont St. Andrews and Craigielaw in East Lothian), one will find the teeing grounds comparatively close to the greens. Clearly, this is to accommodate the walker because this is the preferred way to play the game.

What does all this mean to the visiting golfer? Well, it suggests getting out of the cart and into walking shape. More important, it means one must be aware of cart availability and policy at each course. In "The Directory of Courses," I have indicated specific buggy policy and even the number of buggies available where that information could be gleaned. The following is offered in summation:

• Some courses do not allow buggies at all (e.g., St. Andrews Old Course, Prestwick, Carnoustie, Turnberry, Kingsbarns).

• Many courses have a few buggies available to those with a verifiable medical infirmity or physical disability (e.g., Montrose, Dunbar, Royal Dornoch). In a few cases, age alone may be a qualifier (e.g., St. Andrews New). Age and/or physical condition must be documented.

In Scotland golf is still considered a walking game—a game encouraging quiet conversation with companions while taking a healthful stroll through natural terrain. I am not romanticizing anything here. This is the hallmark of golf in Scotland.

• Some courses have a few buggies available for general hire. This number rarely exceeds four; advance reservation is advised.

• A few courses have a stable of buggies available for general hire. On that score, if you must use a buggy, plan ahead and/or include one or more of the following courses on your itinerary: *Blairgowrie, Craigielaw, Gleneagles PGA Centenary, Fairmont St. Andrews - Kittocks, The Duke's,* and *Whitekirk*. At these courses, advance reservation of a buggy probably won't be necessary.

Practicing for play on a Scottish links course

Except perhaps at Bandon Dunes, a golfer in North America faces difficulty in preparing for an encounter with the prickly gorse of Scotland or, for that matter, even the low-lying, tough, woody heather. Plenty of new "links style" courses feature hillocks and long, wispy grasses. But, to put them all together—with an admixture of wind and rain, blind shots, deep pot bunkers, and rolling fairways—I'm not sure there's any way to fully prepare for golf in Scotland. In bad weather, the courses can be positively brutal but, even in benign conditions, most visiting golfers will play five or six shots above their index. Someone who normally shoots in the high 80s probably will card scores in the 90s and low 100s. A mid-handicapper should be happy with scores in the 80s. The low handicapper may have his or her ego rearranged. In an interesting appendix to his report on a golf trip to Scotland *(Hallowed Ground: A Golf Trip to Scotland)*, Tanner

Stewart notes that, among the eight low-handicap golfers in his group, five of the eight averaged about five strokes over their USGA handicap indices; the other three averaged six or more strokes over their indices. Having said that much, you can still go to your nearest practice range and get a jump start on good golf in Scotland. Here's what to do:

• Hit mid-iron "knock down" shots to targets from 100 to 160 yards. This will help you prepare to play in the wind.

• Find an area of thin lies and practice with all clubs. The links fairways will tend to catch the leading edge of your clubs; you have to work on "nipping" the ball.

• Especially for the St. Andrews courses, practice the longest putts you can find; some of the double greens there are nearly as big as a football field. You'll find plenty of opportunity to use the "Texas Wedge" from well off the greens.

• When you get a blast of lousy weather, think of it as a chance to practice for golf in Scotland. Grab your clubs and head for the course.

Equipment

To help you anticipate the equipment necessary for play in Scotland, I have included a "Golf Readiness Checklist" in "Appendix B" (page 275). From that list, I want to emphasize three items:

• Unless you carry your golf bag, you will probably be using a pullcart or "trolley." If so, take two three-foot bungee cords to secure your golf bag to the trolley. If you don't you'll be cursing all day as your bag repeatedly falls off the trolley amongst the hillocks and uneven rough.

• If you wear glasses, the worst element to deal with in golf is rain. In Scotland, where rain is likely sometime during your trip, you'll be thankful you took a washcloth to tuck into a jacket or pants pocket. A washcloth is easier to handle and stow than a towel.

• Dress in layers. During the typical three to four-hour round of golf, dramatic variations in cloud cover, temperature, wind speed, and precipitation are common. Here's a good way to layer: start with a short-sleeve golf shirt and/or long-sleeve, lightweight jersey; carry a sweater, a windbreaker, and a rain jacket. In the spring and fall, I don't even bother packing short-sleeve shirts. Rather, I start with a long-sleeve pullover and carry a windbreaker, sweater, and rain suit for extra cover.

The author ready for play on a brisk day in March. Note the gloves, stocking cap, and bungee cords.

At the course

• *Confirmation.* Call your scheduled course a day or two before play. This is the time to confirm your presence, change a tee time, request a caddie, or reserve a buggy. The Scots will appreciate your thoughtfulness.

• *Parking.* Upon approaching the golf course, assess the parking situation. Some courses designate a parking area specifically for visitors.

• *Check-in.* Before doing anything else, go directly to the pro shop or starter office to check in for your round. That is where they will have the day's playlist and where you will pay your green fee or submit your prepaid voucher.

• *Clubhouse access.* At some clubs pro shop personnel will give you a numeric code to punch into a keypad near the front door or locker room door, giving you access to the clubhouse for the day. This is a security feature of many private clubs where only members and guests are allowed to use clubhouse facilities.

• *Locker room.* Return to your vehicle for clubs, shoes, and other equipment. It is recommended that you use the locker room for changing shoes, in particular, because golf shoes are not allowed in most clubhouses. Most likely, after the round you'll want to go into the clubhouse—in which case, you'll need your street shoes. Also, many clubs frown on preparing for play in the parking lot. Some (e.g., Glasgow Gailes) specifically state in their club rules that the changing of shoes in the parking lot is strictly FORBIDDEN. Go figure. When in Rome . . . .

• *Yardage books.* Every course has some kind of "stroke saver"—a yardage book with schematic drawings of each hole. They vary in quality but are uniformly indispensable because you won't find yardage markers on most courses. Cost: about £3-5. It's the best scoring investment you will make and an inexpensive souvenir of your trip.

• *Caddies.* This is a thorny subject with objective and subjective facets. First, the objective: Caddies typically cost between £35 and £45. St. Andrews offers trainee caddies for £25 from May onwards. Check with other courses to determine if they have a "junior caddie" program. It's fine for two or three golfers to share the cost of a caddie, but only one bag will be carried and an additional fee for service should be negotiated. Tipping? I think £10 to £15 is fine but you may want to do more or less depending upon the experience you've had. In general, look to the caddymaster or club professional for guidance on costs and caddie policies.

Trolleys ("pullcarts") are universally available and cost about £3-4.

Now, some subjective facets: First, there's no question a good caddie can add special dimension to a round at an historic course like Prestwick, Royal Troon, or the Old Course at St. Andrews. On the other hand, regular use of caddies will add significant cost to a trip—perhaps amounting to as much as lodging if caddies are not shared. Second, by definition, the presence of a caddie or caddies changes group dynamics. That may be good or bad, but it's a fact. Third, some golfers may feel uncomfortable pressure to "perform" for a caddie. Fourth, there are good caddies and bad caddies who create good experiences or bad experiences.

Here's my opinion in a nutshell: Low-handicap golfers can benefit most from having a caddie because they can actually do what the caddie says to do; high-handicappers can expect to enjoy the "local color," but they shouldn't expect a caddie to take ten strokes off their game. Rather than reserve caddies far in advance straight through a trip, the best approach is to assess the caddie situation as a trip unfolds and *call ahead to your appointed course at least two days in advance* to reserve a determined number of caddies. This gives you a chance to make personal contact with the club, confirm your tee time, and perhaps ask for a "senior caddie" who may give you the best experience (or a junior caddie, who may not only need the money but who may be a very good golfer, giving you the best value for money).

For my part, I'm content with a trolley and a yardage book. My objective is to look at a course, make an effort, and not be too concerned about a final score. Even if a caddie can save me four or five strokes on a round, I really don't care enough about that to pay £10 per stroke.

• If you don't hit consistently well with a driver, consider leaving it at home. Direction is more important than distance.

• From the heather and long grass, your first objective should be to get the ball back in play. Don't be a hero and hurt yourself in the process. Take a firm grasp and swing smoothly through the ball; don't thrash at it. If your ball goes into the gorse and you haven't hit a provisional ball, take a penalty drop and play on unless you're playing in a competition.

• Use the toilet before teeing off. Many courses don't provide on-course facilities.

• Take water with you. You won't find that on most courses either. And if you expect a hot dog "at the turn," forget about it. In most cases, there ain't no "turn" anywhere near the clubhouse.

• The biggest complaint Scots have about American golf manners is loud conversation on the putting greens. Remember, in Scotland the tees are close to the greens. Everyone understands you are on vacation and pumped up, but keep a lid on it while on the greens.

Hats off in the clubhouse! It's a custom with respectful social and even mildly religious overtones.

In the clubhouse

• Speaking of lids, *take your hat off upon entering the clubhouse*. This is the Scots' second biggest complaint about American manners and they'll not be shy about reminding you of proper etiquette. Doffing the cap is a custom with respectful social and even mildly religious overtones. You will see that this lends a modest touch of formality to a good time had by all.

• The bar and food service ("catering") are often separate operations. You may pay for a drink separately from your order for food—not always, but sometimes. The usual routine is to go to the bar to order a drink and then put a food order in either at the bar or with waitstaff attached to catering. You may be asked to sign into a visitors book at the bar.

That's about it. Follow these few simple guidelines, smile, greet the members, and you will be welcomed by some of the warmest, most friendly folks on God's green earth. They will be most interested to hear about your experience with their "wee course."

Seventy-Four Great Courses: A Directory with Profiles

THE SEVENTY-FOUR COURSES profiled here constitute about thirteen percent of Scotland's 570+ courses. Ergo, this is a highly selective directory. Of course, any selective list of courses is fraught with danger. The aficionado of Scottish golf will say, "But you've left out Ballater, Braid Hills, and Bruntsfield Links." I would reply: ninety-nine percent of golfers visiting Scotland go to play a handful of courses; they don't go to play Ballater, Braid Hills, and Bruntsfield Links. Maybe they should, but my aim here is to provide useful information rather than to change the profile of Scottish golf tourism. Most directories are not sufficiently selective.

My emphasis is on seaside courses because that is what most visitors to Scotland want to play. In priority order, most first-timers to Scotland want to visit (1) St. Andrews, (2) the Ayrshire coast, (3) Carnoustie, (4) North Berwick/Gullane, and (5) Inverness/Dornoch. In those locations, they are interested mainly in about a dozen courses: St. Andrews' Old/New/Jubilee, Kingsbarns, Royal Troon, Prestwick, Turnberry, Carnoustie, Muirfield, North Berwick, Gullane #1, Royal Dornoch, and Nairn.

If I can get a visitor to Scotland interested in a second tier of lesser-known courses, either on that first trip or on a followup trip, I consider it a victory. These courses might include Lundin Links, Crail, and Elie in Fife; Western Gailes, Barassie, and Irvine Bogside in Ayrshire; Montrose, Royal Aberdeen, and Cruden Bay along the northeast coast; Brora, Tain, Moray, and the Boat of Garten in the north. In short, there's plenty of golf here for both the first-timer and the returnee who has played the big-name courses and is now ready to dip more deeply into the reservoir of great Scottish courses. A treasure-trove of information awaits the careful reader of these pages.

Scotland's new courses: Since the last compilation of this directory in 2009, something like a dozen new championship-level golf courses have opened in Scotland. Some of these are accessible daily-fee courses; others are attached to exclusive private clubs. About half are parkland or heathland courses; the other half are hybrid or links courses. All are unrelentingly expensive. In this edition I have included: Castle Stuart, Dundonald, Machrihanish Dunes, St. Andrews Castle, Spey Valley Golf Club, and Trump International.

On the next two pages are notes on the detail featured at the head of each entry in the Directory. Following these notes, all seventy-four courses included in the Directory are located on a map and categorized in indices by region and price. Directory entrees are arranged in alphabetical order.

2. Blairgowrie Golf Club (1889) - Rosemount

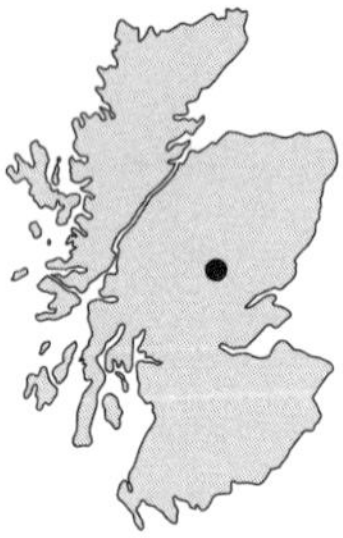

Region #: 7 **Category:** heathland
Architect(s): Tom Morris, Alister MacKenzie, James Braid
Length: 6229-6630 **SSS:** 72 **Par:** 70-72

Address: Golf Course Rd, Rosemount, Blairgowrie PH10 6LG
Directions: A93 from Perth, turn rt at Rosemount sign; from A9, exit Dunkeld, 12 mi to Blairgowrie, 1 mi S on A923

Reservations phone: 01250-872-622 **Fax:** 01250-875-451
Email: office@theblairgowriegolfclub.co.uk
Website: theblairgowriegolfclub.co.uk
Booking Contact(s): Joan Ireland, Liz Harding

Mging Secretary: Douglas Cleeton **Professional:** Charles Dernie
Phone - Starter/Pro shop: 01250-872-594/873-116
Fee(s) (2012): April & Oct £40; May-Sept £60, day tkt w/ Lansdowne £92
Deposit (2012): £10 **Buggies:** 12 - general hire
Visitor Policies: all wk 10-12 & after 1:30; Wed, Fri, Sat frequent club competitions; wkend 2-3:30; hdcps - men 24, women 36
Other: Lansdowne - championship companion course; 9-hole "Wee Course" is one of Scotland's best

AT THE HEAD OF EACH ENTRY, all necessary data is presented to help you book a tee time at seventy-four of Scotland's finest golf courses. It's all here: *address - phone - fax - email - website - key contacts - visitor policies - green fees - deposits.* Following are notes on some data elements and the overall layout of the directory.

• ***Club name and date.*** Each entry starts with the proper name of a club or managing entity. The date in parentheses (1889) is the year the club was formed or was thought to have been formed. This date may or may not be the year when a course was created.

• ***Course yardage: middle tees and medal tees.*** Note that a range of yardage is usually given (5850-6177). The first number is yardage from the "visitor" or "middle" tees. The second number is yardage from the tees for members' competitions or "medal" tees. At most courses, tee markers for visitor and casual member rounds are yellow; the back tees for member competitions are white. Most courses have a set of forward tees (usually red) presumed to be for female golfers and usually referred to as "the ladies tees." *Unless informed otherwise, a male visitor will be expected to play from the yellow tees.* The Scots are a bit finicky about this. If you would like to play from the whites, ask the starter or professional for permission. Most often the answer will be, "I'm sorry, we reserve the medal tees for member play." But it doesn't hurt to ask. A low handicapper might well be allowed to play from the back tees.

A note on Scotland's "short" courses: At first glance, most Scottish courses appear to be considerably shorter than courses in North America. But keep three things in mind before jumping to the conclusion that shorter means easier: First, par at most courses is 69, 70, or 71; a "standard" par 72 is unusual. This means fewer easily-reachable par 5s and par 3s and more long par 4s. Second, yardages usually are measured to the *front* of the green rather than to the center. Add about 270 yards to the total to arrive at a figure comparable to measuring conventions in North America. Third, the elements, particularly persistent winds, tend to have a lengthening effect on the courses. All this adds up to harder, not easier.

• ***SSS: standard scratch score.*** Scotland's "SSS" is comparable to the USGA's course rating. Just as it sounds, the SSS rating on a course is what the scratch golfer should achieve relative to par. If the SSS is 73 against par 69 (e.g., Southerness), a tough round of golf is in store. If, on the other hand, the SSS is 68 against par 70 (e.g., Portpatrick), you're probably looking at something like a stroll in a lovely park.

• ***Booking contact(s) and secretary.*** Though this information is subject to frequent change, I have included it because I think it's nice to be able to make a call and know with whom you might be speaking. Generally, you will *not* speak with the club secretary but rather with a booking secretary or assistant or even the club professional. The best opening gambit is to simply say, "Hello, this is ________ calling from _______. Can you help me with making a visitor tee time?". The conversation will flow on from there.

• ***Phone - starter/pro shop.*** This number is included because most course offices turn over their "diary" to the starter or pro shop within a week of play. To check in before your appointed tee time, this is the number to call.

• ***Fees.*** Generally these are high-season fees April through October. Some courses maintain their "winter rates" through April and return to them in October. When traveling in April or October, it's always a good idea to double-check rates.

• ***Deposits.*** Deposit requirements range from nothing at all to one hundred percent prepayment within a specified time after booking (e.g., Carnoustie, Muirfield, St. Andrews). With some exceptions, the more famous the course the bigger the deposit requirement (e.g., fifty percent at Crail, Royal Troon, and Western Gailes). Generally, these deposits and prepayments are nonrefundable, though they are normally *transferable* to a balance due in those cases where a group has lost one or two of its players. If a complete cancellation occurs well in advance of a booked date and/or a compelling reason for cancellation is made (e.g., death or disability), some clubs will waive their "no-refunds" policy.

• ***Profile.*** Following the club data is comment on each course. This comment often has as much to do with the location, the ambience and feel of a place as with course description. Detailed course descriptions of major courses are available in other books dedicated to that purpose. My aim here is to convey the flavor of a place, put it in perspective, and answer the questions, "Why should I want to play this course?" or "Why should I want to go there?" Area accommodations and nongolf activities are discussed throughout the profiles. Look here also for highlighted TRAVEL TIPS and DRIVE TIME sidebars. Websites noted throughout the profiles are cumulated in "Appendix C."

A note for juniors and professional golfers

Most courses offer reduced rates for juniors, most often defined as persons aged twelve through seventeen years (under eighteen). Sometimes this is a flat rate applicable all week; sometimes it is fifty percent of the adult green fee. Handicap requirements are not necessarily waived for juniors; best to check with each course for their policies.

Members of a national professional golf association (e.g., PGA of America) normally qualify for "courtesy of the course" (no charge) or a reduced green fee. To take advantage of this benefit, professionals must observe every reciprocal courtesy, including a personal call, email, or letter to the head professional and/or secretary and presentation of a current association membership card. Some courses extend courtesy and discounts only to head professionals. Assistant professionals should inquire politely with the philosophy that, "It never hurts to ask."

> On the next six pages are a map and four indices locating seventy-four golf courses in nine regions of Scotland. Following are important notes on how the Directory of Courses is organized.

Directory arrangement and indices. Course entries are numbered from one to seventy-four. They are arranged *alphabetically* because most people are more familiar with course names than with their exact locations. To help navigate the alphabetical entry, several indices preceding the directory give guidance:

- First, there's a *geographic* index in directional order so that one can identify courses in relation to one another.
- Second, all seventy-four courses are arranged *by price* from highest to lowest. This is the most important index. If you play the courses at the top of the list you will have a good trip, go to places most tourists go, and spend a lot of money. If you play courses at the bottom of the list you will have a good trip, go to places most tourists do not visit, and spend a lot less. If you play courses in the middle bracket you will play top-notch courses often described as "hidden gems" and you will spend a middlin' amount of money. There are no wrong answers—only different strokes for different folks. Fully half the courses in the directory are priced between £35 and £65. Generally, these courses best combine quality and value.
- *Tom Morris* and *James Braid*, the giants of Scottish golf architecture, are recognized in the third and fourth indices. It is remarkable how many of the courses listed here are either complete works of their expertise, their imaginative extensions of nine-hole courses, or their redesigns of existing layouts. Students of Scottish golf may find these indices particularly rewarding because they suggest a way of organizing an itinerary—perhaps an all-Braid excursion or an all-Morris pilgrimage. Better yet, consciously combining the two may allow comparison and contrast in design philosophies.

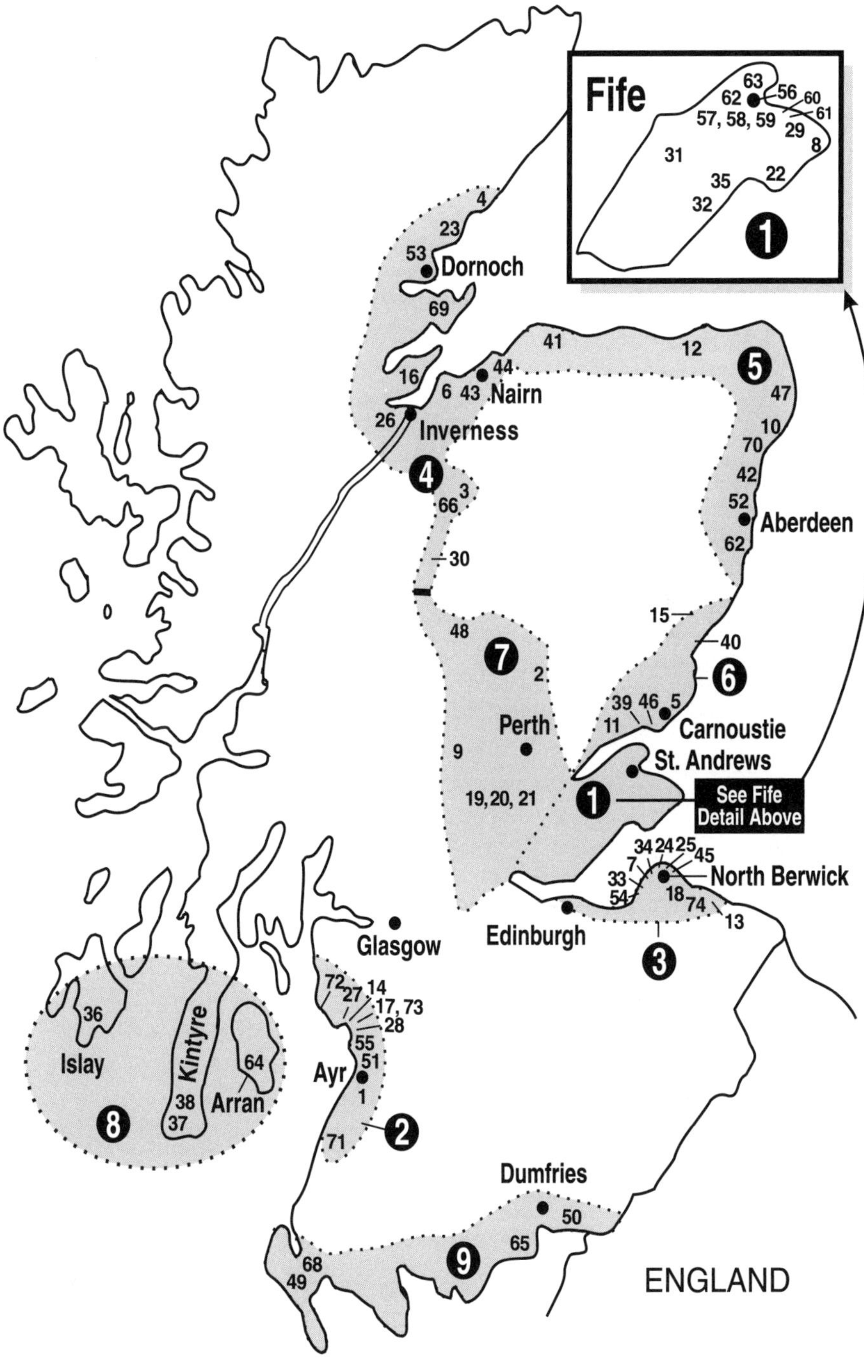

Seventy-four Golf Courses in Nine Regions of Scotland

Index 1 - Geographic Arrangement of Golf Courses

(located by number on map)

+ = Past or current British Open qualifying course

* = Past or current venue for British Open

Region #4 - Inverness/Dornoch (south to north)

Kingussie (30)
Spey Valley (66)
Boat of Garten (3)
Inverness (26)
Castle Stuart (6)
Nairn (43)
Nairn Dunbar (44)
Fortrose & Rosemarkie (16)
Tain (69)
Royal Dornoch (53)
Golspie (23)
Brora (4)

Region #5 - Northeast/North Coast (south to north to west)

Stonehaven (67)
Royal Aberdeen (52)
Murcar (42)
Trump International (70)
Cruden Bay (10)
Peterhead (47)
Duff House Royal (12)
Moray Old (41)

Region #6 - Angus/East Coast (Dundee to Edzell)

Downfield+ (11)
Monifieth+ (39)
Panmure+ (46)
Carnoustie* (5)
Montrose+ (40)
Edzell (15)

Region #7 - Perthshire/Central (south to north)

Gleneagles - King's/Queen's/PGA Centenary (19, 20, 21)
Crieff (9)
Blairgowrie Rosemount (2)
Pitlochry (48)

Region #8 - Arran/Kintyre/Islay (east to west)

Shiskine (64)
Machrihanish (37)
Machrihanish Dunes (38)
The Machrie (36)

Region #9 - South Coast (east to west)

Powfoot (50)
Southerness (65)
Stranraer (68)
Portpatrick (49)

Index 2: Courses by Price

(highest to lowest, weekday high season 2012)

Course	Course #	Price (£)
Kingsbarns	29	195
Muirfield	25	195
Turnberry Ailsa - nonresident	71	180
Royal Troon Old Course (incl optional Portland)	55	175
Castle Stuart	6	170
Gleneagles - all courses - nonresident	19, 20 ,21	160
Turnberry Ailsa - resident	71	150
Trump International	70	150
St. Andrews Old Course	56	150
Carnoustie	5	140
Prestwick	51	130
Western Gailes	73	125
Fairmont Torrance - nonresident	60	125
St. Andrews Castle	59	120
Royal Aberdeen	52	120
Gleneagles - all courses - resident	19, 20, 21	115
The Duke's Course	62	115
Royal Dornoch	53	100
Fairmont Kittocks - nonresident	61	95
Dundonald	14	95
Gullane #1	24	93
Nairn	43	90
North Berwick West Links	45	90
Luffness New	34	80
Murcar	42	78
Golf House Club at Elie	22	77
Glasgow Gailes	17	75
Panmure	46	75
Spey Valley	66	70
Cruden Bay (all-day play)	10	70
St. Andrews Jubilee	58	70
St. Andrews New	57	70
Downfield	11	69
Machrihanish	37	62
Blairgowrie Rosemount	2	60
Craigielaw	7	60

Course	Course #	Price (£)
Dunbar	13	60
The Machrie	36	60
Crail Balcomie	8	60
Kilmarnock Barassie	28	57
Lundin Links	35	57
Scotscraig	63	56
Machrihanish Dunes	38	55
Old Moray	41	55
Leven Links	32	55
Montrose	40	55
Monifieth	39	55
Ladybank	31	53
Nairn Dunbar	44	50
Irvine Bogside	27	50
Southerness	65	50
Longniddry	33	48
Tain	69	48
West Kilbride	72	45
Brora	4	45
Glen GC	18	45
Inverness	26	42
Edzell	15	40
Golspie	23	40
Fortrose & Rosemarkie	16	40
Peterhead	47	40
Powfoot	50	39
Boat of Garten	3	39
Royal Musselburgh	54	38
Crieff	9	37
Pitlochry	48	37
Whitekirk	74	35
Portpatrick	49	30
Duff House Royal	12	30
Kingussie	30	30
Stonehaven	67	30
Stranraer	68	28
Belleisle	1	28
Shiskine	64	20

Index 3: Courses by Tom Morris, Sr. (1821-1908)

Crail (9 holes - 1895; 9 holes - 1899)
Cruden Bay (1899)
Luffness New (1894)
Machrihanish (1879)
Moray Old (1889)
Muirfield (1891)
St. Andrews New (1894)
Scotscraig (1892)
Tain (1890)

Partially designed or expanded

Dunbar (15 holes - 1896)
Elie (1895)
Ladybank (1879)
Lundin Links (1868)
Prestwick (12 holes - 1851)
Royal Dornoch (9 holes - 1887)
West Kilbride (9 holes - 1896)

Index 4: Courses by James Braid (1870 - 1950)

Belleisle (1927)
Boat of Garten (1936)
Downfield (1932)
Gleneagles - King's/Queen's (1919) with C.K. Hutchison
Irvine - Bogside (1926)
Longniddry (1936)
Royal Musselburgh (1926)
Stranraer (1950)

Redesigned or expanded

Blairgowrie Rosemount (1934)
Brora (1920)
Carnoustie Championship (1926 - 1936)
Edzell (1933)
Elie (1921)
Fortrose and Rosemarkie (1935)
Lundin Links (1909)
Nairn (1938)
Prestwick (1918)
Royal Troon (1923)
Scotscraig (1904)
West Kilbride (1914, 1923)

1. Belleisle Golf Club (1927)

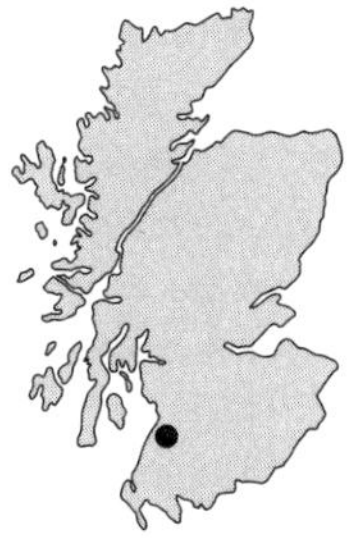

Region #: 2 **Category:** parkland
Architect(s): James Braid
Length: 6040-6446 **SSS:** 70-72 **Par:** 71

Address: c/o S Ayrshire Council, Burns House, Burns SQ, Ayr KA7 1UT
Directions: 1 mi S of Ayr off A719

Reservations phone: 01292-441-258
Email: belleisle.golf@south-ayrshire.gov.uk
Website: golfsouthayrshire.com
Booking Contact(s): senior staffer

Sr. Staffer: Alan Thomson **Professional:** Richard Gordon
Phone - Starter/Pro shop: 01292-441-314
Fee(s) (2012): wkday £28, day tkt w/ Seafield £37; wkend £33, day tkt £40
Deposit (2012): £5
Visitor Policies: all week - public course **Buggies:** no
Other: shorter Seafield Course adjacent (5481 yds)

PARTISANS OF FIFE MAY DISAGREE but, arguably, Ayrshire on Scotland's southwest coast has the greatest concentration of important links courses in the country. Visitors from around the world flock to play Prestwick, Turnberry, and Royal Troon—three past and present sites of British Open history within a coastal span of less than thirty miles. Then there are the increasingly popular courses at Gailes, plus a half-dozen other first-rate courses between Ayr and West Kilbride.

Against this constellation of stars, it's no wonder Belleisle is the Ayrshire golf course most overlooked and underplayed by visitors. In that sense, it qualifies as a true "hidden gem" among Scottish courses—one many consider the finest of Scotland's parkland courses.

And in that word "parkland" lies the truth of Belleisle's anonymity. Though less than a mile from seaside, this is not a links course. At Belleisle, just south of Ayr town center, rich forest ground prevailed over sandy links turf. The fairways are lush. Trees are full and present. Forest OB threatens. This is Belleisle—as full-bodied and robust a parkland course as you're likely to find. If it weren't for the occasional view of the Isle of Arran off in the distance (a *belle isle),* you might think you were miles inland, far away from the sea.

Apart from being one of the best bargains in Scottish golf, the main reason to visit Belleisle is to play a course that is pure James Braid, Scotland's most prolific golf architect. Much of Braid's work involved redesigning or extending existing golf grounds. At Belleisle, Braid was given a clean slate. The result was a "signature" parkland course with a look and feel of modernity. You'll find all the Braid trademarks at Belleisle—challenging par 3s to all points of the compass; long two-shotters that make or break the round; judicious bunkering to indicate the line of play. No tricks. No blind shots.

Everything in full view. Is this James Braid's finest inland course? I'm not sure. I like to think of it as one of the "Four Bs"—the Braid quartet of Belleisle, Blairgowrie, Boat of Garten, and Irvine's Bogside. The setting of each course is different. Each is a gem.

Nongolf notes and lodging - Ayr: Ayr is the "metropolis" of the Ayrshire coast. As such, it has a plethora of hotels, guest houses, and B & Bs extensively listed at ***www.ayrshirescotland.com***.

Ayr was once one of Scotland's prettiest small cities, with attractive public spaces and gardens galore. Alas, the past decade has seen marked decline in Ayr's visual appeal and, apparently, civic pride and/or budget. The north end of Ayr where the town joins with Prestwick is a dreary urban slog where visitors are best advised to avoid lodgings along the busy A719.

Fortunately, the south end of Ayr around Alloway and Belleisle Park remains a leafy, attractive 'burb making a good base for golfers and nongolfers alike. Peaceful gardens and galleries await at Rozelle Park adjacent to Belleisle. And, keep in mind, horse racing is Ayr's main claim to fame. This is where the Scottish Grand National and Gold Cup are run annually in mid-April and mid-September respectively. At those times, available rooms in South Ayrshire are scarce.

This part of Ayr offers a host of lodging options. Large golf parties are well accommodated at the four-star *Fairfield House Hotel* (01292-267-461; ***www.fairfieldhotel.co.uk).*** The twelve-room *Chestnuts Hotel* (01292-264-293; ***www.chestnutshotel.com)*** is a classy hostelry with good food service. The four-star *Greenan Lodge* (01292-443-939; ***www.greenanlodge.com)*** will appeal to the small group looking for a first-rate B & B strategically located between Royal Troon and Turnberry.

For those of literary bent, Ayr is the heart of the Robert Burns industry in Scotland. That fact cannot escape when you are there. It's "Burns this and Burns that." Beneath the hype is the reality of Burns's primary place in Scottish cultural history. Burns enshrined the Lowland Scots dialect. He celebrated common people. He preserved and lyricised Scottish folk music. For all these reasons, "Robbie Burns" became and remains a national folk hero. His birthplace is an informative museum on Alloway's main street and is well worth a visit. On a broader scale, you can follow the "Burns Trail" through the villages and countryside of Ayrshire. One to three-day itineraries are at ***www.ayrshire-arran.com/itineraries/burns.***

The Robert Burns Museum and birthplace on Alloway's main street are well worth a visit.

2. Blairgowrie Golf Club (1889) - Rosemount

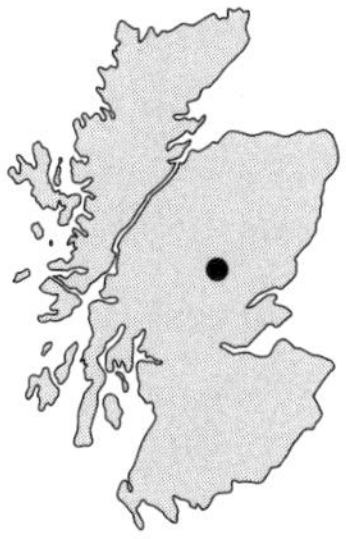

Region #: 7 **Category:** heathland
Architect(s): Tom Morris, Alister MacKenzie, James Braid
Length: 6229-6630 **SSS:** 72 **Par:** 70-72

Address: Golf Course Rd, Rosemount, Blairgowrie PH10 6LG
Directions: A93 from Perth, turn rt at Rosemount sign; from A9, exit Dunkeld, 12 mi to Blairgowrie, 1 mi S on A923

Reservations phone: 01250-872-622 **Fax:** 01250-875-451
Email: office@theblairgowriegolfclub.co.uk
Website: theblairgowriegolfclub.co.uk
Booking Contact(s): Joan Ireland, Liz Harding

Mging Secretary: Douglas Cleeton **Professional:** Charles Dernie
Phone - Starter/Pro shop: 01250-872-594/873-116
Fee(s) (2012): April & Oct £40; May-Sept £60, day tkt w/ Lansdowne £92
Deposit (2012): £10 **Buggies:** 12 - general hire
Visitor Policies: all wk 10-12 & after 1:30; Wed, Fri, Sat frequent club competitions; wkend 2-3:30; hdcps - men 24, women 36
Other: Lansdowne - championship companion course; 9-hole "Wee Course" is one of Scotland's best

CARVED OUT OF MATURE FOREST, each hole at Blairgowrie is lined with silver birch and pine and trimmed by borders of gorse, heather, and broom. It's always beautiful, but especially so in late May and early June. What we remember most about playing golf at Blairgowrie is the springy turf and the peaceful quiet of the forest. There's a peace here both auditory and visual—no housing developments, no golf carts—just you, your companions, and the forest. Even when the course is entirely filled, it can seem you are alone with the golf and the forest, each hole sitting in splendid isolation. The opening hole, "Black Tree," sets the tone: it's a long par 4 requiring two powerful shots to a large, accepting green. Lots of bunkers, expertly placed by Alister MacKenzie and James Braid (at different times), add challenge and define the greens. A straight shooter can score well here. If you spray the ball, you're in for a long day and a lot of lost balls. The one-shotters are among the finest you will see anywhere.

There's a peace here both auditory and visual—no housing developments, no golf carts—just you, your companions, and the forest.

Rosemount's companion course, the Lansdowne, deserves its own place in this directory. Stretched to 7000 yards for tournament play, with narrow fairways and challenging greens, this was far more than a "relief course" designed by Peter Alliss and Dave Thomas during the 1970s. Alterations to several holes have addressed perceived design flaws. A day ticket will get you on both courses for a reasonable fee. If you're up to thirty-six, I recommend this approach when the days are long and you can enjoy a respite between rounds in one of Scotland's most elegant clubhouses.

3. Boat of Garten Golf and Tennis Club (1898)

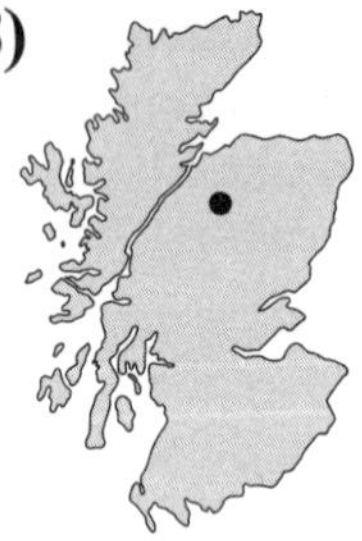

Region #: 4 **Category:** heathland
Architect(s): James Braid (1930-2)
Length: 5648-5876 **SSS:** 68-69 **Par:** 70

Address: Boat of Garten, Nethybridge Rd,
Inverness-Shire PH24 3BQ
Directions: 5 mi N of Aviemore, 2 mi E of A9; through town, turn left at Boat Hotel, then next rt

Reservations phone: 01479-831-282 **Fax:** 01479-831-523
Email: office@boatgolf.com **Website:** boatgolf.com
Booking Contact(s): Debbie Grant

Secretary: Nigel McConachie **Professional:** Ross Harrower
Phone - Starter/Pro shop: 01479-831-282
Fee(s) (2012): wkday £37, day tkt £44; wkend £39, day tkt £49
Deposit (2012): £10 **Buggies:** 2 - general hire
Visitor Policies: all week from 9:20; wkend between 10-4
Other: deposit refundable if cancellation is 30+ days before play

FOR ME, BOAT OF GARTEN brings to mind that old Sara Lee slogan: "Nobody doesn't like Sara Lee." A double negative equals a positive. There's nothing you won't like about "the Boat." The unusual name comes from Garten's history: the golf course sits above the place where in times past a boat ferried people, carts, and livestock across the River Spey. This is one of my favorite courses in all of Scotland.

The Boat exemplifies two aspects of Scottish golf. First, this is a fine example of James Braid's approach to golf course design. Here you can see clearly how Braid used bunkers to indicate a preferred line of play. You can see how he so cleverly and sensitively routed holes through natural landscape to achieve changes of direction, visual appeal, and challenging golf. There's also a rhythm to this course in the sequence of the holes that, in no small measure, is due to Braid's genius. Second, the Boat of Garten is a case study in how a course can be short yet still challenging. Many moderns look at the yardage on a course like this and say something like, "It's only 5876 yards from the back tees. How can that be considered a real golf course?". But then you look at the details and realize there are only two par 5s, most of the par 4s are long and difficult, and par is 70. This is not an easy course.

> ***This is my idea of great golf (and life) in the Highlands . . . A little piece of paradise on Earth.***

Some specifics: The course increases in difficulty as the round progresses. An opening one-shotter plays over flat ground. From there, shots across banks of heather and shots from elevated tees to mogul-filled fairways and elevated greens give the feel of a hilly links course set in a stunning Highland forest. After a relatively easy go of it on the outward nine ("Avenues," #6, is a major exception), you encounter the inward nine featuring several doglegged par 4s where hitting a green in regulation can be accomplished only with two long, perfect shots (e.g., "Tulloch," #13, 422 yards, uphill, dogleg right). The locally-famous "Gully" (#15) requires a mid-iron tee shot to a plateau overlooking a gully, leaving 150 yards to a small green on the other side. To finish the challenge, "Road" (#18) is a punishing 426-yarder to an elevated green. Good luck. It's great fun.

Now for the rest of the Boat story: this is my idea of great golf (and life) in the Highlands. It's in a small town with a good hotel, a steam railway for atmosphere, and an incomparable natural setting in the beautiful Spey Valley. It's reasonably priced, visitors are welcome all week, and the clubhouse and staff are unpretentious and welcoming. I can go to the Boat for a round of golf in the morning, have lunch in the attractive bar of the *Boat Hotel* (01479-831-258; ***www.boathotel.co.uk***), then go for a hike in the nearby Abernethy Forest. It's a little piece of paradise on Earth.

The homey, comfortable clubhouse at Boat of Garten is a gathering spot for locals.

Speyside: Boat of Garten is one of many villages and towns within the greater Spey Valley, one of Scotland's great recreation areas for both warm-weather and cold-weather sports. Fishing, cycling, golf, hiking, skiing—you name it, it's all here. For the more sedate, "Speyside" is also a Mecca for birdwatching (Boat of Garten calls itself "The Osprey Village"). Finally, let us note, this is the region offering Scotland's most extensive network of whisky distilleries. The heart of Speyside is Grantown-on-Spey. Dufftown is the locus of the whisky trade. Aviemore is the ski town and one terminus of the steam railway. Just twenty-five minutes from Inverness, any of these locations makes a good base for Highland fun. First-rate lodgings throughout the area can be viewed at the excellent website ***www.boatofgarten.com***.

4. Brora Golf Club (1891)

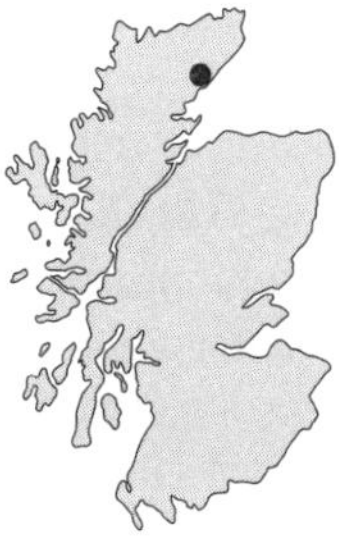

Region #: 4 **Category:** seaside links
Architect(s): John Sutherland (1891); James Braid (1924)
Length: 5854-6110 **SSS:** 68-69 **Par:** 69

Address: Golf Rd, Brora, Sutherland KW9 6QS
Directions: 5 mi N of Golspie on A9; 1st rt after bridge in village center

Reservations phone: 01408-621-417 (no fax)
Email: secretary@broragolf.co.uk **Website:** broragolf.co.uk

Booking Contact(s): secretary
Secretary: Tony Gill **Professional:** none
Fee(s) (2012): wkday £45, day tkt £55; wkend £50, day tkt £60
Deposit (2012): none
Visitor Policies: all wk **Buggies:** 3 - general hire

BRORA IS THE NORTHERNMOST course most golfers play when staying for several days in the Inverness-Dornoch area. This is as pure a seaside links as Scotland offers—nine holes out and nine holes back over rolling topography similar to that at St. Andrews and North Berwick rather than the dune-dominant terrain of Cruden Bay or Royal Aberdeen. Add to that the genius of James Braid who came here in 1924 to re-work and extend a course already touched by Tom Morris of St. Andrews and John Sutherland of Dornoch. Finally, among Scotland's most famous courses, there is a pastoral quality unique to Brora: Due to ancient grazing rights maintained to this day, this is the course memorable for its electric fences protecting the greens from wandering cattle and sheep, as well as the local rules that treat cow pies as "casual water." Brora is rural Scottish golf at its best.

As for individual holes, it's the usual Braidian stew—short, but challenging, and pure fun. The Great One gave us par 3s pointing to all sides of the compass; only one par 5; and the usual "monster" two-shotters (five at 400+ yards). If you're a fan of courses by James Braid (count me in), you'll love this one. Another of those fans, golf writer Jim Finegan, cites Brora "among my dozen favorite seaside courses in Scotland . . . as fine an example of Braid's work at the sea as we are likely to find today." Appropriately enough, Brora is home to the James Braid Golfing Society dedicated to preserving the memory and spirit of James Braid, especially, as they note in their charter, "by playing the lesser-known 'village' courses" (see ***www.thebraidsociety.com***).

Brora is the spiritual home of the great James Braid.

Nongolf notes and lodging: Some folks just like to get away and, if that applies to you, Brora is one of those places to do it. This is a quiet, pretty village with a river running through it (River Brora), so there's plenty of good fishing, beachcombing, hiking, and golf either here or at Golspie five miles southward on the A9. Dornoch and Tain are not much farther afield. Piling on other delights of the good life, Brora has its own local whisky distillery (Clynelish, now owned by the Diageo conglomerate).

The *Royal Marine* (01408-621-252; ***www.hotels-of-distinction.com***) is a handsome, traditional hotel with twenty-two rooms close to the golf course. For those of more modern taste, the Royal Marine manages *The Links Apartments* with spectacular views from high ground across the golf course and out to the open sea; these can be rented short-term or long-term either on a self-catering basis or with breakfast taken at the hotel.

See also: Golspie, Royal Dornoch, Tain

5. Carnoustie Golf Links (1842) - Championship *

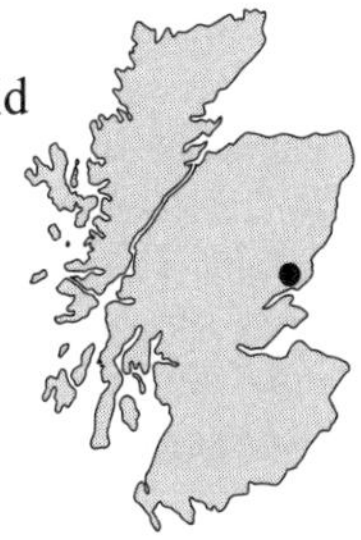

Region #: 6 **Category:** seaside links - no sea view
Architect(s): Allan Robertson, Tom Morris, Willie Park, James Braid
Length: 6692-6941-7400 **SSS:** 74 **Par:** 70

Address: 20 Links Parade, Carnoustie, Angus DD7 7JF
Directions: 3 blks off High St in ctr of town

Reservations phone: 01241-802-270 **Fax:** 01241-802-271
Email: golf@carnoustiegolflinks.co.uk
Website: carnoustiegolflinks.co.uk
Booking Contact(s): Carol McKewan, Nan Hay, Kathleen Blair

Manager: Colin McLeod **Professional:** Colin Sinclair
Phone - Starter/Pro shop: reservations
Fee(s) (2012): £140 all wk; 20% VAT additional if booked by 3rd party (i.e., tour operators, Carnoustie Golf Hotel); diary open early August for following year; various combination tkts with Burnside and Buddon courses
Deposit: 100% prepay **Buggies:** no
Visitor Policies: wkdays; not Sat am or before 11:30 Sun; check on current Carnoustie Golf Hotel preference hrs; unsold hotel times returned to course 8 wks prior to play
Other: hdcps - men 28, women 36; participant in Carnoustie Country Classic early May and Carnoustie Country Dream Ticket; fairway mats on championship mid-Nov - April; course closed to visitors 1st wk in Sept for annual "Tassie" tournament

DRIVE TIME
St. Andrews: 40 min
Aberdeen: 2 hrs
Glasgow Airport: 2 hrs, 30 min

AFTER A PERIOD OF RELATIVE DECLINE following its hosting of the Open in 1975 (won by Tom Watson), Carnoustie has staged two spectacularly successful Opens, first in 1999 (Paul Lawrie) and again in 2007 (Padraig Harrington). In the process, this great golf course has re-emerged as a unique place where golf history is made—in some respects, as much "The Home of Golf" as its more sophisticated sister forty minutes across the water to the south. Now every visiting golfer wants to play Carnoustie. On the demand scale, it's right there behind St. Andrews' Old Course. Look for the Open to return to Carnoustie soon after 2015.

Before 1999 Carnoustie's legendary difficulty was mostly a rumor in international golf circles. Then avid golfers everywhere watched on television as professionals flailed away in knee-high rough and as Jean Van de Velde imploded on the "Home" hole with his name all but etched on the claret jug. For years into the future, Carnoustie will see golfers taking photographs down in the Barry Burn, measuring their success on the infamous eighteenth against Van de Velde's brilliant flameout. In 2007 golfers saw a kinder, gentler Carnoustie but, in the closing battle between Padraig Harrington and Sergio Garcia, they saw a tournament no less stirring than the 1999 edition. From these two tournaments golfers have learned the championship course at Carnoustie can be

BOOKING TIP
All "third parties" (i.e., tour operators) must pay a 20% value-added tax on green fees at Carnoustie. Make a direct booking and save about $195 per foursome—enough to buy a nice dinner at one of Carnoustie's excellent restaurants.

both punishing and fair but, above all, always entertaining.

Among the Open rota courses, Carnoustie suffers from more misinformation than all the others combined. What about Carnoustie's legendary level of difficulty? First, even more than most, this course is made difficult primarily by the vagaries of wind and weather. Nasty weather just seems to cling to Carnoustie like a wet blanket. Second, you'll be playing off the visitor tees at around 6600 yards. That's not exactly a stroll in the park, but neither is it the "Tiger" tees stretching to 7400 yards. To be sure, over 110 bunkers, deep rough, and plenty of gorse, not to mention Jockie's Burn and Barry Burn, await the mis-hit ball. This course is no pushover under any conditions. But, in fine weather, it's not the monster it's made out to be.

Many times I've heard Carnoustie called "boring," "a wasteland," "uninteresting." I would characterize those comments as hasty if not dead wrong. It's true Carnoustie is relatively flat. But a course cannot be labeled boring if it boasts at least half a dozen world-class golf holes, flat or otherwise. And, in that category, I would put Carnoustie's #1 "Cup" hole at the top of my list of the Best Holes in Scottish Golf. It's a complete golf experience. What's more, it's followed by another par 4, "Gulley," that would rank close to the top of that list too. To have such a strong start is unusual in Scottish golf. Throw in "Hogan's Alley" (#6), "South America" (#10), "Spectacles" (#14), and the now-famous closing holes at Carnoustie (#s 16-18) and, in my view, you have one of Scotland's two best golf courses—Carnoustie Championship sitting right alongside St. Andrews' Old Course in a class by themselves.

Punishing rough, yawning bunkers, blind shots, and burns await the golfer at "Car-nasty." Bring your best game.

Now to the important part: How hard is it to get a tee time at Carnoustie? In brief, Carnoustie is the easiest "rota" ticket to get. This is essentially because visitors are welcome all week with only a few restrictions. Tee times are immediately bookable on a first-come-first-served basis from early August for the ensuing year (two to three months before advance tee times are distributed at St. Andrews). An online booking system is available or you can call for personal service from an extraordinarily competent and efficient staff.

If visitor tee times are sold, it is useful to know that the *Carnoustie Golf Hotel* (01241-411-999; ***www.oxfordhotelsandinns.com***) situated behind the eighteenth green has an allotment of a dozen tee times Monday through Friday and six each on Saturday and Sunday. This should not be considered a "last resort"—it's the best hotel in town. But it's also the most expensive. Nevertheless, as Carnoustie starts to get booked up by February-March, the Carnoustie Golf Hotel may be the only answer to your prayer.

Also, note that *the hotel must return any unsold tee times to Carnoustie management eight weeks prior to play*. This may allow you to secure a late booking or move an existing booking to a more favorable time slot.

Carnoustie is the easiest "rota" ticket to get. This is essentially because visitors are welcome all week with only a few restrictions.

In 2012, alongside the first fairway, Carnoustie christened a spanking new building designed to centralize golf services—visitor reception, a pro shop, locker rooms, and catering, topped with a spectacular wraparound viewing gallery on the second floor.

Nongolf notes and lodging: Carnoustie makes a good base for stay-and-play trips on Scotland's east coast. The town is ideally located for driving either north to Royal Aberdeen/Cruden Bay or south to St. Andrews. While Carnoustie will never win any awards for "prettiest town in Scotland," for those of practical bent, lodging is less expensive than in St. Andrews and it's easier to get on the course at Carnoustie than it is to get on St. Andrews' Old Course. Moreover, this is an underappreciated golf Mecca with Panmure, Monifieth, Letham Grange, Downfield, and Montrose all on Carnoustie's doorstep.

Adding to those merits, Scotland's fourth largest city, Dundee, is only fifteen miles distant, offering much to the discerning tourist (don't miss Discovery Point). And the lush Angus countryside holds several of Scotland's top tourist attractions: Glamis Castle and the Angus Folk Museum; historic Arbroath and its famous abbey where Scotland's "Declaration of Independence" was issued in 1320; and the Pictavia Museum at Brechin.

As for lodging, good deals often can be had at the *Carnoustie Golf Hotel*. Better value lodging is available at several substantial guest houses. Try the four-star *Morven House* (01241-852-385; ***www.morvenhouse.com***) or the five-star *Park House* (01241-852-101; ***www.bbcarnoustie.fsnet.co.uk***). Both of these can accommodate groups as large as eight and, working together as they sometimes do, they can fill the bill for even larger groups. Right on the eighteenth fairway of the championship course, June and Phil McConville's four-star *Linksview Guest House* (01241-411-195; ***www.linksviewcarnoustie.com***) is a welcome addition to the Carnoustie scene.

A final fillip for Carnoustie: dining here can be a treat. Both formal and informal food service is available at the *Carnoustie Golf Hotel*. A few blocks away, good food and Carnoustie's past unfold at the historic *Station Hotel* (01241-852-447). Over at 11 Park Avenue, *Ganges* (01241-853-336) reminds us of Britain's commonwealth connection with India. At nearby Arbroath, diners come from miles around to enjoy the ambience and fine food at *But 'n' Ben* (01241-877-223).

Carnoustie's past unfolds at the atmospheric Station Hotel and Restaurant

See also: Downfield, Monifieth, Panmure, Montrose

6. Castle Stuart (2009)

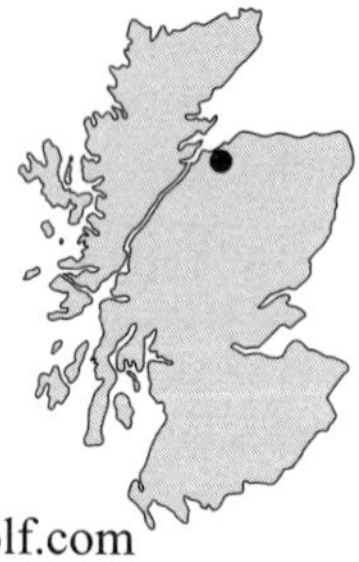

Region #: 4 **Category:** seaside links
Architect(s): Mark Parsinen, Gil Hanse
Length: 6153-7009 **SSS:** not rated **Par:** 72

Address: Balnaglack Farmhouse, Inverness IV2 7JL
Directions: 6 mi E of Inverness, N on B9039 off A96

Reservations phone: 01463-796-111 **Fax:** 01463-796-127
Email: info@castlestuartgolf.com **Website:** castlestuartgolf.com
Booking Contacts: Stefanie Whyte, Kerry Bremner

Manager: Stuart McColm **Professional:** none
Phone - Starter/Pro shop: reservations
Fee(s) (2012): £170 May-Oct, £130 Apr & Nov; 36-hole tkt playable any consecutive 4-day period
Deposit (2012): prepay in full
Visitor Policies: all wk **Buggies:** 2- phys/med
Other: discounts to tour operators; 3-year contract to host Scottish Open, 2011-13

SITUATED MIDWAY BETWEEN Inverness and Nairn, Castle Stuart is the brainchild of Mark Parsinen, co-developer of Kingsbarns in Fife. With American designer Gil Hanse, the two literally have unearthed easily the most dramatic piece of new golf ground in Scotland. Roughly a million cubic feet of topsoil were scraped here to reveal a sand base cascading in tiers from high ground to seaside on land looking across the Moray Firth to the Black Isle.

Due to the varying elevations, every hole on this course claims a sea view. Hole #s 1, 2, 3, and 10, 11, 12 traverse the seaside tier in opposite directions. The rest of the holes trace the upper tier or make the transition from upper to lower. An impressive bank of gorse runs along the face and ridge line of a massive dunescape separating the tiers. Consequently—and this is truly remarkable—when on the upper tier the lower tier is obscured and the eye goes straight to the water. In other words, all the holes on the upper tier also *appear* to be playing along the water. I know of no other course in Scotland that achieves this *trompe l'oeil.* Hole #s 9 and 14 (of course #18) return to the clubhouse. Bunkering combines both the ragged and revetted styles. The greens are traditionally contoured, avoiding the extremes seen at St. Andrews Castle Course. Dune-like contouring helps hide a nearby chipboard plant and isolates some of the holes on the upper level.

It should be said that Mark Parsinen his sidekick Gil Hanse are sincere and true students of Scottish links golf. They've had plenty of practice elsewhere and they've brought their collective experience to bear at Castle Stuart. The salient impression I have had while playing here is that every aspect of the course whispers *thoughtful* design. Playability, walkability, hole sequencing and orientation, visual appeal, shot values, strategic greenside bunkering,—all these and more, just as at Kingsbarns, clearly were in the consciousness of Parsinen/Hanse and combine to form a completely satisfying golf experience front to back. No weak links here.

It did not take long for Castle Stuart's quality and dramatic setting to wow the international golf community. In little more than a year, the course vaulted to the middle ranks of *Golf Magazine's* "World's 100 Best Golf Courses," not so far behind its cousin, Kingsbarns. In 2010 Castle Stuart was awarded a big feather for its cap with a three-year contract to host Barclay's Scottish Open through 2013. Accolades and media attention continue to flow.

So, are there any problems at Castle Stuart? Well, yes, there are. Golf is not Castle Stuart's only *raison d'etre* as it is at Kingsbarns. The golf course is part of a long-term development plan involving a 57-room hotel, 48 additional lodge rooms, and another 30 single units, not to mention another golf course—sort of a Trump development with good taste. If all that comes to pass, we won't exactly feel like we're alone with our boon companions in the dunes.

Because of that, Castle Stuart will be forever caught between trying to be a resort course friendly to all sorts of golfers and a championship-level course designed to host tournaments. Some of the fairways are as wide as a footbal field (thank you very much). And the fairway bunkering is largely ornamental, not much of a threat to the accomplished golfer. Despite miserable weather—and even stretched to 7400 yards—professionals at Castle Stuart's first Scottish Open in 2011 made mincemeat of the course. Can the course be toughened up for tournament play?—maybe, but the jury is out for now.

At the exquisitely-sited, par-3 fourth hole, the designers merged the first Castle Stuart with the new Castle Stuart.

Then there's the matter of cost and attitude in the "down-home" Highlands of Scotland. At £170 (and no doubt rising) Castle Stuart is already among the half-dozen most expensive courses in Scotland. The pitch here is clearly to the upper crust and let the peons be damned. The other most expensive course in the Highlands, Royal Dornoch—surely as good or better than this course—only recently reached the £100 barrier. And while the rest of Highland golf is played on moderately-priced courses and re-lived in relatively simple village clubhouses, Castle Stuart's Florida-inspired ambience (or is it Southern California?) doesn't quite seem to fit. Prices will keep the locals away in droves. Ultimately, I fear Castle Stuart will become another one of those courses that gets played once, maybe twice—another box to tick on the list.

Just as Turnberry, Royal Troon, and Prestwick draw golfers to Ayrshire, the hope is that Castle Stuart, combining with Royal Dornoch and Nairn, will act as a magnet, drawing more golfers for longer stays in the Highlands. If *that* comes to pass, we'll all be winners, for this is the part of Scotland most likely to entice you to "haste ye back" time and time again. As Queen Victoria discovered so many years ago, this is where you'll fall in love with the land and the spirit of the people.

See also: Inverness GC, Nairn, Nairn Dunbar

7. Craigielaw Golf Club (2001) +

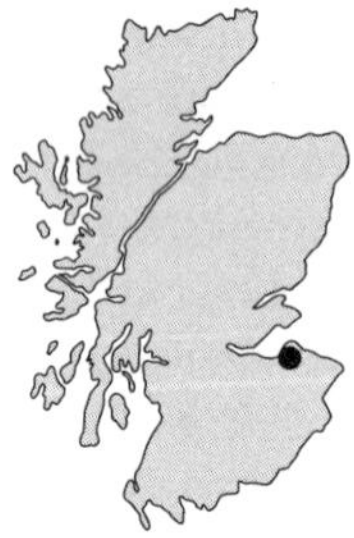

Region #: 3 **Category:** links with a view
Architect(s): Tom McKenzie (Donald Steel & Assocs)
Length: 6043-6601 **SSS:** 70-72 **Par:** 71

Address: Aberlady, E Lothian EH32 0PY
Directions: N side of A198, 3/4 mile W of Aberlady

Reservations phone: 01875-870-800 **Fax:** 01875-870-620
Email: info@craigielawgolfclub.com
Website: craigielawgolfclub.com
Booking Contact(s): starter - Gordon McLanachan

Club Manager: Derek Scott **Professional:** Jonathan Porteous
Phone - Starter/Pro shop: 1875-870-803
Fee(s) (2012): wkday £60, day tkt £80; wkend £80, no day tkt
Deposit (2012): 50%
Visitor Policies: after 9:30 am all wk **Buggies:** 6 - general hire

IF CRAIGIELAW HAD BEEN set down somewhere in the southern United States, it might have been dubbed, "Y'all Come." The democratic spirit of Craigielaw is its most attractive asset. Craigielaw has combined some of the most appealing aspects of golf in America with traditional Scottish touches to create a first-rate, contemporary golf experience. So we have a grass range and practice area; a comfortable clubhouse with no "members only" areas; buggies if you want them; and, out on the course, 150-yard markers and a return to the clubhouse at the ninth hole. At the same time we are given an easily walkable course built on links grazing land framed by rock walls in the heart of Scotland's oldest stretch of golf ground—home to such leathered names as Musselburgh, Kilspindie, Longniddry, Luffness, and Gullane.

Craigielaw was founded specifically to appeal to all the women, juniors, and young men (particularly in Edinburgh) who could not breach the membership walls of all those august golf clubs mentioned above. The membership rolls are filled to overflowing and the average age of the members is about thirty-five. Women and juniors comprise a significant share of membership and, in so many ways, the club is alive and bustling in a way that the older, nearby golf clubs simply can't imagine.

What about the golf course? It's an excellent golf course with lots of memorable holes well designed by the Donald Steel group. Craigielaw sits on high ground above a sand shelf (Kilspindie Golf Club is located directly below at water's edge). At length I could describe the merits of the opening gentle dogleg right, the daunting 424-yarder (#4) uphill into the prevailing wind, the well-bunkered par 3s, the challenging mix of par 5s exceeding 540 yards from the medal tees and, finally, the imaginative holes (#s 13 and 14) threading fairways through handsome old stone walls. It's all good stuff.

But, ultimately, the crux of Craigielaw comes down to the greens, for the greens—their sitings and undulations—are Craigielaw's main defense. The length of the course, even from the back tees, is not enough to deter obliteration of par by the big guys. But the greens—oh, that's another matter, for these are among the most severely undulating greens in Scotland. And, on this score, among all the courses described in this book, I see Craigielaw and St. Andrews' Castle Course as most representative of a fundamental difference between modern golf course architecture and the "traditional" courses that evolved or were designed prior to 1970 (more or less).

In traditional golf course construction, the prevailing philosophy was that getting to the green should be the hard part—the golf equivalent of running the gauntlet or negotiating a mine field. Once on the green, the golfer would find a relatively flat (though perhaps huge) putting surface. This is essentially true of all the "classic" golf courses of Scotland, whether at Troon, Turnberry, Carnoustie, Aberdeen, Cruden Bay, Nairn, or St. Andrews.

At most modern courses the opposite is true: getting through the broad, manicured fairways seems the easy part; getting on and staying on the greens and getting the ball in the hole becomes the challenge. Elevated or crowned greens with sloped sidings reduce the real target area. And, once on a green, the golfer is often faced with severe undulations from all angles. At Craigielaw this description holds to such extent that some have complained about the course being "tricked up." I don't think this is quite the case. Par must be defended one way or another; this is the way they did it here.

At the same time, Craigielaw's setup does make one ponder course design. On the traditional courses of Scotland I can think of numerous short par 4s that can only be played by stroking the ball about 200 yards then playing to a well-protected green perhaps no more than 100 yards away. An easy par 4?—maybe, maybe not—but not at all susceptible to a 290-yard drive. Excepting its devilish opening hole, most of straightaway Craigielaw lies at the mercy of the big hitter (weather permitting). The critical action is at the green. Good design? I'm not sure. I prefer the traditional approach. But I know that Craigielaw is a good golf experience and I appreciate the club's ability to put it all together into an attractive package. So, "y'all come" to Craigielaw. It's a worthy addition to Scottish golf.

8. Crail Golfing Society (1786) - Balcomie Links

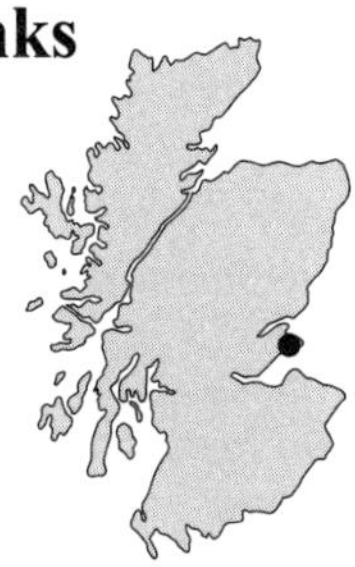

Region #: 1 **Category:** seaside links
Architect(s): Tom Morris (1895 - 9 holes, 1899 - 9 holes)
Length: 5402-5861 **SSS:** 68-70 **Par:** 67-69

Address: Balcomie Clubhouse, Fifeness, Crail KY10 3XN
Directions: well signposted 2 mi E of Crail off A917

Reservations phone: 01333-450-686 **Fax:** 01333-450-416
Email: info@crailgolfingsociety.co.uk
Website: crailgolfingsociety.co.uk
Booking Contact(s): Doreen Mayes, Laura McGilvary

Secretary: David Roy **Professional:** Graeme Lennie
Phone - Starter/Pro shop: 01333-450-278; 01333-450-960
Fee(s) (2012): £60 wkdays, £95 day tkt; £75 wkend, £120 day tkt if clear
Deposit (2012): 50% **Buggies:** 5 - general hire
Visitor Policies: all wkdays; reduced hrs wkends
Other: companion course - Craighead 6221-6722 yds (1999) by Gil Hanse; day tkt w/Balcomie £80 wkdays, £100 wkend

Crail's unusual hexagon-shaped pro shop

I LIKE TO BOOK CLIENTS at the Balcomie Links (pronounced Bal-COMB-ee) in Crail for three reasons: First, this is Fife's most scenic course. Second, at just under 6,000 yards, it's a throwback to nineteenth-century holiday golf—a shotmaker's course—that contrasts nicely with the brawnier tracks at St. Andrews and Kingsbarns. Third, a trip down the road to Crail from St. Andrews gets the traveler onto Fife's coastal route and into the pretty fishing villages of the "East Neuk" between Crail and Leven.

Crail village is ten miles south of St. Andrews. The Balcomie Links are situated another two miles along on the easternmost promontory of Fife where the shore makes its turn westward along the firth. Thus, Balcomie is not only the most scenic course in Fife, it's also the one most exposed to wind and rain from the North Sea. And, to put it mildly, this simple fact tends to have a lengthening effect on a rather short course.

Tom Morris came down here in 1895 from St. Andrews to lay out nine holes for the Crail Golfing Society (the world's seventh or eighth oldest club, depending upon who's reporting). In 1899, he came back to add another nine. This was some of Morris's last work, closing out a productive decade when, well into his seventies, he completed Muirfield, Elie, Luffness New, Scotscraig, and Tain. Balcomie's layout is odd, with the last four holes laid off on a terraced area east of the clubhouse a bit removed from the rest of the course. It's almost as if Old Tom laid out a perfect fourteen and then had to figure out how to cram another four into the picture.

The entire layout can be surveyed from high ground at Crail's clubhouse, newly-refurbished and expanded in 2011. The first hole, "Boathouse," plays down a slope leading to the sea for holes two through five. These latter are among the most stirring in Scottish golf and they will certainly remind one of Pebble Beach, particularly the #5 "Hell's Hole," a brutal beauty playing to 459 yards over the rocky shoreline. Holes six through fourteen play along an OB stone wall lending more atmosphere to the round. After fourteen, a hike of about two hundred yards takes us to the fifteenth tee to begin the homeward "terrace four." Throughout this layout is the presence of Tom Morris in a raft of bunkers, testing par 3s, challenging greens, and one double green. In short, the Balcomie at Crail is a unique course designed by a unique individual in a unique setting—emblematic of all the reasons we go to Scotland to play golf.

LITERARY TIP

Upon leaving the #14 green, glance to the right on the hillside and you will see possible inspiration for "MacDuff's Cave," made famous in Michael Murphy's classic *Golf in the Kingdom* and Michael Konik's *In Search of Burningbush.*

One further note: Craighead, Crail's "second course," is every bit the match of its more famous sibling. Admittedly covering less stirring ground than the Balcomie, the Gil Hanse-designed beauty is a test at 6722 yards from the back tees. If you're up for thirty-six holes, this is a good place to buy a combination ticket.

Lodging - Crail and the East Neuk*:** For some, lodging in Crail or any of the villages in Fife's East Neuk will make an attractive alternative to busy and pricey St. Andrews. In Crail, two budget hotels for golfers are the *Balcomie Links Hotel* (01333-450-237; ***www.balcomie.co.uk) and *The Golf Hotel* (01333-450-206; ***www.thegolfhotelcrail.com***). *The Hazelton* is a good B & B run by Karen and David Rae (01333-450-250; ***www.thehazelton.co.uk***). Farther west along the coast at Anstruther you'll find the popular *Craw's Nest Hotel* (01333-310-691; ***www.crawsnesthotel.co.uk***) and a four-star guest house, *The Spindrift* (01333-310-573; ***www.thespindrift.co.uk***). For more about the East Neuk, see the website ***www.eastneukwide.co.uk***.

See also: Golf House Club (Elie), Leven Links, Lundin Links

9. Crieff Golf Club Ltd. (1891) - Ferntower Course

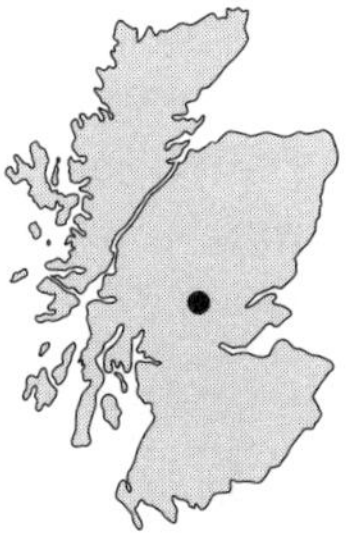

Region #: 7 **Category:** parkland
Architect(s): various, incl James Braid, Robert Simpson, John Stark
Length: 6061-6427 **SSS:** 72 **Par:** 71

Address: Perth Rd, Crieff PH7 3LR
Directions: 1 mi NE of Crieff town center on A85

Reservations phone: 01764-652-909 **Fax:** none
Email: bookings@crieffgolf.co.uk **Website:** crieffgolf.co.uk
Booking Contact(s): professional

Secretary: Roy Hunter **Professional:** David W Murchie
Phone - Starter/Pro shop: 01764-652-909
Fee(s) (2012): wkday (M-Th) £37, day tkt £56; wkend (F-Sun) £43, no day tkt; reduced rates Apr & Oct
Deposit (2012): none **Buggies:** 4 - general hire
Visitor Policies: all wk
Other: 9-hole relief course, "Dornock," 2321 yds

RECONFIGURED AND EXPANDED in 1980, only a few years before the PGA Centenary course was built at neighboring Gleneagles, the Ferntower course at Crieff offers golf over terrain similar to that at Gleneagles at about one-fourth the price. This is a good choice for the golfer on a budget or the golfer already familiar with Scotland's pricier venues. Replete with B & Bs, guest houses, and hotels, Crieff makes a good base for those planning to play at Gleneagles without staying there. Alternatively, it's an easy day trip from St. Andrews, allowing for good inland golf combined with a look at one of Scotland's most interesting towns.

Directly north of Stirling, Crieff long has been a strategic crossroads on routes to and from the Highlands. The ancient feel of this attractive hill town is pervasive in its twisting streets and old stone buildings. When not on the golf course, visitors to Crieff can find historic sites, natural history at Loch Earn to the west, or the commercial history of Scotland's whisky trade at the Famous Grouse Experience.

The Ferntower Course plays east to west along the south-facing slope of a hill called the "Knock," a local landmark. From those heights, golfers enjoy superb views over the Strathearn Valley while hoping (usually in vain) for a level lie. Ferntower's three par 5s and four par 3s offer pleasing variety. Incidentally, the former pro at Crieff is John Stark, who gained a certain measure of immortality as the key figure in Michael Bamberger's delightful book, *To the Linksland.* Stark was instrumental in redesigning the Ferntower to incorporate seven holes from the original Simpson layout and, in the process, creating a good companion nine.

10. Cruden Bay Golf Club (1899)

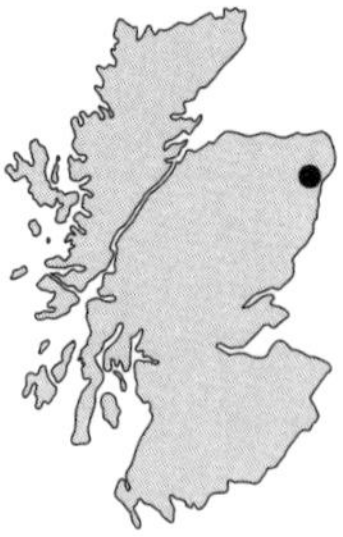

Region #: 5 **Category:** seaside links
Architect(s): Tom Morris and Archie Simpson (1899)
Tom Simpson and Herbert Fowler (1926)
Length: 6022-66287 **SSS:** 71 **Par:** 70

Address: Aulton Rd, Cruden Bay, Aberdeenshire AB42 0NN
Directions: 2 mi off A90 S of village

Reservations phone: 01779-812-285 **Fax:** 01779-812-945
Email: admin@crudenbaygolfclub.co.uk **Website:** crudenbaygolfclub.co.uk
Booking Contact(s): Elaine Stephen

Administrator: Robbie Stewart **Professional:** Neil Murray
Phone - Starter/Pro shop: 01779-812-414
Fee(s) (2012): wkday £70, wkend £75 - for all-day play depending upon course availability, including excellent 9-hole St. Olaf course
Deposit (2012): prepay 30 days prior **Buggies:** no
Visitor Policies: not before 10 M, T; wkend pm only and not before 4:30 on club medal days
Other: Gents Open 3rd wk of July; visitors ok from white tees with hdcp approval

DRIVE TIME
Aberdeen: 30 mins
Nairn: 2 hrs, 15-30 min
Dornoch: 3 hrs, 30 min

HERE'S A MEASURE of Cruden Bay's appeal: after my clients have finished a golf trip, I send a post-trip evaluation asking for a ranking of courses played. In these post-trip evaluations Cruden Bay rarely ranks lower than #2. Usually it is #1—and that's compared to Carnoustie, Dornoch, Turnberry, Troon, and all the courses at St. Andrews. Pete Dye has cited Cruden Bay among his five favorite courses in the world! Readers of *Golf World,* as reported in *Best Courses in Scotland*, rank Cruden Bay sixth among Best Courses and fourth among Best Value Courses.

Many golf writers have described Cruden Bay in loving detail. Suffice to say here, the overwhelming impression made at Cruden Bay is that of a lunar landscape laid down on the gentle curve of an ocean bay. This is nothing less than pure links golf played on the wasteland between fertile soil and raging sea. The course, routed into the natural terrain, traces an elongated "figure-eight" from the elevated clubhouse to

Perched on high ground, Cruden Bay's modern clubhouse affords one of the greatest panoramic views in all of golf.

the equally elevated #10 tee at the far end of the course and back again. In between, it's "Nelly, bar the door!"

Everything you want to find on a Scottish links course is here: long rough, gorse, burns, gullies, dells, dunes, blind shots, elevated tees, sunken greens, raised greens. Golf writer Jim Finegan summarizes: "One of the most awe-inspiring stretches of linksland in Scotland, indeed, in all of the British Isles." I would say Cruden Bay is simply *the* most dramatic duneland in Scottish golf. And, what's more, it's the most *fun* to play. It's so much fun, you hardly care about your score when you reach the comfortable nineteenth hole—incidentally, one of the finest in Scottish golf.

As news of the superb golf experience awaiting at Cruden Bay has spread from one visitor to the next, more and more golfers have made the pilgrimage to this special place. Cruden Bay's busy visitor playlist attests to the fact that this gem of the northeast is no longer hidden—not by a long stretch. Still, it takes a bit of effort to get to the northeast corner of Scotland—not exactly the crossroads of most itineraries. Most golfers make Cruden Bay a stop en route to or from the Highlands or, at least, stay for one night and two rounds. I strongly recommend the latter because this is a course you will want to see and play more than once. If the course is not too busy, Cruden Bay allows all-day play for one green fee—a terrific bargain.

Lodging: Cruden Bay is a small village with limited lodging options. Nevertheless, several small hotels fill the bill for most groups. Overlooking the golf course are two choices: the *St. Olaf Hotel* (01779-813-130; ***www.stolafhotel.co.uk***) near the clubhouse is a family-run place with five rooms (rooms 3 & 4 have golf course views). The *Red House Hotel* (01779-812-215; ***www.redhouse-hotel.com***), a well-known stop for golfers, stands alongside the first fairway (rooms 1, 2, and 5 face the golf course). Down in the village, under the direction of Martin and Lucy Taylor, the *Kilmarnock Arms* (01779-812-213; ***www.kilmarnockarms.com***) offers up good food and solid, three-star lodging. It's a gathering place for villagers when they're not at the golf course and, many years ago, this is where Bram Stoker resided while writing *Dracula*, said to be inspired by the ruins of nearby Slains Castle hovering over Cruden Bay on a promontory north of town.

See also: Royal Aberdeen, Murcar, Trump International

11. Downfield Golf Club (1932)+

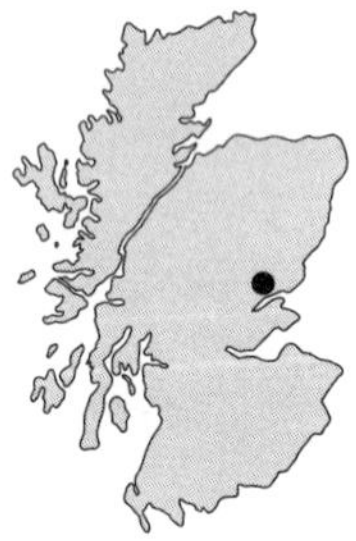

Region #: 6 **Category:** parkland
Architect(s): James Braid (1932); Jack Scrimgeour, Les Wright, C K Cotton (expanded to 18 holes - 1964)
Length: 6247-6817 **SSS:** 71-73 **Par:** 71-73

Address: Turnberry Ave, Dundee DD2 3QP
Directions: NW of Dundee; Exit A923 off ring Rd; left on Harrison Rd to T-junction; left to Turnberry Ave

Reservations phone: 01382-825-595 **Fax:** 01382-813-111
Email: info@downfieldgolf.com **Website:** downfieldgolf.com

Booking Contact(s): Margaret Stewart
Phone - Starter/Pro shop: 01382-889-246 **Professional:** Kenny Hutton
Fee(s) (2012): May-Sept wkday £69, day tkt £77; wkend £45 after 1:45 pm; reduced rates Apr & Oct; 27 and 36-hole pkgs;
Deposit (2012): £20 **Buggies:** 4 - general hire
Visitor Policies: M-F 9:31-11:16, 2:18-3:42; not on Sat; Sun after 2 pm

THE BEST RECOMMENDATION I can make for Downfield is a reminder that, at 6800 yards, this is one of the longest of Scotland's modern classics and one that has been used as an Open Qualifier for tournaments at Carnoustie. This is a course visitors to Carnoustie or St. Andrews should consider as a parkland respite from linksland golf. Situated in northwest Dundee, midway between those two golf Meccas, the course is easily accessible in about twenty minutes from either location.

Originally laid out by James Braid in 1932, Downfield was largely reconfigured in 1964 by members with some assistance from C.K. Cotton. At the time, the course created quite a stir in Scottish golf. Downfield hosted the Scottish Open in 1972, the British PGA Match Play Championship in 1974, and the Scottish Amateur in 1978. Since those halcyon years, Downfield's star has faded a bit as the UK golf establishment has moved on to other venues. Today, this condition makes it all the easier to score a reservation on short notice or even walk on at one of Scotland's finest inland courses.

Downfield may not be the highlight of your trip . . . but it can be a welcome break from the links and it's a lot less expensive than Gleneagles.

The outstanding feature of Downfield is its forest setting with evergreen and deciduous trees unmatched in their multifarious variety except perhaps at Gleneagles and Blairgowrie. The setting is usually described as "mature woodlands," but that antiseptic description does not do justice to the beauty of Downfield. In the fall it is breathtaking. This is rich, midland Scotland at its very best, and it's a good example of why a parkland course should be mixed into an itinerary focused on seaside golf. After playing golf at the links courses—never described as "pretty" or "lush" or "graceful"—it can be a relief to visit a course where all those adjectives apply.

The irony and oddity of Downfield is that, if it's challenge you are seeking, this is a course where one should relish playing off the yellow tees at 6250 yards rather than the medal tees at 6800 yards. The reason: three relatively easy par 5s on the medal course become long, difficult par 4s on the shorter track. The medal par 73 (unusual in golf anywhere) is reduced to par 70 from the second tees. Fairways at #s 4, 5, 7, 15, and 16 are alleys cut through forest; landing areas are generous; and the course is always in "top nick." As golf writer Jim Finegan puts it, Downfield offers "good, honest golf . . . in an exquisite parkland setting, but it is no occasion for hat tossing and dancing in the streets." In short, Downfield may not be the highlight of your trip, but it can be a welcome break from the links and it's a lot less expensive than Gleneagles.

Nongolf notes: Dundee is Scotland's fourth largest city. Approaching from Fife, its setting is dramatic—on a high hill tumbling down to the Firth of Tay. In days past, jute, jam, and journalism made Dundee's reputation. Today, that reputation is associated with high unemployment and related maladies of the modern economy. Dundee has become the place where most visitors take a right turn at the north end of the Tay Bridge to get from St. Andrews to Carnoustie. Near that bridge is anchored Dundee's highest-profile tourist attraction. For a memorable experience, take a left (instead of a right) along the waterfront and you'll find Captain Robert Scott's vessel of Antarctic exploration, the *Discovery*. This ship is now a remarkable museum. An audio-visual introduction precedes a tour of the ship. The *Discovery* is a useful reminder that the Scots were a seafaring people who built great ships and were willing to go places others feared to tread (or sail). This is one of the best nongolf expeditions I can recommend and its 5-star rating from VisitScotland corroborates my experience.

12. Duff House Royal Golf Club (1909)

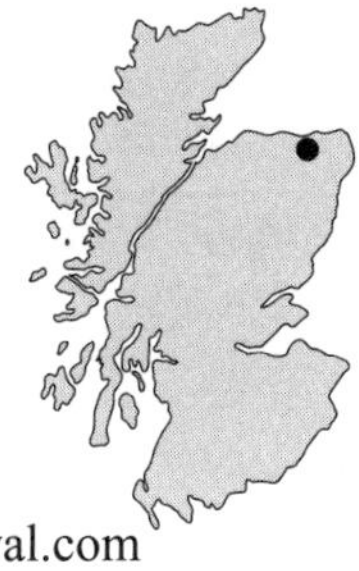

Region #: 5 **Category:** parkland
Architect(s): James Braid (1909), Alister MacKenzie (1923)
Length: 5991-6161 **SSS:** 69-70 **Par:** 68

Address: The Barnyards, Duff House, Banff AB45 35X
Directions: 1 mi S of Banff on A98

Reservations phone: 01261-812-062 **Fax:** 01261-812-224
Email: info@duffhouseroyal.com **Website:** duffhouseroyal.com
Booking Contact(s): secretary
Secretary: James Cameron **Professional:** Gary Holland
Phone - Starter/Pro shop: reservations
Fee(s) (2012): wkday £30, day tkt 40; wkend £36, day tkt £50
Deposit (2012): £10 for groups of 12+ **Buggies:** 2 - med/phys
Visitor Policies: wkdays after 9:36; wkend after 10:32 am

GOLF AT BANFF HAS A LONG HISTORY but, to make the proverbial long story short, Duff House has been part of that history only since 1910 when Alexander Duff, Duke of Fife, donated his parkland estate to the twin towns of Banff and Macduff. Prior to this magnanimous gift to Scottish golf, the game had been played on nine holes on linksland near the Moray Firth. Coincidentally, the duke was married to the daughter of the Prince of Wales, Princess Louise, who secured the "Royal" appellation for the club—the seventh and last in the line of Scottish clubs so designated.

To put an even finer point on the pedigree of Duff House Royal, the course we play today actually dates from 1923-5 when Alister MacKenzie was engaged by the club to give them a course worthy of the royal designation. As a last gesture before his relocation to America, where he created Augusta National, that's exactly what the master of wartime camouflage did. And, because Scotland boasts so few MacKenzie courses, Duff House Royal must be included in a selective directory of this sort.

Just to toughen up a one-shotter a bit, this raft of massive bunkers guards the sixteenth green at Duff House Royal.

Though not far from seaside, MacKenzie worked with flood plain parkland turf fronting the River Deveron. Here he created a challenging venue featuring huge, double-tiered greens protected by dozens of bunkers. Deceptively short at 6161 yards, the course has only one par 5, leaving us at par 68 against an SSS of 70. This kind of profile promises a collection of monster par 4s—a promise kept on the road home as we encounter #14 (434 yards), #15 (468 yards), and #17 (462 yards). Yes, I skipped #16: that's a 242-yard one-shotter reachable only by the power hitter. The eighteenth home hole will feel like sweet relief after playing this stretch of closing holes among the most punishing in Scottish golf.

Nongolf notes: For those traversing northeast Scotland's "Coastal Trail," Duff House Royal is situated about twenty-six miles west of Fraserburgh. It's just off the A98 where that highway returns to the coast at Banff-Macduff after an inland bend. Given some time and inclination, this is an area to savor and explore. For example, one can combine a day of golf with art at Duff House itself. The Palladian mansion designed and built by William Adam in the 1730s is now managed by Historic Scotland and is part of the National Gallery's network of "Country House Galleries" (see ***www.nationalgalleries.org***).

When in Scotland, SLOW DOWN and enjoy the gift of life.

The inland attraction of the northeast corner of Scotland is the "Castle Trail." The seaside attraction is the collection of small fishing villages that dot the coastline. One of these is Pennan, twelve miles east of Banff-Macduff on the B9031. I mention this tiny village because scenes in a feature film, *Local Hero*, were shot here. Written and directed by a Scot, Bill Forsyth, this movie captures a part of the spirit of Scotland without any of the usual clichés. It's a movie about North Sea oil and the transformation of a small village or, more precisely, how a small village manages to retain its character in the face of "modernization." In the opening scenes of the movie, two American oil executives—buttoned-down, intense, and efficient—arrive in the small town to "make a deal" and get out as quickly as possible. By the end of the movie these fellows have shed their shirts and ties and are lazing about on the sand with an old beachcomber. I hope this is something like what happens to you on your trip to Scotland. The message: when in Scotland, SLOW DOWN and enjoy the gift of life.

See also: Moray Old

The Duke's Course *- see St. Andrews - Old Course Hotel - Duke's Course*

13. Dunbar Golf Club (1856) +

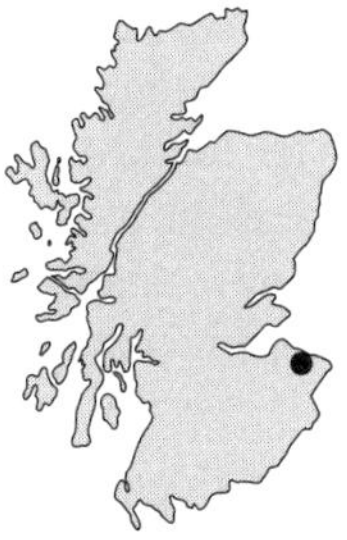

Region #: 3 **Category:** seaside links
Architect(s): Tom Morris (1894) re-design; extended by James Braid and Ben Sayers (1922-24)
Length: 6200-6597 **SSS:** 70-72 **Par:** 70-71

Address: East Links, Dunbar EH42 1LT
Directions: S of town ctr off A1087

Reservations phone: 01368-862-317 **Fax:** 01368-865-202
Email: secretary@dunbargolfclub.com **Website:** dunbargolfclub.com
Booking Contact(s): Verena Wilthew

Manager: Liz Thom **Professional:** J Montgomery
Phone - Starter/Pro shop: 01368-862-086
Fee(s) (2012): wkday £60, day tkt £80; wkend £85, day tkt £105; twilight rate
Deposit (2012): £10 **Buggies:** 3 - med/phys
Visitor Policies: M-F after 9:30 except Th, wkend 10-12 and after 2 pm

TWENTY MINUTES SOUTHEAST of North Berwick, just off the A1, at the attractive port/resort of Dunbar, golfers will find a classic links where the game has been played since at least the early seventeenth century. It's another course where the long hand of Tom Morris remains. After evolving from twelve holes to fifteen holes before graduating to eighteen holes in 1880, Dunbar was extended and redesigned by Morris in 1894. Later, the course was further extended by James Braid and Ben Sayers.

Unusual in Scottish golf—or golf anywhere for that matter—the first two holes are par 5s. The first hole shoots straight away from the starter house and the second, like a boomerang, returns to place. Then #3, a par 3, makes a ninety-degree turn, heading straight to the ocean. After this quirky start, dictated by available land, the oldest holes proceed along a narrow strip of linksland, out and back, in classic fashion. Along the way exhilarating ocean views and excellent golf holes are highlighted by a stone wall on the right side of the outgoing nine. This is no course for a slicer, for, once free of the outgoing wall, the ocean sits starboard coming home. At the final hole it will be abundantly clear why Dunbar is used as a qualifying course when the Open is held at Muirfield. Back at the clubhouse you'll find no warmer welcome in Scottish golf.

TRAVEL TIP
Locals pronounce their town with the accent on the last syllable (i.e., Dun-BAR). Same with Inver-NESS, Aber-DEEN, and Dum-FRIES. On the other hand, it's LUFF-ness, so you never know.

Anyone interested in an additional eighteen holes will find the short but intriguing Winterfield golf course on the opposite (northeast) end of town. This course features a bundle of wild and woolly one-shotters (the first hole across a vast, grass gully is worth the price of admission), played first on the bluffs above the ocean, then out on a promontory fully exposed to the forces of nature. I know of only one other course in Scotland quite like this one and that is the promontory layout at Fortrose. Great stuff.

The town: Dunbar has always occupied a strategic position relative to England, so you'll see here a collection of castle ruins and historic buildings. Of greatest interest to many Americans is the birthplace of John Muir, the most influential conservationist of our nineteenth century and fountainhead of America's system of national parks. The John Muir Country Park is located outside Dunbar and his birthplace, now an excellent museum, is in the middle of town at 126 High Street. Interested in a brewery tour?—this is the home of the Belhaven Brewery, Scotland's largest regional brand. It's on the main drag into town.

14. Dundonald Links (2003)

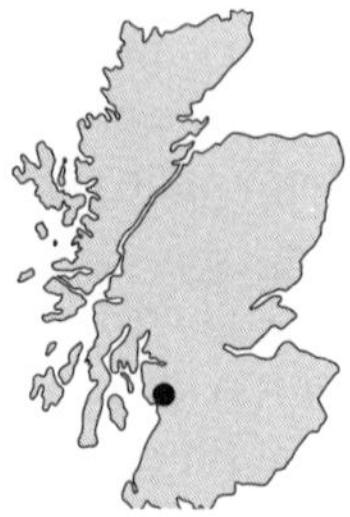

Region #: 2 **Category:** inland links
Architect(s): Kyle Phillips
Length: 6340-6725 **SSS:** 72-74 **Par:** 72

Address: Ayr Rd, Gailes, Ayrshire KA11 5BF
Directions: service rd 4 mi N of Troon at Gailes off A78

Reservations phone: 01294-314-000 **Fax:** 01294-314-001
Booking Contact: Janice Borys
Email: dundonaldlinks@lochlomond.com **Website:** dundonaldlinks.com

Manager: Guy Redford
Fee(s) (2012): £95; £70 after 2pm; Apr & Oct £70; tour operator discounts
Deposit (2012): none
Visitor Policies: all wk **Buggies:** 1 - phys/med
Other: participant in Ayrshire Golf Pass and The Gailes Experience (with Western Gailes and Glasgow Gailes)

WHAT A TRIAL IT HAS BEEN to get this great course up and running! Originally billed as "Southern Gailes," developer intentions were to build an American-style resort course with a Spanish-themed clubhouse, a 130-room hotel, cabana-style cottages, etc. In the wake of September 2001 and international economic dislocation that followed, it didn't take long for that project to go bust. Clubhouse construction was well underway when Lyle Anderson's oh-so-private Loch Lomond Golf Club acquired the course in unfinished condition in 2003. Lyle Anderson didn't like the clubhouse design, so he had it torn down . . . or so the story goes. And nothing on that front has happened since—the club still operates out of a temporary port-a-cabin, albeit a deluxe edition with bar/restaurant, pro shop, and offices.

Flash forward to 2012: Lyle Anderson is bankrupt and Loch Lomond is owned by the members. After years of languishing underplayed and being perennially up for sale, Dundonald is rising like the proverbial Phoenix, having aggressively sought public play since about 2008—in effect, being told to live or die on the strength of its own resources. Today, the important fact to know about this star-crossed course is that it is "the other" Kyle Phillips course in Scotland—the course intended to be Phillips' exclamation point on Scottish golf after having completed Kingsbarns near St. Andrews. And we must hope and pray it does not go away, for it is, indeed, magnificent.

Kyle Phillips was working with topography far less dramatic than Kingsbarns when he created "Southern Gailes" on land north of Troon adjacent to Western Gailes and Glasgow Gailes. The ground was essentially flat, having been commandeered for use as a military training ground in 1936 (from 1911 it had been another "Dundonald" 18-holer). To complicate matters, an unfortunate and immutable fact of the site was the presence of a huge paper plant to the east across the Gailes service road.

Knowing all this, one can only marvel at the genius of Kyle Phillips. The designer's response to visual pollution from the paper plant was to move tons of sand to create funnels of faux dunes and, thus, isolate holes on the east side of the course. Design creativity continued: Constant changes of direction (no less than seven on the second nine); doglegs alternating left and right; par 3s offering variety, challenge, and even a nod to iconic Scottish one-shotters. Then there is the Phillips style: The clean, sharp look of revetted bunkers; brilliantly strategic bunkering in the fairways and at the greens; and interesting, sensibly-undulated greens in the best Scottish tradition. A salutary feature of this otherwise unpromising ground was the Montgomery Burn running to the sea—used by Phillips to add a fillip of challenge and visual appeal to six of Dundonald's eighteen.

If it would seem the author is a fan of Kyle Phillips, he pleads guilty. In my view, Phillips is the most imaginative and yet most traditional of the course designers working today. I like Dundonald just as it is—the simple port-a-cabin, the friendly staff, the price (half the rate of Kingsbarns). And I don't for a minute miss the fancy clubhouse that was torn down or the 130-room hotel that was never built. Perhaps some other developers working in Scotland could learn something from the experience at Dundonald.

See also, Glasgow Gailes, Western Gailes, Kilmarnock Barassie

15. Edzell Golf Club (1895)

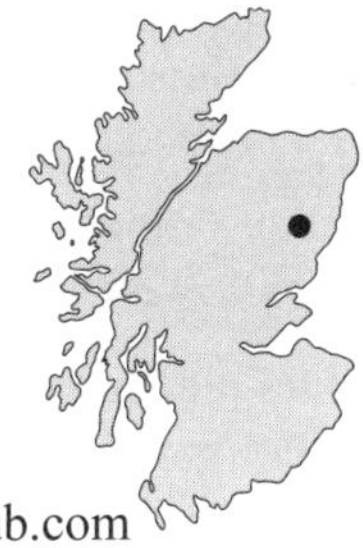

Region #: 6 **Category:** parkland
Architect(s): Robert Simpson (1895), James Braid (1933-34)
Length: 6042-6299 **SSS:** 71 **Par:** 69-71

Address: High St, Edzell, Angus DD9 7TF
Directions: 4 mi W of A90 on B966; left just past Edzell archway

Reservations phone: 01356-647-283 **Fax:** 01356-648-094
Email: secretary@edzellgolfclub.com **Website:** edzellgolfclub.com
Key Contact(s): secretary

Secretary: Ian Farquhar **Professional:** Alistair J Webster
Phone - Starter/Pro shop: 01356-648-462
Fee(s) (2012): wkday £40, day tkt £52; wkend £44, day tkt £60
Deposit (2012): £5
Visitor Policies: all wk, call on wkend **Buggies**: 4 - general hire
Other: excellent 9-hole "West Water" course, par 32, 2057 yds

FOR GOLFERS IN TRANSIT from north to south or vice versa, Edzell Golf Club is an elegant way to break up the drive. For 36-holers staying in Angus, this is a highly-regarded parkland course to pair with one of the historic seaside courses. Still another way to enjoy Edzell is to combine golf with a drive up Glen Esk on a narrow road that crosses the B966 about a mile north of Edzell. A twelve-mile jaunt on this road, through a

TRAVEL TIP
To see Scotland's most dramatic scenery, drive "the glens." Near Inverness try Glen Affric. At Ballater there's Glen Muick. In the south drive the "Waters of Moffat" (A708).

broad, verdant glen, leads to the Glenesk Folk Museum, castle ruins, and abbey ruins on the rim of Loch Lee. A great place for a picnic! Back in Edzell are more castle ruins and gardens. Lots of fishing, hiking, and hunting in this area too. In short, Edzell is a good example of how a savvy traveler can combine golf with excursions into the Scottish countryside in a way that will never show up on the typical tour. As for the golf, it's a challenge on a course planned by Bob Simpson of Carnoustie. Relatively flat and compact, Edzell is easy to walk despite its location at the foot of hills that rise to 1,000 feet. Pleasant views abound. The River West Walter plays a role here and out-of-bounds is a constant factor—in the case of #15, on both sides of a tight fairway. This one's a *real* hidden gem.

***Elie** - see Golf House Club at Elie*
***Fairmont St. Andrews Kittocks** - see St. Andrews - Fairmont Hotel*
***Fairmont St. Andrews Torrance** - see St. Andrews - Fairmont Hotel*

16. Fortrose and Rosemarkie (1888)

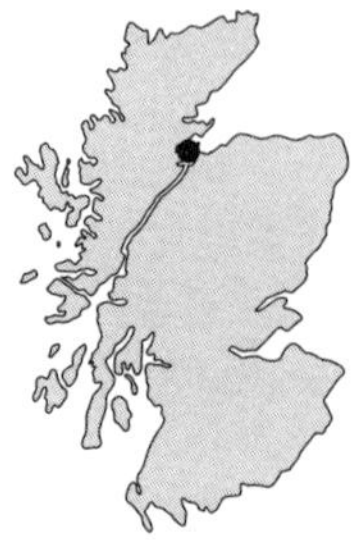

Region #: 4 **Category:** seaside links
Architect(s): James Braid (1932-35)
Length: 5657-5890 **SSS:** 69 **Par:** 71

Address: Ness Rd East, Fortrose, Ross-Shire IV10 8SE
Directions: 12 mi N of Inverness; E on A832 at Tore roundabout; rt at Fortrose police station, follow signs

Reservations phone: 01381-620-529 **Fax:** 01381-621-328
Email: secretary@fortrosegolfclub.co.uk **Website**: fortrosegolfclub.co.uk

Booking Contact(s): secretary
Secretary: Michael MacDonald **Professional:** none
Phone - Starter/Pro shop: 01381-620-733
Fee(s) (2012): wkday £40, day tkt £56; wkend £47, day tkt £62
Deposit (2012): no
Visitor Policies: all wk **Buggies:** 3 - general hire

GOLFERS VISITING THE INVERNESS/DORNOCH region generally have their sights set on Royal Dornoch, Castle Stuart, Nairn, Tain, and maybe Brora—in about that order. Once those are played, this is a good course to squeeze into the itinerary—a quick morning or afternoon round perhaps but, better yet, on a day's outing to the "Black Isle" (actually a peninsula) just a few miles northeast of Inverness.

Fortrose and Rosemarkie is another James Braid design extended between 1932 and 1935 from nine holes laid out when the golf club was formed in 1888. At only 5657 yards from the visitor tees, with an SSS of 69, the course may remind one of the short but difficult track designed by Braid at Boat of Garten. But the setting here is dramatically different: the golf course is crammed into a promontory (Chanonry

Point) jutting into the Moray Firth. Just across the water, on another point of land, is Fort George, a military outpost built by the English after the Jacobite rising of 1745. These two pincer-like points of land aimed at one another form a natural harbor wall between Inverness and the sea.

Golf tour operators like to tout the "Hidden Gems" of Scotland. The trouble is, most of them are not hidden at all. Fortrose and Rosemarkie is an exception. Relatively speaking, it is a hidden gem and it's also one of the best bargains in Scottish golf. This is a course you will not soon forget.

Nongolf notes: If lodging in a small town away from Inverness appeals, Fortrose is a good choice. It's a handsome, homey village where everybody knows everybody. And quite a few of them eat and drink at an award-winning hotel/restaurant, *The Anderson* (01381-620-236; ***www.theanderson.co.uk***), operated by Jim and Anne Anderson, American expats who came here to stay in 2003.

A trip to Fortrose also gives the traveler an opportunity to visit a "Clootie Well." This is a kind of site once widespread in Celtic lands and, indeed, in other parts of the world, but found now in only a few places in the United Kingdom and Ireland. In brief, a clootie well is a sacred spring with supposed healing powers and "cloot" is the Scots Gaelic word for cloth. Combining these concepts, we have a place where people in need of physical or spiritual healing come to wash themselves, then hang all manner of cloth, from strips of muslin to brassieres and BVDs, on the trees and bushes surrounding the well. In spiritual theory, as the cloot deteriorates the treated affliction subsides too. The effect created is surreal in a kaleidoscopic, even phantasmagoric, riot of color. Some will find this fascinating and fun; others may find it just plain creepy. In *The Naming of the Dead*, Scottish mystery writer Ian Rankin found it creepy enough to make a clootie well the locus of a murder. In any case, a clootie well gives us a glimpse at a remnant of paganism and will add an indelible image to your traveler's mental notebook .

Two clootie wells are located on the A832 eastward from the Tore Roundabout to Fortrose. The one most easily found is visible on the right side of the road a few miles from the roundabout and about one mile west of the turnoff to Munlochy. There's another one farther along the road at Avoch.

Here's something you probably won't find in your home town—a "clootie well" with mythic medicinal properties.

17. Glasgow Golf Club (1892) - Glasgow Gailes +

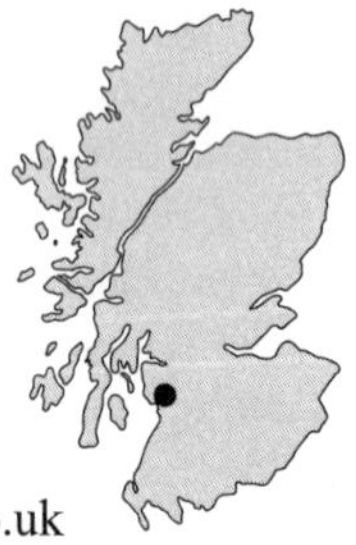

Region #: 2 **Category:** seaside links - no view
Architect(s): Willie Park, Jr. (1892)
Length: 6322-6535 **SSS:** 71-72 **Par:** 71

Address: Gailes Rd, Irvine KA11 5AE
Directions: 2 mi S of Irvine off A78; 4 mi N of Troon town ctr

Reservations phone: 0141-942-2011 **Fax:** 0141-942-0770
Email: admin@gaileslinks.co.uk **Website:** gaileslinks.co.uk

Booking Contact(s): Claire Middleton
Secretary: Alan G McMillan **Professional:** John Greaves
Phone - Starter/Pro shop: 01294-311-561
Fee(s) (2012): wkday £75, day tkt £90; wkend £80; reduced rates Apr & Oct
Deposit (2012): 50% **Buggies:** 3 - general hire
Visitor Policies: after 10:30 and 2 pm; wkend after 1:30
Other: white tees for hdcp 6 and below; participant in The Gailes Experience w/ Western Gailes and Dundonald; 10 percent tour operator discount

GLASGOW GAILES IS AMONG the "dazzling dozen" that line the Ayrshire coast from West Kilbride to Turnberry. A common thread among them is the coastal railway that made the courses easily accessible to residents of Glasgow in the late nineteenth century. The Glasgow Golf Club opened its course at Gailes in 1892 to relieve member pressure on its home course at Alexandra Park in Glasgow. Willie Park, Jr., was asked to design the course and he did a magnificent job of it.

TRAVEL TIP
For complete fitness and spa facilities, a driving range, and two 9-hole warmup tracks, check out the North Gailes Health Club and Spa directly east of Glasgow Gailes.

This is a classic heather-filled links course that could hardly be more different than its dune-filled neighbor, Western Gailes. The course is relatively flat. Most holes are straightaway, putting the emphasis on accurate driving and quality second shots to well-guarded, rather small greens. The par 3s are treacherous. There's plenty of length for the average golfer, and for the professionals who come here to qualify for the Open Championship the course can be stretched to 6900 yards (SSS 74). A lasting impression I have of playing here is walking off the eighteenth green thinking these are the best greens I've experienced anywhere. If this sounds like a course too often overlooked by visiting golfers, you would be reaching the right conclusion.

In context, Glasgow Gailes is one of the three excellent golf courses within spitting distance of one another on linksland four miles north of Troon town center. These are the courses of "The Gailes Experience." Western is situated on the west side of the rail line between the railway and the sea. Glasgow lies away from the water, on the east side of the line and a little to the north across a service road. Dundonald, designed by Kyle Phillips of Kingsbarns fame, resides across the road to the south of Glasgow Gailes.

The classic red stone clubhouse at Glasgow Gailes

The courses at Gailes will not likely supplant the royal triumvirate of Turnberry, Troon, and Prestwick on the golf traveler's list of Ayrshire priorities. But, for those who have extra time to give to this golf Mecca, Gailes is the place to go. Western Gailes certainly has gained in international notoriety, having appeared on many "Best of Scotland" lists; Glasgow Gailes has achieved the distinction of having been named Scotland's *only* final qualifying course for the Open for the years 2014-17; and Loch Lomond's Dundonald course fills out the dance card with a contemporary twist. This triumvirate of classic and contemporary courses in such proximity is matched in Scotland only by the courses at St. Andrews.

My recommendation: At this writing, one of the best deals in Scottish golf is "The Gailes Experience" involving play on all three of the courses at Gailes for something approximating a one-third discount on green fees. The promotion is administered by Western Gailes.

See also: Dundonald, Western Gailes

18. Glen Golf Club (1906) - (North Berwick East Links)

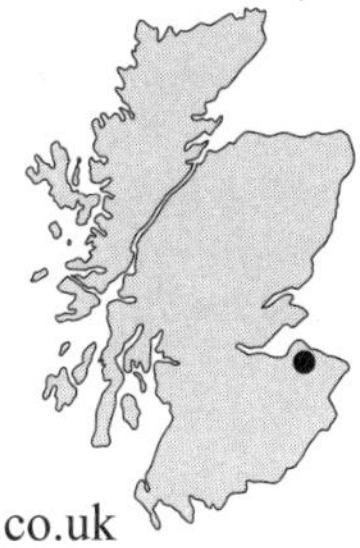

Region #: 3 **Category:** seaside links
Architect(s): Ben Sayers, James Braid (1906), Philip Mackenzie Ross
Length: 5791-6043 **SSS:** 68 **Par:** 69

Address: East Links, Tantallon Terrace, N Berwick EH39 4LE
Directions: E of town ctr off Beach Rd

Reservations phone: 01620-892-726 **Fax:** 01620-895-447
Email: secretary@glengolfclub.co.uk **Website:** glengolfclub.co.uk
Booking Contact(s): Charlie Shearer

Manager: Rita Wilson **Professional:** none
Phone - Starter/Pro shop: 01620-892-726
Fee(s) (2012): wkday £45, day tkt £60; wkend £58, day tkt £73; check for pm after 2 pm 35 & 48; and reduced twilight rates (after 4 pm)
Deposit (2012): £15 **Buggies:** 12 - general hire
Visitor Policies: all wk 9:30-noon and after 1 pm; Sat after 2 pm; Sun 9:30-11 and after 2:30 pm

AMONG THE MOST SCENIC courses in Scotland, this track on the opposite end of town from the historic "West Links," is worth a visit either in its own right or paired with the West Links on a day of 36-hole golf.

The ski-slope second shot at Glen GC's opening hole.

On a crisp fall day alternating between sunshine and a Lothian burst of showers, I played a round of golf at Glen Golf Club with then Captain John Wellwood. Briefly stated, I have never played a more invigorating eighteen holes in Scotland. The reasons? Apart from the presence of good company, first, Glen GC is a course that can be fully enjoyed by the average golfer. The mid-to-high-handicapper can play this course without feeling like a lightweight boxer thrown into the ring with a heavyweight. Though you'll find plenty of challenge here, no great banks of gorse or heather lie in wait to swallow up errant balls. Second, even if you're not playing well you'll still enjoy panoramic ocean views encompassing the coastal south, monumental Bass Rock, and The Kingdom of Fife to the north.

When not admiring the scenery, you'll find a collection of memorable golf holes—all consistently good, some outstanding. In the latter category, I would include all the one-shotters, particularly the signature #13, a 144-yarder where a blind shot leads to a green set in a hollow (with beach to the right) in a gully some one hundred feet below the level of the teeing ground. This is one of those unforgettable, quirky holes found only on the older courses of Scotland.

The mid-to-high-handicapper can play this course without feeling like a lightweight boxer thrown into the ring with a heavyweight.

Number fourteen, at 370 yards, requires a solid drive across the aforementioned gully to achieve position for a clear second shot to a small green. Back to the beginning (and the end), the par 4 #1 hole ("The Haugh") plays straight out about 220 yards, then up a steep hill to a blind green. Number eighteen ("Jacob's Ladder") traverses adjacent ground in the opposite direction, plunging from the hilltop to a broad fairway and a narrow, deep green at the home hole.

Upon completing the eighteenth, you'll return to one of the newest and most dramatically-situated clubhouses in Scotland. At their centenary in 2006, members at Glen Golf Club sprang for a beauty with wraparound glass on a second story looking out to the sea on one side and the golf course on the other. Here we have one of the great panoramic seaviews in Scotland—perhaps the envy of members at the prestigious West Links in their more confined and traditional clubhouse. Whatever that case may be, let it be known that North Berwick has *two* great courses to engage the visiting golfer.

For North Berwick lodging and nongolf notes, see North Berwick - West Links

The Courses at Gleneagles

19. King's Course 20. Queen's Course
21. PGA Centenary Course

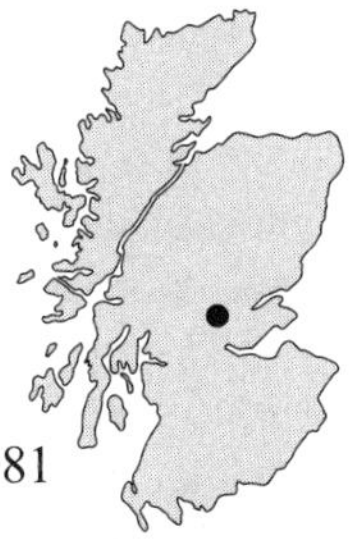

Region #: 7 **Category:** parkland
Architect(s): James Braid, C.K. Hutchinson (King's, Queen's); Jack Nicklaus (PGA Centenary)
Length: King's 6125-6790; Queen's 5660-5965; Centenary 5605-7081
SSS: King's 73; Queen's 70; Centenary 71-73
Par: King's 68-70; Queen's 68; Centenary 72

Address: Auchterarder PH3 1NF
Directions: well signposted 3 mi S of Auchterarder off A9

Reservations phone: 01764-694-469; UK freephone 0800-389-377; USA freephone1-866-881-9525 **Fax:** 01764-694-387
Email: resort.sales@gleneagles.com **Website:** gleneagles.com

Professional: Andrew Jowett **Pro shop:** 01764-694-362
Fee(s) (2012): Apr 1 - mid-May hotel res £80, non-res £115; mid-May thru mid-Oct hotel res £115, non-res £160; tour operators 15% on bookings
Deposit (2012): hotel residents - none; visitors 100% prepay
Visitor Policies: 14-day cancellation policy - full refund
Buggies: Centenary - plenty; med/phys on King's/Queen's with driver-caddie
Other: Scottish PGA early July, Johnnie Walker Championship last wk of August - both on PGA Centenary; host to Ryder Cup 2014

DRIVE TIME
St. Andrews: 1 hr, 15 min
Glasgow Airport: 1 hr, 30 min
Pitlochry: 50 min

PLAYING HOST TO THE RYDER CUP IN 2014, Gleneagles will be in the brightest spotlight since world leaders met here at the G8 in 2005. The place can be described in the plainest of words: This is an international resort with three superb golf courses. But to put it that way is a little like describing the Empire State Building as a large edifice.

So, let's start over. Gleneagles is *the* finest international resort hotel in Scotland and, very likely, among the half-dozen classiest golf hotels in the world. With its amenities and grounds on the breathtaking edge of the Scottish Highlands, Gleneagles puts Turnberry a bit in the shade.

As for the golf courses, it might suffice to say that the two courses by James Braid and C.K. Hutchinson (King's and Queen's) and the one course by Jack Nicklaus (PGA Centenary, formerly known as Monarch's) are at or near the top of the list of Scotland's best inland courses. But that would be putting it too plainly also—especially when golf writers have worn their thesauri thin from looking for words to describe these courses in this lovely land. In *Blasted Heaths and Blessed Greens,* Jim Finegan waxes positively rhapsodic in describing the Gleneagles courses as "no less than wonderful, a collection of arresting golf holes painted with bold brush strokes on a canvass of hills and valleys, of heather and bracken and gorse, of majestic hardwoods and equally majestic evergreens." I'll leave the Gleneagles poetry to those who have done it so well over the years. The visiting golfer will appreciate more pedestrian information from me: If you are looking for traditional Scottish course design, you'll want to choose the King's Course or the Queen's (vintage1919). These are hilly venues—be prepared to climb. The King's Course features half-a-dozen par 4s in the 400+ range and par ranging from 68 to 70 depending upon the tees used. Braid offers *no* par 5s on the 6115-yard track. At 5965 yards, the Queen's Course is the shorter of the two. But don't be fooled. The course has only one par 5.

The Nicklaus PGA Centenary course looks and feels like a modern American course, right down to the raft of buggies available for general hire. Distances between green and tee are considerable. Five par 5s make up for their absence on the King's and Queen's. Carved fairways, heavy bunkering, water, and undulating greens are all "Jack." This course is home to the annual Scottish PGA Championship in July and the Johnnie Walker Championship in late August.

No handicap or gender restrictions apply at Gleneagles. With five sets of tees on both the King's and Centenary courses, and with four on the Queen's, there's a track for golfers of every level. Though hotel guests have tee-time priority, it's normally easy to book a time at Gleneagles on *one* of the courses on short notice. You won't be disappointed in any of the choices.

My advice: The courses are most beautiful in the spring (April to mid-May), and in late October. That's also when bargains can be had at the courses and in the hotel.

22. Golf House Club at Elie (1875)

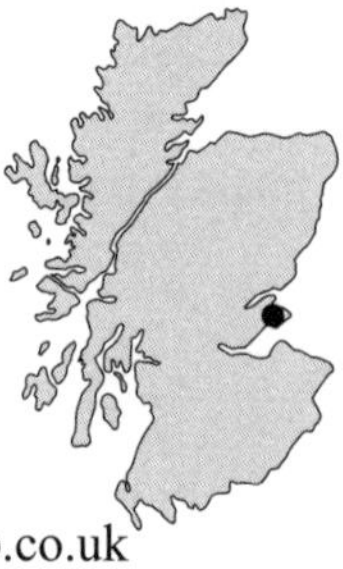

Region #: 1 **Category:** links-heathland hybrid
Architect(s): evolution w/ help from Tom Morris (4 holes - 1895-6)
Length: 6000-6273 **SSS:** 70 **Par:** 70

Address: Elie, Fife KY9 1A5S
Directions: signposted near town center off A917

Reservations phone: 01333-330-301 **Fax:** 01333-330-895
Email: secretary@golfhouseclub.co.uk **Website:** golfhouseclub.co.uk
Booking Contact(s): Moira Lawrie or secretary

Secretary: Graham Scott **Professional:** Ian Muir
Phone - Starter/Pro shop: 01333-330-955
Fee(s) (2012): wkdays £77, day tkt £97; wkend £88, day tkt £108
Deposit (2012): 50% **Buggies:** none
Visitor Policies: wkdays after 10 am; wkend - flexible; mid-July to mid-August only after 3 p.m.

WHEN I THINK OF ELIE, the phrase, "Sherman's March to the Sea," springs to mind. None of the typical links "out and back" along a coast line here. At Elie you start perhaps three-quarters of a mile from seaside at the clubhouse and then you *march*—albeit, to and fro—for six holes before approaching the water. Even then, it's back and forth until, finally, three exquisitely challenging holes present themselves for play along the rocky shore (#s 11, 12, and 13). And, yet, the sea is never out of sight. It's out there—tantalizing and omnipresent. You know you're at a seaside links, but it comes and goes like a lover pursued, then found, then lost. With the holes twisting and turning to all points of the compass, the rhythm of the course—from heathland to sea and back to heathland—is thrilling and fulfilling.

Elie's starter house and "Excalibur," the periscope for viewing the first fairway.

Now, if you've ever wondered where James Braid acquired his preference for the testing two-shotter, look no farther than Elie. This is where Braid was born and raised and, by no mere coincidence, the golf course here has *no* par 5s and only two par 3s! If it weren't for the imagination and variety applied to the par 4s, this could get plain boring. Elie provides the key to understanding Braid: length—incidental; tough but fair; above all, imaginative and fun.

Elie is loaded with memorable features. There's the opening blind drive up the #1 fairway ("Stacks") over a sharp rise—but even more memorable, a periscope mounted at the starter house to view play over the rise. You'll only tee off after getting the call, "Play away!" from the starter. This periscope, vintage 1938 and called "Excalibur," came to the club in 1966 and has become a beloved landmark in Scottish golf.

Next, you'll be struck by the proximity of town buildings along the fourth, fifth, and sixth fairways—among them, the Golf Tavern, once the meeting site of Elie's golf clubs. Farther along, memorable is the only way to describe Elie's three seaside holes that begin at the precipitously perched teeing grounds at #s 11 and 12 and follow the coast to "MacDuff's Cave"—a cliff rising above the 190-foot-wide green at the #13 "Croupie." In a flight of hyperbole, James Braid called this testing seaside two-shotter "the finest hole in all the country." And who are we to quarrel?

Starter Ken Murray surveys the first fairway before giving the call to "play away."

Not done yet, you'll remember the narrow neck of land, two fairways wide, joining the four holes near the clubhouse to the twelve holes nearer the sea. No surprise, this odd feature has its history too: this was a part of the linksland contested by a landowner on one side and the town golfers on the other. It became the subject of an important legal decision adjudicated in favor of the golfers in 1822 after many years of squabbling—important because it helped establish case law supporting public access to linkslands.

Finally, the clubhouse with its banks of plate glass windows looking out over the course will leave its impression too. In a word, memorable—an important word when it comes to judging golf courses. Incidentally, Elie is home club for a passel of luminaries in Scottish golf—folks like Sir Michael Bonallack, Peter Thomson, Peter Dawson, and Malcolm Campbell.

See also: Crail, Leven Links, Lundin Links

23. Golspie Golf Club (1889)

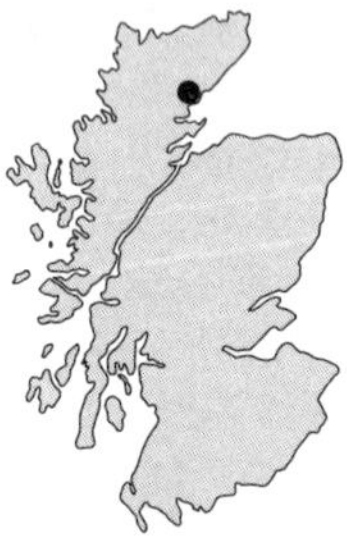

Region #: 4 **Category:** links-parkland-heathland hybrid
Architect(s): James Braid (1905); revisions made in 1967 & 2010
Length: 5816-6021 **SSS:** 70 **Par:** 70

Address: Ferry Rd, Golspie, Sutherland KW10 6ST
Directions: 10 mi N of Dornoch on the A9; S end of town, hard rt at playing fields

Reservations phone: 01408-633-266 **Fax**: 0148-633-393
Email: info@golspiegolf-club.co.uk
Website: golspie-golf.co.uk
Booking Contact(s): Jeanette Cumming

Fee(s) (2012): wkday £40, day tkt £50 **Deposit (2012):** £10
Visitor Policies: all wk **Buggies:** 2 - general hire

GOLSPIE LIES TEN MILES NORTH of Dornoch on the A9. Golf at Golspie and neighboring Brora is for travelers who have decided to spend a few days based in the Dornoch-Tain area while exploring the northern reaches of Scotland. Golspie may be the least among the four northern courses featured in this directory but, due to its pedigree (another James Braid design), its location, and its unique composition, Golspie deserves its place, for this is the only Scottish course that so clearly breaks into an even six holes each of links turf, heathland, and parkland pasture.

Alterations have been made to the course since 2009 to give it more teeth, yet, at 5816 yards from the visitor tees, the course is still among the shortest included here (ask to play from the white tees; it probably will be ok). After five opening holes along the shore, we turn inland with a magnificent par 3 at #6 and only re-emerge at the close of the round. If your trip has included Braid's creation at Boat of Garten, Golspie's #9 ("Paradise") will remind you of the testing doglegs there. Paradise is followed by a fine par 3, "Lochy," playing across a deep hollow to a two-tiered green. Still more enjoyable golf follows in the strong closing three: Braid gave Golspie two challenging par 3s followed by the "Drum Brae" par 4 at 445 yards—a typical Braid home hole that says to the golfer, "You think this course is so easy? Try making par here."

Nongolf notes: Another reason for making the trip to Golspie is to visit Dunrobin Castle ***(www.dunrobincastle.co.uk)***, home of the Dukes and Earls of Sutherland since at least the fourteenth century. One of Scotland's oldest, continuously-inhabited castles, Dunrobin's stately rooms, formal gardens, and falconry exhibitions make a great half-day diversion from golf.

See also: Brora, Royal Dornoch, Tain

24. Gullane Golf Club - Gullane # 1 (1882) +

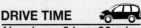

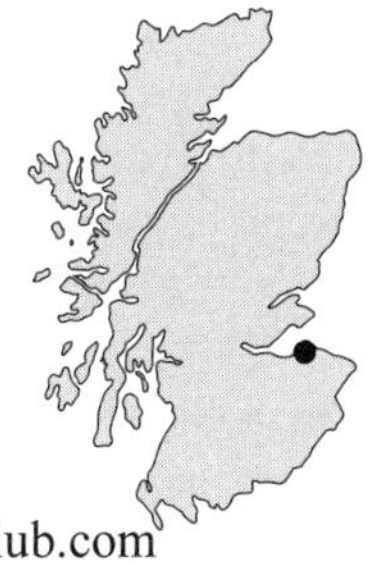

Region #: 3 **Category:** seaside links
Architect(s): various
Length: 6077-6466 **SSS:** 72 **Par:** 71

Address: East Lothian EH31 2BB
Directions: W side of village on A198; h'way bisects golf courses
Reservations phone: 01620-842-255 **Fax:** 01620-842-327
Email: bookings@gullanegolfclub.com **Website:** gullanegolfclub.com
Booking Contact(s): June Lawther, Angela Neisen

Secretary: Derek Thomson **Professional:** Alasdair Good
Phone - Starter/Pro shop: 01620-842-255
Fee(s) (2012): wkday £93, day tkt £128; wkend £108, no day tkt
Deposit (2012): £25 **Buggies:** 4 - general hire
Visitor Policies: wkday 10:30-noon and 2:30-4 pm; wkend tee times limited
Other: hdcp - men 24, women 30; combo tkts with Gullane #2 & #3

DRIVE TIME
Aberdeen: 3 hrs, 30 min
Carnoustie: 2 hrs
St. Andrews: 1 hr, 45 min
Troon: 2 hrs, 45 min

GULLANE GOLF CLUB IS AT THE EPICENTER of golf along the coastline and countryside east of Edinburgh. Arguably, this swath of land called "East Lothian" offers Scotland's densest concentration of golf courses—and that's saying quite a lot. Within ten miles of Gullane village lie some twenty golf courses of varying price and quality—all good, some great. Now, with the development of private clubs and courses on the Archerfield links between Muirfield and North Berwick, virtually all the accessible coastline between Musselburgh and North Berwick is utilized for golf.

A year in the life of this rich Lothian land, with golf and Gullane at its center, is described in an evocative book *Playing Through* by Canadian writer Curtis Gillespie. And now, with the help of Mr. Gillespie, we might get to the root of one of the most burning issues in Scottish golf—i.e., Is the name of this town properly pronounced GULL-an or GILL-an? Having previously reported the pronouncement of Mrs. Sheila Montgomery, former booking secretary at Gullane ("There are no gulls in Gullane"), I have since learned that Mrs. Montgomery perhaps did not tell the whole story. As Mr. Gillespie reports, it seems the gentry who live on the hill overlooking the sea pronounce it GILL-an, while the common folk down on the flats call it GULL-an. Villagers whose Gullane ancestors extend to centuries past, often call the village by its ancient name, "GOOL-in." Mr. Gillespie suggests that, in striking up a conversation about Gullane with a local, the true diplomat will wait to hear how the local pronounces Gullane and then follow suit!

Now that we have that settled, I'd like to be able to say I favor the championship course at Gullane as much as I like the town and its East Lothian surroundings—but I don't. There's no doubt that, at the seventh tee of Gullane #1, you can experience one of the most awesome panoramic views available on a Scottish golf course. To the north sits the Kingdom of Fife; off to the east lies Muirfield; and to the west, on a clear day, you can see all the way to the Forth Bridge on the west side of Edinburgh. There's also no doubt my somewhat negative view of Gullane #1 has been influenced by the ferocious gales blowing off the North Sea when I've been there. I know it can't be like that all the time or no one would live in Gullane. Nevertheless, to my mind, this is the most overrated of Scotland's marquee courses.

I have my logical reasons too: First, the setting of the courses at Gullane, for all its promise in a pretty village, just past Aberlady (another pretty village), is remarkably pedestrian for its plain openness without the bracing virtue of views to the open sea. The main impediment to a sea view is Gullane hill where championship golf is played. Second, you have to climb that hill. And, rather than provide a graceful "switchback" of the sort found at Pitlochry, for example, the golfer is given a straight-away chute up a wind tunnel at #2 ("Windygate"), then a ski-slope ride back down to sea level at #17 ("Hilltop"). In between are fourteen holes routed around and through the crevices and flats of Gullane hill. The great views come at the aforementioned #7 "Queen's Head"—a hole that shoots practically straight downward for 400 yards. With a tailwind, a strong driver can reach the green, but I'm not sure that qualifies as great design. On the other hand, this is a tough, highly-regarded qualifying course when the Open is held at Muirfield; golf has been played on these grounds for over three hundred years, so it can't be all bad. As I've said elsewhere, "I could be wrong. Go judge for yourself."

I'd like to be able to say I favor the championship course at Gullane #1 as much as I like the town and its East Lothian surroundings—but I don't.

For the 36-holers out there, Gullane #1 is complemented by the more benign Gullane #2, a 6200-yard track that flanks #1 on the slopes of Gullane Hill and sweeps down toward Aberlady Bay before turning back toward the clubhouse. The #3 course is on flatter ground and is highly regarded as an enjoyable short course to pair with one of the others on a combination ticket offered by management.

Despite my lack of appreciation for the championship course, everything about Gullane is nothing short of terrific. The clubhouse, opened in 1993, is comfortable, modern, and efficiently run. Just behind the clubhouse is a nine-hole layout for kids (adults are not allowed unless accompanied by a child). The presence of this little gem reminds us of how completely integral golf is to Scottish life. And near the children's nine sits the "Old Clubhouse," now a bar/restaurant not to be missed by any visitor to Gullane.

Gullane's pro shop and adjacent Heritage of Golf Museum run by Archie Baird

Speaking of golf, history, and culture, another not-to-miss attraction at Gullane is the Heritage of Golf Museum located next to the pro shop just off the first tee of the championship course. Here you can commune with Archie Baird, perhaps the most avid living collector and interpreter of Scottish golf history and memorabilia. Tours of his museum are by appointment only. Call the pro shop or phone him in advance at 01875-870-277. Make an appointment before or after your round and, if available, he'll meet you for a personalized tour. Nothing is behind glass. Archie will let you feel the weight and texture of old clubs, feathery balls, gutta percha balls, and Gene Sarazen's original sand wedge. He'll take you on a memorable tour through the history of golf.

Lodging and food in and around Gullane: The village and surrounding area are well stocked with quality lodging. Adjacent to Muirfield, the elegant *Greywalls Hotel* (01620-842-1444; ***www.greywalls.co.uk***) tops the charts in old-world ambience and price. A few fee times at Muirfield during high season are available for residents of the hotel on Mondays and Fridays. More reasonably priced is the ivy-clad *Golf Inn* on the main street (01620-843-259; ***www.golfinn.co.uk***). Four-star B & B lodging is available at *Faussetthill House* (01620-842-396; no website). Out in the countryside, nicely situated in Dirleton between Gullane and North Berwick, you'll find the popular *Open Arms Hotel* (01620-850-241; ***www.openarmshotel.com***) and the recently-refurbished *Castle Inn* (01620-850-221; ***www.castleinndirleton.com***), a 19th-century coaching inn with five rooms on the village green. And, in nearby Aberlady, Edinburgh restaurateur, Malcolm Duck, has reinvigorated the 17th-century vintage *Kilspindie House Hotel* (01875-870-682; ***www.kilspindie.co.uk***).

La Potiniere in Gullane captures the Scottish-French connection in fine dining.

Good food deserves special mention here, partly because it is unusual to have so much variety and quality in Scotland's village life. All the hotels mentioned above feature food and drink and each is excellent. Then, check out Gullane's *Old Clubhouse* (01620-842-008) for one of Scotland's most atmospheric pubs. Across the street from the Golf Inn, *La Potiniere* (01620-843-214) thrives on the Scottish/French connection in fine cookery. Add to these the ethnic and traditional restaurants in North Berwick's High Street and you have a cornucopia of quality to defy those who complain about food in Scotland.

See also: Craigielaw, Honourable Company of Edinburgh Golfers, Longniddry, Luffness New, Royal Musselburgh

25. Honourable Company of Edinburgh Golfers (1744) - at Muirfield, Gullane *

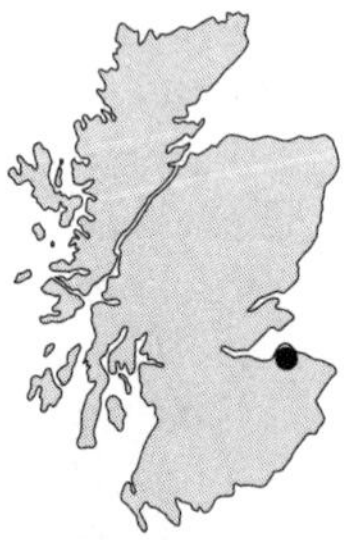

Region #: 3 **Category:** seaside links
Architect(s): Tom Morris (1891), Tom Simpson, Henry Colt
Length: 5980-6728 **SSS:** 73 **Par:** 70-71

Address: Muirfield, Duncur Rd, Gullane, E Lothian EH31 2EG
Directions: through Gullane, left on Duncur Rd at S edge of town

Reservations phone: 01620-842-123 **Fax:** 01620-842-977
Email: hceg@muirfield.org.uk **Website:** muirfield.org.uk
Booking Contact(s): Anne McCarthy

Secretary: Alastair Brown
Fee(s) (2012): £195, day tkt £250
Deposit (2012): 100% prepayment **Buggies:** no
Visitor Policies: Tues & Thurs, 8:30-9:50 am; foursomes ("alternate shot") in pm; maximum of 12 in visiting groups; Mon & Fri - some times for residents of Greywalls Hotel, April - September
Other: hdcps - men 18, women 24; no cell phones on course or in clubhouse; jackets/ties in dining room; women may not lunch in clubhouse and must be accompanied by a man on the course

DRIVE TIME
Aberdeen: 3 hrs, 30 min
Carnoustie: 2 hrs
St. Andrews: 1 hr, 45 min
Troon: 2 hrs, 45 min

A TEE TIME AT MUIRFIELD, the oldest golf club in the world, is easily secured if a golfer can plan well ahead. Once run like a nineteenth-century counting house, Muirfield took a giant leap into the modern age in 2004 with the addition of credit-card processing and an excellent website where visitors can make bookings online *up to fifteen months* prior to date of play (e.g., March 2012 for dates through June 2013, April 2013 for July 2014, etc.).

To the private club's credit (and bank account), visitors are allowed to play at this historic course on Tuesdays and Thursdays. A comparison of this policy to the members-only approach at private clubs in the United States makes Scotland's most exclusive clubs look warmly welcoming.

Muirfield took a giant leap into the modern age in 2004 with the addition of credit-card processing and an excellent website where visitor bookings can be made online up to fifteen months prior to date of play.

Here's how Muirfield works: In the morning, nine tee times are allotted for stroke play off the first and tenth tees. That's eighteen tee times. In the afternoon, after lunch in the clubhouse, all play is "foursomes" (alternate shot). You can buy either one round in the morning or a day ticket to include the afternoon foursomes. In either case, lunch is optional (and expensive).

With a tee time at Muirfield securely in hand, you will encounter a course quite unlike any other in Scottish golf. Though the turf is links turf and the sea is in sight, the course sits away from the sea in a vast field of billowing rough and gently rolling terrain. No strip of linksland here. Old Tom Morris had a lot of ground to work with at Muirfield. Applying his talent and imagination to that ground in 1891, Morris developed a uniquely creative layout in which the first nine, moving clockwise, encircles the second nine holes that run counter-clockwise. The result: constant shifts of direction and—unusual in links golf—a pattern that placed the #1 and #10 teeing grounds near the clubhouse. Given the relatively flat ground at Muirfield, all targets are in view—no blind shots. Challenge is provided by length; large, undulating greens; narrow fairways and unforgiving rough; and over 160 bunkers—most of them severely penal, with sides so steep the only play is up and out but not far forward. Most holes present at least eight bunkers for the golfer to avoid. This is among the most heavily-bunkered courses in Scottish golf.

Anne McCarthy, the friendly "voice of Muirfield"—the farthest thing from stuffy.

Golfers great and not-so-great have applauded this design for over one hundred years. James Braid was so taken by the course that he gave the name Muirfield to one of his sons. This was Harry Colt's favorite course and, in the mid-1920s, he re-worked the Morris original to achieve the course we have today. More recently, Jack Nicklaus named his most famous early project Muirfield Village. Tom Watson, winner of the British Senior Open at Muirfield in 2007, is another devotee of the course. Among the rest of us mere mortals, when readers of the UK's *Golf World* were polled a few years back, they named Muirfield the best course in Scotland and third most difficult. One measure of the greatness of Muirfield is simply to note the winners of the British Open tournaments held here since 1959. They are: Gary Player, Jack Nicklaus, Lee Trevino, Tom Watson, Nick Faldo, and Ernie Els. Stay tuned: Another luminary will join the list when the Open is played here again in 2013. Muirfield invariably provides a level of drama seen only on the truly great courses—and, among those, this one must be counted at the top rung with St. Andrews, Carnoustie, and Turnberry.

TRAVEL TIP

For the surest shot at playing Muirfield, visit in March or October. Example: at this writing, ten of eighteen visitor times were available on March 29, 2012, and fourteen of eighteen times were available on October 2, 2012.

Lodging and nongolf notes: see Gullane and North Berwick - West Links

26. Inverness Golf Club (1883)

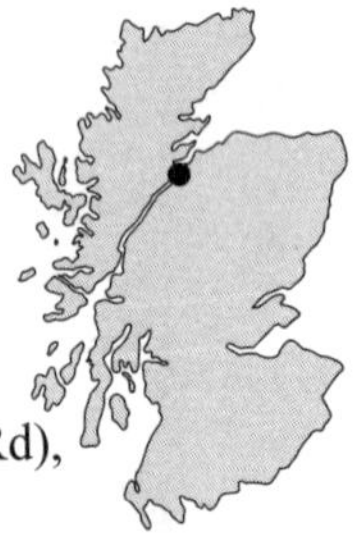

Region #: 4 **Category:** parkland
Architect(s): members; bunkering by James Braid (1937)
Length: 5686-6087 **SSS:** 67-69 **Par:** 67-69

Address: The Clubhouse, Culcabock Rd, Inverness IV2 3XQ
Directions: From town center, follow B853 (Old Edinburgh Rd) to Culcabock Rd; E to clubhouse. From A9, exit B9006 (Old Perth Rd), 1.5 mi to clubhouse

Reservations phone: 01463-239-882 **Fax:** 01463-240-616
Email: manager@invernessgolfclub.co.uk **Website:** invernessgolfclub.co.uk
Booking Contact(s): managing secretary

Secretary: Ewan Forbes **Professional:** Alistair P Thomson
Phone - Starter/Pro shop: 01463-231-989
Fee(s) (2012): £42 all wk; day tkt £55
Deposit (2012): none **Buggies:** no
Visitor Policies: 10-12 and 2-4 wkdays; call W & Sat; after 10:30 Sun

DRIVE TIME
Glasgow Airport: 4 hrs
Aberdeen: 3+ hrs
Dornoch: 1 hr
St. Andrews: 3 hrs, 30 min

INVERNESS GOLF CLUB IS A PARKLAND course bisected by a busy thoroughfare and surrounded by residential Inverness. This is *not* the club profile most golf tourists are seeking when they go to Scotland. However, several years after having played at Inverness Golf Club, I can honestly say that at least a half dozen holes here have left an impression on my mind equal to that of any other half dozen holes in all of Scottish golf. That amounts to the strongest possible recommendation I can make for a golf course. My advice is to take a day's break from seaside golf and play this course. I guarantee you won't forget it.

As at Downfield in Dundee, Inverness Golf Club is tougher from the second (yellow) tees than from the back (white) tees. Two long par 4s from the yellows (#s 3 and 5) play at par 5 from the whites; yet the whites measure only thirty yards longer. This makes no sense.

That's about the only thing that makes no sense about Inverness—well, not quite. Five of the holes at Inverness are on hilly land on the east side of Culcabock Road (pronounced Cul-KAY-bock). This is a busy urban thoroughfare with no walk light for the golfers! Trolley in hand, one must hope for a break in the traffic before making a dash for the safety of the other side. This makes no sense either. A pedestrian-controlled walk light at that crossing would not bring the apocalypse to Inverness.

Enough with the complaining. After a placid start on Inverness's first two holes, the visitor encounters three attention-getting par 4s at 444+ yards over rather flat ground. Now the fun begins. From #6 straight through #15 we are given ten of the most consistently arresting holes in Scottish golf. Number six ("Wyvis"), at 291 yards, asks for a blind mid-iron layup before a second shot to a small, elevated green protected by a burn no more than five yards off the front of the green. Number seven ("Spion Kop") measures 169 yards to a green perched atop a steep, grassy embankment perhaps sixty feet above the level of the teeing ground. Number eight ("Meadows") is one of those short but perfect, doglegged par 4s that cannot be overwhelmed by a big hitter; instead, it requires a precise shot to the corner enabling a mid-iron second shot to a well-bunkered green. After a temporary finish on the west side of Culcabock Road at #9 and #10, we dash over to the east side for #s 11-15—five excellent holes, including two of the most difficult holes (#s 14 and 15) I have encountered anywhere in the wide world of golf.

These latter two holes deserve special attention. Number Fourteen ("Midmills"), the club's signature hole, is a diabolical par 4 dogleg right set at 435 yards from the yellow tees and 475 yards from the white tees. A huge poplar guards the right corner. A bunker guards the left corner at 220 yards. If this wicket is negotiated, the golfer faces a 200+-yard second shot to a long, narrow green through a funneling shoot bounded by OB on the right and a steep, grassy hill on the left. Making this shot with a golf club is akin to threading a needle with gloves on. A golf-ball-shooting rifle would be the better instrument. A professional golfer might make this shot, but the wise amateur will probably lay up. In this respect, Midmills has a lot in common with St. Andrews' Road Hole. It's just as tough.

A half dozen holes here have left an impression on my mind equal to that of any other half dozen holes in all of Scottish golf.

Following Midmills, we come to "Curling Pond" or, to put a more American twist on the name, one might call it, "Bowling Alley." It's a 150-yard par 3 with a margin for error of perhaps fifty feet before one's ball is kicked off an embankment to OB on the right or swallowed up by bunkers and tall grass on the left side of a long, narrow green. Whew!—you should be sweating by now.

Now it's back to the west side of Culcabock Road for the closing holes featuring a 446-yard par 4 home hole sporting no less than nine bunkers! This is one that brings to mind that old saw, "It takes three good shots to get there in two." 'Nuff said; it's one of the toughest closers in Scottish golf.

Two other points of aesthetic interest that make Inverness such a memorable golf course: First, all but a few of the greens are thoughtfully framed by stands of pine, poplar, or tall flowering shrubs. This design element not only lends visual appeal to the course but also aids the golfer at approach. Second, if there were a beauty contest for bunkers, the large, graceful bunkers filled with light brown sand at Inverness would surely win the contest.

Lodging and nongolf notes: Inverness is the acknowledged capital of the Highlands—a fast-growing small city in a lovely setting. All major northern highways and rail lines converge at Inverness and it's loaded with accommodations in every price category. At last count, Inverness had some two hundred B & Bs and guest houses and at least fifty more hotels. A good inventory is at ***www.scotland-info.co.uk.*** Tourism drives the local economy and, accordingly, lodging values can be had in an atmosphere of fierce competition.

Since this is not a general travel book, I am hesitant to open the subject of nongolf activities in this part of Scotland. Suffice to say Inverness is a logical jumping off point for compelling and uniquely Scottish tourist experiences—the beauty and mystery of Loch Ness, the Speyside whisky trail, the northern coastal fishing villages, Ullapool

TRAVEL TIP
For a scenic day trip, take the round trip train ride from Inverness to Kyle of Lochalsh on the west coast. It's two and one-half hours each way with a two-hour break in Lochalsh for lunch or sightseeing on the Isle of Skye.

and the amazing sub-tropical gardens of the west coast, the Isle of Skye, the barren reaches of the far north and the wild and lonely island chains of the Outer Hebrides and the Orkneys. Closer to home base, most tourists visit historic Culloden Battlefield where Bonnie Prince Charlie and Scotland's Jacobite supporters were defeated in 1746 in the last battle fought on British soil. Not far from Culloden, Cawdor Castle draws thousands of tourists annually to walk the beautiful grounds and re-visit the history and legend of Macbeth. In town, Inverness offers the best shopping and range of services to be found in the Highlands. The attractive High Street is restricted to foot traffic. There's a castle to tour on a high bluff overlooking the downtown, and the placid Ness River flows through the heart of the city on its way to the Moray Firth and the open sea. In short, Inverness is one of Scotland's enchanted places and you'll soon realize why so many people come up here to start their vacations in the country's northern Highlands—also why this is the UK's fastest-growing city, filled with escapees from the pricey, overcrowded south.

For more notes on lodging: see Brora, Nairn, Royal Dornoch

27. Irvine Golf Club (1887) - "Bogside" +

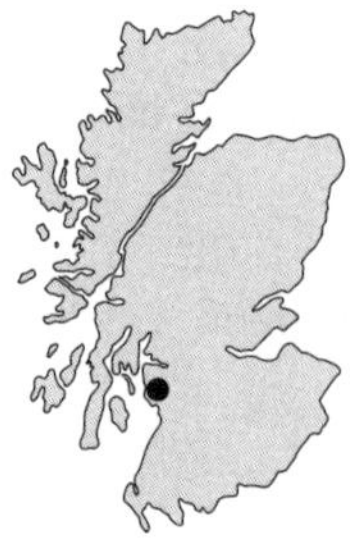

Region #: 2 **Category:** links - no view
Architect(s): James Braid
Length: 6423 **SSS:** 72 **Par:** 71

Address: Bogside, Irvine KA12 8SN
Directions: N of Irvine town center (A737), poorly marked road nr Ravenspark Academy

Reservations phone: 01294-275-979 **Fax:** 1294-278-209
Email: secretary@theirvinegolfclub.co.uk **Website:** theirvinegolfclub.co.uk
Booking Contact(s): secretary (a.m. only)

Secretary: WJ McMahon **Professional:** James McKinnon
Phone - Starter/Pro shop: 01294-275-626
Fee(s) (2012): wkday £50, day tkt £60; wkend £60, no day tkt
Deposit (2012): £5 **Buggies:** no
Visitor Policies: M-F anytime; wkend after 3 pm

ONE MIGHT BEST THINK of Irvine's Bogside in league with the nearby courses at West Kilbride, Gailes, and Barassie. These courses offer alternatives to the more famous Ayrshire courses at Troon, Prestwick, and Turnberry. Understandably, most first-time visitors to the Ayrshire coast want to play the area's fabled trio. The returning veteran may well be looking for the next tier of courses and, in that tier, Bogside should be on everyone's must-play list.

At Bogside we experience another James Braid classic. Here, Mr. Braid—Scotland's caped crusader for the unforgiving two-shotter—showed his ultimate disdain for the stroke-saving par 5 and the pushover par 3. Bogside sports only two par 3s and one par 5. The remaining fifteen holes are two-shotters! Thus, what at first glance seems a course of average length, in typical Braidian style, turns out to be a bearcat where most golfers will not play to their handicap.

Visitors to Bogside applaud the remarkable variety of holes that Braid created on this expanse of links turf. Another striking feature: the silky-smooth, well-tended greens. This is a characteristic not only of Bogside but of all the courses along the Ayrshire coast. I think it's fair to say these are the best greens in all of Scotland, from West Kilbride and Irvine right on down to Turnberry.

These are the best greens in all of Scotland, from West Kilbride and Irvine right on down to Turnberry.

Nongolf notes: Only twenty-six miles from Glasgow, near the mouth of the Firth of Clyde, Irvine reminds us that Scotland is a land of seafaring folk. We get that reminder at the Scottish Maritime Museum in Irvine's Harbourside area, an urban renewal project lending a modern interpretation to Scotland's coastal past. This is Burns country, so Irvine boasts a Robert Burns Museum. A few miles south of town, between Troon and Irvine, you'll find the ruins of Dundonald Castle, first home of Scotland's Stewart kings and Scotland's third most important castle site after the better-known (and better-preserved) structures at Edinburgh and Stirling.

See also: Dundonald, Glasgow Gailes, Kilmarnock, West Kilbride, Western Gailes

28. Kilmarnock Golf Club (1887) - Barassie +

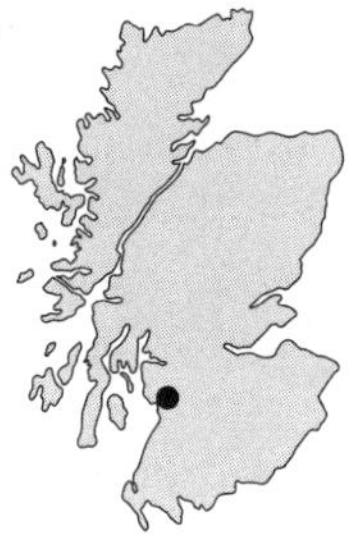

Region #: 2 **Category:** seaside-heathland hybrid
Architect(s): various
Length: 6484-6852 **SS:** 73 **Par:** 72

Address: 29 Hillhouse Rd, Barassie, Troon KA10 6SY
Directions: follow signs at corner near oceanside where B746 (Kilmarnock Rd) turns into/out of Troon

Reservations phone: 01292-313-920 **Fax:** 01292-318-300
Email: golf@kbgc.co.uk **Website:** kbgc.co.uk
Booking Contact(s): Margaret Boyd

Secretary: Donald Wilson **Professional:** Gregor Howie
Phone - Starter/Pro shop: 01292-311-322
Fee(s) (2012): wkday £57, day tkt £82; wkend £67, no day tkt
Deposit (2012): £25 **Buggies:** 4 - general hire
Visitor Policies: M, T, Th, Fri ; limited times on Wed & Sat; Sun after 2 pm
Other: participant in Ayrshire Golf Pass; 9-hole Hillhouse Course (2756 yds)

IF YOU WANT TO PLAY "KILMARNOCK," don't look for it in the town of Kilmarnock. You need to go to Barassie, adjacent to Troon, about ten miles westward. That's because this is a coastal course built in the late 1880s by inland Kilmarnock merchants for their sporting pleasure. That was the time of the first big "boom" in golf—a time when outstanding golf courses were built along the railway running out of Glasgow down the Ayrshire coast. These courses at Irvine, Gailes, Barassie, Troon, Prestwick, Ayr, and Turnberry have stood the test of time. They're just as good today as they were then (or better).

"Barassie" will appeal primarily to the seasoned traveler who, having played the "rota" courses, is looking for golf on new ground. It's interesting how reputations within this second tier of courses seep through the international golf community. In this case, even though Barassie abuts Western Gailes, it is Western that has captured the attention of visitors. No denying the greatness of Western Gailes, but neither are the classics at Barassie, Glasgow Gailes, Irvine, and West Kilbride far behind.

At Barassie you'll find most of the course compactly wedged on rather flat ground between two converging rail lines. Barassie has everything you're looking for in a links layout—heather-lined fairways, pot bunkers, gorse, and those wonderful Ayrshire greens. All this, including the rail lines, might make you think you're playing Prestwick for half the price. Three par 5s, three par 3s, and twelve par 4s typify the Scottish approach to a "traditional" round with par at 72. In other words, this is tougher than your average par-72 track and, with a head wind off the water, the course can be severely challenging. With medal tees stretching to 6852 yards, it's easy to understand why Barassie is used as a qualifying course when the Open is held at Royal Troon. Most golfers will be quite adequately challenged from the yellow tees set at 6484 yards.

"Forget some of the 'name' courses and try this one." That advice could apply to about fifty of the seventy-four courses in this directory.

In sum, I would relay the comment of a visitor who sent his observations on Barassie to an internet chat room: "Forget some of the 'name' courses and try this one." That advice could apply to about fifty of the seventy-four courses in this directory. And I'll say it again: to the extent a golf visitor to Scotland can disengage from the grip of the "name" courses, that visitor will have a less expensive, more interesting trip.

See also: Belleisle, Dundonald, Glasgow Gailes, Irvine (Bogside), Royal Troon, West Kilbride, Western Gailes

Telephone/Fax Calling Procedures

From the United States:

Dial 011 (international long distance), then 44 (country code), then the number in Scotland without the leading "0" (i.e., 011-44-1334-466-666).

29. Kingsbarns Golf Links (2000)

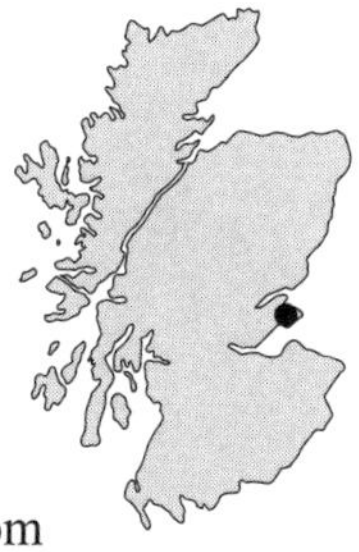

Region #: 1 **Category:** seaside links
Architect(s): Kyle Phillips, Mark Parsinen
Length: 6174-7126 **SSS:** 73 **Par:** 72

Address: Kingsbarns, nr St. Andrews, Fife K16 8QD
Directions: 8 mi SE of St. Andrews (A917) past Kingsbarns village

Reservations phone: 01334-460-861 **Fax:** 01334-460-877
Email: info@kingsbarns.com **Website:** kingsbarns.com
Booking Contact(s): Teresa Stewart, Maureen Macdonald, Julie Gerrard

General Manager: Stuart McEwan
Phone - Starter/Pro shop: reservations **Professional:** Alan Purdie
Fee(s) (2012): April £175 all wk; May onward £195 all wk; 2nd round played within 7 days, April £87.50, May onward £97.50; tour operator incentive scheme
Deposit (2012): 50%; balance 1st day of month preceding month of play
Visitor Policies: all wk **Buggies:** no
Other: closed Dec - March; Dunhill Cup late Sept/early Oct

I'VE BEEN WATCHING and occasionally playing Kingsbarns since its opening in 2000 and my feelings about the course remain the same: decidedly mixed. The operation's American ownership is felt in businesslike attention to every detail. From its entrance, straight through to the nineteenth hole, everything about Kingsbarns is first-class. Better yet, it is "down home" in the most important, human way. There's no phony fawning. The excellent staff—from the booking secretaries to the caddies—are efficient, personable, and sincerely interested in providing a golf experience without the snobbery often attached to high-end courses, private or public. Even the clubhouse and food menu are straightforward Americana—no blue blazers, club ties, and stuffed shirts here. In many respects, Kingsbarns has succeeded in combining the best of Scotland with the best of America.

On the other hand, Kingsbarns raises all kinds of questions in my mind—like, Is this really why we go to Scotland? Is this the future of Scottish golf for visitors? Is any golf course worth £195? Why does this golf course cost £45 more than either St. Andrews' Old Course or Carnoustie? Or, for that matter, why does it cost £100 more than its equally new neighbors at the Fairmont Hotel and at Dundonald Links, another course by Kyle Phillips? Is this course really as good as its reviews? A little background is in order: Kingsbarns and golf course architect Kyle Phillips fairly exploded onto the international golf scene in 2000—so completely that, within two seasons, the course had gathered up virtually every "Best New . . ." award around and had leaped into the upper tier of *Golf Magazine's* rankings of "World's Best Courses." In 2001 Kingsbarns was invited to join Carnoustie and St. Andrews' Old Course in hosting the annual Dunhill Cup, now played as a pro-am event—all pretty heady stuff for the new kid on the block.

Was all this hoopla and hype justified? In a few words: well, yes, probably. Kingsbarns is, indeed, a world-class course and, given four sets of tees, players of all levels can enjoy the challenge. The terrain at Kingsbarns has a wonderful rolling

The first tee and handsome stone clubhouse at Kingsbarns

quality about it and sea views abound from every corner of the course. Six holes skirt the rocky shore, offering a scene reminiscent of Pebble Beach, particularly at the 566-yard, doglegged par 5 #12 hole that sweeps the shoreline à la Pebble, as well as the "signature" par 3 #15 hole playing from elevated tee to elevated green across a roiling inlet from the sea. Modern routing returns the golfer to the clubhouse between nines.

In retrospect, we see that Kingsbarns came upon Scotland's golf stage at precisely the right moment—when the golf travel industry and Scots were starved for something new and bold and different, yet at the same time traditional. Scotland really had not turned out a new world-class venue since Mackenzie Ross re-worked the Ailsa at Turnberry. Oh, there was the stray and underappreciated course like Craighead down the road at Crail. But Kingsbarns was something special and the world responded. This, we were told, might be the last and greatest seaside course ever built in Scotland. Praises and hosannas were fulsome and continuous.

A few years later, in St. Andrews alone, we have three new courses practically next door to Kingsbarns—the Torrance and Kittocks at the Fairmont Hotel, plus the new Castle course by David McLay Kidd adjacent to those. Add to these Castle Stuart in the north and Machrihanish Dunes in the west and, in this context, Kingsbarns is not so novel today as it was in 2000. I guess if Alan Greenspan were a golfer (and he may be, for all I know), he might suggest that the golf world reacted to Kingsbarns' arrival with a mild case of "irrational exuberance."

If I can play three historic courses in Fife for the price of one Kingsbarns, you know what I'm going to do—and I think I'm pretty representative of a whole lot of golfers.

As for cost, there's no doubt a new course has startup expenses that older clubs have put behind them—land costs, course construction, a clubhouse, etc.—and these costs justify above-average green fees. But Kingsbarns has raised the high-season visitor fee from £85 in 2000 to £195 in 2012—a stunning 130 percent in thirteen years. Don't you wish you could do that with your paycheck!

To my mind, prices like this have a deadening effect in several ways on all of Scottish golf: By economic definition, it discourages untold numbers of golfers from playing a great course because it's just too darned expensive; it propels price increases at neighboring courses; and it ensures that few visitors will ever play the course more than once. It seems to me that's just the opposite of what Scottish golf should be doing.

After thirteen years, my judgment: A wonderful golf experience—no doubt. But, value for money?—no way. For me, the solution is simple: If I can play three historic courses in Fife for the price of one Kingsbarns, you know what I'm going to do—and I think I'm pretty representative of a whole lot of golfers.

30. Kingussie Golf Club (1890)

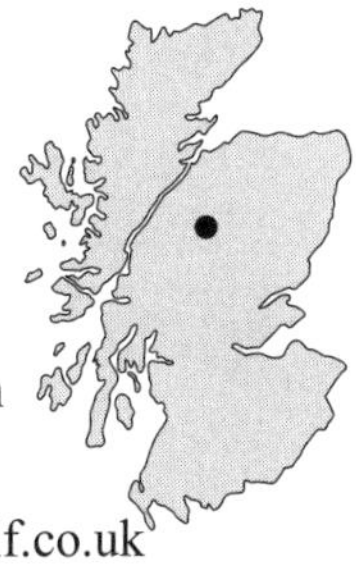

Region #: 5 **Category:** parkland
Architect(s): Harry Vardon extended existing nine (1908)
Length: 5411-5615 **SSS:** 68 **Par:** 67

Address: Gynack Rd, Kingussie, Inverness-shire PH21 1LR
Directions: 1/2 mi N of town center off A78, turn at Duke of Garten

Reservations phone: 01540-661-600 **Fax:** 01540-662-066
Email: sec@kingussie-golf.co.uk **Website:** kingussie-golf.co.uk
Booking Contact(s): secretary

Secretary: Ian Chadburn **Professional:** no
Phone - Starter/Pro shop: 01540-661-374
Fee(s) (2012): wkday £30, day tkt £38; wkend £34, day tkt £40
Deposit (2012): no
Visitor Policies: all wk **Buggies:** 3 - general hire

THE COURSE AT KINGUSSIE (pronounced king-YEWsie) is included in this guide for two reasons: First, it was designed largely by the great Harry Vardon and that, alone, is cause for inclusion. Second, it is representative of the many "wee" courses found in the resort towns strung out in "Strathspey" south of Inverness. In addition to the excellent course at Boat of Garten, you'll find eighteen-hole delights at Newtonmore (Kingussie's twin town just a few miles away on the A86) and Grantown-on-Spey, and little Carrbridge has a nine-hole charmer. The common denominator here is not championship golf, but "holiday golf" in the Highlands—relaxed, scenic, invigorating, and plenty challenging to most golfers.

TRAVEL TIP
Look out for the lefties! This is "shinty" country, where kids learn to strike a ball from both the right and left sides. The upshot: Kingussie and Newtonmore share the prize for most left-handed golfers.

Like Boat of Garten, Kingussie is more than a pleasant walk in pretty surroundings. Though quite short, there are no par 5s here. Thus, five of the twelve two-shotters extend well over 400 yards. Hilly terrain adds to the challenge. The Vardon emphasis is on shotmaking rather than length—and one could say, the "Scots emphasis" just as well, for this is a characteristic of most Scottish courses. Nevertheless, it's the scenery you'll remember as much as the golf. From high points on the course, the Monadhliath Mountains are visible to the west and the Cairngorms to the east. In between you'll marvel at the melange of soft colors and the crisp Highland air.

Nongolf notes: The nongolf reasons for lingering in this lovely part of Scotland are just as compelling as the golf. Kingussie itself is widely known as the location of one of Scotland's most interesting "living museums"; that's the Highland Folk Museum located on Duke St. near town center. Here is assembled a collection of relics and reconstructed buildings, including a thatch-roofed "Black House" modeled after those common on the Isle of Lewis ("black" because it was a smoky, windowless home to both animals and people). In the summer you'll find "citizens" of the village out tending the gardens and working at spinning wheels, all quite happy to welcome you into their homes and talk about their way of life. A companion folk museum is at nearby Newtonmore.

Before arriving at Kingussie, many people stop at the Dalwhinnie Distillery just a mile along where the A889 meets the A9. After Kingussie, one can spend hours or days exploring the forests and moors around Aviemore and Garten. Here, on the Rothiemurchas Estate and in the Glenmore and Abernethy forests you can walk quite literally for hundreds of miles on groomed trails. Rothiemurchas has Scotland's largest stand of ancient, native Caledonian or Scots Pine. A particularly fine display of this remarkable tree can be seen on the easy hike around Loch an Eileen. The visitor center for Rothiemurchas is on Ski Road, one mile from Aviemore. Railroad buffs will delight in the steam train that runs from Aviemore through Boat of Garten to Broomhill (see ***www.strathspeyrailway.co.uk***). In short, lots to see and do in this territory twenty to forty miles south of Inverness.

The Black House at Kingussie's Highland Folk Museum

See also: Boat of Garten

31. Ladybank Golf Club (1879) +

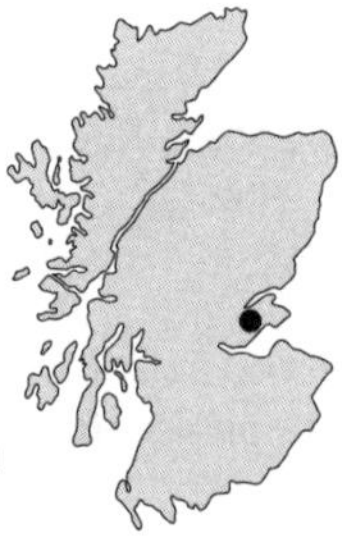

Region #: 1 **Category:** heathland
Architect(s): Tom Morris and others; extended to 18 holes in 1962
Length: 6300-6580 **SSS:** 72 **Par:** 71

Address: Annsmuir, Ladybank, Fife KY15 7RA
Directions: From St. Andrews, 1/2 mi from Melville Lodges roundabout off A92; toward St. Andrews, 1/2 mi on rt past town sign

Reservations phone: 01337-830-814 **Fax:** 01337-831-505
Email: info@ladybank.co.uk **Website:** ladybankgolf.co.uk
Key Contact(s): Lynne Melville

Mging Secretary: Fraser McCluskey **Professional:** Sandy Smith
Phone - Starter/Pro shop: 01337-830-725
Fee(s) (2012): wkday £53, day tkt £79; wkend £63, no day tkt; reduced Apr & Sept
Deposit (2012): £20 **Buggies:** 6 - general hire
Visitor policies: wkdays 9:30-noon, 1:15-4 pm; phone wkends

LADYBANK IS A BEAUTIFUL PLACE in the heart of Fife. This flat, tranquil heathland course offers respite from the rigors of Fife's seaside links, yet presents its own challenge. Ladybank is a thinking golfer's course, requiring accuracy off the tee to stay clear of thick growths of heather, broom, and pine and birch forest. But beyond accuracy, it requires every shot in the bag.

Ladybank is all positive and popular with Fife residents. The course and clubhouse are well managed and manicured. There's a good practice area. Staff are helpful and friendly. It's an historic Open Qualifying Course and, though many changes have been made since its conception in 1879, Ladybank traces its roots to six original holes laid out by Tom Morris.

So, given its popularity and polish, why, on the gut level, does Ladybank disappoint ever so slightly? I can only think it's because this course is so much like dozens of superb American courses in forest settings. No single hole is truly memorable, yet none is entirely pedestrian either. The best measure I can suggest is against other great Scottish inland courses and, when I contemplate a comparison between Ladybank and Blairgowrie, Belleisle, Boat of Garten, or the courses at Gleneagles, Ladybank finishes second every time. In short, though it certainly is *Fife's* finest inland course, I don't think it is *Scotland's* finest inland course. As I've said elsewhere, "I could be wrong." Go experience Ladybank for yourself. You won't be sorry.

32. Leven Links Golf Course (1820) +

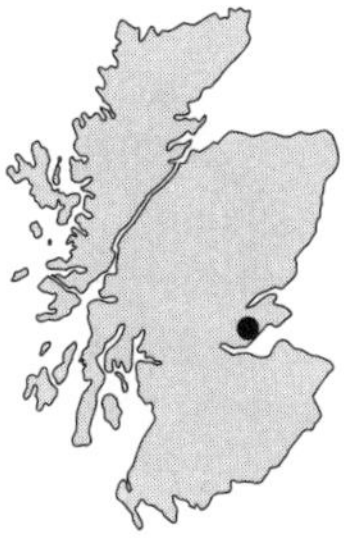

Region #: 1 **Category:** seaside links
Architect(s): Tom Morris, others
Length: 6250-6506 yds **SSS:** 71-72 **Par:** 69-71

Address: The Promenade, Leven, Fife KY8 4HS
Directions: off A915 from Leven town center; left on Church Rd, rt on Links Rd

Reservations phone: 01333-428-859 **Fax:** 01333-424-229
Email: secretary@leven-links.com **Website:** leven-links.com
Booking Contact(s): secretary

Secretary: Jen Low **Professional:** no
Phone - Starter/Pro shop: 01333-421-390
Fee(s) (2012): wkday £55, day tkt £70; wkend £60, day tkt £75
Deposit (2012): £10 **Buggies:** no
Visitor Policies: all wk after 9:30, sunday after 10:30; sat - 6 days in advance

LITERALLY CHEEK BY JOWL with Lundin Links Golf Club, Leven Links occupies the ground to the west of a stone fence ("Mile Dyke") separating the two courses. In many respects these courses are something like Siamese twins and, if you're playing one, it's easy enough to play the other.

Not surprisingly, the two clubs are joined (and were separated) by history. Leven is the older of the two. In the early 1800s golfers played eastward from Leven on nine holes. Then in 1868 Tom Morris laid out a new nine on the Lundin side of Mile Dyke. Until 1909, golfers played eighteen holes starting from opposite ends of the two nine-hole layouts! This amounted to the ingenious, but, as golf became more popular, it was neither practical nor safe. Ultimately, the nines were split at the Mile Dyke and each club went its own way.

In terms of course design, what follows is the most interesting part of the history. When the nines were split to achieve eighteen holes, there was nowhere to go but inland to the north side of the railway. Eventually the railroad went out of business leaving the rail embankment as an out-of-bounds waste area running the length of both courses. Lundin has left its rail embankment largely intact, while Leven has rather leveled its embankment. This is the sort of history that makes golf in Scotland—and these courses in particular—unique and fun.

Frankly, they don't do a very good job of promoting themselves at Leven. The course does not get the visitor play it deserves. But, keep in mind, for decades Leven has been used as a tough qualifying course (USGA slope 135) for the Open and, truth be told, this is among the purest of links courses in Scotland. Why? Because every hole is on a sand base; because it fronts the sea; because it is not over-watered and, thus, it browns out in dry weather; because natural dunes isolate many of the fairways; because at #18 "Scoonie," Leven gives us one of the great closing holes in golf. Get thee to Leven—it's the real deal.

See also: Lundin Links

33. Longniddry Golf Club, Ltd. (1921)

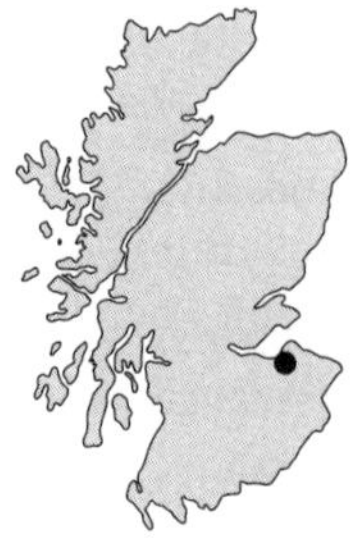

Region #: 3 **Category:** links-parkland hybrid
Architect(s): Harry Colt (1922), James Braid (1936), Phillip Mackenzie Ross (1945), Donald Steel (1998)
Length: 5969-6230 **SSS:** 71 **Par:** 68

Address: Links Rd, Longniddry EH32 0NL
Directions: from A1, exit B6363; off A198 (Main St), W of town

Reservations phone: 01875-852-141 **Fax:** 01875-853-371
Email: secretary@longniddrygolfclub.co.uk
Website: longniddrygolfclub.co.uk

Club Mgr: Robert Gunning **Professional:** John Gray
Phone - Starter/Pro shop: 01875-852-228
Fee(s) (2012): wkday £48, day tkt £75; wkend £70, day tkt - inquire
Deposit (2012): £10 **Buggies:** 4 - general hire
Visitor Policies: wkday, 9:30-4:30; wkend - call

I LIKE LONGNIDDRY for its imaginative design crafted by four great golf architects. Like Royal Musselburgh, Longniddry is near the Firth of Forth but presents distinct parkland characteristics. Forested ground approaches the sea on this stretch along the south coast of the firth, giving the golf courses from Aberlady Bay to Musselburgh a lushness uncharacteristic of the courses from Gullane eastward. This makes for a visual treat with water in view but framed by woodlands. In this case, Longniddry is blessed with stands of Scots Pine scarcely represented in the Scottish lowlands.

The design of Longniddry is, at once, traditional and modern. The course is essentially two fairways wide—out-and-back in classic links fashion—with a three-fairway bulge in the middle. But, instead of linking one hole to another in a relatively straight line, the primary designers, Harry Colt and James Braid (at separate times), concocted exhilarating changes of direction on virtually every one of the outgoing nine holes. On return, along the shore, the course straightens but, even so, there's a twist at the end—for, just as at Western Gailes, the clubhouse here sits at the "finish line" of a racetrack routing rather than at one end or the other.

Though relatively short by modern standards, one should not be fooled by a glance at the Longniddry scorecard. There are no par 5s here and SSS is 71 against par 68. This profile forewarns a stiff challenge ahead—no less than seven two-shotters of 400+ yards. The #3 hole stretches to 450 yards. At 432 and 430 yards respectively, the home holes (#17 "Arthur's Seat" and #18 "Hame") will test your mettle. With the wind up, shelter afforded by trees from the #3 hole to #11 will sing sweet relief.

Looking for a "hidden gem"?— Longniddry is a good choice to combine wth the better-known courses of East Lothian. On a self-catering stay in this region of Scotland, it should be on the "must-play" list.

34. Luffness New Golf Club (1894) +

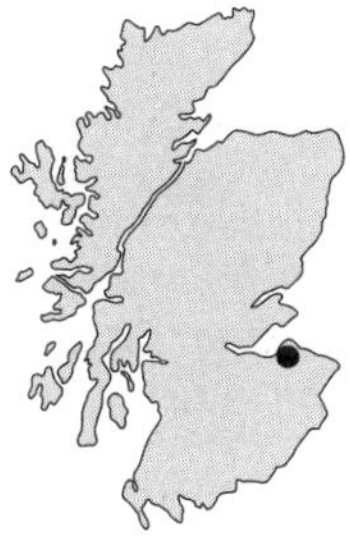

Region #: 3 **Category:** links-minimal sea views
Architect(s): original layout Tom Morris, re-routing by James Braid (1924)
Length: 5958-6328 yds **SSS:** 69-71 **Par:** 70

Address: Aberlady, E Lothian EH32 0QA
Directions: between villages of Aberlady and Gullane; clubhouse on E side of A198

Reservations phone: 01620-843-336 **Fax:** 01620-842-933
Email: secretary@luffnessnew.com **Website:** luffnessnew.com
Booking Contact(s): secretary

Secretary: Group Captain AG Yeates **Professional:** none
Fee(s) (2012): £80, day tkt £95
Deposit (2012): £20 **Buggies:** no
Visitor Policies: M-F only

LUFFNESS NEW IS A MAJOR LEAGUER in Scottish golf and has been for a long time. Its design pedigree traces directly to James Braid and Old Tom Morris, and it has been used as an Open qualifying course for Muirfield.

Luffness has still more in common with Muirfield: It's a "gentlemen's club" where ladies must be accompanied on the course and in the clubhouse by a member; foursome play ("alternate shot") is a popular format here; and the professional ranks of Edinburghian businessmen are well represented in the membership.

Luffness is easy to miss because, upon approaching Gullane village on the A198, one's eye falls upon a vast field of golf courses where it is quite impossible to tell where one course begins and the other ends. It's a case of not seeing the trees for the forest.

Luffness is the first one on the right—and the left—for the course is bisected between its fifth and sixth holes by the A198. Five holes play to the east while thirteen holes play on the west side of the highway.

Over the years this simple fact of life at Luffness has led to some interesting re-routing of the golf course. What was once a rather conventional circular layout has given way to an unconventional series of three counter-clockwise loops that bring the fourth and twelfth holes near to the clubhouse. Consequently, it's not at all unusual at Luffness to find members playing a quick four, eight, twelve, or fourteen holes for some salutary exercise and a little practice on the links. How convenient. And all because the early routing had shots sailing back and forth over the highway. Those picky drivers of the horseless carriage!

The opening and closing holes at Luffness are classics. "Luffness Mill" starts the round on a gentle rise to a green only 332 yards away. Easy enough, one might say. But from the tee the view might lead one to think about hitting a shot into craters of the moon, for the green is shielded behind five deep bunkers completely blocking the fairway. It's a wonderful hole. The closing hole is a long par 4 (416 yards) featuring a wide fairway aslant to the teeing ground and a small green surrounded by a grassy embankment designed to keep balls from skipping OB onto the A198.

In between these beauties, Luffness plays over ground that, as the management likes to say, is "sensibly flat apart from minor undulations associated with seaside courses" (a wry dig at neighboring Gullane #1). I might put it a little differently, for, in my view, Luffness suffers from its location on the rather bland Gullane plain fronting Gullane Hill. Individual holes have merit and the greens at Luffness are superb but, overall, this is some of the least interesting ground among the major courses in Scottish golf. Just one man's opinion.

The joker here is the deepest, thickest, most luxuriant rough only a grazing animal could enjoy.

The wild card at Luffness (and other courses at Gullane) is the brutal wind that either barrels down the firth from the west or swirls off the North Sea and up the Forth estuary from the other direction. The joker here is the deepest, thickest, most luxuriant rough only a grazing animal could enjoy. Golfers might describe the experience as a "challenge" but, the fact is, you cannot wander even a foot or two off the fairway without the likelihood of losing a ball. This is one course where short and straight is the only way to play. Anything off line is most likely long gone. If you are not a straight driver of the ball, I'd advise leaving the "woods" in the clubhouse and playing Luffness with the irons. You'll score better.

See also: Gullane

35. Lundin Golf Club - Lundin Links (1868) +

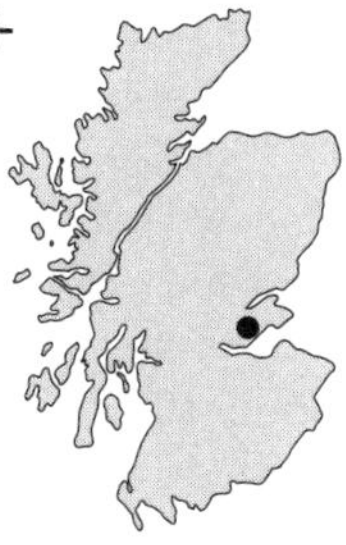

Region #: 1 **Category:** seaside-parkland hybrid
Architect(s): Tom Morris (1868) James Braid (1908-09)
Length: 6138-6371 **SSS:** 71 **Par:** 71

Address: Golf Rd, Lundin Links, Leven KY8 6BA
Directions: From St. Andrews via A915; sharp left turn 3/4 mi W of Largo town center just past Old Manor Hotel

Reservations phone: 01333-320-202 **Fax:** 01333-329-743
Email: secretary@lundingolfclub.co.uk **Website:** lundingolfclub.co.uk
Booking Contact(s): Amanda Clunie

Secretary: Alistair MacDonald **Professional:** Ron Walker
Phone - Starter/Pro shop: 01333-320-051
Fee(s) (2012): wkday £57, day tkt £77; wkend £65
Deposit (2012): £20 **Buggies:** no
Visitor Policies: wkday 9 am-3:30 pm; Sat after 2:45 pm; Sun 11:30-3 pm

IF I WERE PLAYING GOLF regularly in Fife, I would sooner play at Lundin Links than on any course in St. Andrews. Why? First, the price is right. Next, looking over the Firth of Forth to North Berwick and Musselburgh, the setting is dramatic. Third, the course combines elements of seaside links and parkland terrain. And, finally, not a single hole disappoints and several will stay forever in your memory even if played only once: There's the stunning first hole that plays down to a broad fairway then back up to a tabletop green; farther along the seafront, moving away from the clubhouse, before the course makes a turn to the north, there's an impossibly difficult (often copied) 452-yarder to another elevated green set behind a burn and a steep embankment; the par 3, #12, takes you straight uphill to another tabletop green; then #14, advisedly named "Perfection," plunges back down Lundin's bluff to a green far below. Then it's on toward the clubhouse as each of the finishing holes becomes more demanding. "Home," at 442 yards into a prevailing wind, finishes a great golf experience.

Not a single hole disappoints and several will stay forever in your memory even if played only once.

But Lundin Links is a lot more than a beauty. It has *character*. For where do you find out-of-bounds running through the middle of the entire course? This phenomenon is due to club history: the original nine holes laid out by Tom Morris in 1868 utilized the linksland between the sea and a rail line; the course, like many in Scotland, was only two fairways wide. Later, the course was redesigned and extended to the other (north) side of the rail line, thus creating the parkland component of the course. When the railroad went out of business, the rail embankment was left alone. Consequently, the possibility of "OB" follows the golfer around Lundin Links, first on one side, then on the other, even in the middle of the course! Other qualities of Lundin Links: shared fairways, lots of bunkers, a few burns, and high ground (#13 and the teeing ground of #14) overlooking the entire course set against the Firth of Forth. All in all, simply grand.

Lodging: Lundin Links is a great place to base while playing courses in St. Andrews and Fife. Several lodgings deserve special mention: the *Old Manor Hotel* (01333-320-368; ***www.theoldmanorhotel.co.uk***) overlooks Lundin Golf Club; the half-timbered *Lundin Links Hotel* (01333-320-207; ***www.lundin-links-hotel.co.uk***) provides food and lodging in the middle of town; and the *Crusoe Hotel* (01333-320-759; ***www.crusoehotel.co.uk***) is a classic three-star hotel on the harbor in Lower Largo. *Hampton House* (0791-493-4227; ***www.hampton-house.co.uk***) is an excellent four-star guest house on the main road near the golf club.

See Crail, Leven Links, Golf House Club at Elie

36. The Machrie Golf Links (1891)

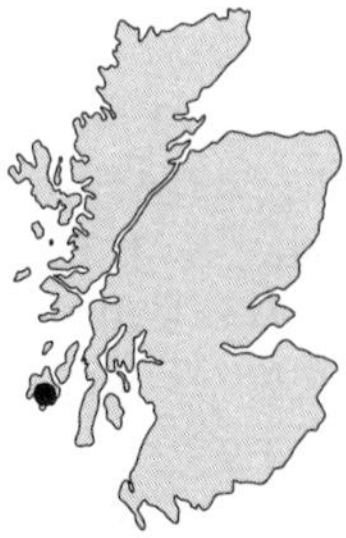

Region #: 8 **Category:** seaside links
Architect(s): Willie Campbell (1891), Donald Steel (1978)
Length: 5964-6250 **SSS:** 70 **Par:** 71

Address: Port Ellen, Islay PA42 7AN
Directions: From Port Ellen ferry dock, 3 mi toward airport, left off A846; from Port Askaig, about 15 mi, rt past airport

Reservations phone: 01496-302-310 **Fax:** 01496-302-404
Email: machrie@btconnect.com **Website:** machrie.net
Booking Contact(s): mgr

Mgr: Ian Brown **Professional:** none
Fee(s) (2012): £60, day tkt £97.50
Deposit (2012): none **Buggies:** 4 - general hire

FOLKS ON ISLAY (pronounced EYE-la) breathed a huge sigh of relief in July 2011 when it was announced that Gavyn Davies, former Goldman Sachs executive and retired chairman of the BBC, had purchased the defunct Machrie Hotel and Golf Links, home of one of Scotland's most revered and historic golf courses.

That's a long lead sentence, but it sums up the potentially dire circumstances The Machrie was facing earlier in the year, with the Machrie Hotel in "administration" (i.e., basically bankrupt) and the future of the golf course uncertain. Now, with that future assured, golfers can make their travel plans and the citizens of Islay can expect to have a vastly improved golf complex for many years to come.

Gavyn Davies is one of the good guys. He's obsessed with links golf. He's respectful of tradition. He's welcomed by the locals. It is hoped he won't turn The Machrie into a rich man's playground. The hotel will be refurbished and eventually there will be a new clubhouse. But the process will be gradual and low-key and may take most of the next decade to spin out. For now, golfers will have The Machrie to play—as unique and rewarding a links experience as Scotland offers up.

Machrie is cut from the same cloth as Cruden Bay, Western Gailes, North Berwick, and Machrihanish. Here you'll find, as Jim Finegan puts it, "a bona fide relic . . . a priceless example of the way golf courses were once brought into being." And, as you might imagine, Machrie and those mentioned above are on a short list of my favorite courses in Scotland. Natural ground defines them all, with minimal sculpting from the hand of man; each presents a fair share of blind shots over dunes and hillocks to big, undulating greens; each is a bit quirky, carrying with it a piece of the nineteenth century and golf history into our time; each brings sheer fun to the golfer on a scale no modern course can approach; each is in a magnificent location relatively removed from the most heavily-traveled tourist trails.

"Brought into being"—that nicely-turned Finegan phrase—says a lot about the old process of coaxing a golf course out of the natural landscape; of giving life to a golf course already there, just waiting to be born; of finding the best green sites, then working back through the landscape to the most arresting teeing grounds. The gem at Machrie was brought into being in this way in 1891 by one Willie Campbell of Musselburgh. Campbell was a young and leading light in Scottish golf when he came to Machrie to lay out a championship course. He left for America soon after completion of his work on Islay and became head professional at The Country Club in Brookline, Massachusetts, where he died way before his time in 1900. His wife, Geraldine, lived on to become a pioneering female golf professional.

Willie Campbell's aim was to create a long and difficult course challenging enough to bring golfers from the mainland to visit the Machrie Hotel and Golf Links. At more than 6000 yards, with no hole less than 200 yards, and with blind shots on virtually every hole, he succeeded. Within ten years, Machrie was attracting Scotland's finest golfers to compete for the Kildalton Cross Trophy and a prize of £100—at that time the highest stake in the world of golf. With such riches to be won in such a fine setting, Harry Vardon, James Braid, and J.H. Taylor came here to compete in 1901. Today the Kildalton Cross Trophy Tournament continues as an amateur open event held the first full week of August. Incidentally, the Kildalton Cross is Islay's prized historic relic: the only remaining Celtic "High Cross" in Scotland. It dates from the late eighth century and can be seen at the Kildalton Chapel five miles northeast of Port Ellen.

"CalMac" car-ferries serve golf destinations on Arran, Kintyre, and Islay. The "Hopscotch 16" ticket allows four crossings at reduced rates to cover the three areas.

To bring the story of the course design up to date, in 1978 Donald Steel was asked to eliminate at least some of the blind shots imposed by Machrie's terrain and Campbell's brain. He did that mainly by shortening the par 3s and thereby lengthening the remaining two and three-shotters (only two of those). In common consensus, the result was an improved course—one more suited to the modern game while retentive of the spirit and character of Campbell's creation.

Nongolf notes and lodging: Though one can fly to Islay from Glasgow, the best way to visit Machrie is on a leisurely sojourn encompassing the Isle of Arran and the Kintyre Peninsula. Starting by ferry from Ardrossan on the mainland, to Brodick on the Isle of Arran, allow at least five days to do justice to this wild and wonderful part of Scotland. On Arran you'll have an opportunity to play Shiskine, a twelve-hole throwback to the nineteenth century. Kintyre and Machrihanish (and now Machrihanish Dunes) deserve two days before pushing on to Islay, where vacationers are drawn to the golf, the whisky distilleries, and the open spaces. Jura—home of one famous whisky distillery (The Isle of Jura) and about 200 permanent population—lies just northeast of Islay. Finished with this island-hopping and ready to return to the mainland, you will have passed through a total population of perhaps 15,000 souls. So, if you're looking to get off the beaten path, this is the way to do it.

Whether such an island journey begins or ends at Islay, you will need to get familiar with the Caledonian MacBrayne ferry schedules available at their excellent website ***www.calmac.co.uk.*** The connection to Islay is at Kennacraig, a few miles south of Tarbert at the isthmus of the Kintyre Peninsula. Plan to reserve space in advance during the busy summer months. Always check the website and/or call for most current information.

Late March to Late October Ferry Crossings, Kennacraig - Islay
Crossings take 2 hrs, 20 min and arrive at either Port Ellen or Port Askaig.

(M, T, Th, F, Sat) - Depart Kennacraig
7 a.m., 9:45 a.m., 1 p.m., and 6 p.m.
Return ferries from Port Ellen or Port Askaig:
7 a.m., 9:45 a.m., 3:30 p.m., and 6 p.m.

Wednesday and Sunday schedules vary - check *www.calmac.co.uk*
phone 08705-650-000.

Tourism is the main industry on Islay; thus, lodging is plentiful. Near the golf course is the venerable 4-star *Glenmachrie B & B* where you can do bed, breakfast, and dinner with one of the best cooks in the land, Mrs. Rachel Whyte (01496-302-560; ***www.glenmachrie.com***). Mrs. White and her husband, Alasdair, also run the five-star *Glenegedale House* on the same farm ground (01496-300-400; ***www.glenegedalehouse.co.uk***). Meals at both Glenmachrie and Glenegedale are taken at Glenegedale House. In Port Ellen, the *Islay Hotel* (01496-300-109; ***www.theislayhotel.com***) has risen in grand style from the dust of its predecessor. Nearby, at Laphroig, golf pro Ron Goudrie and wife Emma take small parties in their two-room gem of a B & B, *The Old Excise House* (01496-302-567; ***www.theoldexcisehouse.com***). At Bridgend there's the classic, ten-room *Bridgend Hotel* (01496-810-212; ***www.bridgend-hotel.com***). I particularly like this Bridgend location because, from here, one can proceed in either direction on the forked main highways of Islay—either toward Port Ellen or toward Port Charlotte. At handsome and prosperous Bowmore, you'll find the classy *Bowmore House* on Shore Street in the middle of town (01496-810-324). General information about Islay can be had at ***www.islayinfo.com.*** The Islay Whisky Society has its own site, ***www.islaywhiskysociety.com.*** Jazz fans!—for a special treat, plan to be on Islay in mid-September for some of the best mainstream jazz available in the UK in memorable settings (***www.islayjazzfestival.co.uk***).

See also: Machrihanish, Machrihanish Dunes, Shiskine

37. Machrihanish Golf Club (1876)

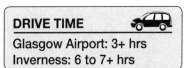

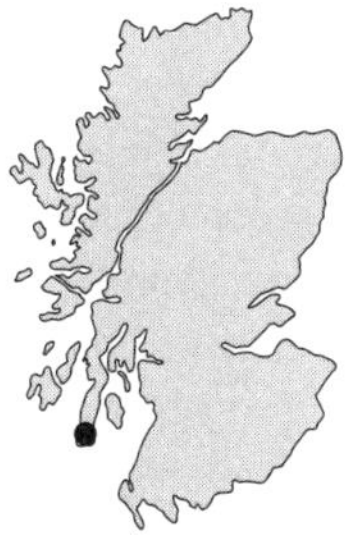

Region #: 8 **Category:** seaside links
Architect(s): Tom Morris (1879); J.H. Taylor (1915); Sir Guy Campbell
Length: 5971-6335 **SSS:** 71 **Par:** 70

Address: by Campbeltown, Argyll PA28 6PT
Directions: 5 mi W of Campbeltown on B843

Reservations phone: 01586-810-277 **Fax:** 01586-810-221
Email: pro@machgolf.com **Website:** machgolf.com
Booking Contact(s): professional

Professional: Kenneth Campbell **Starter/Pro shop:** 01586-810-277
Fee(s) (2012): all wk £62, day tkt £93; 5-day tkt £300
Deposit (2012): none
Visitor Policies: all wk **Buggies:** no

DRIVE TIME
Glasgow Airport: 3+ hrs
Inverness: 6 to 7+ hrs

MACHRIHANISH. MOCK-RI-HON-ISH. The syllables roll off the tongue, conjuring visions of Celtic clans, pipers, and warrior kings in a mythical medieval kingdom. Out on the golf course you encounter "Balaclava" (#6), "Bruach Mor" (#7), "Gigha" (#8), "Ranachan" (#9), "Nocmoy" (#10), and Kilvian (#13)— at this point, you're likely to wonder, "Where am I? And what language is this anyway?".

In this peninsular part of Scotland—not so far away from Glasgow as the crow flies, but poles apart in spirit—Scotland's kinship to Ireland is more apparent than in other parts of the country. Indeed, from the southernmost tip of the peninsula—the Mull of Kintyre—the Emerald Isle is clearly visible (on most days), no more than twelve miles away.

The pastoral beauty of Kintyre, the romance of Celtic history, and the reputation of the golf course at Machrihanish, have combined to make a trip to this place something of a pilgrimage. In recent years, with the advent of Machrihanish Dunes, visitors are showing up in increasing numbers. Machrihanish is no longer a "secret" known only to a few.

The challenge of Machrihanish is getting there. This is remote territory. By automobile, the golf course is about 135 miles of mostly two-lane driving from the Glasgow airport. Plan on three to four hours. Unless it's your jet-lagged day of arrival, the drive is a delightful one along the west side of lovely Loch Lomond, then down the west side of Loch Fyne to Tarbert at the isthmus of Kintyre. From Tarbert, forty more miles on the A83 southward through stirring coastal countryside deliver you to the promised land.

To my mind, the most satisfying way to make the pilgrimage to Machrihanish is within the context of an "island-hopping" trip by ferry through what I've designated as Region #8, encompassing the Isle of Arran, the Kintyre Peninsula, and Islay. With this approach, we ferry across from Ardrossan to Brodick (on the Isle of Arran), linger at least long enough to play the twelve-hole gem at Shiskine, then go on to Kintyre from Lochranza to Claonaig.

This approach allows one to sink into the pace and pleasure of a magical landscape. At the course, it encourages one to *play more than one round.* For at Shiskine, Machrihanish, and Machrie, the golfer will encounter a host of "blind shots"—shots from tee and fairway to unseen landing areas. It's true, "The shots are only blind once," but to realize that truism, more than one round is required. I firmly believe the *only* way to play Shiskine, Machrihanish, and Machrie is to leave time for multiple rounds.

For those who want to make a day trip out of Machrihanish, two options are available where the tradeoff is essentially money for time. Loganair operates two flights daily from Glasgow to the Campbeltown airstrip midway between Machrihanish and Campbeltown. For most current schedule and special offers combining golf and air travel, check with the carrier at 01392-268-500 or ***www.flybe.com***. From Troon on the Ayrshire coast, the *Kintyre Express* (01586-555-895; ***www.kintyreexpress.com)***, runs a 12-seat chartered speedboat that cuts travel time to Campbeltown to one hour and fifteen minutes. Assuming a good seafaring constitution, this can be a worthy adventure for a group of eight to twelve golfers based in Ayrshire.

Not only playing at Machrihanish, but getting there and being there, are among the most treasured memories of my trips to Scotland.

Is the course at Machrihanish as good as its reputation? Is it worth the effort required to get here? How much of the allure of Machrihanish lies in its setting? All I can say is there's magic in the air of Kintyre and, as with all great golf courses, the setting of the course is part of a total experience. Not only playing at Machrihanish, but *getting* there and *being* there, are among the most treasured memories of my trips to Scotland.

Kintyre and Machrihanish have had the same effect on others. Beatle Paul McCartney came here to vacation and ended up buying a farm, writing a song ("The Mull of Kintyre"), and recording that song with the Campbeltown Pipe Band. Golf writer Malcolm Campbell has concluded, "If there is a golfing heaven somewhere, then it is a safe bet that Machrihanish will have to be passed to get there." Not to be outdone, Michael Bamberger, in his modern classic *To the Linksland*, sought the mystery of the Scottish game and found it at Machrihanish, waxing rhapsodic with words like, "ambrosial," "exquisite," and "Nirvana" to describe the course and his experience. Bamberger finished, "If I were allowed to play only one course for the rest of my life, Machrihanish would be the place." That's a pretty strong endorsement.

So, what is it about this course that turns grown men to mush? The romance starts right at the first hole ("Battery")—universally regarded as one of the great experiences in Scottish golf. James Finegan calls it, "my favorite first shot in all the world." Battery is a 423-yarder requiring a drive over Machrihanish Beach to a fairway aslant to the line of play. It's a risk-reward setup—the more beach you risk, the shorter your second shot. Four bunkers are set to capture any ball hit through the fairway from 230 yards to 290 yards.

Now it's on to the second and third holes and the first two of Mac's blind shots. The first one, from the #2 fairway, takes you across the Machrihanish Water (a burn running through the course to the sea) to another rolling green high up on a grassy knoll. The second, from the #3 tee, now changing direction toward the sea, requires a 200-yard carry over and through dunes to a sloping landing area. A good drive here is a must and is rewarded with a bird's-eye view of a green shaped like a jelly-bean set in a hollow below the fairway.

The fourth and fifth holes offer more exquisite links golf—first a short par 3 across a grassy swale, then a dogleg-left requiring two perfect shots to negotiate another route through duneland. From here, the string of four two-shotters with the Celtic names begins: varying yardage at 315, 432, 337, and 354 likely will have you using every club in the bag. Thus ends what, in my experience, is the best "front nine" in Scottish golf.

Notice that the outward nine presents no par 5s and only one par 3. Now, on the inward nine, moving away from the sea to less dramatic ground, the pattern changes: here we have two 5s, three 3s, and four 4s—an entirely different arrangement lending spice to what must be described as the more bland of the two nines. Two holes are particularly memorable: first, #14, a 442-yard two-shotter over billowing ground; then, the extremely difficult 233-yard, par 3, #16 over wasteland to a smallish green protected by mounds and a deep bunker. Mac's two closing holes play over relatively plain ground and often are disparaged but, with OB lurking all the way down the left side, a good card can be easily ruined on "The Burn" and "Lossit." Reaching the clubhouse door, you'll find a convivial place to while away a few hours with a good book, a pint or two, and an occasional glance through large windows to watch the golfers teeing off on "Battery." Bamberger was right: this is Nirvana.

"Battery"—the first tee at Machrihanish. Consensus opinion among course critics ranks this the "best first shot in golf"

Lodging and nongolf notes*:** When the Ugadale and Royal Hotels associated with the Machrihanish Dunes project open in 2012, Kintyre will be overrun with high-end lodging. Simpler choices are available. Near the golf course, *The Warren* (01586-810-310) run by Judy and Bryan McClement is a good mainstream guest house. On the highway into the village, Linda Peacock's *East Trodigal Cottage* (01586-810-305) gets consistently good reviews. Midway between Campbeltown and Machrihanish, on the B842 that runs down to Southend, you'll find the bucolic *Oatfield House* (01586-551-551; ***www.oatfield.org), a Georgian mansion with a fascinating history and four-star standing. Back in Campbeltown, the best choice is *Craigard House* (01586-554-242; ***www.craigard-house.co.uk***), one mile from city center on the north side of the Campbeltown Loch. It's a twelve-room small hotel with an intimate dining room and a resident pooch named "Beanie" who will be more than happy to take you for a stroll along the loch. These and more options for both short-term and longer self-catering stays can be reviewed on the website of Machrihanish Golf Club (***www.machgolf.com***).

For some of the most dramatic scenery on Kintyre, take time to drive down to Southend, then westward along the coast on a single track as far as you can go. When the

"Beanie," the resident pooch at Craigard House, is always ready for a walk along Campbeltown Loch.

road dead-ends, you can walk another mile—sharply downward, then sharply upward—to a high point with views to a lighthouse on the coast far below and westward to Ireland and Islay. At the end of the trail is a memorial to servicemen killed in a Chinook helicopter crash that occurred off the coast in 1994. Here at the bottom of Kintyre, you'll also find ancient ruins, cemeteries, standing stones, and the short but challenging Dunaverty Golf Course (4800 yards) where a sign suggests that you deposit your fee in an "honesty box" before starting play. On the course you will be joined mainly by four-legged creatures chewing the cud—another memorable experience available only in the remote regions of Scotland.

See also: The Machrie Golf Links, Machrihanish Dunes, Shiskine

38. Machrihanish Dunes (2009)

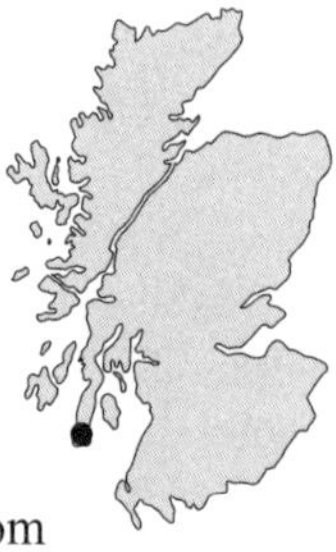

Region #: 8 **Category:** seaside links
Architect(s): David McLay Kidd
Length: 5815-7175 **SSS:** not rated **Par:** 72

Address: Machrihanish, Kintyre PA28 6PT
Directions: 5 mi W of Campbeltown on B843

Reservations phone: 01586-810-000 **Fax:** 01586-550-160
Email: info@machdunes.com **Website:** machdunes.com
Booking Contact(s): Kirsty Martin, reservations mgr

Mgr: Jeanette Jansson
Fee(s) (2012): £55, £79 all-day play; discounted resident rates, twilight rate
Deposit (2012): none; prepay 30 days prior
Visitor Policies: all wk **Buggies:** no
Other: 30% tour operator discounts

"This special place offers a simplicity and honesty that feeds the soul of all who spend time here." —David McLay Kidd

I DON'T LIKE THE "SHOULDS" IN LIFE. But every lover of Scottish golf should go to Machrihanish. Today we are fortunate to know that the trip to Machrihanish can include play on Machrihanish Dunes as well as the great Old Course at Machrihanish Golf Club (and Dunaverty down the road to Southend).

The words highlighted above are *heartfelt* words from course designer David McLay Kidd who, as a boy, vacationed with his family on the Kintyre peninsula. Machrihanish Dunes is likely to be his most lasting legacy. The irony: This is the course where he moved the least dirt and sand—where his hand was lightest on the land. I don't mean that in a disparaging way. It's just a fact imposed upon him by the land and Scotland's protector of the environment, Scottish Natural Heritage.

Machrihanish Dunes sits on duneland north of Machrihanish Golf Club—the two billed as "Old Tom Morris meets new McLay Kidd." Unlike Kidd's Castle Course in St. Andrews, Mach Dunes was coaxed out of the natural landscape within a Site of Special Scientific Interest (SSSI). Restrictions regarding what could and could not be done on the land were severe and enforced by a resident environmental consultant. That meant no fertilizers, no pesticides, no irrigation, no heavy machinery. "Building" was done only on tees and greens. The result was a uniquely "natural" golf course uncommon in this day and age.

A little background: Banking on the mystique of Machrihanish, a consortium of investors led by Southworth Development LLC of Newton, Massachusetts, has envisioned a "Bandon Dunes model" on the Kintyre Peninsula ("Build it and they will come"). Their broader vision imagines creating a new locus of international golf stretching from Scotland's Ayrshire coast westward through the Kintyre peninsula and Islay to the Antrim coast of Northern Ireland (Portrush, Portstewart, etc.).

The "cottages" at Mach Dunes—two-bedroom duplexes for rent by the night or time-share ownership.

The Southworth development involves resurrection and refurbishment of the original Machrihanish clubhouse (now the Old Clubhouse Pub); thirty-six time-share "cottages" at Machrihanish Village (also available for nightly rental by visitors); refurbishment of the twenty-two room Ugadale Hotel across from Machrihanish Golf Club; and refurbishment of the twenty-three room Royal Hotel in downtown Campbeltown. The hotels are scheduled to open in March 2012.

Southworth's grand vision is inspired and inspiring. Yet, I'm a skeptic. Like the Trump development on the northeast coast of Scotland, these grandiose plans are at the mercy of often miserable weather for six to eight months of the year and, more important, they are competing for the attention of the golfing visitor with St. Andrews, Carnoustie, East Lothian, and the Highlands of Scotland. For most golfers, especially first-timers, the lure of Kintyre will not displace the lure of mainland Scottish golf. Let me put it this way: I would not be an investor in the enterprise—but maybe that's why I'm a lowly scribe rather than a venture capitalist.

In any case, everything at Machrihanish Dunes—from the website to the course guide to facility design and hotel refurbishment—has been done to the highest standard of professionalism. It's clear these people really care about what they are doing. Unusual in today's world, there has been "congruence" between promise and performance—the promises of Southworth have been delivered on time and in spades. No expense has been spared.

But let us turn to the golf course . . . because all will be for naught if the golf course is not sufficiently compelling. Is it sufficiently compelling?—yes and no.

YES: It is truly thrilling to walk on this natural ground—and that includes the weeds, coarse grasses, rocks, rabbit scrapes, sand blowouts, and the browned out fairways and lush rough of summer. Like it or not, this really is "the way golf began" (the course motto). In that respect, Mach Dunes is not entirely unique; similarly unmanicured golf can be played on remote village courses at places like Askernish, Colonsay, and Traigh. Apart from the land itself, what *is* unique is the contemporary take on the concept—the brawny length, the imaginative routing, the big and occasionally astonishing greens concocted by McLay Kidd. Five sets of tees marking the course from 5200 to 7200 yards assure that golfers of all levels can enjoy this experience.

I say "yes" to the price too. Unlike most of Scotland's new high-end courses by "name" designers, Mach Dunes is pitched at the middle of the market. They're not creating another golf ghetto for the rich here. While sitting next door to such a reasonably-priced and outstanding golf course like Machrihanish, Mach Dunes can hardly go off into the stratosphere with price—nobody would play the course if they could play two or three rounds on Machrihanish for the price of one round on Machrihanish Dunes. And I think we can count on the price staying pretty reasonable. Southworth sells real estate. That's how they make their money. They're not going to make it selling tee times on Machrihanish Dunes.

NO: The marketing slogan at Mach Dunes may be "The Way Golf Began," but it could have been "Home of the Five-Hour Round." The problem is the distances between tees and greens. The first time I came here I gave up on the course after taking two and one-half hours to play nine holes as a single golfer with no one either in front or behind me! I was absolutely "knackered." Management has worked hard on this problem with improved signage and walking paths, but I can assure them that golf didn't begin with one-eighth mile traipses from green to tee. This will be a continuing issue; I count no less than eight long hikes from green to tee and that's about eight too many. The course is hard enough and hard enough to walk without wearing us down with two miles of walking between tees.

A related problem is the distance between Machrihanish village and the golf course. It's about four miles out to the golf course. By the time you check in at the Dunes Village, get shuttled out to the golf course, warm up, then play the course and have a post-round libation, you're looking at a minimum six-hour investment of time, energy, and money. That's not the recipe of enjoyment for a lot of people.

Finally, the course is just damned difficult. The course has been rated USGA slope 141 from the back tees (about as high as a course can get). And, as at McLay Kidd's St. Andrews Castle Course, some of the greens are over-the-top to the point of silliness. Instead of giving us sensibly-modulated greens on a difficult course in the great Scottish tradition, it seems, perhaps in an effort to create a "signature" look, McLay Kidd just cannot contain himself. Also, as at St. Andrews, some "softening" of several greens has occurred already. Upon leaving the eighteenth green after a second round on Mach Dunes, as a typical middle-handicapper, my main thought was that I might really enjoy this course if I played it from the yellow tees at 5800 yards or even from the forward tees at 5200. At 6400 yards the whites were a struggle. The fourth and fifth tees at 6800 and 7200 yards are out of the question for the average golfer.

Bottom line: Machrihanish Dunes is a work in progress. As Anthony Pioppi has written in one of the most informative course guides in Scottish golf: "Because of its location, Machrihanish Dunes, much like the earliest links layouts, will always be evolving. The course you stand on today will not be the same one, five, ten or twenty years from now." The process will be interesting to watch. The jury is out on Machrihanish Dunes—both the real estate development and the golf course—and it is likely to be out for quite a long time.

See also: Machrihanish

39. Monifieth Golf Links - Medal Course + (1858)

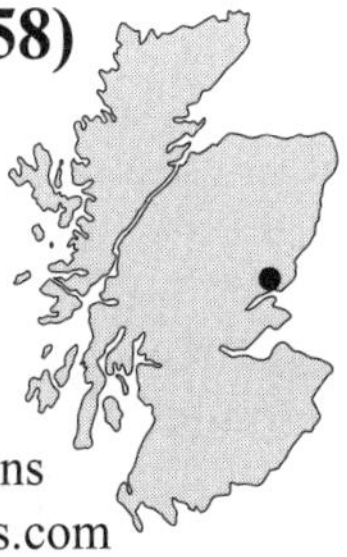

Region #: 6 **Category:** links - heathland hybrid
Architect(s): Allan Robertson, Alexander Pirie
Length: 6459-6655 **SSS:** 72 **Par:** 71

Address: Princes St, Monifieth DD5 4AW
Directions: N of town center, S on Tay St off A930

Reservations phone: 01382-532-767 **Fax:** same as reservations
Email: secretary@monifiethlinks.com **Website:** monifiethlinks.com
Booking Contact(s): Steve MacFarlane - golf mgr

Secretary: Jan Brodie **Professional:** Ian McLeod
Phone - Starter/Pro shop: 01382-532-767
Fee(s) (2012): wkday £55, wkend £65; day tkt £80 - medal, £75 w/ Ashludie
Deposit (2012): 25% **Buggies:** 6 - general hire
Visitor Policies: M-F after 9:32 am; Sat after 2 pm; Sun after 10 am
Other: participant in Carnoustie Country Classic early May and the Carnoustie Country Dream Ticket; 18-hole relief course, Ashludie (5123 yds) by James Braid

MONIFIETH IS A BRAWNY COURSE well paired with the even brawnier Carnoustie Golf Links. In between the two, Panmure sits as a relatively delicate gem. These three, strung out along the A930 northeast of Dundee, encourage a prolonged stay based in Carnoustie. No more than forty minutes from St. Andrews, Monifieth also can fit an itinerary based in that fair city.

The impression made at Monifieth—both around the course and on the course—is unique in Scottish golf. At bottom, the most important aspect of this part of Scotland is its working-class character. To me, Monifieth represents "lunch bucket" golf. There's nothing pretentious or ritzy here. This is a municipal course, flanked by another municipal course (the Ashludie). Situated between the coastal railway and the town in a remarkably plain neighborhood of stone flats and commercial buildings, the links are played mostly by common folk. And that's the way it has always been at Monifieth, where one of Scotland's oldest clubs was organized by artisans and foundry workers in the mid-1800s. Lining the eighteenth fairway are four golf clubhouses and assorted stone row houses, all equally stolid and nondescript. In short, you'll see nothing graceful or light or scenic at Monifieth. Just good, solid, affordable golf and sociability.

On the course, we arrive with knowledge that this is ancient golf ground. Public records show golf being played here for at least 450 years! Thus, at a course like Monifieth, the golfer sensitive to history can actually see and feel the evolution of the game. After several centuries of haphazard play along the links, nine holes were laid out in 1856 by Alexander Pirie and the legendary Allan Robertson of St. Andrews. In 1880, after institutionalization of the idea of eighteen holes for a "round" of golf, nine more holes were added. The course underwent other major changes in 1912, 1930, and 1968. Along the line, especially during the 1950s, long groves of pine trees were planted, creating a links course with lots of trees! Unfortunately, the trees look as if they were planted in rows all on the same day. So they stand like Wellingtonian brigades of soldiers lined up along one or another side of the fairways, particularly on the outgoing nine. Design modifications are not always positive. On the other hand, Monifieth boasts plenty of good holes. On balance, as golf writer Jim Finegan notes, "Monifieth has neither the weaknesses nor the strengths of Panmure." It's a straightforward, no-nonsense course with several long two-shotters, excellent one-shotters, and at least one great par 5 (#9). All said and done, you *will* remember Monifieth's unique working-class setting and those stands of pine trees lining the fairways.

Monifieth represents "lunch bucket" golf. There's nothing pretentious or ritzy here.

Monifieth's pine trees seem out of place on a links course

See also: Carnoustie, Panmure

Telephone/Fax Calling Procedures

From the United States:

Dial 011 (international long distance), then 44 (country code), then the number in Scotland without the leading "0" (i.e., 011-44-1334-466-666).

40. Montrose Golf Links (1810) - Medal Course +

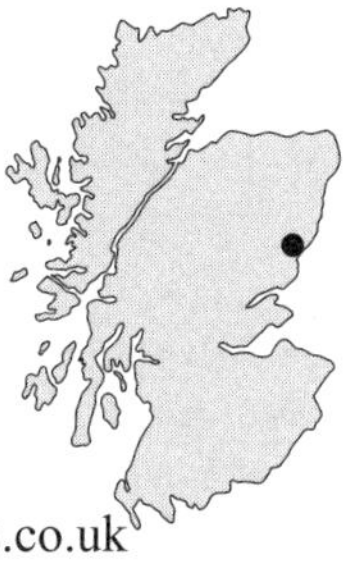

Region #: 6 **Category:** seaside links
Architect(s): evolution; Tom Morris (1901); Willie Park, Jr. (1903)
Length: 6229-6495 **SSS:** 70-72 **Par:** 71

Address: Traill Dr, Montrose DD10 8SW
Directions: N of town center off A92

Reservations phone: 01674-672-932 **Fax:** 01674-671-800
Email: secretary@montroselinks.co.uk **Website:** montroselinks.co.uk
Booking Contact(s): Wendy

Secretary: Claire Penman **Professional:** Jason Boyd
Phone - Starter/Pro shop: 01674-672-634
Fee(s) (2012): wkday & Sat £55, day tkt £70; Sun £40; £40 7-9 a.m. and after 3 p.m.
Deposit (2012): £10 **Buggies:** 2 - med/phys
Visitor Policies: all wk; Sat after 2:45 pm; Sun after 10 am
Other: 18-hole companion course, Broomfield (4830 yds); participant in Carnoustie Country Classic early May and Carnoustie Country Dream Ticket

ON THE EAST COAST, situated halfway between Dundee and Aberdeen, about thirty-five minutes north of Carnoustie, Montrose Medal is in a bit of a no-man's land for golf tourists. On a two-day stay in Carnoustie, it makes a good pairing with that great course—superior, in my opinion, to both Panmure and Monifieth. It's just a little farther away.

Montrose fits well with any itinerary prepared to turn its back on the golf Meccas of Fife, Ayrshire, and East Lothian. For example, on a second or third trip to Scotland, the now-seasoned aficionado of Scottish golf, might focus on the east coast northward from the Firth of Tay. This focus takes us from the wealth of courses around Carnoustie, to Montrose and nearby Edzell, then on to the linksland north of Aberdeen. Montrose also fits well with any itinerary combining the Highlands and the east coast.

In any event, the reward is great when we arrive at Montrose. Golf history books tell us about the ancient pedigree of this linksland that rivals all the better-known "homes" of golf. Records show golf being played here in the middle of the sixteenth century. The course is usually described as the fifth oldest in the world and its oldest associated golf club dates its articles of incorporation to 1810 with records of informal activity stretching much farther back into the eighteenth century. Until the idea of a golf round finally settled on eighteen holes during the 1870s, Montrose was famous for playing the game on twenty-five holes. While Prestwick was hosting the Open with twelve holes during the 1860s, in 1866 Montrose hosted its own Open played to all twenty-five holes! The winning score was 112 (quick math: that's about 81 for eighteen holes).

I like the Montrose course. It's a bit of a patchwork. On one hand, it's everything you expect from a seaside links—towering sandhills; long wispy beach grass; rumpled fairways; and deep, revetted bunkers. On the other hand, when the course veers off on the bias toward town for six holes, you get the distinct feeling you're on an entirely different course. That's not all bad. But, at Montrose, the change seems rather abrupt and you think there might be a story behind this routing. There is. The Montrose golf clubs have had to fight more than once for their linksland and some compromises have been made along the way. Most recently, some modifications to hole #s 1 and 2 have been necessary to accommodate coastal erosion along Montrose Bay.

The important fact is that a lot of good golf awaits you at Montrose. In my view, the aptly named one-shotter, "Table" (par 3, #3), is as good as the famous "Redan" hole at North Berwick. From the teeing grounds at #s 2, 3, and 6, you have views of beach and sea equal in wild flavor to anything in Scottish golf. The holes, themselves, happen to be very good too, especially #6, "Sandy Braes," where I once finished with a "snowman" after landing in an innocent-looking bunker next to the green. The redeeming moment in that round was my par on the superb two-shotter, "Rashie's" (#17), where, it is said, "it takes three good shots to reach the green in two." Holes ten through fifteen are the ones that jut inland in a loop before the course resumes its more traditional links routing back to the clubhouse. You'll decide for yourself whether you like this configuration. Personally, I rather like the change in direction and character. Montrose should be on everyone's list of Top Twenty historic links courses in Scotland. It might creep into my Top Ten because it's a bit off the beaten path.

See also: Edzell

41. Moray Golf Club (1887) - Old Moray

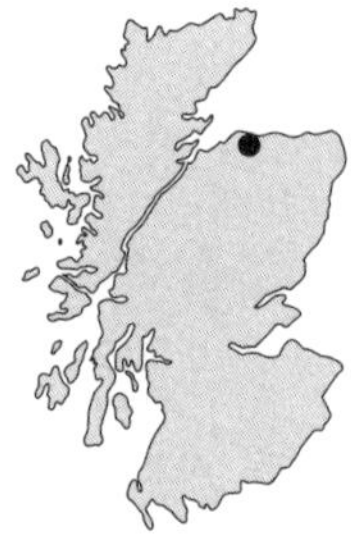

Region #: 5 **Category:** seaside links
Architect(s): Tom Morris (1889), Henry Cotton (1970)
Length: 6004-6643 **SSS:** 72 **Par:** 69-71

Address: Stotfield Rd, Lossiemouth, Morayshire IV31 6QS
Directions: well signposted from center of town

Reservations phone: 01343-812-018 **Fax:** 01343-815-102
Email:

Booking Contact(s): secretary
Secretary: Steven M Crane **Professional:** A Thomson
Phone - Starter/Pro shop: 01343-813-330
Fee(s) (2012): wkday £55, day tkt Old £75; wkend £65, day tkt £85; combo day tkt with New Course £70 wkday, £80 wkend
Deposit (2012): £10 **Buggies:** 4 - general hire
Visitor Policies: wkdays & Sun after 10 am; Sat after 2 pm
Other information: adjacent RAF base is quiet on wkends; New Moray, companion course (6258 yds); Scotland's largest amateur open 3rd full week of July; 10% tour operator discounts

NORTH AND WEST OF CRUDEN BAY along northeast Scotland's "Coastal Trail," a remarkable array of courses awaits the visitor. Three of these courses are featured in this directory (Peterhead, Duff House Royal, and Moray Old). Other good eighteen-hole courses can be played (in order, east to west) at St. Combs, Fraserburgh, and Buckie.

A little farther along we come to Moray at Lossiemouth—a classic links course by Tom Morris (1889) and arguably the finest pearl in the strand. Situated twenty-five miles east of Nairn and six miles north of Elgin, "Lossie" is about the last westward stop before the northeast coast becomes the Western Highlands. This makes Moray Old a great course to combine with the championship course at Nairn and/or inland courses to the south (e.g., Boat of Garten, Grantown-on-Spey). This is also an excellent base for making a foray along Scotland's "Whisky Trail," a seventy-mile, signposted jaunt encompassing most of the country's best-known, single-malt distilleries (including Glen Grant, Glenfiddich, Glenlivet, and Strathisla).

Moray Old is among those most classic of Scottish courses that begin in town (in this case, one block off the main street), proceed outward, then return to a handsome stone clubhouse overlooking a dramatic home hole. Thus, Moray Old stands in atmospheric league with St. Andrews' Old, Montrose, North Berwick, and Prestwick. Moray, in fact, is best known for its challenging 423-yard, par-4 finishing hole. Scots golf writer David Hamilton calls it "the noblest finishing hole in Scotland." With a steep dropoff to the left, a rising grassy slope to the right, and the clubhouse beckoning from behind a plateaued green, golfers will return to town where, as Hamilton puts it, "a small, well-informed audience is usually present to watch futile attempts at the difficult second shot."

There's much to remind one here of a course that came six years later in Morris's work—namely, the New Course at St. Andrews.

In some respects this is my favorite among the courses by Tom Morris. I know part of that judgment comes from Moray's northern location in a small town that sees relatively few visiting golfers from North America. But there's more to it: there's a beguiling, straightforward purity here that contrasts with Morris's work at Dornoch. All the usual links features abound—deep rough, dunes, ocean views—but there are no blind shots, no severely-convoluted greens, no deep swales fronting greens. In fact, there's much to remind one here of a course that came six years later in Morris's work—namely, the New Course at St. Andrews: seven holes out, then a collection of holes featuring directional changes before the return to the clubhouse. Straightforward, no nonsense. I love this northern setting on the relatively dry Moray Firth. And, excepting the noise from the jets flying in and out of the Royal Air Force base at Lossiemouth, you'll love it too. And what about that funny name "Lossiemouth"? Well, Moray and Lossiemouth are at the *mouth* of the River Lossie. This is literal Scotland.

As at Blairgowrie, Crail, and Royal Dornoch, the "companion" course here (New Moray) is a full-blown, full-blooded 18-holer at 6258 yards, making for one of the better 36-hole days in Scotland.

See also: Boat of Garten, Duff House Royal, Nairn

Muirfield *- see Honourable Company of Edinburgh Golfers*

42. Murcar Golf Club (1909)

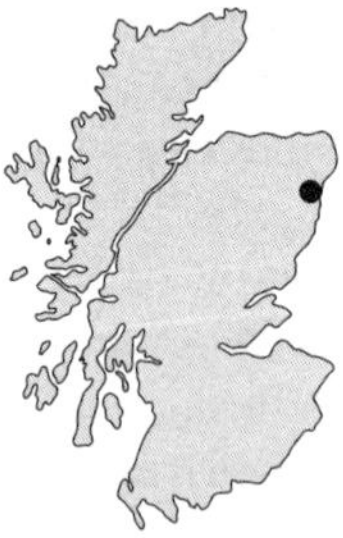

Region #: 5 **Category:** seaside links
Architect(s): Archie Simpson (1909), James Braid, George Smith (1930s)
Length: 5809-6287 **SSS:** 73 **Par:** 69-71

Address: Bridge of Don, Aberdeen AB23 8BD
Directions: from Aberdeen rt at 3rd roundabout from River Don; on A90 lft at 1st roundabout toward Aberdeen (Exhibition Ctr)

Reservations phone: 01224-704-354 **Fax:** 01224-704-354
Email: golf@murcar.co.uk **Website:** murcar.co.uk
Booking Contact(s): secretary

Secretary: Carol O'Neill **Professional:** Gary Forbes
Phone - Starter/Pro shop: 01224-704-370
Fee(s) (2012): wkday £78, day tkt £95; wkend £94
Deposit (2012): £10 **Buggies:** no
Visitor Policies: all wk; Sat after 2:30 pm; Sun after 11 am
Other: 9-hole course, "Strabathie" (2684 yds) by James Braid

WHILE TRAVERSING THE HUMPS and bumps of Murcar a few years back, I had the distinct feeling of playing golf inside a pinball machine. "The luck of the bounce" never had so much meaning as it has found at Murcar. With Royal Aberdeen and Cruden Bay, this must be among the most convoluted, crumpled pieces of duneland in Scotland. Of course these tracks all lie along the same stretch of coastline and, indeed, Murcar abuts Royal Aberdeen on the Royal's north side. This latter fact places Murcar and Royal Aberdeen among the best thirty-six hole combinations in Scottish golf along with the courses at St. Andrews, Nairn, North Berwick, Gullane, and Gailes.

At #1 we're off to a gentle downhill start through a mogul-strewn fairway, but it's not until we reach the third hole, "Ice House," that the full impact of Murcar's duneland emerges. Here, over steeply falling ground strewn with mounds and hillocks and a pathway through the dunes, one can only hit and hope the golf gods are with you. To quote from the club's hole-by-hole guide, "The golfer on looking back from the rear of the green may be under the impression that he has just negotiated a lunar landscape."

Murcar is plain fun with lots of memorable holes . . . I had the distinct feeling of playing golf inside a pinball machine.

Holes four through nine play along and through the coastal dunes in one of the longest stretches of great seaside golf in Scotland. Among these holes, Scottish golf historian David Hamilton rates the 423-yard #7 "Serpentine" among the finest eighteen holes in the country. And, with many elevated tees along this stretch, Murcar affords the best sea views among the great courses north of Aberdeen.

Playing away from seaside, the second nine inevitably fades a bit in comparison (rather like Royal Aberdeen in this respect). Still, Murcar's second nine presents plenty of good holes to remember. Particularly striking are two more classics at #15 and #16—the first a short par 4 requiring a second shot across a burn to a green perched atop a steeply-embanked hill; then a peak-to-peak par 3 that plays across the fifteenth fairway to a severely undulating green protected front left by a heart-shaped bunker. Course architects today would not even dream of two holes like these—let alone in proximity to one another. This is course design from another time.

While the course is an antique, there's nothing old-fashioned about Murcar's refurbished and expanded clubhouse (2006) and practice facilities. Murcar's expansive grass range and short-game ground adjacent to the clubhouse are rarities among old-line Scottish clubs. All in all, it's a first-rate golf experience in the reasonably-priced class with Cruden Bay, Glasgow Gailes, Irvine Bogside, and Kilmarnock Barassie. Certainly, if Royal Aberdeen is not available, the visiting golfer loses nothing (and retains a few quid) by making a stop at Murcar.

See also: Cruden Bay, Royal Aberdeen, Trump International

43. The Nairn Golf Club (1887)

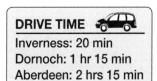

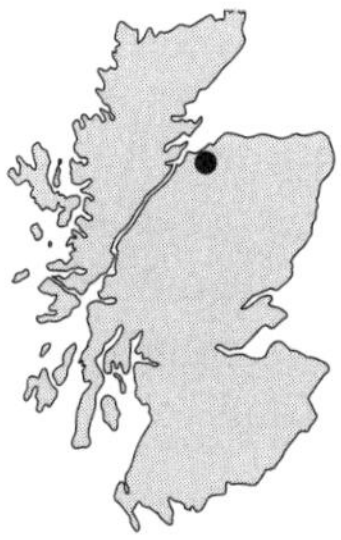

Region #: 4 **Category:** seaside links
Architect(s): Archie Simpson, Tom Morris (1890), James Braid (1910-1926)
Length: 6140-6774 **SSS:** 73-74 **Par:** 72

Address: Seabank Rd, Nairn IV12 4HB
Directions: 16 mi E of Inverness; W side of town off A96

Reservations phone: 01667-453-208 **Fax:** 01667-456-328
Email: secretary@nairngolfclub.co.uk **Website:** nairngolfclub.co.uk
Booking Contact(s): Tracey Davidson

Club mgr: Yvonne Forgan **Professional:** Robin Fyfe
Phone - Starter/Pro shop: 01667-452-787
Fee(s) (2012): wkday £90, wkend £100 May-Sept; 2-round tkt £145 may be played any time in 4-day period; £65 April & Oct, 2-round tkt £95; 10% tour operator discounts
Deposit (2012): prepay 30 days prior **Buggies:** no
Visitor policies: all wk; hdcp - men 28, women 36
Other: 9-hole course, the Cameron, by James Braid

DRIVE TIME
Inverness: 20 min
Dornoch: 1 hr 15 min
Aberdeen: 2 hrs 15 min

MOST GOLF VISITORS TO SCOTLAND'S northern Highlands have Nairn and Royal Dornoch at the top of a short list of priority courses. The courses have a lot in common, including the long hand of Tom Morris. Both are attractive, out-and-back, seaside courses featuring challenging greens and dense banks of gorse and heather. But Nairn has neither the dramatic elevations of Dornoch nor Dornoch's spectacular setting on a crescent bay. Nevertheless, the Moray Firth is quite nice and is visible from virtually every hole. The course is impressive in its own way. As a frequent venue for major professional and amateur tournaments, Nairn deserves to be on everyone's Top Twenty list.

This is a course where ordinary golfers can lose a lot of balls; tight fairways lined with gorse and a proximate sea await the errant drive. More than one hundred bunkers dot the fairways and surround the silky greens. The greens are not so undulating as those at Dornoch, but they are bigger.

Nairn's design pedigree is about as good as it gets. The course was conceived by Archie Simpson of the famous Carnoustie Simpson family. In 1890 Tom Morris was called in to extend and modify the course. Between 1910 and 1926, James Braid tinkered here, until the present design was achieved. Since then, to accommodate the longer modern game, new tees have extended the course to 6700+ yards for tournament play.

Most golfers will remember Nairn for its gorse and its abrupt three-hole loop (#s 13-15) in the otherwise straightforward, out-and-back design. Apart from that feature, there's a raft of memorable holes starting with all the first seven along the seashore and the closing three holes that follow the inland loop. Among the closers is the par 4, #16—418 yards of pure challenge first across a waste area to a rolling fairway, then across a burn fronting a green surrounded by five bunkers. The next hole crosses another burn, then a brawny par 5 at 516 yards takes you to the clubhouse—incidentally, one of the newest and finest in Scottish golf.

Lodging and nongolf notes: At the turn of the twentieth century, Nairn made a transition from fishing village to Edwardian seaside resort and, in that respect, resembles North Berwick in East Lothian. One can still see this dichotomy between Nairn's old "Fishertown" and fancier digs on the north side of the A96 that splits the town of 11,000 more or less in half.

Major bequests from members have allowed Nairn to build one of the newest and finest clubhouses in Scottish golf.

I prefer Nairn to Inverness as the golfer's "home base" on Scotland's Moray coast. Nairn is quiet and accessible. It's big enough to have everything the traveler needs, yet small enough to be enjoyably walkable. With two championship golf courses, a wide range of lodging options, and seaside or riverside strolls awaiting outside one's doorstep, Nairn, like North Berwick, offers the complete package. Moreover, the town is ideally located for easy access to Inverness, the Whisky Trail, castle sites, and golf courses along the north coast and in the Spey Valley.

The high-end hotels here are the *Golf View Hotel* (01667-452-301; ***www.golfviewhotelnairn.co.uk***) and the *Newton Hotel* (01667-453-144; ***www.oxfordhotelsandinns.com***). Each sits on extensive grounds down by the water. Lots of locals gather at the three-star *Braeval Hotel* (01667-452-309; ***www.braevalhotel.co.uk***) and the recently-refurbished *Clubhouse* (01667-453-321; ***www.clubhousenairn.co.uk***). The latter hostelry, formerly the *Claymore House Hotel*, has long been known as one of Scotland's outstanding "golf hotels." Under new ownership, the small hotel has taken on a cruise atmosphere with a vivacious riot of bright color—great fun for the post-round gabfest. All these offer formal and informal dining and are joined in this category by the eight-room *Sunny Brae Hotel and Restaurant* (01667-452-738; ***www.sunnybraehotel.co.uk***).

"Can't miss" B & Bs and guest houses include Shelagh Southwell's *Greenlawns* (01667-452-738; ***www.greenlawns.uk.com***); Liz Burgess's five-star *Sandown House* (01667-451-363; ***www.sandownhouse.com***) overlooking Nairn Golf club on the edge of town; Rosemary Young's classy *Inveran Lodge* (01667-455-666; ***www.inveranlodge.co.uk***), and Angela and George Mackay's *Glebe End* (01667-451-659; ***www.glebe-end.co.uk***). For longer, self-catering stays, both *Inveran Lodge* and *Glebe End* have two-bedroom units adjacent to their main houses. These properties and many more can be viewed at ***www.visitnairn.com***.

See also: Castle Stuart, Inverness GC, Nairn Dunbar, Moray

44. Nairn Dunbar Golf Club (1899)

Region #: 4 **Category:** seaside links
Architect(s): members
Length: 6290-6765 **SSS:** 72-74 **Par:** 72

Address: Lochloy Rd, Nairn IV12 5AE
Directions: 18 mi E of Inverness; E side of town off A96
Reservations phone: 01667-452-741 **Fax:** 01667-456-897

Email: enquiries@nairndunbar.com **Website:** nairndunbar.com
Booking Contact(s): Sarah MacPherson, Gail MacKenzie

Secretary: Jim Gibson **Professional:** David Torrance
Phone - Starter/Pro shop: 01667-453-964
Fee(s) (2012): Apr & Oct £40; May-Sept £50 all wk, day tkt £70; twilight rates (after 4 pm high season); 15% tour operator discounts
Deposit (2012): £15 **Buggies:** 4 - general hire
Visitor policies: all wk **Other:** excellent practice ground

IN COMMON WITH NORTH BERWICK, Nairn has two excellent golf courses— one on the west side of town, one on the east side; one known far and wide, one known far less. This is the one known far less, especially by visitors.

Nairn Dunbar is Nairn's "mechanics club," conceived and dedicated to the proposition that working men and women have a right to play golf too. Sir Alexander Dunbar of Boath donated sixty acres of a much larger estate to create the club in 1899 and it's been onward and upward ever since. This is an interesting, challenging golf course that has hosted a variety of national amateur tournaments over the years and deserves its rank among the best of Scotland's "hidden gems."

Some distance from seaside, Nairn Dunbar is a hybrid links course with a collection not only of the requisite gorse and broom but of heather, dense bushes, conifers, and willows. This is partly due to the considerable amount of water flowing through the course in a network of channeled ditches that run to the sea. These "burns" add both visual interest and challenge to the golf course. In fact, the distinguishing mark of Nairn Dunbar is its visual appeal. From the ditch-lined par 4 #4, through the classic par 3 at #8, to the strong finishing hole, this course delivers eye appeal and superb golf in a linksy-heathland setting—most like Scotscraig in my experience.

Nairn Dunbar is one of those courses in Scotland offering good value for money. That puts it in class with places like Cruden Bay, Southerness, Monifieth, Irvine Bogside, and Longniddry to name but a few. A combination ticket with Nairn Golf Club is available, increasing the appeal of multiple rounds in Nairn. Without traveling far, combining the courses at Nairn with play at Moray, Duff House Royal, Inverness GC, and Hopeman, the visiting golfer can enjoy a full week of bracing, value golf along the Moray Firth.

See also: Duff House Royal, Moray, Nairn, Inverness GC

45. North Berwick Golf Club (1832) - West Links

Region #: 3 **Category:** seaside links
Architect(s): evolution
Length: 6033-6420 **SSS:** 71 **Par:** 71

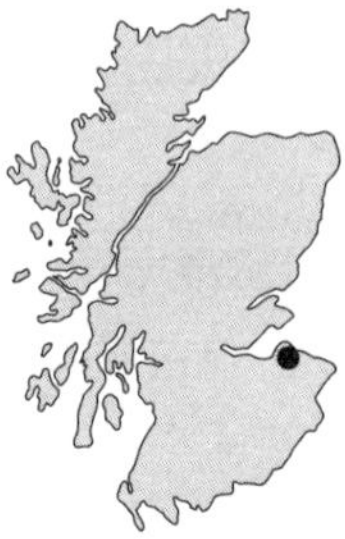

Address: Beach Rd, North Berwick, E Lothian EH39 4BB
Directions: W end of town center, 1 blk off A198
Reservations phone: 01620-892-135 **Fax:** 01620-893-274

Email: secretary@northberwickgolfclub.com
Website: northberwickgolfclub.com
Booking Contact(s): Norma Ogg, Sally Dawe

Mging Secretary: Christopher Spencer **Professional:** Martyn Huish
Phone - Starter: 01620-892-666
Fee(s) (2012): wkday £90, day tkt £120; wkend £95, no day tkt
Deposit (2012): £20 **Buggies:** no
Visitor Policies: wkdays 10:09 am - 4:09 pm; Sat after 3:00; Sun after 12:30

FOR NORTH BERWICK (pronounced BARE-ick) I'll go out on a limb: If I had to choose my favorite golf course in Scotland—a course to play day in and day out—it would be the West Links at North Berwick. North Berwick offers pure links golf on a beautiful stretch of land bordered by the town on the south, grand homes and the Marine Hotel on the west, and broad ocean vistas to the north and east—if you will, a bit of St. Andrews with a view and the crowds long gone.

If I had to choose my favorite golf course in Scotland—a course to play day in and day out—it would be the West Links at North Berwick.

Another part of the reason is North Berwick's ambience and location. It's a small, attractive seaside town, self-contained yet only thirty minutes by train from Edinburgh. And, since I like small towns and big cities, this combination places North Berwick among my favorite spots in Scotland.

A few more details: First is the West Links' extraordinary setting one block off the town's High Street. Just as at St. Andrews, golfers start at the first tee in town, play down the strand to the ninth, then return to town on the second nine. You'll arrive at the eighteenth green no more than seventy-five yards from a road tracing the beach to the East Links (Glen Golf Club) less than a mile away. There's a "connectedness" in this setting that, at once, exudes the history of golf and its central place in the social and cultural life of Scotland. Among Scotland's most venerable courses, only St. Andrews, Prestwick, Lossiemouth, and Montrose so clearly transmit this sense of history and unity with their town surroundings.

North Berwick is thirteenth on the list of Scotland's oldest golf clubs. The course is one of those designed more by evolution than by any individual. Historians indicate that, after several centuries of play along the links, club members settled on the current layout by about 1895—with little change since. Thus, there's an historic unity about the West Links surpassed only by that at the Old Course in St. Andrews.

As for individual holes on the West Links, there's not a weak link to be found. In fact, several are so striking as to be unforgettable. Start with #1 "Point Garry (Out)," where a second shot is made to a black and white target perched behind an elevated green adjacent to rocks and beach below and to the right. Then come two long par 4s where, on the #3 "Trap," the first of North Berwick's famous stone walls makes its appearance. Next follows a 175-yard one-shotter called "Carlekemp" that should be called, "Precision" ("Perfection" comes later—that's #14). If all that weren't enough to announce a round of joyful challenge, bumps and humps and hollows follow over more exhilarating ground to close out the first nine.

Down in the trough of the tri-partite green on North Berwick's #16, "The Gate"

Not to be outdone, the inward nine, if anything, exceeds the outward half in eccentric appeal. Here one finds, from the thirteenth to the eighteenth, a string of holes among the most famous in Scottish golf. Number thirteen, "Pit," is one of those you'll never forget—a 365-yarder whose sunken green is separated to the left side of the fairway by a low stone wall. Only a perfect second shot can find the green; more likely, you'll be laying up with the hope of getting close in three. Next comes the aforementioned "Perfection," where a second shot toward the beach to a blind green requires just that. After ringing a bell to announce a clear green at Perfection, it's on to the par 3 "Redan"—one of the most copied holes in golf, sitting at an angle to the line of play across a grassy divide and pitched front to back. Par is a good score at the Redan. With no pause in the action, #16 ("The Gate") plays to one of the most unusual greens in Scottish golf—a raised tri-partite tabletop with two large flats separated by a trough about three feet deep by nine feet wide! Number seventeen—"Point Garry (In)"—is another long two-shotter that once shared a green with Point Garry (Out). Finally, as at St. Andrews, the short home hole (274 yards) presents opportunity for heroics in front of onlookers ranged along the road and at the clubhouse windows. But wait! The green here, flat as the proverbial pancake, sits on a sharply-cut tabletop, surrounded by a grass moat. After a strong drive, a short pitch shot requires a deft touch to enable a closing birdie or par.

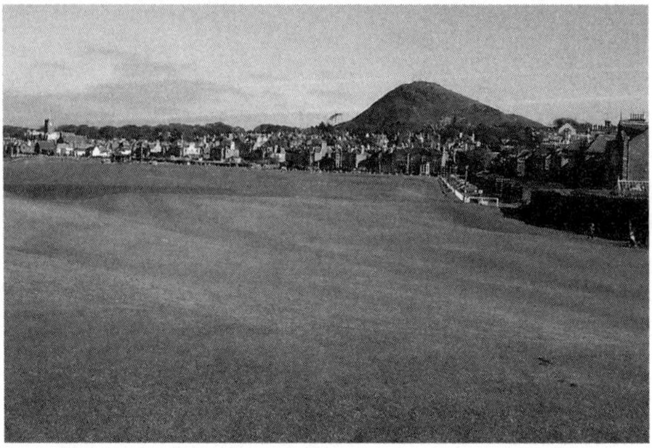

As at St. Andrews, North Berwick's 1st and 18th holes leave from and return to town on a broad expanse of shared fairway.

Does this sound like fun? Indeed, it is. I first played North Berwick in a rain storm only briefly interrupted by relative calm and glimpses of sunshine—yet it was among the most enjoyable rounds of golf in my experience. Since then I've had opportunity to play the West Links when I could relax, look around, and savor the setting. Rain or shine, North Berwick delivers the best of what Scotland has to offer on a golf course. Silver-tongued Jim Finegan sums it up best: "For sheer golfing pleasure—a pleasure bred of variety, unpredictability, challenge, and proximity to the sea—few courses surpass North Berwick's West Links. Admittedly, it is old fashioned and, on occasion, even odd. But it is irresistibly old fashioned and irresistibly odd."

Back at the handsome stone clubhouse behind the eighteenth green, newly expanded in 2010, we look out over the gray slate roofs of the town to landmark Bass Rock—now a bird sanctuary but once home to political prisoners—and on toward Dunbar on the eastern shore. It's a perfect end to a perfect round of golf.

TRAVEL TIP
Interested in spending time in Edinburgh? Stay in less expensive North Berwick and take the train into the city. Travel time: 32 minutes to city center - no parking, no hassles.

Lodging and nongolf notes: For such a high-profile golf destination, North Berwick suffers a bit from a dearth of middle-of-the-road choices. Thus, when thinking about lodging here, it's best to cast one's eye over all of East Lothian. To extend your range of options, try ***www.visiteastlothian.org*** and see the lodging and nongolf notes in my description of Gullane Golf Club.

In North Berwick proper, overlooking the sixteenth fairway of the West Links, high-end lodging is covered by the *Macdonald Marine Hotel & Spa* (01620-892-406; ***www.macdonaldhotels.co.uk***). Fully renovated and expanded in 2006, the Marine is now on par with St. Andrews' Rusacks and Troon's Marine Hotel among the grand turn-of-the-century stone palaces fronting Scotland's oldest and most famous golf courses. Another renovated property, the *Nether Abbey* (01620-892-802; ***www.netherabbey.co.uk***) is North Berwick's best small hotel.

Lined with restaurants and shops, North Berwick's graceful High Street is one of Scotland's finest.

Also on the high end, but in the self-catering category, is Tom and Emma Hill's *North Berwick Golf Lodge* (01620-892-457; ***www.northberwickgolflodge.co.uk***). This is an historic coach house, luxuriously appointed, and rented for a flat-fee with a minimum stay of three nights; optional food service is available. It's ideal for a party of eight to twelve (depending upon gender composition of the party).

Several of my favorite lodgings in Scotland are in North Berwick's B & B and guest house category. On Dirleton Avenue, the main drag into town, Tom and Emma Hill also have the *Golf Lodge B & B* (01620-890-064); Charlotte Souter's *Kaimend B & B* (01620-893-557; ***www.kaimend.com***) is down by the Marine Hotel on the sixteenth fairway of the West Links. Private baths here (rather than en suite facilities) could be a stopper for some, but for peaceful surroundings and pure elegance this one is hard to beat. Mid-town, two blocks south of the main street on Law Road, Gwen and Jake Scott preside over a walled Georgian mansion once attached to church land in town center. Here, at *The Glebe House* (01620-892-608; ***www.glebehouse-nb.co.uk***), guests can enjoy an astonishing collection of fine furniture, prints, paintings. and bric-a-brac. Private parking, friendly hosts, and a touch of seclusion in the heart of town make this a captivating choice.

When not on a golf course or at your lodging, the interesting streets of this attractive town beckon. North Berwick's gracefully curving High Street is among Scotland's finest. And, for such a small town, culinary choices abound: there's Thai, Indian, Italian, Chinese, and traditional Scottish fare—all within a few hundred yards of one another. If the legs can tolerate another workout, you can climb nearby "Berwick Law," an extinct volcano rising to 613 feet and visually dominating the relatively flat Lothian coastal plain for miles around. North Berwick's Scottish Seabird Centre is fascinating and informative. Two enticing castle ruins—Tantallon to the east and Dirleton to the west—offer historic ramblings. With Dunbar only twenty miles farther east along the coast and vibrant Edinburgh only thirty minutes away by train, North Berwick has it all without the hoopla of St. Andrews.

See also: Craigielaw, Dunbar, Glen GC, Gullane, Luffness New, Whitekirk

46. Panmure Golf Club (1899)

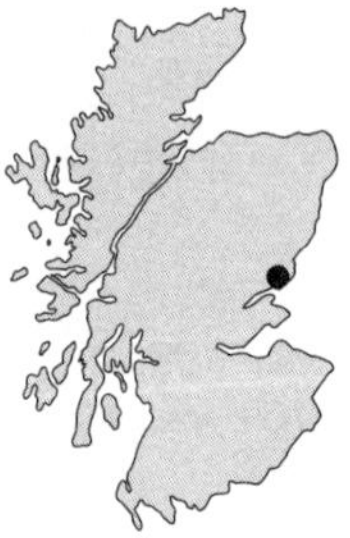

Region #: 6 **Category:** links/parkland hybrid
Architect(s): members, James Braid (1922)
Length: 6085-6360 **SSS:** 71 **Par:** 70

Address: Burnside Rd, Barry by Carnoustie DD7 7RT
Directions: first village SW of Carnoustie on A930; from Carnoustie, first left after passing through two roundabouts
Reservations phone: 01241-855-120 **Fax:** 01241-859-737

Email: secretary@panmuregolfclub.co.uk **Website:** panmuregolfclub.co.uk
Booking Contact(s): Jeanne Kirk or secretary

Secretary: Charles Philip **Professional:** Andrew Crerar
Phone - Starter/Pro shop: 01241-852-460
Fee(s) (2012): £75 all wk, day tkt £100; 9+ golfers £65 & £90
Deposit (2012): £20 **Buggies:** 2 - general hire
Visitor Policies: Sat after 3:30 pm; Sun after 10:00; no Tues am times
Other: participant in Carnoustie Country Classic early May and Carnoustie Country Dream Ticket

AFTER PLAYING THE CHAMPIONSHIP course at Carnoustie, Panmure is a logical choice for the next round of golf. For half the price of its prestigious neighbor, Panmure offers superb golf on a delightful, challenging course. In fact, at a more reasonable length of 6085 yards from the visitor tees, the game here may be more enjoyable to the average golfer than the test of strength at Carnoustie.

Hogan went away trumpeting the #6 hole at Panmure . . . as one of the best two-shotters in the world.

Panmure has been characterized by some golf writers as twelve great holes surrounded by six holes of sheer banality. Personally, I think it's more like fourteen and four. Nevertheless, the critique bears some truth. Panmure's opening three holes and closing three holes play over flat, uninteresting pastureland. Yet this presumed weakness adds variety and symmetry to the layout. The flat holes at each end bracket the hillocky, gorse-laden interior. To me, that composition makes the course memorable; I like its pace and rhythm.

Club historians remind us that this is where Ben Hogan practiced before winning the British Open in 1953 at Carnoustie—and that Hogan went away trumpeting the #6 hole (now called "Hogan's Hole") as one of the best two-shotters in the world. As usual, he was right. Other memorable holes include #8, where a flat green is guarded by a large, conical sandhill; #12, a long par

Panmure's classic clubhouse with filigreed latticework in the gables.

4 requiring a precise second shot over the Buddon Burn to an elevated green; and the 234-yard par 3 fifteenth hole.

Panmure Golf Club has a long and proud history. Organized in 1845, the club shared playing time at neighboring Monifieth until its own clubhouse and course were finished in 1899. With its dormers and gables and filigreed latticework, Panmure boasts one of Scotland's most attractive golf clubhouses. Lovers of historic architecture can only hope the structure will be forever preserved.

See also: Carnoustie, Monifieth

47. Peterhead GC (1841) - Old Course

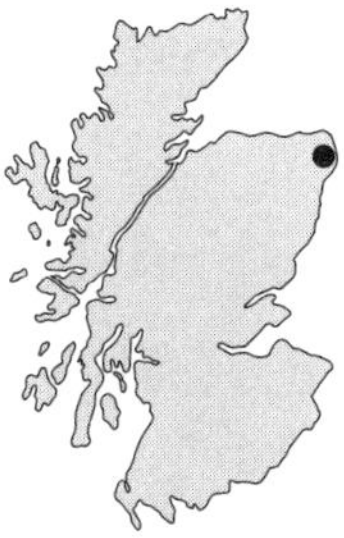

Region #: 5 **Category:** seaside links
Architect(s): Willie Park, Jr. (1891), Laurie Auchterlonie and James Braid (1920s)
Length: 5758-6173 **SSS:** 68-71 **Par:** 69-70

Address: Riverside Drive, Peterhead AB42 1LT
Directions: N side of town; rt at T-junction of A90 and A198 (Waterside Inn); left at 1st roundabout, then left at 2nd roundabout
Reservations phone: 01779-472-149 **Fax:** 01779-480-725

Email: enquiries@peterheadgolfclub.co.uk **Website:** peterheadgolfclub.co.uk
Booking Contact(s): secretary or professional

Secretary: John Stewart **Professional:** Harry Dougal
Phone - Starter/Pro shop: 01779-472-149
Fee(s) (2012): £40 wkday, £55 day tkt; £50 wkend, £65 day tkt
Deposit (2012): £5 **Buggies:** no
Visitor Policies: anytime M-F & Sun; after 2 pm Saturday
Other: 9-hole "New" course (1923), 2230 yds by Laurie Auchterlonie surrounds large practice area

MORE THAN MOST CLUBS, Peterhead has experienced the ups and downs that come with the tides of history and the tides of the North Sea. One of the ups and downs starts quite literally with the rather strange parking lot situated every bit of one-eighth of a mile from the clubhouse over a bridge crossing the Ugie River that flows around the linksland here into the North Sea. It's a long, uphill trudge

More important, the club has struggled perennially with the tides of the local economy—first as an east coast center of the volatile fishing trade and, more recently, as one locus of the even more volatile oil industry. Founded in 1841, the club makes rightful claim to being the eighteenth oldest golf club in the world—as the club brochure notes, older than venerable Prestwick. Yet, some five decades passed before the club secured land adequate for a home and nine holes on the Craigewan links north of Peterhead. In 1891, two-time Open winner Willie Park, Jr., was commissioned to lay out those first nine. In 1908 the course was extended to eighteen holes. Still more land acquisition led to an additional eighteen designed by Laurie Auchterlonie in 1923 (thus Peterhead's "Old" and "New" tracks). But this promising configuration did not stand the test wrought by mid-century wars and economic dislocation. The New fell into disrepair to become a nine-hole relief course (and a very good one, by the way). Fortunately, for the modern golfer who likes to practice and warm up a bit, much of that land became today's excellent practice area with target greens and a short-game facility—a rarity in Scottish golf.

Now we come to the more daunting tides of the sea. Among the great links courses along Scotland's east coast, Peterhead has the unfortunate distinction of having been most seriously affected by beach erosion. Since World War II, the Old Course's original sixteenth, seventeenth, and eighteenth holes have been lost to the sea. In fact, one can now stand on the sea-facing side of the clubhouse and look down on the site of the abandoned eighteenth green. It's a sad sight—and not unique to Peterhead. Other great courses along this northeast stretch, including Royal Aberdeen, have had to deal with this formidable challenge from Mother Nature. It is a continuing storyline in Scottish golf.

And now for the course: Peterhead's experience with the power of the sea has led to significant changes to the original course (new holes) and re-routing. Three new holes were laid out in 1969 along the Ugie River and these, though they are fine holes, don't have much in common with the rest of the course. The first hole, "Ugie," is mildly reminiscent of the great first hole at Machrihanish—which means it's a pretty darned good hole. As for re-routing on the rest of the old ground, I sense a certain strain to make it all "work" and this leads to some awkward moments.

Nevertheless, it should be understood that Peterhead is an excellent course with duneland characteristics comparable to those at Cruden Bay, Murcar, and Royal Aberdeen. Elevated tees at many holes provide exhilarating sea views and Peterhead's remaining four holes that thread the seaside dunes are as good as any in Scottish golf. Relatively small greens and a persistent upward grade on the northward holes (usually into the wind) make this course play considerably longer than the official yardage suggests.

Any golf party traversing northeast Scotland's "Coastal Trail" en route to or from Cruden Bay and Royal Aberdeen, will be rewarded by a stop at Peterhead. It's one of those historic, intriguing courses too often overlooked by visitors.

See also: Cruden Bay, Duff House Royal

Telephone/Fax Calling Procedures

From the United States:

Dial 011 (international long distance), then 44 (country code), then the number in Scotland without the leading "0" (i.e., 011-44-1334-466-666).

48. Pitlochry Golf Club (1909)

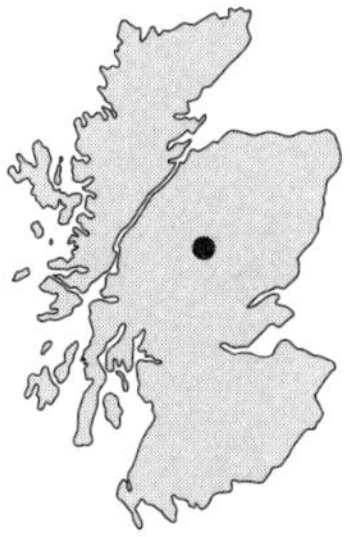

Region #: 7 **Category:** parkland
Architect(s): Willie Fernie (1909), Cecil Hutchinson (1920s)
Length: 5414 - 5670 **SSS:** 69 **Par:** 69

Address: Golf Course Rd, Pitlochry PH16 5QY
Directions: N of town off the A924 (Atholl Rd)
Reservations phone: 01796-472-792 **Fax:** 01796-473-947

Email: pro@pitlochrygolf.co.uk
Website: pitlochrygolf.co.uk
Booking Contact(s): professional

Professional: Mark Pirie
Phone - Starter/Pro shop: 01796-472-792
Fee(s) (2012): May-June-Sept wkday £32, day tkt £42, wkend £40, day tkt £47; July-Aug wkday £37, day tkt £47, wkend £42, day tkt £52; reduced Apr & Oct wkend £38, day tkt £48
Deposit (2012): none, prepay 30 days prior **Buggies:** no
Visitor Policies: all wk; members only until 9:30 am

DRIVE TIME
Glasgow airport: 1 hr, 30+ min
Inverness: 1 hr, 45 min

I FELL IN LOVE WITH SCOTLAND at Pitlochry—the golf course and the town. It was the first course I encountered in Scotland and quite unlike anything I had seen in my part of the world. From the opening shot to a fairway split by a gully; then up a great hill for #s 2 and 3; then on to the blind shot at "Queen Mary's Rest" (#5); and the dramatically elevated teeing ground at #6 "Druid's Stone," here we have one of Scotland's most scenic courses, with spectacular views westward across the Tummel Valley. After playing holes #4 through #17 back and forth, 'round and about, on top of Pitlochry's graceful hill, the golfer descends to an attractive and welcoming clubhouse situated next to the #18 "Home" green. Not incidentally, among these eighteen holes, I would rank four as highly as any in Scottish golf for memorability (#s 1, 5, 10, and 16). As for the rest, they're all enjoyable, though, as a whole, they add up to only mildly-challenging golf on one of the shortest courses in this directory. As Scotland's Malcolm Campbell puts it, "Pitlochry is not the most testing golf course in the wide world of golf—and who is to say it is not the better for it—but it certainly is one of the most delightful to play." And, oh, those views!

Nongolf notes and lodging: Equally delightful as the golf course is the town itself. About thirty miles north of Perth on the A9 (Scotland's main artery northward), Pitlochry is at the geographic center of Scotland

The Moulin Hotel near Pitlochry is vintage 17th century with a modern brew pub attached.

and bills itself, "The Gateway to the Highlands." The town is a destination resort and has been since Victorian times. In summer the place can be crawling with visitors perusing the shops of the main street (Atholl Road). But don't let that scene get you down on Pitlochry. Off the main street, there's much to see and do here and the crowds can be avoided. This is an excellent base for making day trips throughout Perthshire and central Scotland. Stirring, scenic drives meander westward from the A9 on narrow roads along Loch Rannoch, Glen Lyon, and Loch Tay (be sure to make a photo-op stop at Queen's Rest seven miles west of town). To the east, one of Scotland's most scenic highways, the short A924 connecting the A9 to the equally-scenic A93, starts from Pitlochry in the middle of town. Just a few miles along the A924, at a leftward bend, as the narrowing road starts to climb, you'll find the entrance to Edradour Distillery, renowned as Scotland's smallest distiller of single-malt whisky (tours are free). A few miles to the north on the A9 lies Blair Castle, one of Scotland's most popular castle parks, and just a bit farther along is the House of Bruar, a prodigious gift emporium (***www.houseofbruar.com***). A hike to the Falls of Bruar is worth the effort; you'll find the trailhead behind the House of Bruar.

I fell in love with Scotland at Pitlochry—the golf course and the town.

But you don't have to leave town to have a good time. Pitlochry's winding streets invite exploration. The Heather Gem Factory located behind the Tourist Information office is fascinating. Hiking and nature trails are close by (some surrounding the golf course). And the River Tummel awaits just below town where you'll also find the Pitlochry Dam and Fish Ladder and the Pitlochry Festival Theatre that draws visitors from miles around throughout the summer season (01796-484-626; ***www.pitlochry.org.uk***).

The bright orange roof of Pitlochry's refurbished clubhouse is probably visible from space (use your imagination).

As a tourist magnet, Pitlochry is loaded with lodgings in every budget category. One of the best, able to accommodate large golf parties, is the ten-room *Beinn Bhracaigh* run by Alf and Ann Berry (01796-470-355; ***www.beinnbhracaigh.com***). A four-star entry in the B & B category is the *Dunmurray Lodge* operated by Tony and Irene Willmore (01796-473-624; ***www.dunmurray.co.uk***). Both of these establishments underscore my premise that one need not spend more than £40 to £50 per person per night for first-rate lodging. Among the full-service hotels, on the north end of Atholl Road, the *Claymore House Hotel* (01796-472-888; ***www.claymorehotel.com***) does a good job with food and mid-price lodging. Three-quarters of a mile up the A924 (Moulin Road) is the *Moulin Hotel* (01796-472-196; ***www.moulinhotel.co.uk***), one of my favorite hotels in Scotland. The Moulin is an historic coaching inn (1695) with seventeen comfortable rooms, an attached pub, and its own microbrewery. The hotel pub is a hangout for locals as well as visitors. It's a great place to meet and be met.

49. Portpatrick Golf Club - Dunskey Course (1903)

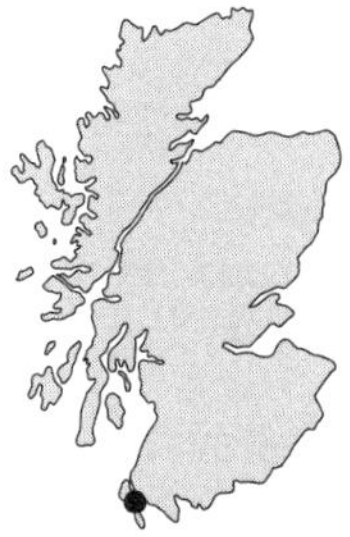

Region #: *9* **Category:** seaside links - heathland
Architect(s): C W Hunter
Length: 5622-5913 **SSS:** 68-69 **Par:** 70

Address: Golf Course Rd, Portpatrick DG9 8TB
Directions: signposted NW of village
Reservations phone: 01776-810-273 **Fax:** 01776-810-811

Email: enquiries@portpatrickgolfclub.com
Website: portpatrickgolfclub.com
Booking Contact(s): Leona Connor

Club Mgr: James Gaffney **Professional:** James Erskine
Phone - Starter/Pro shop: 01776-810-273
Fee(s) (2012): M-Th £30, day tkt £50; Fri - Sun £34, day tkt £60
Deposit (2012): £10
Visitor Policies: all wk **Buggies:** 12 - general hire
Other: 9-hole par-3 Dinvin course, 1504 yds

TUCKED AWAY AS IT IS in the southwest corner of Scotland, few golf tourists from North America visit the Dumfries-Galloway region. That's a good reason to consider a trip to this beautiful area. Beginning just south of Turnberry, that trip might include golf at Stranraer, Portpatrick, Southerness, and Powfoot with an admixture of inland courses at Newton Stewart, Selkirk, Kelso, and other "Borders" towns—all set in a paradise of rolling green hills and picturebook villages and towns perched beside sparkling rivers. Different from the rugged beauty of the Highlands, the Dumfries-Galloway beauty is of the soft, rolling sort found in England's Yorkshire district and in Ireland.

Among the southern courses mentioned above, Portpatrick is perhaps the most dramatically situated on the rocky coast of an anvil-shaped piece of land dead across the water from Belfast, Northern Ireland, just twenty miles away. On a clear day you can see Ireland (#10 is "Erin View"), the Mull of Kintyre to the northwest, and the Isle of Man off to the south.

Wind, rain, and long rough are the main determinants of a golf score at Portpatrick. With few bunkers and no two-shotters over 400 yards from the visitor tees, the main distraction here is the scenery. However, in the whole scheme of weather in Scotland, this is one of the most benign areas, washed as it is by the warm waters of the Gulf Stream. Given a day of sparkling weather on the "Rhinns of Galloway," most will find this short course a lovely pushover and, in either case—blustery or calm—this is one place I would ask for permission to play from the medal tees at 5913 yards.

See also: Powfoot, Southerness, Stranraer

50. Powfoot Golf Club (1903)

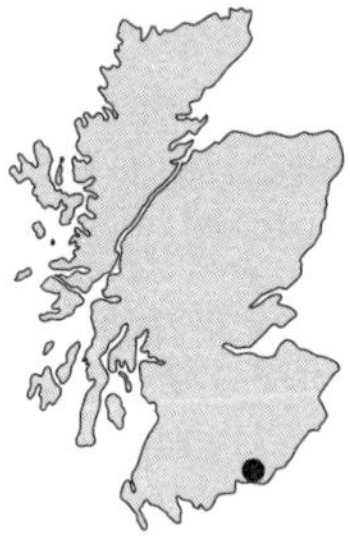

Region #: 9 **Category:** seaside links/parkland hybrid
Architect(s): Alex "Sandy" Herd (1903)
Length: 5993-6275 **SSS:** 70-71 **Par:** 70-71

Address: Annan, Dumfries-shire DG12 5QE
Directions: B724 off A75 at Annan, then 1/2 mi S of Cummertrees
Reservations phone: 01461-204-100 **Fax:** same

Email: info@powfootgolfclub.com
Website: www.powfootgolfclub.com
Booking Contact(s): mgr

Office Manager: Stephen Gardner **Professional:** none
Phone - Starter/Pro shop: 01461-204-100
Fee(s) (2012): wkday £39, day tkt £50; wkend £50, day tkt £60
Deposit (2012): £10 **Buggies:** 5 - general hire
Visitor Policies: M-F 9-11 am and 1-3:30 pm; Sat 2:30 - 3 pm; Sun 10:30-11:15 am and 1-3:30 pm

AFTER WINNING THE OPEN CHAMPIONSHIP in 1902, Alex "Sandy" Herd traveled down to the bottom of Scotland the following year to help locals lay out nine holes for a burgeoning resort development at Powfoot on the Solway Firth. The golf course was extended to eighteen holes by 1913 when Powfoot ran smack into complications wrought by two world wars. Like most of the golf courses on Scotland's strategic southwest coast, Powfoot's wide open spaces made for a perfect military base. Consequently, the course was reduced to thirteen holes and did not regain its full stature as an eighteen-holer until 1949. World War II left a particularly marked imprint on Powfoot—in one dramatic and one less obvious way. The dramatic residue of the war is at #9 "Crater" where a sizeable depression created by a German bomb remains as an "unnatural hazard." The less obvious legacy is the rather flat eastern half of the course on ground leveled for military purposes. The last five holes, played largely over parkland terrain, were reconstructed after the war.

I'll bet you don't have one of these on your home course. Powfoot's #9 "Crater" features a depression created by the explosion of a German bomb during World War II.

The layout at Powfoot is a little unusual for a seaside links. The acreage here is rather rectangular. Off to a typically straightforward opening par 4 from the front windows of the clubhouse, hole #s 2 through 4 turn toward the sea and then down the coastal side of the rectangle. The middle nine holes march back and forth through a pleasing series of one and two-shotters until #13 is reached back in front of the clubhouse. This is where the course ended for so many years. The next five post-war holes meander about on the parkland side of the rectangle until returning once again to the welcoming "nineteenth hole." A quirky feature of Powfoot, not so unusual on Scottish linksland, is an estate road that runs to the sea and bisects the course on its way. Four of Powfoot's holes play across this Ryehill road.

Hadrian's Wall—less than an hour from Powfoot, an educational diversion for the itinerant golfer.

Powfoot is a busy little club serving over 800 members in a catchment area that includes Dumfries, Annan, and Gretna in Scotland and Carlisle on the English side of the border. Situated as it is, Powfoot is often played by visiting golfers traveling from England to one of Scotland's golf Meccas farther north. For all the reasons cited in my descriptions of Portpatrick, Stranraer, and Southerness, these courses and the beautiful Dumfries-Galloway countryside deserve more than a drive-through.

Nongolf notes: This is a fascinating area relatively untrammeled by visitors from North America. No more than an hour's drive from Powfoot, the great tourist attraction for many is Hadrian's Wall. Here, one can spend a few hours or a few days exploring Roman ruins and hiking along the wall. The B6318 parallels much of the wall; informative visitor centers are at Housteds Roman Fort and Vindolanda (***www.vindolanda.com***). In the opposite direction, midway between Annan and Dumfries lies the medieval stronghold at Caerlaverock, one of Scotland's best castle stops. About twenty miles southwest of Dumfries are the Threave Estate and Gardens (a National Trust property; see ***www.nts.org.uk***) and the attractive fishing village and "artists town" of Kirkcudbright (pronounced Kir-COO-bree), associated with a clique of turn-of-the-century artists, largely from Glasgow, who came here to escape the dismal city in favor of easy living and inspiration in an historic seaside setting (see ***www.kirkcudbright.co.uk***).

For more nongolf notes, see Southerness. See also: Portpatrick, Stranraer

51. Prestwick Golf Club (1851)

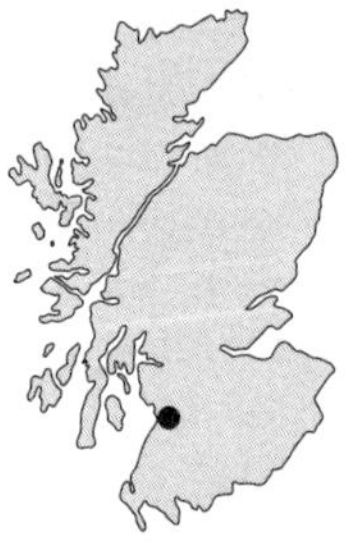

Region #: 2 **Category:** seaside links
Architect(s): Tom Morris - 12 holes (1851); others
Length: 6544-6700 **SSS:** 73 **Par:** 71

Address: 2 Links Rd, Prestwick, Ayrshire KA9 1QC
Directions: From N on A79, 1 mi S of Prestwick Airport; rt at Station Rd (light); under rail bridge 400 yds toward beach. From S, left at Station Rd in Prestwick town center off A79 (Main St)
Reservations phone: 01292-671-020 **Fax:** 01292-477-255

Email: bookings@prestwickgc.co.uk **Website:** prestwickgc.co.uk
Booking Contacts: Margaret Campbell, Morven English

Secretary: Ken Goodwin **Professional:** David Fleming
Phone - Starter/Pro shop: 01292-479-483
Fee(s) (2012): wkday £130, day tkt £185; Sun £155
Deposit (2012): £70 **Buggies:** 1- med/phys w/ caddie
Visitor Policies: wkdays except Th pm; Sat after 4 pm; limited hrs on Sun
Other: hdcps - men 24, women 28

WHEN MY CLIENTS INCLUDE the Ayrshire coast on an itinerary, I like to start them out at Prestwick Golf Club if possible. This is where you return to an older age of golf—to the nineteenth century and the historic days of the first Open championships. At Prestwick, on the course and in the clubhouse, you can soak in the aura and origins of professional tournament golf in an atmosphere little changed by the passage of time. And though its time has come and gone as a venue for the British Open, Prestwick remains among the most challenging courses in Scottish golf. And the word "challenging" really doesn't get to the heart of the matter. The course is also vexing, devilish, and entertaining in ways unique among the classic courses, past and present, on the Open "rota."

This unassuming cairn in a corner of Prestwick Golf Club marks one of the most important spots in golf history. This is where golfers teed off in the first Open Championship in 1860.

Between 1860 and 1925 Prestwick was the main venue for the Open Championship. Twenty-four of the first sixty-five Opens were held here. And, as testimony to the quality of Prestwick's course, those twenty-four tournaments were dominated by all the great names in the first two generations of Scottish golf: the Morrises from St. Andrews, the Parks from Musselburgh, the Simpsons from Carnoustie, and, later, Harry Vardon and James Braid. Tom Morris, Jr., considered the finest golfer of his day, won the Open at Prestwick three years in a row between 1868 and 1870 and thus was allowed to keep the original Open prize—a red

Moroccan leather belt with silver buckle. Subsequently, a new prize was produced—the now famous "claret jug" engraved with the name of each winner of the Open since 1872.

Prestwick is another course where you will find the living presence of golf's nineteenth-century father figure, Tom Morris. Morris moved from St. Andrews to Prestwick in 1851 as a young man to lay out twelve holes, assume a position as Keeper of the Green, and, not incidentally, to raise a family. Today, some of that early layout remains, including seven of Morris's green sites. Morris returned to St. Andrews in 1864. Prestwick's clubhouse was constructed in 1868, and in 1883 the course was extended to eighteen holes. By that time the club was firmly established as one of the preeminent clubs in Scottish golf.

"You would like to gather up several holes from Prestwick and mail them to your top ten enemies."
— Dan Jenkins

Upon stepping to the first tee at Prestwick you will be struck immediately by the vexing, devilish side of the place. A slicer of the ball will cringe, for tight up against the right side of the entire first fairway is a stone wall flanking a rail embankment (OB). But, compensate too far leftward and you're into the gorse and rubble. The second shot isn't any easier. Prestwick's first lesson: accuracy will beat distance every time. The first hole, a mere 369 yards, will remind you, as Jim Finegan puts it, "this course may be a monument to the era of the gutta percha ball. But it is no tombstone. The golf here continues to be gloriously vital."

Now on to the attractively deceiving par 3 second hole before tackling the famous "Cardinal" par 5 with its strategically-placed, mammoth bunkers stretching the width of the fairway and lined with railroad ties ("sleepers" in Scots parlance). If this sight brings Pete Dye to mind, it's no coincidence. Pete came here to play in 1963 and went away a changed man. You can read about his Scottish epiphany in the book, *Bury Me in a Pot Bunker*.

"Cardinal" and "Bridge" (#4) play alongside the Pow Burn—a critical natural feature of Prestwick that cuts into the course behind the second green and then runs the full length of the layout. Thirteen of Prestwick's holes are crammed into the west side of the burn, while only five holes (#s 5-9) lie on the more expansive east side of the burn. This configuration gives the course a certain rhythm I like: tight at the beginning and end; open in the middle.

With all this excellent terrain covered in the first four holes, you can hardly expect it to get better—and, yet, it does—for now we approach the equally famous "Himalayas," a blind one-shotter (206 yards) over a 25-foot-high sandhill to a green surrounded by five bunkers. This is antique Scottish golf at its best.

Well, I could go on and on, hole after hole. Just two more: First, "Arran" (#10), is one of my favorite holes in Scottish golf. It's a 454-yard, par 4, dogleg right across the Pow Burn and then straight down a bunkered fairway aimed at the Isle of Arran off in the distance. Par is a good score, but the setting is so spectacular you don't care that much if you don't meet the test. Prestwick's most famous hole is the #17 "Alps" (one of the Morris originals). It's a 391-yarder with a drive up a hill, then a blind shot to a green fronted by a bunker so cavernous you need steps to get in and out (more Pete Dye material). With the course largely unchanged in one hundred years, Prestwick links the past and present of golf course design. The line between Tom Morris, the most influential designer of the nineteenth century, and Pete Dye, the most influential designer of the twentieth century, cuts right through Prestwick Golf Club.

Back at the clubhouse you'll find a priceless collection of golf memorabilia, including a replica of Young Tom Morris's red Moroccan leather belt (the original is in possession of the Royal and Ancient Golf Club). Lunch is available 10 a.m. to 3:30 p.m. in the casual Cardinal Room. The more formal Long Room requires coat and tie and advance reservation (men only).

The line between Tom Morris . . . and Pete Dye, the most influential designer of the twentieth century, cuts right through Prestwick Golf Club.

Lodging and food: Prestwick's "main street," the busy A79 with its constant flow of traffic, can be a bit off-putting. But you don't have to go far to find a quiet place to lay your head, and food options along the strip are plentiful. The key intersection here is Station Road and Main Street. Here sits the historic Red Lion pub and restaurant where the "Golf Club of Ayrshire" was formed in 1851 and where the idea for an Open championship was hatched in 1860. This is a "must" stop for golfers. The big, handsome rooms of the Red Lion are warmly inviting and the food service is down-home delicious.

Station Road takes us to the rail depot, Prestwick Golf Club, and a more peaceful precinct. About 200 yards along that road, on the right, *The Hollies* (01292-473-514) is a welcome addition to Prestwick lodging. Big enough to comfortably lodge a group of eight golfers, The Hollies is a classy house with plenty of history and character. Past the rail bridge, about 200 yards from Prestwick's first tee, Alison and Neil Ferguson's four-star *Golf View* (01292-671-234; ***www.golfviewhotel.com***) is a highly-recommended guesthouse. Still farther along, one block off Links Road on the seafront, we come to the *Parkstone Hotel* (01292-477-286; ***www.parkstonehotel.co.uk***), a full-service hostelry with eleven single rooms (highly unusual!) and excellent food service in an attractive restaurant/bar.

Back on Main Street a remarkable array of restaurants and watering holes awaits visitors and locals alike. From tapas (Caprice) to tandoori (Taj), from traditional (The Bank) to *chic moderne* (Elliots), from lasagna (La Porovia) to libations and bar food (The Golf Inn), Prestwick has something for every palate. Taken together—lodging, food, transportation, and proximity to courses—these attributes make Prestwick an excellent base for golf travel along the Ayrshire coast.

See also: Royal Troon for more lodging and nongolf notes

52. Royal Aberdeen Golf Club (1780) - Balgownie Course

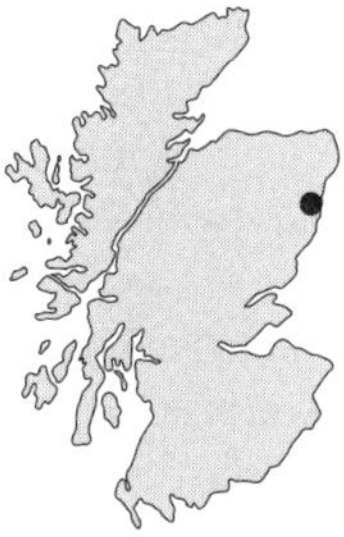

Region #: 5 **Category:** seaside links
Architect(s): Willie Park, Sr., Robert Simpson, others
Length: 6104-6415 **SSS:** 70 **Par:** 71

Address: Balgownie, Bridge of Don, Aberdeen AB23 8AT
Directions: 1st light N of Bridge of Don on A92; signposted at Links Rd
Reservations phone: 01224-702-571 **Fax:** 01224-826-591

Email: admin@royalaberdeengolf.com **Website:** royalaberdeengolf.com
Booking Contacts: Sandra Nicolson, Shona Milne

Dir of Golf: Ronnie MacAskill
Phone - Starter/Pro shop: 01224-702-571
Fee(s) (2012): wkday £120, day tkt £170; wkend £120; reduced in Apr & Oct
Deposit (2012): 25%; bal 1 month prior **Buggies:** no
Visitor Policies: wkday 10-11:30 am, 2-3:30 pm; wkend after 3:30 pm
Other: limited pullcarts & caddies; hdcp - men/women 24; the Silverburn - 18-hole companion course (4021 yds), par 64

DRIVE TIME
Glasgow Airport: 3 hrs, 45+ min
Gullane: 3 hrs, 30 min
Inverness: 2 hrs, 30 min
Carnoustie: 2 hrs

SINCE HOSTING THE SENIOR BRITISH OPEN in 2005 (won by Tom Watson) and the Walker Cup in 2011, Royal Aberdeen's stock has risen in the eyes of visiting golfers. This is a great course and, if it were located in Scotland's central belt of population, it would be as well-traveled as Carnoustie, Troon, and Scotland's other "rota" courses outside St. Andrews.

So it's just a matter of location, location, location. Scotland's northeast corner is a bit off the beaten path, but the wise traveler who finds it will uncover all the best the country has to offer: a vibrant city, castles, country house hotels, whisky distilleries, fishing villages, mountains, rich pastureland, and outstanding golf courses, both seaside and inland. It's no accident that this is the part of Scotland where Britain's royal family likes to hang out (i.e., at Balmoral Castle in the Dee Valley). They've been coming here for well over a century.

Nor is it an accident that Royal Aberdeen and the great course at Cruden Bay are often considered in tandem. Only thirty miles apart, their moonscape terrains are cut of the same coastal cloth patterned by towering dunes and rumpled fairways in such extreme that they form a pair nearly unique in Scottish golf. Readers of *Golf World* ranked these two courses sixth (Cruden Bay) and seventh (Royal Aberdeen) in a "Best Courses" poll a few years ago. My guess is that they would rank even closer to the top if more golfers made the trek northward. Now, with the addition of the links at Trump International and the discovery of Murcar, the "hidden gem" next door to

Golf writers, in virtual unanimity, acclaim the first nine among the finest in the country.

Royal Aberdeen, the likelihood is that the stock of the entire northeast will rise along with that of Royal Aberdeen.

Despite its relatively short length (the medal tees stretch only to 6600 yards), the Balgownie is one tough customer. Golf writers, in virtual unanimity, acclaim the first nine among the finest in the country. Part of this acclaim derives from the first three holes that combine a 410-yard opener with a 530-yard par 5 and a 223-yard par 3—no "warm-up" typical of Scottish golf here! These are monsters that can wreck a scorecard before you know what hit you. A little farther along, the brutal 453-yard ninth hole, doglegging to the right as it falls off to the left, achieves star status: David Hamilton (*Scottish Golf Guide*) places it among the best holes in Scotland. In comparison, the inward nine may disappoint a bit but, played into the customary wind off the North Sea, it's no pushover even though 300 yards shorter.

A little history: One of the seven "royal" clubs of Scotland, Aberdeen Golf Club received its designation in 1903 when King Edward VII agreed to become Patron of the Club. Such was the momentary culmination of a proud history that began officially in 1780 but clearly stretched back to the middle of the sixteenth century when some form of golf developed along Scotland's eastern seaboard. In short, when the Society of Aberdeen Golfers formed in 1780 it became Scotland's sixth oldest golf club, joining the distinguished company of clubs that played at Leith, Edinburgh, Musselburgh, and St. Andrews.

In 1903, the Royal Aberdeen Golf Club had been at its current Balgownie location, about a mile north of Aberdeen, only since 1888. Prior to golf's explosion of popularity and standardization in the late 1800s, the club had played its golf along the linksland nearer town between the Rivers Don and Dee. Balgownie was just a suburban jump away to the north side of the Don and, there, several golf architects from Carnoustie's Simpson family had the principal hand in creating one of Scotland's finest. Though Willie Park, Sr., was involved early on, it is Robert Simpson who is generally given credit for the Balgownie Course.

Royal Aberdeen's splendid clubhouse is one of the woodiest in Scottish golf. It's another one of those overlooking the first tee and eighteenth green, thus providing continual entertainment for members and guests within. A priceless collection of golf memorabilia is housed within.

Nongolf notes and lodging: With a population of about 225,000, Aberdeen is Scotland's third largest city; its moniker is "the Granite City." Massive, gray stone buildings dominate the central part of town giving the place a stoic façade. But, beneath the gray aesthetics of Aberdeen lies Scotland's most dynamic city, driven by its university and North Sea oil. Take a look at downtown Aberdeen and you'll see the High Street crawling with shoppers on a mission. As a university town, all the modernity, promise, and energy of youth infuses the city. If Edinburgh is Scotland's history book and Glasgow is its warehouse, then Aberdeen is Scotland's "E-commerce" window on the future. It's an exciting little city with a personality all its own. For more

If Edinburgh is Scotland's history book and Glasgow is its warehouse, then Aberdeen is Scotland's "E-commerce" window on the future.

information, see ***www.aberdeencityandshire.com***.

Aberdeen presents a bit of a lodging challenge for golfers. Most of the golf to be played is north of the city, while the best lodging is south and west of the city. This state of affairs is complicated by the difficulty of getting through the city on the traffic-choked A90—the main north-south thoroughfare. Plans for a by-pass around Aberdeen have been on board for at least a decade. Once promised by 2012, Aberdonians and their visitors will be lucky if they see it before by 2015.

Long a staple among Scotland's great "golf hotels," the Udny Arms in Newburgh is strategically located midway between Royal Aberdeen and Cruden Bay.

In the meantime, popular on high-end golf trips are the baronial *Mercure Ardoe House* (01224-860-600; ***www.mercure.com***) and the five-star *Marcliffe at Pitfodels* (01224-861-000; ***www.marcliffe.com***). More reasonably-priced and more centrally located on Kings Gate near the A90 is the *Atholl Hotel* (01224-323-505; ***www.atholl-aberdeen.co.uk***). This is a handsome, thirty-four-room, family-run hotel offering good value for money, especially at weekends when rates are reduced.

On the north side of town, strictly utilitarian but well located near Royal Aberdeen and Murcar golf courses, are a *Holiday Inn* (0870-400-9046) and a *Premier Travel Inn* (08701-977-012). Another solution is to seek the countryside. Midway between Aberdeen and Cruden Bay, at the village of Newburgh is the *Udny Arms* (01358-789-444; ***www.udny.co.uk***), a long-time "golf hotel" popular on many mid-price tours. And, if you're looking for a true "hidden gem," the Udny Arms backs up on the town's eighteen-hole, gorse-laden course, Newburgh on Ythan. Finally, if the idea of a farmhouse retreat appeals, you'll find *Savock B & B* one mile south of Foveran village off the A90. This four-star property is the home of Pat and George Booth (01358-789-602; ***www.aboutscotland.com/aberdeen/savock.html***). Theoretically, the Trump development not far from Newburgh will add a surfeit of high-end lodging to this mix—but don't hold your breath; my guess is that won't come any sooner than the Aberdeen by-pass.

See also: Cruden Bay, Murcar, Trump International

53. Royal Dornoch Golf Club (1877)

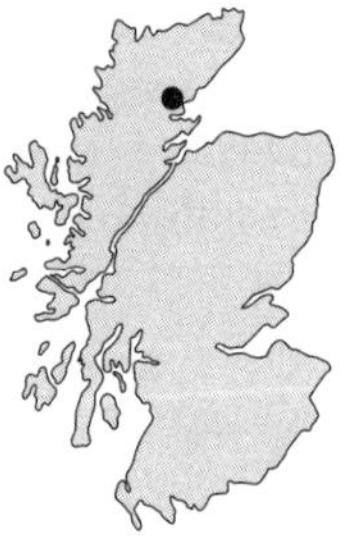

Region #: 5 **Category:** seaside links
Architect(s): Tom Morris (1891), Donald Ross (1900), John Sutherland & J.H.Taylor - various yrs; George Duncan (holes 7-11)
Length: 6222-6595 **SSS:** 71-73 **Par:** 70

Address: Golf Rd, Dornoch IV25 3LW
Directions: 45 mi N of Inverness on A9; rt on A949; rt at town square, left to clubhouse
Reservations phone: 01862-810-219 **Fax:** 01862-810-792

Email: bookings@royaldornoch.com **Website:** royaldornoch.com
Booking Contact(s): Donna Sutherland, Claire Riddell, Audrey Turner

Secretary: Neil Hampton **Professional:** Andrew Skinner
Phone - Starter/Pro shop: 01862-810-902
Fee(s) (2012): M-F, £100, day tkt £160; wkend £110; day tkt £175; combo tkt w/ Struie £100 wkday & £120 wkend (may be played over 2 consecutive days); reduced rates Apr & Oct
Deposit (2012): £40
Visitor Policies: all wk; Sat after 2 pm **Buggies:** 4- med/phys
Other: hdcps - men 24, women 35; companion csourse - Struie (5727-6192 yds) designed by Donald Steel

IN 1886, WHEN OLD TOM MORRIS came up to Dornoch to help John Sutherland and friends lay out "nine proper golf holes" and plan nine more, he is said to have remarked, "The a'mighty had gowf in his eye when he made this ground." Of course, Tom Morris—not only the father of modern golf, but golf's greatest diplomat—said something like that about every course he planned. At Dornoch, there's every reason to think Morris meant exactly what he said. I am personally convinced that, when Morris saw this ground, he saw an opportunity to create the most difficult classic links course in his repertoire—classic in its "out and back" setup; difficult in its elevation changes, its natural sitings for greens, and its susceptibility to every trick in the Morris bag.

Despite a host of alterations in ensuing years—first by Donald Ross in 1900, by John Sutherland over a long stretch of years, then by George Duncan in the 1940s—Dornoch is through and through a Morrisonian course, for its successive architects were decided followers of Morris. Dornoch native Donald Ross even went to St. Andrews to work with Tom Morris before returning to Dornoch to serve for a few years as its first professional and greenkeeper. Ultimately, of course, he emigrated to the United States where he became the most prolific golf course architect of the twentieth century. He returned to Dornoch in 1900 only to lengthen the course in response to introduction of the rubber-cored golf ball.

Thus, the hallmarks of Dornoch stand as a collective monument to Tom Morris and his disciples: large, heavily-contoured, shaved greens sitting on plateaus; bunkers by the dozens; green-fronting swales; elevated teeing grounds; a few blind shots; tight driving areas often to aslant fairways. Natural phenomena add further difficulty to Dornoch: first, the wind, then the acres of ball-eating gorse. The net result: stroke for stroke, in my view, one of the two or three most difficult courses in Scotland. Also, one of the most beautiful. Indeed, in May and early June, at the elevated third, fourth, and fifth tees, set amidst thick banks of gorse in full yellow bloom stretching down the entire left side of the course, this is among the most breathtaking seaside vistas in all of Scotland.

Golf was played at Dornoch long before the nineteenth century. Public records dating to 1616 give Dornoch status as the third oldest locus of golf after St. Andrews and Leith (Edinburgh). True or not, the historical record is significant as an indicator that, by the seventeenth century, golf had secured a certain hold on Scotland over the entire length of the eastern seaboard—even in the most remote parts of the country.

A cloudy day on the first tee at Dornoch.

After organizing as a club in 1877, Dornoch came into its own at the turn of the century, partly as a result of the area's association with Andrew Carnegie—CEO of U.S. Steel and library-builder nonpareil. Born in Dumfermline in Fife, Carnegie never left his Scottish roots entirely behind. He built Skibo Castle in the northern Highlands outside of Dornoch, and he learned to play golf on a course built for him there. In 1901 he presented the Dornoch Golf Club with a silver shield as reward to the winner of a tournament held annually ever since during August. In 1903, the railway reached Dornoch, enabling vacationers to make an overnight journey from London to the far reaches of the northern Highlands. In 1906, Dornoch received its "royal" designation from King Edward VII via the patronage of the Duchess of Sutherland. In 1909, Carnegie paid for a clubhouse at the newly-christened "Royal Dornoch."

Despite this flurry of attention, throughout most of the twentieth century Royal Dornoch remained largely unvisited by the international community of golf travelers. It was simply too far north—at least until 1985. That was the year new bridges spanning the Cromarty Firth and Dornoch Firth cut driving time from Inverness by about one hour. Suddenly, Dornoch became more accessible. Tom Watson and Ben Crenshaw came to Dornoch and went away raving (having left behind quotable tidbits). Then, adding fuel to the fire, golf writer Lorne Rubenstein's hymn to Dornoch, *A Season in Dornoch*, published in 2001, brought still more pilgrims to catch a glimpse of what Rubenstein and his wife experienced over a summer in this magical place. The upshot: these days Dornoch is one popular place to play golf.

If you can play good golf at Dornoch, you can play good golf anywhere. Leave some extra time. It's a course to play more than once.

I've expended more ink here on the history of Dornoch than on the course itself. But here's the bottom line: if you can play good golf at Dornoch, you can play good golf anywhere. Leave some extra time. It's a course to play more than once.

Nongolf notes and lodging - Dornoch/Tain: If Royal Dornoch is the only northern golf course on your itinerary and your time is short, your preferred base may be Inverness or Nairn. On the other hand, if one can linger awhile in the northern Highlands above Inverness, a logical base is the Dornoch/Tain area. There's plenty of golf to be played and, from here, one can explore the coast all the way up to John O' Groats—Scotland's "land's end"—and the interior of Sutherland, Caithness, and Easter Ross.

The best deal in Tain—the four-star Golf View B & B overlooks Tain Golf Club.

After being out of commission for several years, Dornoch's four-star, twenty-two room *Royal Golf Hotel* (01862-810-283; ***www.royalgolfhoteldornoch.co.uk***) is back in business. From its location behind Dornoch's clubhouse, you can practically roll out of bed to land on the first tee. On the main street is the historic, twenty-four room *Dornoch Castle Hotel* (01862-810-216; ***www.dornochcastlehotel.com***). Small groups (up to four) are well served at Isla Fullerton-Smith's *Highfield House* (01862-810-909; ***www.highfieldhouse.co.uk***) and Marelle Mackay and Ed Sierra's *Amalfi B & B* (01862-810-015; ***www.amalfidornoch.com***). Expat Ed Sierra is also known as a first-rate caddy at the golf club. Larger groups (up to eight) can lodge comfortably at Paul and Irene Hart's five-room *Bank House* (01862-811-717; ***www.dornochbankhouse.com***). For more choices see the golf club's website, ***www.royaldornoch.com*** and ***www.visitdornoch.com***

Nearby Tain is home to the world-famous Glenmorangie Distillery and several good hotels. The *Morangie House* (01862-892-281; ***www.morangiehotel.com***) is a Victorian gem complete with woody bar and attractive dining room. Under the same ownership is the equally atmospheric *Mansfield Castle Hotel* (01862-892-052; ***www.mansfieldcastle.co.uk***). On the south side of the A9, in 2005 Derek and Heather Wynne launched the *Carnegie Lodge Hotel* (01862-894-871; ***www.carnegiehotel.co.uk***). The draw here is owner hospitality in a first-rate dining room and a golf-themed bar. Rooms are plain but functional-modern. My favorite B & B in Tain is Bill and Sue MacDougal's four-star *Golf View House* (01862-892-856; ***www.golf-view.co.uk***). Set on two acres of land on a bluff overlooking Tain Golf Club, it's the best deal in town.

See also: Brora, Golspie, Tain

54. Royal Musselburgh Golf Club (1774) and The Old Links at Musselburgh

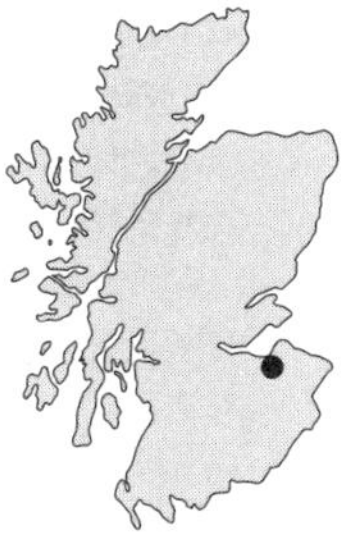

Region #: 3 **Category:** parkland
Architect(s): James Braid (1926), Mungo Park (1939)
Length: 6237 **SSS:** 70 **Par:** 70

Address: Prestongrange House, Prestonpans EH32 9RP
Directions: W of Prestonpans off A198
Reservations phone: 01875-810-276 **Fax:** same

Email: royalmusselburgh@btinternet.com **Website:** royalmusselburgh.co.uk
Booking Contact(s): administrator

Professional: John Henderson
Phone - Starter/Pro shop: 01875-810-139
Fee(s) (2012): wkday £38, day tkt £48; wkend £45, no day tkt
Deposit (2012): £10
Visitor Policies: wkdays except Fri pm **Buggies: 5 -** general hire
Other: no credit cards

SITUATED BETWEEN MUSSELBURGH and Prestonpans on the estate of the Barons of Prestoungrange, Royal Musselburgh (pronounced muscle-bruh) is drop-dead gorgeous—a tree-lined beauty sporting a collection of imaginative holes designed by James Braid in the 1920s with his usual emphasis on long par 4s, a mix of par 3s, and a de-emphasis on round-saving par 5s. Even though near the sea (and with occasional views out to the Firth), Royal Musselburgh is played on parkland turf reminiscent of Belleisle at Ayr (another Braid course). This is one of Scotland's prettiest parkland courses. The clubhouse of the RMGC—also one of the finest in Scottish golf—is housed in a mansion the Barons of Prestoungrange occupied from the sixteenth century to the early twentieth century.

Of course there's far more to the Musselburgh story than its present verdant location. Toward the sea, not far from the RMGC lie the Old Links of Musselburgh, These two courses shall be forever intertwined in golf history, for it was at the Old Links that some kind of golf took root in Scotland as early as the 1400s. The original course at Musselburgh was a seven-hole affair. An eighth hole was added in 1832 and a ninth followed in 1870. Since then the routing has remained essentially unchanged, though re-sequencing moved the former par-three closing hole to today's opening hole. The course comprises three par 3s, five par 4s, and one par 5.

Royal Musselburgh was the last of four major clubs to vacate the Old Links in favor of more expansive digs. The others were the Honourable Company of Edinburgh Golfers (Muirfield), Royal Burgess Golf Club, and the Bruntsfield Golfing Society. Between 1868 and 1889 this ground was the site of six British Opens. And, when the last Open was played at Musselburgh in 1889, a chapter in the history of golf closed.

To get a great golf trip underway in East Lothian, I recommend an opening round on the Old Links. For this is not only the most historic ground in golf but the most unusual site as well—since 1816, the course has shared common ground with a 3.5-mile horse racetrack! The course plays inside and over the racetrack, and the grass track and railings made of pvc pipe are in play. Horse races in the UK are run clockwise while the golf course plays in anti-clockwise rotation—fortunately, not at the same time.

An additional attraction at Musselburgh: The course can be played with hickory sticks. I tried this once. To say the least, it was challenging. I was issued a driving club, a mid-iron, and a putter. With these three clubs my goal was to negotiate the course in something like fifty strokes. Somehow I did it. But it wasn't easy and the driver felt like a ball and hammer in my hands. The trick was to swing slowly and let the weight of the clubs work whatever magic they had left in them. It was a good experience that made me appreciate not only modern clubmaking technology but the ability of our golfing ancestors to play the hands they were dealt.

Of note, an £11 million proposal by the racetrack management to build a floodlit all-weather track (that would have neutered the Old Links) was vetoed by the national Scottish Executive in September 2007 (after having been approved by the local council). The very existence of the Old Links has always been susceptible to public and private pressures because this is simply not a great golf course, nine-hole or otherwise. Yet, at least three of the nine holes at the Old Links are truly memorable and completely challenging (#s 4, 8, and 9) and that's not bad for an old codger. This is where the diameter of the golf hole was established (four and one-quarter inch); and this was the home course of five Open champions—Willie Park, Sr. and Jr., Bob Ferguson, David Brown, and Mungo Park. Allowing the Old Links to disappear would be tragic. Instead, putting an end to the persistent threats to its existence, the course should be made a national heritage site. For more information about the Old Links at Musselburgh, see ***www. musselburgholdlinks.co.uk*** (ph/fax: 0131-665-5438).

"Mrs. Forman's" pub, where for centuries golfers paused for a pint slipped through a trap door in the wall behind the fourth green of the Old Links.

So, when discussing Royal Musselburgh, golf fans, we are talking history. We're talking about a golf club formed two years before the issuance of the Declaration of Independence, housed in a sixteenth-century mansion, with a history of play on ground dedicated to golf since the time of Columbus. For all these reasons, I encourage my clients to make a day of the courses at Musselburgh with a nine-holer on the Old Links in the morning, followed by lunch at the Royal Musselburgh clubhouse, before an afternoon round on Braid's twentieth-century creation. This combination makes for an unforgettable day of Scottish golf.

55. Royal Troon (1878) - Old Course

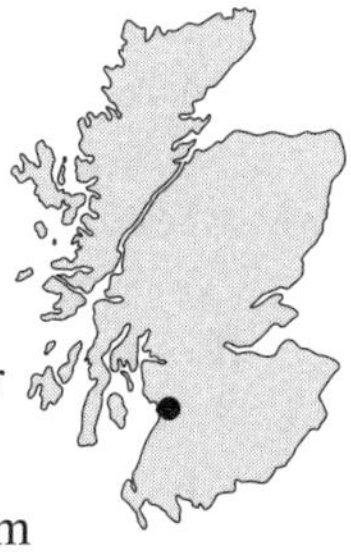

Region #: 2 **Category:** seaside links
Architect(s): Willie Fernie (1888)
Length: 6201-6641-7175 SSS: 71-75 **Par:** 71

Address: Craigend Rd., Troon, Ayrshire KA10 6EP
Directions: terminus of B749 at corner of Craigend and Bentinck Dr
Reservations/starter: 01292-311-555 **Fax:** 01292-318-204

Email: bookings@royaltroon.com **Website:** royaltroon.com
Booking Contact(s): Peter Mackie

Professional: Kieron Stevenson
Fee(s) (2012): £175 (includes optional play on Portland Course)
Deposit (2012): 50% within 21 days; balance 60 days before play
Visitor Policies: mid-April thru mid-Oct: M, T, Th only, 9-10:30 am & 2:30-4 pm; no jrs under 16 on Old Course
Buggies: 2 - med/phys; must hire driver
Other: hdcp - men 20, women 30; companion course, Portland (6102-6289 yds)

DRIVE TIME
Turnberry: 35 min
Carnoustie: 3 hrs
St. Andrews: 2 hrs, 45 min
North Berwick: 2 hrs, 30 min

RARELY DO WE HAVE THE CHANCE to laud a golf club for lowering green fees, but that's exactly what happened in 2009 to the great credit of Royal Troon. Prior to that date the club required visitors to pay for lunch and two golf courses, whether or not the second (Portland) was played. For this questionable policy, visitors were charged £220—the most expensive tab in Scottish golf. Visitors started staying away in droves.

Then, with the departure of a certain club secretary who mercifully shall go unnamed, all that changed. The green fee for Old Course play was reduced and the Portland was thrown in as an option at no additional cost. Lunch was made optional as well. For golfers who want to make a day of it, this arrangement offers a certain kind of Nirvana—a perfect day in a perfect place at a now more reasonable price. The setting is superb; the championship course is excellent; the Portland is good; the clubhouse is grand; the staff is first-rate.

Royal Troon's comfortable lounge capped a £5 million renovation and extension of its magnificent clubhouse—visitors welcome Monday, Tuesday, and Thursday.

Other salutary changes have brought Royal Troon emphatically into the twenty-first century. In 2003 women with a handicap of thirty or below were allowed to play the Old Course for the first time. In 2008 the club completed a £5 million extension of its magnificent clubhouse, and a new team of young professionals was hired and moved into a spiffy new pro shop.

Royal Troon is a great golf experience and, because visitors are accepted on only three weekdays, a tee time at Troon can be difficult to get in high season. In this regard, two important notes: First, unlike St. Andrews and Carnoustie, Troon will advance-book a single golfer. Second, if a date is booked up, it's a good idea to go onto the "waitlist" with the hope of a cancellation. Because full payment is not required until sixty days before play, Troon is the target of some speculative booking by tour operators; thus, cancellations occur as deadlines for payment come and go.

Royal Troon is a classic links course—out and back, anti-clockwise, first along a gently-curving bay; then, after meandering a bit at the turn, back to the clubhouse on an inland track. In this respect, among Scotland's Open courses, Troon is most similar to St. Andrews' Old Course. The course is essentially the work of Open champion Willie Fernie who came to Troon in 1888 to serve as club professional and to extend an existing small course to eighteen holes. The main changes since then have largely involved adding bunkers and lengthening the course to a 7175-yard championship stretch. Most visitors will play the course at a considerably easier 6200 yards. Single-digit handicappers may be allowed to play from the medal (white) tees at 6641 yards.

The topography at Troon lacks the dune-filled drama found on the linksland at places like Cruden Bay, Aberdeen, and Dornoch. Requisite humps and bumps and wispy beach grasses are ever-present, but the terrain is relatively flat. Troon's six opening holes and six closing holes march in a rather straight line away from and returning to the clubhouse. It's the inside six holes (#7 through #12) that give the course its character and reputation. These holes feature constant changes of direction, doglegs to left and right (four of the six), a straightaway par 4 at 438 yards (#10, "Sandhills"), and one of the most famous par 3s in the world ("Postage Stamp," #8)—all in all, six of the best holes you will play on your trip to Scotland. The homeward nine is nearly three hundred yards longer than the first nine and, into the wind, can make for a rather trying experience.

Troon is the youngest of Scotland's "royals" but not the youngest of its Open venues (that honor goes to Turnberry). The royal designation was granted by Queen Elizabeth II on the occasion of Troon's centenary celebration in 1978. Open championships have been held here since 1923. Troon was the logical west coast heir to Prestwick's place in the Open rota. Indeed, as at all the Open venues, the quality of Royal Troon's challenge is reflected in its parade of champions. South African Bobby Locke won here in 1950. Since then, it's been an all-American parade: Palmer ('62), Weiskopf ('73), Watson ('82), Calcavecchia ('89), Leonard ('97), and Hamilton ('04). Look for the Open to return to Troon soon after 2015.

Nongolf notes and lodging: Troon is an ideal base for enjoying golf along the Ayrshire coast. The courses at Barassie, Gailes, and Irvine lie a few miles to the north. Prestwick and Ayr are the next towns south. Troon boasts three municipal golf courses, two of them comparable to Royal Troon's Portland (the Darley and Lochgreen). Most important, there's a relaxed, inviting air about Troon that you don't find on the busy streets of its larger neighbors. The town is big enough to support a variety of shops and restaurants. There's easy access to the beaches and to a harbor where P & O ferries make two daily runs between Troon and Larne, Northern Ireland, about thirty-five miles north of Belfast. Thus, Troon can be a base for golf combining Scotland and Ireland (see ***www.poferries.com***). Troon harbor is also home to the Kintyre Express (01294-270-160; ***www.kintyreexpress.com***), a charter speedboat service specializing in day trips to the Kintyre peninsula.

B & B/guest house options in Troon are low in quantity but high in quality. A popular choice about four hundred yards from the first tee at Troon is Norma McLardy's *Copper Beech* at 116 Bentinck Dr. (01292-314-100; ***www.copperbeech.freeservers.com***). The setting here is Tudor elegance. Another good choice on the edge of town overlooking the Portland course is the classy *Sandhill House* (01292-311-801; ***www.sandhillhouse.com***).

While short on B & Bs, Troon is well served by hotels of varying size and distinction. In the middlin' category, one of the most popular golf hotels on the Ayrshire coast is the *South Beach Hotel* (01292-312-033, ***www.southbeach.co.uk***) about one-half mile from Royal Troon. The superior doubles here are spacious and reasonably-priced for such an auspicious location. The classic *Anchorage Hotel* (01292-317-448; ***www.anchoragehoteltroon.co.uk***) is a three-star choice with history as a coaching inn on Troon harbor. Its woody pub with a touch of sports bar about it is popular with locals—always a good sign.

The South Beach Hotel in Troon—one of Scotland's unique 3-star "golf hotels."

Moving up the price scale, the massive *Marine Hotel* (01292-314-444; ***www.barceló-hotels.co.uk***) overlooking the eighteenth fairway at Royal Troon is a famous golf hotel in vintage comparable to Rusacks in St. Andrews and the Marine at North Berwick. Catty-corner from the Marine is the *Piersland House Hotel* (01292-314-747; ***www.piersland.co.uk***), ancestral manse of the Johnnie Walker (whisky) estate. Two sister establishments in the country-house category are *Lochgreen House* (01292-313-343) and *Highgrove House* (01292-312-511), owned and operated by master chef Bill Costley (***www.costley-hotels.co.uk***). The Lochgreen House is on the B749 about a mile from Royal Troon. Highgrove House is a few miles east on the A759 at the "Loans" crossroads. Both hotels feature comfort in small-scale surroundings and "Four-Rosette" dining (the best). In the same category, outside town off the A77, is the award-winning *Enterkine Country House* (01292-520-580; ***www.enterkine.com***). All these lodgings are superb in their own way and give Troon an unmistakable ambience of class and quality.

See also: Dundonald, Glasgow Gailes, Irvine, Kilmarnock, Prestwick, Western Gailes, West Kilbride

The Courses at St. Andrews
56. The Old Course *

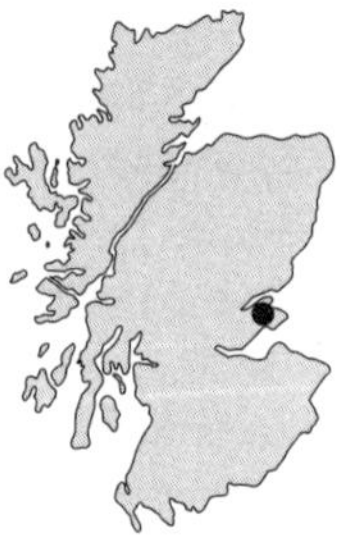

Region #: 1 **Category:** seaside links
Architect(s): evolution, Tom Morris
Length: 6566 **SSS:** 72 **Par:** 72

Address: St. Andrews Links Trust, St. Andrews KY16 9SF
Directions: A91 to St. Andrews; 2nd left at Golf Pl
Reservations phone: 01334-466-666 **Fax:** 01334-477-036

Email: reservations@standrews.org.uk
Website: standrews.org.uk
Booking Contact(s): Advance Reservations Office; apply on or after 1st Wed in Sept for advance booking in the ensuing year

Fee(s) (2012): £150; 20% VAT on 3rd-party bookings (tour operators)
Deposit (2012): 100% non-refundable prepay
Visitor Policies: closed Sun (see Part II, Chapter 2, for more detail)
Buggies: none
Other: no trolleys in am; hdps men - 24, women 36

DRIVE TIME
Edinburgh Airport: 1 hr, 10 min
Glasgow Airport - 2 hrs, 15 min
Carnoustie: 40 min
Gullane (Muirfield): 1 hr, 45 min

SO MANY THOUSANDS OF DESCRIPTIVE words have been written about this storied, historic course there is no good reason for me to add to the word count. Most of what I have to say of a practical nature is in Part II, Chapter Two. All I want to add here is that, when people ask me, "Allan, what are your favorite courses?", I always start by saying, "First, the Old Course is in a class by itself." I really believe that. The moonscape setting, the huge double greens, the monstrous bunkers, and the grand scale of the Old Course are enough to distinguish it from all others. Layered on top of all that is the weight of history. And there's still another factor I find equally compelling about the Old Course: On no other course do I get such a clear appreciation for the interplay of skill and fate. Lady Luck plays a huge role here—for good and ill, just as in life. And, to me, that's why every golfer should play the Old Course at least once. It will keep you humble and appreciative of life (and of Tiger Woods).

A goal of every serious golfer—the 1st tee and 18th green at St. Andrews' Old Course.

57, 58, 59. St. Andrews - New, Jubilee, Castle

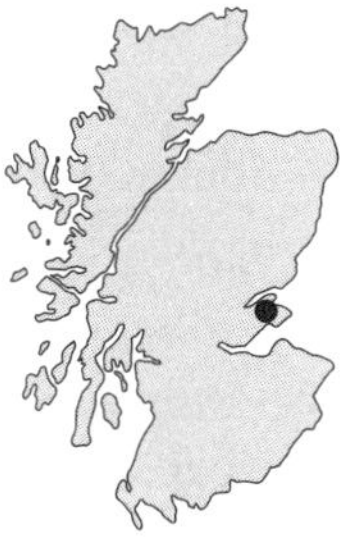

Region #: 1 **Category:** seaside links
Architect(s): New - Tom Morris (1895); Jubilee - various incl Willie Auchterlonie (1936-48), Donald Steel (1988-9), and Martin Hawtree (2011); Castle - David McLay Kidd (2008)
Length: New 6362-6625, Jubilee 6424-6742, Castle 5460-6759
SSS: New 72-73, Jubilee 71-73, Castle 72-74
Par: New 71, Jubilee 72, Castle 71

Address: St. Andrews Links Trust, Pilmour House, St. Andrews KY16 9SF
Directions: A91 to St. Andrews; 2nd left at Golf Pl; Castle course 3 mi S of town on A917
Reservations phone: 01334-466-666 **Fax:** 01334-479-555

Email: reservations@standrews.org.uk **Website:** standrews.org.uk
Key Contact(s): Advance Reservations Office

Fee(s) (2012): New £70, Jubilee £70, Castle £120; 20% VAT on 3rd-party bookings
Deposit (2012): 100% prepayment
Visitor Policies: all wk
Buggies: New Course - 2 - med/ phys and seniors (men 65+, ladies 60+)

ST. ANDREWS' NEW AND JUBILEE courses sit side by side and are often considered in tandem, as I am doing here (The Castle Course follows). These are the two courses most golfers weigh when looking for play on another St. Andrews course. They are less expensive than the Castle Course and they are in town; the Castle is three miles southeast of town.

Considering the New and Jubilee, invariably the question arises, "Which course is better?". Ask that question of twelve St. Andrews golfers and you'll likely get "six of one, half dozen of the other." At 6800 yards from the white tees, the Jubilee is the longer of the two and is often cited as, "the toughest course in St. Andrews." The New Course, not much changed since it was laid out by Tom Morris in 1895, is considered the natural heir to Old Course tradition. Apropos to that, the New Course lies next to the Old Course while the Jubilee occupies a strip of land between the New Course and the sea.

Play on the New and Jubilee begins at the attractive Links Clubhouse overlooking the second fairway of the Old Course. This is where visiting golfers will find parking and course facilities: a reception desk, locker rooms, bar, restaurant, gift shops, practice putting greens, plus the starter office and first tees for both the New and Jubilee. A panoramic view of the links can be gained from an observation deck atop the clubhouse.

In comparing the courses, similarities are more important than differences. Obviously, they play over similar terrain. Given its position, the Jubilee offers more ocean views but, since there is really no seriously high ground on the links at St. Andrews, this factor is negligible. Both courses are out-and-back classics. And, even in length, the 200-yard difference is insignificant when spread over eighteen holes. Both courses feature great banks of gorse that line the fairways and frame the greens. Both courses have an astounding number of bunkers filled with soft St. Andrews sand. Both have large, undulating greens and one double green. Indeed, the similarities indicate a toss-up.

"Which course is better?". Ask that question of twelve St. Andrews golfers and you'll likely get "six of one, half dozen of the other."

That much said, my own preference is for the New Course. Why? First, the New Course carries the indelible stamp of Old Tom Morris and thus sports a certain pedigree and integrity of design. The Jubilee first opened as a twelve-hole course for women and children in 1897 and has passed through several incarnations. Donald Steel brought championship length and wholesale redesign to the course in 1988-89 and, most recently (2010-11), Martin Hawtree carried out extensive work on the middle eight holes of the golf course. Consequently, the Jubilee has a more layered history than the New.

More important, land available to the two courses has had its effect. While the Jubilee is shaped like the sheath of a dagger, the New Course resembles the more graceful shape of a spoon. Five opening holes traverse the "handle" of the New Course, while three return to the clubhouse—all in a straight line. In the "bowl" of the spoon, Tom Morris exercised his imagination, creating ten varied holes with frequent changes of direction. In contrast, the Jubilee rather resembles a straightaway forced march out (seven holes), with a brief respite (six holes back and forth), before the return to the clubhouse. Some zig-zag routing increases the angles, but, overall, I much prefer the greater variety and grace of the New Course.

St. Andrews - The Castle Course (2008)

FROM THIS PERSPECTIVE, several years on from its opening in 2008, the jury is still out on Andrews' vaunted "seventh course" designed by David McLay Kidd and his associate Paul Kimber. As with McLay Kidd's project at Machrihanish Dunes, opinion is deeply divided and probably will remain divided for a long time to come.

In the meantime, we know the Castle is radically different than the other six courses at St. Andrews and we know David McLay Kidd can create controversy. The points of greatest controversy have been, first, Kidd's willy-nilly scattering of "Don King heads"—grassy mounds—in the middle of a number of fairways to penalize even the straightest of drives and, second, the most severely undulating greens anywhere in the wide, wide world of golf.

Both of these issues have been addressed by the powers that be. Many of the grassy mounds have been removed, recontoured, or mown; and several greens have been "softened" (I love that term) to mitigate the fun-house experience and/or create more pin positions on the greens. The Links Trust might have been justified in billing McLay Kidd for having to "fix" his course. On the other hand, golf courses take time to mature and evolve, and, as at Mach Dunes, this one too must be considered a work in progress. Check back in about one hundred years.

Some facts: In contrast to the natural terrain of the courses on the links at St. Andrews, the Castle Course was manufactured. Thousands of tons of dirt were moved and thousands more tons of sand were imported to create a faux dunescape on farm ground a mile southeast of town. Spectacular views look toward the picturesque town from land gently falling from high ground to a seaside escarpment. The course is seriously exposed to the elements. Artfully formed teeing grounds allow play from 5400 to 7200 yards. The Castle's greens depart from the subtlety characteristic of St. Andrews' other courses. Green depths average about forty yards; most are tiered or feature multiple humps and swales. At least one St Andrews tradition is upheld: a huge double green is shared by hole #s 9 and 18 near a brilliantly-designed circular clubhouse—a cliffside eyrie with stunning views to the sea.

There's a hole down there somewhere! Variously described as "fun house" greens or burial grounds for dinosaurs, several of the Castle greens have been "softened" since the course opened in 2008.

More detail: Rather than traditional out-and-back routing, the course spreads out over 220 acres with the ninth hole returning to the clubhouse. Maximum use is made of the Castle's cliffside setting; seven greens are sited on the cliff and five holes play along the imposing hazard. The sea is visible from every part of the course. The first nine is an easier walk on low ground; the second nine climbs to relatively higher ground. The five par 3s are superb; the diabolical "signature" hole (#17) plays across a ravine. Most tee shots on the par 4s and par 5s are semi-blind. Generous fairways tolerate some wayward driving but also reward the straight shooter. Rough is deep and penal. Burns front the greens at #4 and #15. Bunkering is of the ragged, natural sort.

One element I really like and one I really don't like: The designers have celebrated the hallmark of links golf—the running shot. Most of the greens are open in front, challenging the golfer to navigate around and over and through the hazardous landscape. That's fun. What I don't like has nothing to do with the oft-criticized fairway mounds and fun-house greens. It's the McLay Kidd "dunes" that, to me, look like something cooked up for Disneyland. For real dunes, go to Cruden Bay, Royal Aberdeen, or to almost any links course in Ireland, but don't come here. Compared to Kyle Phillips's faux dunes at Dundonald, these look kind of silly.

Finally, one more similarity to the McLay Kidd project at Machrihanish Dunes: If the golfer can come here with a sense of humor—just to enjoy the course without being too concerned about scoring—a good time can be had by all. For the mid-to-high handicapper this could even be a place to play off the forward tees. In short, pick the right tees, blast away, have fun, and then decide for yourself whether this course will stand the test of time.

See also: Part II, Chapter Two, for more detail on the courses at St. Andrews and Links Trust policies.

St. Andrews - Fairmont Hotel (2002)
60. The Torrance + 61. The Kittocks

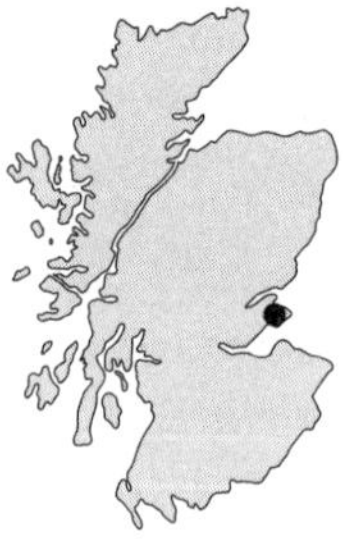

Region #: 1 **Category:** seaside "links-style"
Architect(s): Torrance - Sam Torrance, Gene Sarazen, Gary Stephenson (2009)
Kittocks - Denis Griffiths & Assocs, Bruce Devlin
Length: Torrance 5509-7230, Kittocks 5195-7049

SSS: Torrance 70-74, Kittocks 74 **Par:** both 72
Address: St. Andrews, Fife KY16 8 PN
Directions: 3 mi S of St. Andrews on the A917
Reservations phone: 01334-837-000 **Fax:** 01334-471-115

Email: standrews.scotland@fairmont.com
Website: fairmont.com/standrews
Booking Contact(s): Director of Golf: Jason King

Phone - Starter/Pro shop: 01334-837-023
Fee(s) (2012): Torrance - May-Sept M-Th non-resident £105, resident 80; Fri-Sun non-resident £125, resident £100; twilight discounts after 4 pm; reduced rates Apr & Oct; green fee and hotel discounts for tour operators
Deposit (2012): none
Visitor Policies: all wk
Buggies: Kittocks - 36 for general hire; Torrance - limited, med/phys

FAIRMONT ST. ANDREWS RECEIVED a big boost in 2008 from the Royal & Ancient Golf Club when the R & A named the Fairmont Torrance a qualifying course for the 2010 Open Championship in St. Andrews. In preparation for the event, significant redesign of all teeing grounds and eight holes on the Torrance made a good course better and spurred a new level of interest in golf at the Fairmont.

The Torrance and Kittocks are the main attractions at this monumental, 209-room hotel developed near St. Andrews in 2002-03 by the American-owned Château Elán group led by Donald Panoz, inventor of the Nicotine Patch. Christened the St. Andrews Bay Golf Resort and Spa, the development was built with intent to join Turnberry, Gleneagles, and the Old Course Hotel on the short list of Scotland's five-star international golf resorts.

After five years of ho-hum acceptance from the golf community, St. Andrews Bay was purchased by the high-flying Fairmont Hotels in 2007. After pumping £13 million or so into the hotel and the golf courses, Fairmont Hotels may yet realize the promise of this location on 520 acres of rolling, high ground three miles south of St. Andrews on the coastal route (A917).

As one might expect, Fairmont St. Andrews is fully outfitted for conspicuous consumption, from five restaurants to at least as many "anti-stress" therapies available at the hotel spa. In other words, if you want to go to Scotland but feel like you're on a luxury cruise, or maybe never left home, Fairmont St. Andrews may be the place for you. If you want to discover the real Scotland, I suggest you look elsewhere. The visiting golfer is best advised to lodge in St. Andrews or down on the Fife coast and use Fairmont St. Andrews as “filler” on an itinerary. These courses are good for (a) walk-on play; (b) weekends, when member clubs are not available; (c) Sunday, when the Old Course is closed; and (d) when you’re too pooped to pop and ready for a buggy on the Kittocks. Of special note: Given the quality of these courses, the twilight rates constitute a huge bargain in golf around St. Andrews.

Fairmont St. Andrews is fully outfitted for conspicuous consumption . . . . If you want to discover the real Scotland, I suggest you look elsewhere

The Torrance and Kittocks were built shortly after the successful project at nearby Kingsbarns, yet, here, green fees are little more than half the rate at Kingsbarns. With stunning views out to the North Sea and greater proximity to the skyline of St. Andrews, Fairmont St. Andrews has every bit the visual appeal of Kingsbarns. Both feature modern course design on similar ground. In short, if Kingsbarns seems a bit pricey, but you still want to play a modern “championship” course in Scotland, Fairmont St. Andrews offers two good alternatives.

At the same time, keep in mind that this is not links golf. Like St. Andrews’ Castle Course, the Fairmont courses sit well above the sea. They were carved out of old farm ground and were seeded with a grass mixture of thirty-five percent rye rather than the bents and fescues of traditional linksland. The ball sits up on these “American-style” or “links-style” fairways. On the Kittocks this is particularly evident and there’s barely a hummock or mogul to be found until we reach the tenth fairway. None of this is necessarily bad; it’s just a fact.

Finally, visitors should be aware that, like other destination resorts, Fairmont St. Andrews indulges in substantial discounts on bookings to tour operators. These are always described as “incentive discounts,” but that’s just fancy language for “steering” business to the hotel. So, when an operator extols the virtues of Fairmont St. Andrews, just ask yourself: What’s in it for him or her? Why should I want to stay at that hotel? Is that the best choice for me—on a hill three miles outside of town? And why should I play one of these courses when I could play one of the historic courses in Fife for half the price? In other words, be suspicious. Go to Fairmont St. Andrews for the right reasons—for golf at the right time on good modern courses—but don’t go because it is recommended by a tour operator.

62. St. Andrews - Old Course Hotel The Duke's Course (1995)

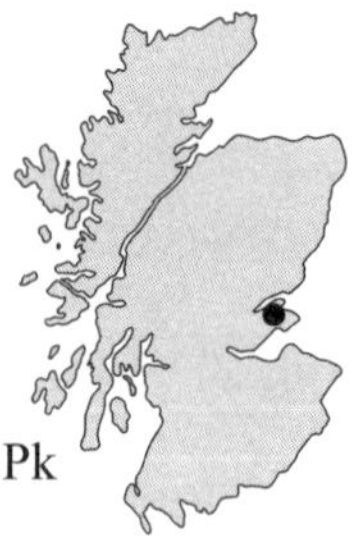

Region #: 1 **Category:** heathland
Architect(s): Peter Thomson (1995), Tim Liddy (2006)
Length: 6130-7512 **SSS:** 72-76 **Par:** 71

Address: Craigtoun, St. Andrews, Fife KY16 8NS
Directions: from town, Hepburn Gardens Rd 2 mi SW to Craigtoun Pk
Reservations phone: 01334-474-371 **Fax:** 01334-477-668

Email: reservations@oldcoursehotel.kohler.com
Website: oldcoursehotel.kohler.com
Professional: Ayden Roberts-Jones **Golf Manager:** David Scott

Phone - Starter/Pro shop: 01334-470-214
Fee(s) (2012): hotel residents - varying rates or incl in package rates - call hotel; nonresidents – April- mid May £75, mid-May-mid-Oct £115
Deposit (2012): none; 7-day cancellation **Buggies:** 30 - general hire
Visitor Policies: all wk
Other: green fee and hotel discounts for tour operators

AS IF ST. ANDREWS did not already offer an embarrassment of golf riches, in 1995 the five-star Old Course Hotel unveiled this gem by Peter Thomson, the celebrated Aussie who won the British Open five times between 1952 and 1965. In 2004 the hotel was acquired by Herb Kohler—he of bathroom fixture fame. Since then, extensive modifications have been carried out by Tim Liddy, an acolyte of Pete Dye. These have included new teeing grounds, complete re-bunkering, several new greens, and re-routing of hole #s 15-18.

Just two miles southwest of town, The Duke's occupies high ground affording excellent views over St. Andrews to the waters beyond and, on a clear day, off to Angus in the far distance. Usually billed as an alternative to links golf, the real beauty of The Duke's Course is that it is such a fine heathland course in proximity to links golf. It's a rare combination. So, yes, The Duke's serves as an alternative to the St. Andrews links, but it happens to be an outstanding golf course worthy of

Overlooking the famous "Road Hole," the Old Course Hotel owns and operates The Duke's Course on the outskirts of town. The hotel is not involved with management of St. Andrews' Old Course.

play in its own right. A lot of Brits think so too, as evidenced in various magazine polls ranking the Duke's "Best Parkland Course in the UK." High praise, indeed.

In expansiveness and length, The Duke's reminds us of Jack Nicklaus's PGA Centenary Course at Gleneagles. But that's about as far as the comparison goes, for Peter Thomson's idea of course design contrasted sharply with that of the Golden Bear. While Nicklaus never met a water hazard or forced carry he didn't like, Thomson eschewed both, giving the golfer every opportunity to play the game along the ground as well as in the air. This is not to say The Duke's is without challenge. With 121 bunkers and several "wee burns" to negotiate, along with punishing rough, there's plenty here to keep one's attention. Moreover, at 7512 yards from the championship tees, this is Scotland's longest inland course. Most male visitors will play the course at 6550 yards or even the next step down at 6130 yards. Five sets of tees at the Duke's make the course playable by golfers of every level of ability.

This is a good course to play on Sunday when the Old Course is closed. As a daily fee course it is easier to get on than many other courses in Fife.

Since lines of ownership in St. Andrews can be confusing, let me reiterate: The Duke's Course is owned and operated by the Old Course Hotel Golf Resort & Spa and is entirely independent of the St. Andrews Links Trust. Hotel residents receive priority treatment, but the course is rarely full up, so a visitor normally can secure a tee time with no problem. Another practical tip: this is a good course to play on Sunday when the Old Course is closed. As a daily fee course, it is easier to get on than many other courses in Fife.

The Jigger Inn, restaurant and pub, was preserved when the Old Course Hotel was built in 1968.

I am not keen on places like the Old Course Hotel, but there's no questioning the hotel's quality or its superb setting overlooking the #17 "Road Hole" on the Old Course. Room rates are breathtaking and vary wildly depending upon season, size, and location within the hotel. Tour operators and travel agents are granted substantial discounts at both the hotel and the golf course.

63. Scotscraig Golf Club (1817) +

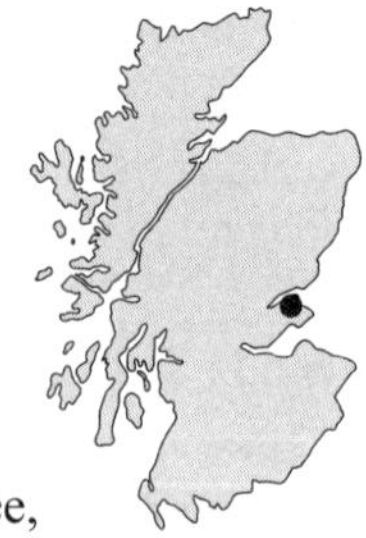

Region #: 1 **Category:** links/heathland hybrid
Architect(s): Tom Morris (1892), Robert Simpson (1904), James Braid (1923)
Length: 6310-6669 **SSS:** 72 **Par:** 71

Address: Golf Rd, Tayport, Fife DD6 9DZ
Directions: from Dundee, E at Tay Bridge roundabout to Tayport town center, left on Elizabeth St; from St Andrews, direction Dundee, then 3 mi on B945, rt on Elizabeth St
Reservations phone: 01382-552-515 **Fax:** 01382-553-130

Email: admin@scotscraiggolfclub.com **Website:** scotscraiggolfclub.com
Booking Contact(s): Alison Harvey
Secretary: Barry D Liddle **Professional:** Craig Mackie

Phone - Starter/Pro shop: 01382-552-855
Fee(s) (2012): wkday £56, day tkt £75; wkend £72 am, £62 pm, day tkt £100
Deposit (2012): £25 **Buggies:** 2 - general hire
Visitor Policies: M-F 9:30-11:28, 2:30-4:00; wkends call

SCOTSCRAIG IS AN OPEN QUALIFIER course that pulls rank as the thirteenth oldest golf club in the world. Despite its historic status and lineage that runs to members of the Royal and Ancient Golf Club, this congenial club often gets overlooked in Fife's flurry of golf flak. When booking a course outside St. Andrews, visitors often choose Crail, Kingsbarns, or the courses at Fairmont St. Andrews—all toward the southeast corner of Fife. Rarely do they consider driving ten miles north to Tayport on the Fife side of the Tay Bridge. That's their mistake.

> **PLANNING TIP**
> Schedule low-deposit Scotscraig as a "fallback course" when balloting for play on St. Andrews' Old Course. If successful at the Old Course, cancel or reschedule Scotscraig.

Tayport is a bedroom community for Dundee and a bit on the "other side of the tracks"—though in this case we're talking about the other side of the firth. No pretense here. Scotscraig is a solid, old-line golf club with a classic clubhouse. Nothing fancy on the course either.

Here, you'll experience a challenge some people judge as demanding as that at Carnoustie. The course is sensibly flat, an easy walk. It's a seaside links with splashes and dashes of heather and trees, most reminiscent of the land at Monifieth and Glasgow Gailes. The par 4 #4 "Westward Ho," played to a plateau green, will leave a lasting impression. Attractive, strategic bunkering reminds us this was a course crafted by Carnoustie professional Robert Simpson and, later, James Braid—plenty of pedigree and plenty of good golf. If not on my list of Scotland's top twenty links courses, it's close—in a group with other Open qualifiers like Barassie, Irvine, and Leven.

64. Shiskine Golf and Tennis Club (1896)

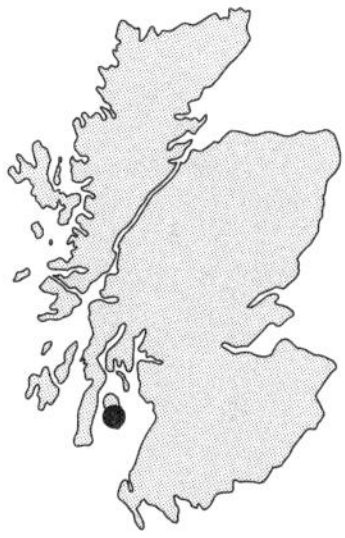

Region #: 8 **Category:** seaside links
Architect(s): Willie Fernie (1896), Willie Park, Jr. (1910)
Length: 2996 **SSS:** 41 **Par:** 42

Address: Shore Rd, Blackwaterfoot, Isle of Arran KA27 8HA
Directions: NW of village from either A841 coastal route or B880 "String Rd"
Reservations phone: 01770-860-226 **Fax:** 01770-860-205

Email: info@shiskinegolf.com **Website:** shiskinegolf.com
Secretary: Pietra Johnston **Professional:** Douglas Bell
Fee(s) (2012): wkday £20 (12 holes), 24 holes - £35; wkend £25 & 39

Deposit (2012): none **Buggies:** 4 - general hire
Visitor Policies: all wk; July - Aug all reservations one day in advance

SHISKINE IS SCOTLAND'S WONDROUS twelve-hole attraction on the Isle of Arran just fifty-five minutes by ferry off the Ayrshire coast. While the least expensive course among the seventy-four in this directory, Shiskine sits atop the list among those played for pure fun—with Machrihanish, Machrihanish Dunes, The Machrie, and Cruden Bay. These are the courses that evoke a time when golf was a quirky game of chance and skill played at seaside over natural, scruffy ground to greens hidden by hills and surrounded by burns and hollows—the places visited by the ghosts of Willie Fernie, Willie Park, Jr., and Old Tom Morris.

Two of those old Scots had a hand at Shiskine. Willie Fernie laid out nine holes for the new club in 1896. Fifteen years later, Willie Park, Jr., was commissioned to alter and extend the course to eighteen holes. During World War I the linksland was commandeered for defensive purposes. After the war, parts of the course were neglected until the club found its identity in the twelve holes we have today. Little remains of what Fernie and Park did.

"The Crow's Nest" at Shiskine—somewhere up there is a green.

Shiskine features seven par 3s, four par 4s, and one par 5. Seven of the twelve holes are blind or semi-blind. At the 368-yard #1 hole, we're off to a straightforward Scottish start with sea, beach, and OB on the left. Then it's on to "Twa' Burns" where the photocopied course guide advises that the target off the tee is a "white tyre." The #3 hole, "Crow's Nest," is of a kind seen only in Scotland. It calls for a 130-yard shot up the grassy slope of an outcropping from the Drumadoon cliffs some seventy-five fee above the teeing ground. Somewhere up there is a green. From the tee the golfer sees only a white signal flag, meaning either "I surrender" or "all clear." What goes up must come down and that's what happens at the next hole, "The Shelf," featuring a seventy-five foot drop to the water's edge. By this time, anticipating "The Himalayas," "Drumadoon," and "Paradise," you're in thrall of magical stuff from another era. Descending from high ground at #10 Paradise, we return to an attractive new clubhouse christened by the proud members in 2010

Nongolf notes and lodging: In some cultures, a place like the Isle of Arran would be turned into a glitzy, glamorous getaway for the rich. But, bless the down-to-earth Scots, they're just not very impressed by glitz and glamor. Arran remains an affordable, unassuming place where thousands of Scots and English go to "get away from it all" for a few days or an extended stay. Arran's tourism moniker is "Scotland in Miniature," reflective of its rugged northern terrain and its rolling, green southern hills. Brodick is the port here and is home to about 1,000 of the island's 5,000 citizens. Shops, restaurants, and hotels line Brodick's beachfront boulevard. Since tourism is Arran's main concern, moderately-priced lodging options abound (see ***www.ayrshire-arran.com***.) Just outside town, the luxury category is represented by the *Kilmichael Country House Hotel* (01770-302-219; ***www.kilmichael.com***), where good food is a special attraction. Speaking of good food, try *The Brodick Bar* (01770-302-169) on Alma Road in the center of town. Here, my wife, Ruth, and I once experienced Scotland's finest, most decadent, sticky toffee pudding. A few miles south of Brodick, at Lamlash, you'll find the four-star *Lilybank Guest House* (01770-600-230; ***www.lilybank-arran.co.uk***) looking out across peaceful Lamlash Bay to the Holy Isle. Down near the golf course at Blackwaterfoot, Ian and Ann Relf preside over the *Blackwaterfoot Lodge* (01770-860-202; ***www.blackwaterfoot-lodge.co.uk***), a classic late Victorian small hotel.

Standing stones on Machrie Moor—one of Arran's many attractions.

Elsewhere I have recommended Arran in the context of a peninsula-and-island-hopping trip encompassing Kintyre (Machrihanish) and the Isle of Islay (Machrie). But it's easy enough to make a daytrip to Arran from a base in Ayrshire. From March through October the first ferry out of Ardrossan is at 9:45 a.m. and the last ferry off the island leaves Brodick at 4:40 p.m. In between there's plenty of time for lunch and twenty-four holes at Shiskine. See ***www.arran.net*** or ***www.calmac.co.uk*** for the Ardrossan-Brodick schedule and prices. Whether for a day or for longer, the Isle of Arran is a special place well worth the time of a visiting golfer.

65. Southerness Golf Club (1947)

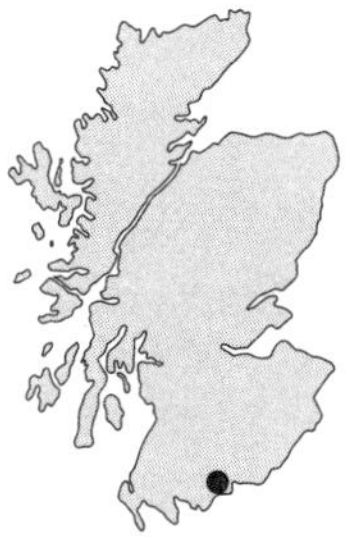

Region #: 9 **Category:** seaside links
Architect(s): Mackenzie Ross (1947)
Length: 6110-6566 **SSS:** 70-73 **Par:** 69

Address: Southerness, Dumfries DG2 8AZ
Directions: 3 mi S of Kirkbean off A710
Reservations phone: 01387-880-677 **Fax:** 01387-880-644

Email: bookings@southernessgolfclub.com
Website: southernessgolfclub.com
Booking Contact(s): secretary

Secretary: J R Handley **Professional:** none
Fee(s) (2012): wkday £50, day tkt £65; wkend £60, day tkt £75
Deposit (2012): £10 UK residents; foreign visitors, none
Visitor Policies: M-F 10-12, 2-4; wkend 10-11:30, 2:30-4pm **Buggies:** no

AMONG ALL THE COURSES in this book, Southerness is far and away the best course played by the fewest visitors, at least visitors from North America. Looking for a true "hidden gem"?—look no farther than Southerness. Like Royal Aberdeen, if this course were located anywhere in Scotland's central belt of population, it would probably be on the Open rota. It's that good—easily in my personal Top Ten list of links courses in Scotland.

The designer responsible for this southern gem was Mackenzie Ross, who resurrected Turnberry from its role as an air landing strip after World War II. Ross came to Southerness in 1947 to create what Malcolm Campbell has called, "arguably the only truly championship-standard seaside links to have been built on the British mainland since the Second World War." Though now we must make room for Kingsbarns, Castle Stuart, and others in that assessment, Campbell's words are an extraordinary endorsement of a great golf course.

Among all the courses in this book, Southerness is far and away the best course played by the fewest visitors.

The routing at Southerness is brilliant, most similar to the anti-clockwise perambulations at Western Gailes and Royal Troon. The difference here is that, while circling a vast pasture, most of the holes simultaneously tack left and right, backward and forward, to create a constantly changing relationship to ever-present winds off the Solway Firth. Five excellent par 3s of varying length play to five points of the compass. Five two-shotters play to more than 400 yards even from the visitor tees; from the medal tees, the number reaches eight. Two short par 5s offer us only mild respite. Note that from the white tees SSS here is 73 against par 69. That's about

The birthplace of John Paul Jones—American hero, British traitor.

The comfortable clubhouse and big, flat 18th green at Southerness—a warm welcome assured and one of the best opportunities for birdie at this challenging course.

as big a gap as you are likely to find in Scottish golf, rivaling Carnoustie's gap from the championship "Tiger" tees. Yet Southerness is fair enough. All the elements of links golf are present, but nothing is hidden from view. It's all in front of you and—set in pastureland, lined with gorse and heather, surrounded by the Solway Firth and Galloway hills—it's all a visual treat. Moreover, at £50 circa 2012, among all the courses in this book, Southerness best represents value for money—the highest level of course design at a reasonable price.

Nongolf notes: Most visitors likely might encounter Southerness on a journey from England to the more northerly golf Meccas of Scotland. On its approach to Scotland, England's M6 becomes the A74. Just inside the Scottish border at Gretna, the A75 branches westward twenty-five miles to Dumfries, a large town of considerable interest and good accommodations. That's the place to stop for a rendezvous with Southerness, fifteen miles south of town.

Dumfries is a handsome town with a river running through it (River Nith), a pedestrian mall in city center, and a ruddy complexion cast by hundreds of stately red sandstone buildings of Victorian vintage. This is where Robert Burns died in 1796 and his wife, Jean Armour, lived until 1834. Burns and his wife are buried in St. Michael's churchyard in central Dumfries. Arbigland Gardens can be found at nearby Kippford and only one mile from Southerness you can see the birthplace of John Paul Jones—an American revolutionary war hero widely regarded as a traitor in Britain. Lockerbie, site of the infamous Pan Am bombing, is twelve miles northeast of Dumfries and well worth a visit. A moving memorial, "Garden of Remembrance," is located in a cemetery on the A709 at the edge of town.

The modest Burns House, where Robbie died in 1796 and his wife, Jean Armour, lived until 1834.

See also: Portpatrick, Powfoot, and Stranraer

66. Spey Valley Golf Club (2006)

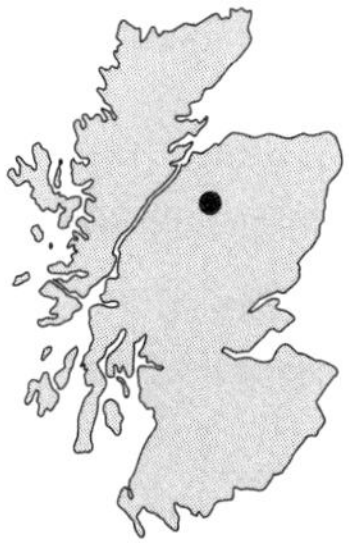

Region #: 4 **Category:** heathland
Architect(s): Dave Thomas
Length: 6653-7017 **SSS:** 73-75 **Par:** 72

Address: Aviemore, Inverness-shire PH22 1PN
Directions: N side of town, E on Dalfaber Dr off B9152
Reservations phone: 01479-811-725

Email: golf@ahresort.co.uk
Website: macdonaldhotels.co.uk
Booking Contact(s): course mgr
Professional/course mgr: Murray Urquhart

Fee(s) (2012): £70 all wk, 4-ball rate £60; residents of resort £50
Deposit (2012): £15 **Buggies:** 25 - general hire
Visitor Policies: all wk

SIXTEEN HOLES AT SPEY VALLEY GC (attached to the Macdonald Aviemore Resort) constitute a perfect golf course in a perfect setting on the heather-filled banks and fields fronting a languid sweep of the incomparable River Spey. I have no reservation in claiming that in late summer, with the heather in purple bloom, this could be on a short list of the most beautiful places in the world.

Unfortunately, hole #s 1 and 18 are so far removed from the rest of the course (about one-quarter of a mile) that a buggy is recommended to maintain pace of play. Quite a pity that, too, for both of these are first-rate starting and finishing holes. Upon querying the professional, I was told that the split is about even between walkers and riders. The division between these two holes and the rest of the course was dictated by road access and a ravine and burn that split the property as water channels from the surrounding hills to the river.

The great attraction here is, first, the land, and then the design work of Englishman Dave Thomas—in my view, the most underrated course architect of the past half-century. His signature bunkering is never overdone, but is both perfectly strategic and visually stunning. Several short, doglegged par 4s contrast with four of the longest par 5s in Scotland to promote sustained interest and careful shot selection. Six holes skirt the Spey while another half dozen play through great banks of beautiful but diabolical heather. Two holes play around a man-made lake on low ground. Four sets of tees, in the modern style, give every golfer a suitable challenge. And plenty challenge it is: USGA slope ratings from the yellow to the championship tees range from 134 to 138. Complaints?—only the ball-gobbling heather that really should be cut back and the long walks between the opening and closing holes.

Aviemore is about thirty minutes south of Inverness and is an ideal locus for holiday golf in and around the Spey Valley at Boat of Garten, Grantown-on-Spey, Carrbridge, Newtonmore, and Kingussie—all a rewarding day away from links golf.

See also: Boat of Garten, Kingussie

67. Stonehaven Golf Club (1888)

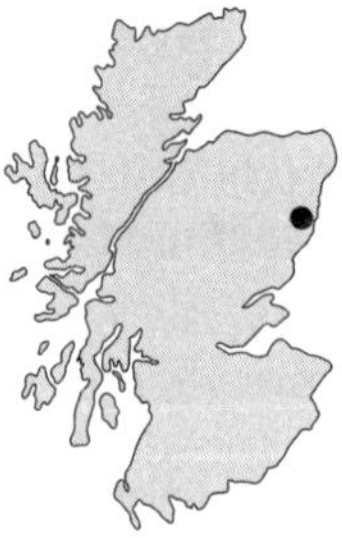

Region #: 5 **Category:** links/parkland hybrid
Architect(s): Artie Simpson (1897)
Length: 4804-5103 **SSS:** 65 **Par:** 67

Address: Cowie, Stonehaven AB39 3RH
Directions: 1 mi N of Stonehaven off B947
Reservations phone: 01569-762-124 **Fax:** 01569-765-973

Email: stonehaven.golfclub@virgin.net
Website: stonehavengolfclub.com
Secretary: Morag Duncan **Professional:** none

Fee(s) (2012): wkday £30, day tkt £35; Sun £35, day tkt £40
Deposit (2012): £10 **Buggies:** no
Visitor Policies: M-F anytime; Sat after 4 pm

LOCATED FIFTY MILES NORTH of Carnoustie and fifteen miles south of Aberdeen, Stonehaven, by any measure (4800-5100 yards), is not much more than an "executive" course. Apart from twelve-hole Shiskine, it is the shortest course included in this directory. Yet, Stonehaven is here because those 5100 yards pack quite a wallop perched atop perhaps the most dramatic seascape in Scottish golf.

Sited largely between the scenic coastal rail line and the sea, on steep cliffs above the North Sea, Stonehaven is also among the most exposed of courses to brutal winds and weather. A nasty day of wind and rain can make this course unplayable. But a calm day will leave the golfer with nothing less than a golden memory of golf in an unforgettable location. In either case you'll be surprised to discover how challenging a short course can be.

A calm day at Stonehaven will leave the golfer with nothing less than a golden memory of golf in an unforgettable clifftop location.

Stonehaven town is an historic fishing village boasting population of about 10,000 hardy souls. It's a good place to poke around a bit after a stop for lunch in the attractive town center. Another reason to put Stonehaven on the itinerary: a mile or so south of town are the remains of Dunnottar Castle—like the golf course, perched dramatically atop a broad escarpment overlooking the sea. Dunnottar was used as the setting in Franco Zefferelli's treatment of *Hamlet* starring Mel Gibson.

My advice on Stonehaven: Make it a half-day stopover between points north and south. It's not only a bargain but a scenic wonder to put in your mental scrapbook of Scottish images.

68. Stranraer Golf Club (1905)

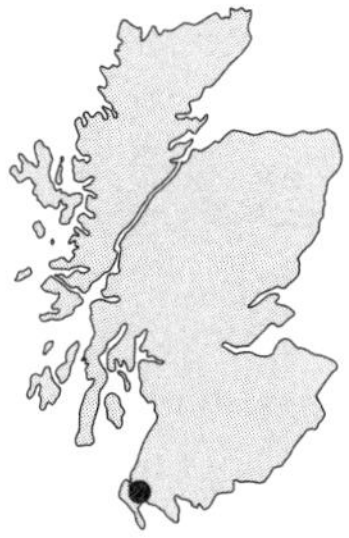

Region #: 9 **Category:** parkland (seaside)
Architect(s): James Braid (1950)
Length: 6056-6308 **SSS:** 72 **Par:** 70

Address: Creachmore, Leswalt, Stranraer DG9 0LF
Directions: 3 mi NW of Stranraer on A718

Reservations phone: 01776-870-245 **Fax:** 01776-870-445
Email: enquiries@stranraergolfclub.net
Website: stranraergolfclub.net
Booking Contact(s): secretary

Secretary: James Burns **Professional:** none
Fee(s) (2012): wkday £28, day tkt £40; wkend £33, day tkt £44
Deposit (2012): £10 **Buggies:** 7 - general hire
Visitor Policies: all wk; 9:30 am-12:30 pm and after 1:30 pm

AMONG THE QUARTET of southern courses featured in this book—Stranraer, Portpatrick, Southerness, and Powfoot—Stranraer is the first in line along the coastal route southward from Turnberry (just 40 miles on the A77). Stranraer is a ferry port with service to Belfast (see ***www.stenaline.co.uk***) and is also on the rail line from Glasgow. Competitive ferry service to Larne in Northern Ireland departs from nearby Cairnryan (see ***www.poferries.com***).

Stranraer sits at the south end of Loch Ryan, an inlet from the North Channel, at the neck of the anvil-shaped peninsula called the "Rhinns of Galloway." In this location, far from Scotland's golf Meccas to the north, James Braid created another fine golf course with a typically unusual combination of holes—this time only one par 5 and three par 3s, leaving fourteen two-shotters including three stretching beyond 450 yards! Of the rest, the golfer is given a pleasing variety of shapes and lengths in holes varying from 315 to 397 yards, all artistically and thoughtfully framed by leafy backdrops of bushes, deciduous trees, and pine. It was James Braid's last creation before he died in 1950 (Stranraer Golf Club was formed in 1905, but the original course was abandoned when it became a military post during World War II). Since 1950, Stranraer has gained a sterling reputation for its excellent greens and general course conditioning and maintenance. This is attributable in part to the relatively mild Gulf Stream weather found in this part of Scotland. The rest of it is attributable to local pride in "Braid's Last" exemplified in more than £100,000 spent on unseen drainage work on three holes susceptible to standing water during years of exceptionally wet weather. Though seaside, Stranraer is a parkland course positioned largely on high

The 18th at Stranraer—literally, James Braid's last contribution to Scottish golf in 1950.

ground overlooking the sea. Several holes skirt the shoreline, but the rest of the course is inland and quite hilly. This one's a seaside beauty.

So, why visit Stranraer? First, it's an excellent course. Second, like most of the courses at the bottom of Scotland, it's a bargain. Third, getting there is half the fun. Fourth, if you're coming to Scotland from England, heading for the Ayrshire coast, it's not much out of the way at all. Fifth, at the clubhouse, refurbished for Stranraer's centenary in 2005, you'll experience a particularly warm Scottish welcome; they don't see a lot of visitors here, so your presence will be noticed and appreciated. Need more reasons? I would add the attractions of southern Scotland. This is Clan Kennedy country and near Stranraer you'll find the magnificent 75-acre Kennedy Castle Gardens. Fourteen miles south of Stranraer on the Rhinns of Galloway is Logan Botanic Garden where you can see plants from the southern hemisphere flourishing on a Gulf Stream coast.

See also: Portpatrick, Powfoot, Southerness

69. Tain Golf Club (1890)

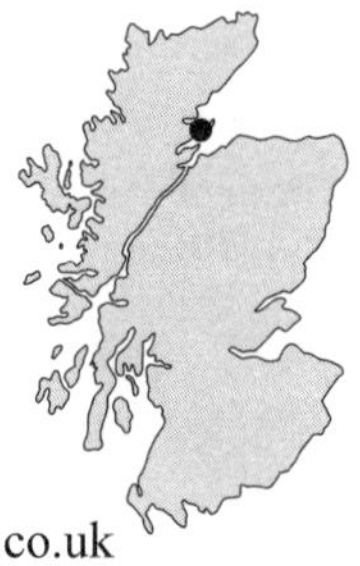

Region #: 4 **Category:** seaside links
Architect(s): Tom Morris
Length: 6109-6404 **SSS:** 71 **Par:** 70

Address: Chapel Rd, Tain, Ross-shire IV19 1JE
Directions: signposted from ctr of town

Reservations phone: 01862-892-314 **Fax:** 01862-892-099
Email: info@tain-golfclub.co.uk **Website:** tain-golfclub.co.uk
Booking Contact(s): admin secretary

Admin Secretary: Maggie Vass **Professional:** Stuart Morrison
Phone - Starter/Pro shop: 01862-893-313
Fee(s) (2012): rates vary by month Apr, May, Oct; June-Sept £48 all wk, day tkt £65; twilight reduced rates May-July
Deposit (2012): £10 **Buggies:** 5 - general hire
Visitor Policies: all wk; wkend after 11:30 am

GOLF WRITER JIM FINEGAN describes Tain as "golf in a minor key," and that says it pretty well. Tain simply lacks the grandeur of its near neighbor Royal Dornoch. It is always seen in the shadow of that magnificent course.

Having said that, let me quickly add that Tain, in its minor key, is one of the most unusual and enjoyable courses in the entire country. It's a Tom Morris layout, so it comes replete with penal bunkers, green-fronting swales, a few blind shots, and imaginative one-shotters. The first hole alone is worth the price of admission: from the first tee it looks straightforward enough, but, out in the fairway, you realize you are about to make a blind second shot over a public byway and a fence to a tucked away, smallish green. Welcome to quirky Tain! Most of the first nine holes hump and bump along in extremis before the ground smoothes out a bit on the inward half. Anti-clockwise routing takes us out and back, perambulating through bucolic pastureland and some of the heaviest gorse plantations on any Scottish course. Tain is beautiful but can be lethal; straight is good. "Alps," a two-shotter (#11), is reminiscent of Carnoustie's "Spectacles" and two superb par 3s over a burn at #16 and #17 bring the round to an unusual close. The home hole is plain vanilla made venturesome only by the proximity of the green to the plate-glass windows of the attractive clubhouse built in 1998.

For some reason, a lot of pesky black flies inhabit Tain. In calm weather they can be annoying. You can hope for a stiff Scottish breeze. And a final note on the setting of Tain Golf Club: On Golf Road, a one-lane track leading to the clubhouse, you'll drive the length of a striking gothic cemetery and, if you're a golfer, you can't help but think, "Here lies the ultimate 19th hole." Indeed, Tain Golf Club leaves an indelible imprint on the mind.

See also: Brora, Golspie, Royal Dornoch

70. Trump International Golf Links (2012)

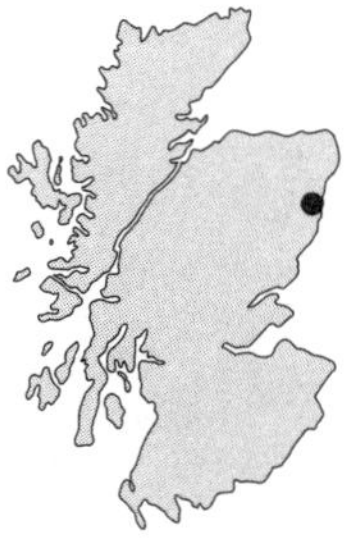

Region #: 5 **Category:** seaside links
Architect(s): Martin Hawtree
Length: 4 tees to 7400 yds **SSS:** not rated **Par:** 72

Address: Menie Estate, Aberdeenshire AB23 8YE
Directions: at Balmedie, 7 mi N of A92/A90 junction

Reservations phone: 01358-743-300; in USA 212-836-3234
Fax: in USA 212-980-3821; in Scotland 01358-743-325
Email: info@trumpgolfscotland.com **Website:** trumpgolfscotland.com
Booking Contact(s): administration **Professional:** none

Fee(s) (2012): £150 wkday, £200 wkend, 15 July - 31 Oct 2012; closed winter
Deposit (2012): 50%
Visitor Policies: all wk **Buggies:** med/phys

IN LATE 2011, TRUMP INTERNATIONAL quietly started accepting requests for tee times on "the greatest golf course in the world" beginning July 15, 2012. It was to be a short season with play only through October 31. Thus closed a rather prosaic chapter in a tumultuous story that is far from over.

The melodrama began in 2006 when Donald Trump resolved to build a golf course north of Aberdeen within a Site of Special Scientific Interest (SSSI) including Scotland's highest sand dunes. Too convoluted and occasionally infantile to report here, the ensuing saga, at least through late 2010, has been best detailed by George Peper in an article in the fall issue of *Links Magazine* from that year. The nut of the story: While admitting his project would have "major adverse impact" on one of Scotland's most environmentally-sensitive coast lines, and opposed every step of the way by the government-funded Scottish Natural Heritage, other environmental organizations, and adjacent landowners, Trump enlisted local and national politicians to work his will. Along the way, the Trump team did almost everything it could possibly do to alienate the local population and, especially, the people who own land adjacent to the Trump project. Fever pitch was reached in 2010 when the Trump organization threatened to pursue Compulsory Purchase Orders (condemnation) to gain control of nearby private land, including a 23-acre farm that Trump called "a pigsty." Opposition gained apace and Trump ultimately backed down.

At least Donald Trump can claim a couple of "firsts" in Scottish golf history. He's the first man ever to inspire both a documentary film and an organization dedicated to sabotaging a golf resort. The film is *You've Been Trumped* (***www.youvebeentrumped.com***) and the organization is Tripping Up Trump (***www.trippinguptrump.com***). At this point, Trump is also the first man ever to inspire the filing of more than 800 formal objections with the Aberdeenshire Council to whatever he proposes at the Menie Estate. Contrast this pathetic performance to the diplomatic involvement with Scottish Natural Heritage and locals at Kingsbarns, Castle Stuart, and Machrihanish Dunes—where developments have been welcomed in Scotland and carried out by not-so-ugly Americans.

But that's all about Donald Trump. What about the golf course designed by Martin Hawtree? Given the land it is on and the designer involved, it had to be good. Most of the holes play two fairways wide in anti-clockwise routing through a set of gigantic dunes. At the north end of the course six holes play around a huge sand blowout called the "Menie Dome." As Hawtree has said, the course will remind us more of courses on the west coast of Ireland—Doonbeg, Ballybunion, Waterville, and Tralee— than anything in Scotland except parts of nearby Royal Aberdeen, Murcar, Cruden Bay, and Peterhead. Four sets of tees will mitigate what can only be a treacherous test for any golfer, especially with some typically windy weather barreling off the North Sea.

The problem, of course, is price. Management calls the opening entry fee (£150) an "introductory price," which can only mean that £200 is on the near horizon—and that means the Trump development will be just another ghetto for the rich and the course will be little more than another "trophy" for some few to collect. Trump does not want a course where the *hoi polloi* might enjoy a casual round on interesting terrain (as at Machrihanish Dunes); he wants a world-famous course where, someday, the Open Championship might be held.

Reportedly, the golf course is being built for something like £100 million. The rest of the promised investment (£750 million to £1 billion) is slated for another golf course, a 450-room hotel, 950 apartments, and 500 residential homes on a 1,400-acre estate. The size of that promised hotel, by the way, is twice the size of the mammoth Fairmont St. Andrews, which has trouble filling its rooms even in summer.

Here's a prediction: The projected 450-room hotel will not be built; and, if it is built, it will be a much smaller "white elephant" (otherwise known as a tax write-off). Most Scots in golf tourism along the northeast coast welcome the development, believing it will boost visitor play in the region. But, as I have said many times to those willing to listen: As far as golfers are concerned, no matter what Trump builds or when it is built, northeast Scotland will always be *fifth* on the visitor's list after St. Andrews, Carnoustie, Ayrshire, East Lothian, and the Northern Highlands. It's a very nice fifth—but fifth nonetheless. Trump International is not going to change the priorities that visitors bring to Scotland.

71. Turnberry Hotel – Ailsa Course *

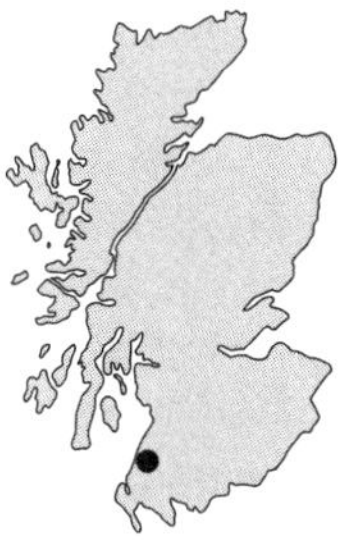

Region #: 2 **Category:** seaside links
Architect(s): Mackenzie Ross (1946-51), Donald Steel (2007)
Length: 6493-7211 **SSS:** 72 **Par:** 69-70

Address: Turnberry, Ayrshire KA26 9LT
Directions: rt at junction of A77 and A719

Reservations phone: main desk 01655-331-000
Fax: 01655-331-152
Email: turnberry@turnberry.co.uk **Website:** turnberry.co.uk
Booking Contact(s): reservations office for hotel and courses

Director of Golf: Chris Card **Professional:** Richard Hall
Phone - Starter/Pro shop: 01655-334-048
Fee(s) (2012): May-Sept resident £150 all wk, £230 day tkt; non-resident £180 M-Th, £199 F-Sat- Sun, no day tkt; reduced rates Apr & Oct; twilight reduced rate
Deposit (2012): res - none; non-res 100% prepay **Buggies:** 3 - med/phys
Visitor Policies: all wk; hotel residents have priority; non-res may book 2 wks prior to date of play - call pro shop
Other: companion course, the Kintyre, redesigned in 2001 by Donald Steel

DRIVE TIME
Troon: about 35 min on the A77-M77
1 hr on the coastal route (A719)
Glasgow Airport: 1 hr, 15 min

GOLF FANS THE WORLD OVER were reacquainted with the Ailsa course at Turnberry in 2009 as Tom Watson battled a battalion of younger men to come within one stroke and a playoff of capturing his sixth Open Championship. It was one for the ages—as have been all the Opens played on this remarkable golf ground.

With its seaside setting, expansive layout, rolling terrain, and wispy, waving grasses, I like to think of Turnberry as "Muirfield with a view." Surely this is one of the two or three most beautiful seaside courses in Scotland. Hole #s 4 through 11 play along the water in Scotland's finest stretch of sustained seaside golf—first, tacking leftward along Turnberry Bay to the promontory where the famous #9 tee is perched; then cutting ninety degrees to the right past Turnberry's landmark lighthouse.

These magnificent sea holes are bracketed by superb inland combinations of three parallel opening holes (par 4s of varying length) and seven closing holes featuring imaginative changes of direction, length, and variety. There is simply no weak link here—all told, some of the most memorable holes in Scottish golf.

The history of golf at Turnberry falls into two distinct periods: the War Years and the Post-War Years. Britain's engagement in the twentieth century's two world wars wreaked havoc at Turnberry. Twice within thirty years, the linksland was commandeered as an airstrip by the Royal Air Force. After World War I, James Braid and C.K. Hutchinson were hired to reconstruct the golf courses. With the coming of World War II, land was bulldozed and runways were built (fortunately, most of the damage was done a bit inland below the hotel, away from the seaside links). By 1945, Turnberry was as exhausted as the British nation.

Into this breach stepped a determined hotel director, Frank Hole, who would not allow his parent company to abandon the golf courses at Turnberry. Hole persevered and ultimately contracted with Mackenzie Ross to design a new course. Work began in 1946 and continued over a period of five years. When it was done, Ross had achieved a course widely recognized as a classic of championship quality equal to its setting—the first such course built in Scotland in many years and the first of the post-war period (ultimately, the only twentieth-century course included on the "rota" of the Open Championship).

Tournament golf found its way to Turnberry immediately, culminating, first, in its hosting of the Walker Cup in 1963, then in its designation in 1977 by the Royal and Ancient as the newest venue for the Open. Turnberry arrived on the international golf scene as the stage for one of the two or three most dramatic tournaments in Open history—the famous "Duel in the Sun" between Tom Watson (the winner by one stroke) and Jack Nicklaus. Since 1977, Turnberry has hosted three additional Opens—in 1986 (Greg Norman); in 1994 (Nick Price); and 2009 (Stewart Cink). Interesting, isn't it, how these Scottish tracks seem to bring the cream to the top!

Would that the ownership history at Turnberry were as consistent. Like the great hotels of the Canadian Rockies, Turnberry Hotel was a product of the golden age of rail transportation. Built in 1906, it was owned and operated by the Glasgow and South Western Railway as a destination resort. From Scottish to Japanese to American to Arab hands, over the years the hotel has been an expensive piece on the Monopoly board of international business.

Now in the hands of Dubai World and managed by the Luxury Collection under the Starwood umbrella, the hotel is finding new life with new money. After undergoing a stunning £44 million makeover prior to hosting the Open Championship in 2009, Turnberry remains one of the jewels in the five-star Scottish crown otherwise bedecked in the golf regions only by Gleneagles and the Old Course Hotel.

Situated on a high bluff overlooking the sea, Turnberry is Scotland's premier seaside resort.

Regardless of ownership, Turnberry's place on the planet seems timeless. This is Robert Burns's romantic countryside where the Ayrshire coastal plain gives way to the rolling, green hills of Galloway. Expansive views from high bluffs over the Turnberry links look out over a seascape encompassing the Isle of Arran, the Kintyre Peninsula, and, on a clear day, Ireland on the far-off southwest horizon. Ten miles offshore, the Ailsa Craig—a tortoise-shaped volcanic rock (1208 feet high)—anchors the scene with primeval certitude. In this setting, the great hotel appears a natural and indispensable part of the poetic picture. Sitting atop the great bluff overlooking the linksland, with its russet roof and white façade, the building looks as if it might have been transferred wholesale from colonial America—maybe George Washington's Mt. Vernon on steroids. Edwardian or neo-colonial, in either case it's a classic—timeless in its appeal; at the same time, a monument to times gone by.

> ***Is Turnberry worth the cost at whatever price? Remember that classic bumper sticker: "We're not extravagant. We're just spending our kids' inheritance."***

Poetic, yes, but this is a practical book. Travelers want practical information—like, "Do you have to stay at the hotel to play the golf course?" and, "If you stay at the hotel, how much does it cost?".

Do you have to stay at the hotel to play the golf course? Hotel residents have priority position for tee times. But, because Turnberry is, in effect, a daily-fee course, one can usually get onto the Ailsa Course, even in high season, without staying at the hotel. For regular tee times (before late afternoon), the way to do that is to request a tee time two weeks prior to the desired date of play. In 2010 the hotel started selling twilight times beginning at 5 p.m. for about half-price with nonrefundable payment any time in advance. During shoulder season (April and October) twilight tee times have started as early as 3 p.m. (check with hotel reservations for current policy).

How much does it cost to stay at the hotel? Date-specific rates, promotional deals, and varied room options make this difficult to answer but, essentially, the "rack rate" in high season is about $300 per person double occupancy in the least expensive rooms. Add the cost of golf on the Ailsa and you have a one-day hotel/golf experience in the neighborhood of $500-600 per person, per day. This one is worth shopping around because deals are always on offer and rates are significantly discounted for tour operators. But, is Turnberry worth the cost at whatever price? Only you can decide. It's not an easy decision, but remember that classic bumper sticker: "We're not extravagant. We're just spending our kids' inheritance."

Nongolf notes: A few miles north of Turnberry, you'll find historic Culzean Castle (pronounced Coo-LANE), the most visited of Scotland's "National Trust" properties. The home of Robert Adam, Scotland's leading architect of the eighteenth century, this perfectly-preserved Georgian mansion is surrounded by forest walks, expansive grounds, and formal gardens. It was an elegant office site for General Dwight Eisenhower during World War II and should be seen when in the area.

Alternative to the pricey food, drink, and lodging at Turnberry, drive two miles north to the village of Maidens where you'll find *Cotter's Restaurant* at the *Malin Court Inn* (01655-331-457; ***www.malincourt.co.uk***) and, nearby on a picturesque half-moon bay, *Wildings Hotel and Restaurant*. Wildings, in particular, is wildly popular with the locals. Reservations recommended (01655-331-401; ***www.wildingshotel.com***). As the names imply, both of these establishments have rooms to let. For a budget b & b near Turnberry the *Fairways B & B* (01655-331-522; ***www.fairways-turnberry.co.uk***) fills the bill. For pub life, drive five miles southward from Turnberry on the A77 to Girvan.

72. West Kilbride (1893)

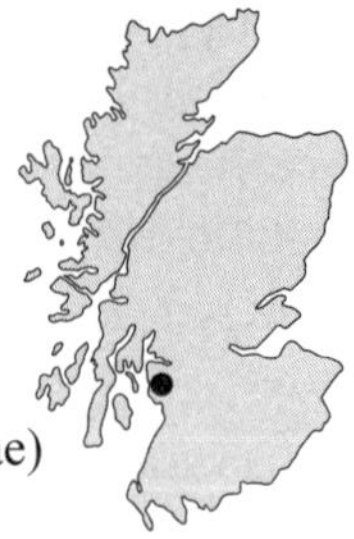

Region #: 2 **Category:** seaside links
Architect(s): Tom Morris (1893), Willie Fernie (1905), James Braid (1914)
Length: 5896-6452 **SSS:** 71 **Par:** 71

Address: 33-35 Fullarton Dr, Seamill WK, Ayrshire KA23 9HT
Directions: left toward sea at junction of A78 and B781 (Yerton Brae)

Reservations phone: 01294-823-911 **Fax:** 01294-823-911
Email: golf@westkilbridegolfclub.com
Website: westkilbridegolfclub.com
Booking Contact(s): secretary for 8+ groups; otherwise pro shop

Secretary: Hamish Armour **Professional:** Iain Darroch
Phone - Starter/Pro shop: 01294-823-042
Fee(s) (2012): wkday £45; day tkt £60
Deposit (2012): none
Visitor Policies: after 3 pm wkend **Buggies:** 3- med/phys

WEST KILBRIDE GOLF CLUB is best described with the word "most." This is the most northern linksland along Ayrshire's golf coast stretching some sixty miles from West Kilbride to Turnberry. West Kilbride sits about twenty-four miles north of Troon and five miles north of Ardrossan (where CalMac ferries embark for the Isle of Arran). Despite its pedigreed design history involving Tom Morris, Willie Fernie, and James Braid, West Kilbride is easily the *most overlooked and most underrated* of Ayrshire's great links courses. This is due in part to its location a bit removed from the golf magnet at Troon. Among all the golf courses of Scotland—not just those of Ayrshire—West Kilbride is among the *most exposed* to the open sea. Situated on a sand shelf below sharply rising bluffs, the course sits defenseless against whatever the western seas and skies care to unleash. Part and parcel of that siting, West Kilbride enjoys the *most panoramic* views to the open sea (at eye level) of any golf course in Scotland. With no hills or dunes to obscure the view, the water is simply there, visible from every hole, and, on the occasional sunny, calm day, there can be no finer place on God's green earth. Essentially three fairways wide, bounded on one side by the proximate sea and on the other by private property, West Kilbride presents the *most out-of-bounds* of any course I have encountered. Out-of-bounds is a factor on twelve of eighteen holes, including seven of the last nine. Finally, West Kilbride has the *most laid-back*, classiest clubhouse in Scotland. We're not talking Ritz here, but down-home, comfortable digs with Louis Armstrong, Billie Holiday, and Sarah Vaughan on the sound system. It doesn't get any better than that.

See also: Royal Troon and Prestwick for area lodging

73. Western Gailes Golf Club (1897) +

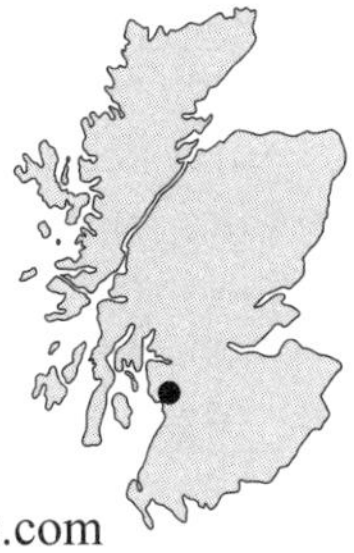

Region #: 2 **Category:** seaside links
Architect(s): Willie Park, Sr. and Jr., Fred Hawtree (1975)
Length: 6179-6639 **SSS:** 73 **Par:** 71

Address: Gailes, Irvine KA11 5AE
Directions: 8 mi N of Troon off A78 (2 mi S of Irvine)

Reservations phone: 01294-311-649 **Fax:** 01294-312-312
Email: enquiries@westerngailes.com **Website:** westerngailes.com
Booking Contact(s): Vicky O'Dowd, Lynn Scott

Secretary: Jerry Kessell **Professional:** no
Phone - Starter/Pro shop: call reservations #
Fee(s) (2012): £125 wkday, £165 day tkt (incl buffet lunch M, W, F); Sat, Sun £125, no day tkt
Deposit (2012): 50% **Buggies:** no
Visitor Policies: M, W, F 9-12, 2-4:30 pm; Sat 3-4:30 May - Sept; Sun 2-3:30 pm
Other: participant in The Gailes Experience with Dundonald and Glasgow Gailes

IN COMPANY WITH COURSES like Nairn, Cruden Bay, Royal Aberdeen, and Royal Dornoch, Western Gailes has joined a second tier of elite courses increasingly familiar to golf tourists. This is due largely to its presence on package tours and then the word-of-mouth buzz that follows such experiences. If price is a measure of self-worth, Western Gailes has put itself in the company of Carnoustie and Prestwick and only a notch or two below St. Andrews' Old Course.

Is the reputation and price of Western Gailes justified relative to the rest of Scottish golf? In a word, yes. This is among Scotland's finest linkslands. It's in my personal Top Five list along with Cruden Bay, The Machrie, Machrihanish, and North Berwick. That's a list that has much to do with location, cost, accessibility, and clubhouse ambience as with the golf courses themselves. I like this northern part of the Ayrshire coast and, though Western is not in the bargain category, it is a uniquely satisfying place.

The great draw at Western Gailes, as at Cruden Bay, is the extraordinarily convoluted links terrain and the powerful challenge of golf on a characteristically windy venue. Here, a kaleidoscope of sandhills, hillocks, humps, bumps, depressions, marram grass, gorse, and heather present an ever-changing visual treat and persistent challenge to the shotmaker. Holes #5 through #13 parallel the coast—one of the longest stretches of seaside play in Scottish golf. And it is here that the gales common to Gailes come so frequently into play, for this is a course fully exposed to

The elegant whitewashed clubhouse at Western Gailes—winner of an award for the UK's "Best Dirty Bar"(casual lounge for golfers).

the prevailing winds. And, though the visitor tees play to only about 6200 yards, these middle holes can often make you feel like you're grappling with a 7000-yard monster. Certainly, the average golfer will be adequately challenged from the yellow tees; if you are allowed to play from the white tees (ask the starter), you'll fully understand why Western Gailes is used as a qualifying course when the Open is held at Royal Troon or Turnberry.

Western Gailes sits on a narrow strip of land between the coastal rail line and the sea. The course is basically two fairways wide—at first glance, a classic out-and-back links. The difference at Western is the position of its elegant white-washed clubhouse. Rather than residing at one end of an out-and-back chain of holes, this clubhouse sits on high ground nearly at mid-point in the chain. Thus, the routing is a racetrack loop—off to the first turn (#1 to #5), down the backstretch (to #13), then on to the wire (#14 through #18). Just as at a racetrack, the Gailes clubhouse looks out over the finish line. There's no stopping at the ninth hole; that's way off on the other side of the track!

With Glasgow Gailes and Dundonald Links just across the rail line, there's a powerful attraction to spend a full day playing golf at the Gailes. Certainly any combination of these courses makes for one of the strongest one-two punches in Scottish golf.

See also: Dundonald, Glasgow Gailes, Kilmarnock, Royal Troon

74. Whitekirk Golf and Country Club (1995)

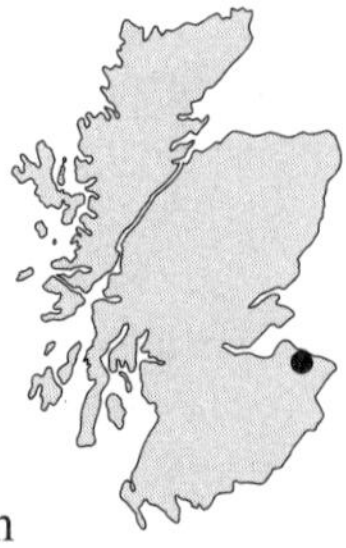

Region #: 3 **Category:** parkland
Architect(s): Cameron Sinclair
Length: 6225-6526 **SSS:** 72 **Par:** 72

Address: Whitekirk nr N Berwick, E Lothian EH39 5PR
Directions: 5 mi SE of N Berwick off A198

Reservations phone: 01620-870-300 **Fax:** 01620-870-330
Email: countryclub@whitekirk.com **Website:** whitekirk.com
Booking Contact(s): club mgr **Professional:** Paul Wardell

Club Mgr: David Brodie
Fee(s) (2012): wkday £35, day tkt £52.50; wkend £39, day tkt £58.50
Deposit (2012): £10
Visitor Policies: all wk **Buggies:** 10 - general hire

SURROUNDED BY ROLLING FARMLAND, Whitekirk Golf and Country Club is perched on and around a high, graceful hill that dominates the terrain near Whitekirk hamlet midway between North Berwick and Dunbar. This place reminds me of the movie Field of Dreams: "Build it and they will come." Landowner-developer George Tuer built it in 1995 and they are coming. It's a popular place with locals for miles around.

Americans will feel right at home at Whitekirk. Visitors are welcome at all times. Indeed, the whole idea of Whitekirk is daily-fee visitor appeal. To that end, the facility features a comfortable, classy clubhouse with good food service and a full-blown leisure club (unfortunately, not available to visitors). Outside, golf carts are lined up just like at home and a 300-yard, American-style practice range encourages a proper warm-up (a rarity in Scottish golf). Plans are on the drawing board for a sixty-to-seventy room hotel and an additional eighteen holes of golf.

So, Mr. Tuer has not missed a beat when it comes to marketing. Furthermore, the course itself happens to be a worthy addition to Scottish golf. British designer Cameron Sinclair did the work here and he did a good job of it. Four sets of tees accommodate golfers of all abilities. Strong par 3s and several long par 4s put a lot of starch in this golf experience. Numerous amateur and professional tournaments have been held here. Elevated teeing grounds provide outstanding views over the rolling Lothian countryside—to nearby Tantallon Castle and out to the sea five miles away. This is a good bargain in Scottish golf and ideal for a buggy candidate.

See also: North Berwick West Links and Gullane GC for area lodging

APPENDICES

APPENDIX A

Most Frequently-Called Reservations Telephone Numbers

(From outside the United Kingdom, dial 011-44, then the following)

Brora 1408-621-417
Carnoustie 1241-802-270
Castle Stuart 1463-795-440
Crail Golfing Society 1333-450-686
Cruden Bay 1779-812-285
Dunbar 1368-862-317
Fairmont St. Andrews 1334-837-412
Gleneagles 1764-694-469
Golf House Club - Elie 1333-330-301
Kingsbarns 1334-460-861
Leven Links 1333-428-859
Lundin Links 1333-320-202
Montrose 1674-672-932
Nairn 1667-453-208
North Berwick West Links 1620-892-135
Prestwick 1292-671-020
Royal Aberdeen 1224-702-571
Royal Dornoch 1862-810-219
Royal Troon 1292-311-555
St. Andrews Links 1334-466-666
Scotscraig 1382-552-515
Turnberry 1655-331-000
Western Gailes 1294-311-649

Caledonian MacBrayne (ferries) 8705-650-000

APPENDIX B

Golf-Readiness Checklist

- ❑ Golf bag with hood
- ❑ Golf balls: at least 3 per round - or buy them there
- ❑ Tees; divot repair tool; ball markers; pencils
- ❑ Golf shoes - two pairs ❑ or rubber overshoes
- ❑ Hat (preferably waterproofed) ❑ stocking cap or earmuffs
- ❑ Waterproof rain suit ❑ Windbreaker
- ❑ Umbrella
- ❑ Sweater(s) (dress in layers)
- ❑ Two towels and/or washcloths (for cleaning ball, glasses in the rain)
- ❑ Winter gloves (even in summer it can get cold)
- ❑ Sunscreen
- ❑ First-aid kit: tape/band aids/ibuprofen or aspirin/lanolin
- ❑ Water bottle (there won't be any drinking water on most courses)
- ❑ Ziploc bags (to keep food, etc., separated/dry)
- ❑ One or two 2 to 3-foot bungee cords (to secure bag to trolley)

Nongolf items

- ❑ Proof of USGA handicap index
- ❑ Allan Ferguson's *Golf in Scotland* - print or e-book
- ❑ Passport ❑ Driver's license

APPENDIX C

Useful Internet Sites

Following is a list of websites of general interest and of lodgings mentioned in the text. Sites of golf courses are in Part III, "The Directory of Courses."

General Interest

aboutscotland.com - general, incl lodging
bta.org.uk - British Tourist Authority
dcs.ed.ac.uk - malt whisky information
eif.co.uk - Edinburgh International Festival
electricscotland.com - general interest and history
golftravelguide.com - especially for airline guidelines
historic-scotland.gov.uk - Historic Scotland
islaywhiskysociety.com - Islay Whisky Society
houseofbruar.com - House of Bruar nr Pitlochry - gift emporium
kropla.com - electricity around the world
news.bbc.co.uk - British Broadcasting Co.
nationalgalleries.org - National Galleries of Scotland
nms.ac.uk - National Museums of Scotland
nts.org.uk - National Trust for Scotland
packinglight.net - lightweight travel gear
ricksteves.com - travel gear
robertburns.org - all things Burns
scotch-whisky.org.uk - association of whisky distillers
scotchwhisky.net - all things whisky
scotland-info.co.uk - general
scotsman.com - Edinburgh, national newspaper
smws.com - Scotch Malt Whisky Society
spinfish.co.uk - fly fishing in the UK
timeanddate.com - world time zones and weather
usga.org - United States Golf Association
visitscotland.com - VisitScotland (formerly the Scottish Tourist Board)
walking.visitscotland.com - hiking
yell.com - international yellow pages

Transportation and Communication

arnoldclarkrental.co.uk - Arnold Clark rental cars (other car companies, see p. 74)
ba.com - British Airways (other airlines - see, p. 69)
britrail.com - rail transportation
calmac.co.uk - Caledonian MacBrayne ferries
dialahuman.com - short-circuiting phone trees
firstgroup.com - rail transportation
insurance4carhire.com - independent insurance broker
inter800.com - toll-free telephone numbers
kintyreexpress.com - speedboat service, Troon to Kintyre and N Ireland
lochlomondseaplanes.com - charter seaplanes

multimap.co.uk - online mapping service
poferries.com - P & O ferries
squaremouth.com - travel insurance
stenaline.co.uk - Stena Line ferries
streetmap.co.uk - mapping service

Scottish Golf

europeantour.com - Senior British Open and other information
opengolf.com - official site of the British Open
randa.org - The Royal and Ancient Golf Club
scottishgolfunion.org - Scottish Golf Union
scottishgolfhistory.net - Neil Laird, golf historian
scottishgolfsociety.com - Scottish Golf Society
thebraidsociety.com - James Braid Golfing Society

Golf Discount Cards and Open Competitions

carnoustiecountry.com - Carnoustie Classic and Carnoustie Dream Ticket
greensavers.co.uk - Bunkered Magazine's 2-for-1 program
openfairways.co.uk - UK-wide offers (4 for 3, 2 for 1)
2-fore-1golf.com - UK-wide offers
weeyellowbook.com - The Wee Yellow Book (club open competitions)

Fife and St. Andrews

eastneukwide.co.uk - East Neuk Promotional Group
eatingoutinfife.co.uk - Fife restaurants
st-andrews.ac.uk - University of St. Andrews
standrews.org.uk - St. Andrews Links Management
standrews.co.uk - St Andrews official tourism site
saint-andrews.co.uk - Town Council
visit-standrews.com - St. Andrews Merchants Association

Other Regions and Towns

aberdeencityandshire.com - Aberdeen and Grampian Highlands
angusanddundee.co.uk - Angus and Dundee
arran.net - Isle of Arran
ayrshirescotland.com - Ayrshire
ayrshire-arran.com - Ayrshire and Isle of Arran
boatofgarten.com - Boat of Garten and Speyside
dufftown.co.uk - Dufftown and whisky country
gael-net.co.uk - West Highlands
grantown.co.uk - Grantown-on-Spey
islayinfo.com - Islay
north-berwick.co.uk - North Berwick
pitlochry.org.uk - Pitlochry Festival Theatre
pitlochry.org - Pitlochry
scot-borders.co.uk - Borders tourist board (southeast)
visitarran.net - Isle of Arran
visitdornoch.com - Dornoch
visithighlands.com. - VisitScotland's highlands tourist board
visitnairn.com - Nairn

LODGING

$$ = £40 - 50 per person per night (most 4-star B & Bs and many 3-star hotels)
$$$ = £55 - 100 (some 3-star hotels and most 4-star hotels)
$$$$ = over £100 (some 4-star hotels and all 5-star resort hotels)

General
aboutscotland.com - private promotional service
assc.co.uk - Association of Scotland's Self Caterers
hotels-scotland.co.uk - private promotional service
scotland-info.co.uk - private promotional service
scotland2000.com - private promotional service
smoothhound.co.uk - private promotional service
theaa.com - UK Automobile Association - including route planner, restaurants
visitscotland.com - VisitScotland (Scottish tourist board)

Lodging - Region #1 (Fife)
ardgowanhotel.co.uk - Ardgowan Hotel, St. Andrews $$$
aslar.com - Aslar Guest House, St. Andrews $$
balbirnie.co.uk - Balbirnie Park Country House Hotel nr Glenrothes $$$
balgeddiehouse.com - Balgeddie House nr Glenrothes $$
balmashie.co.uk - Balmashie Cottages, nr St. Andrews $$
castlemount.net - Castlemount B & B, St. Andrews $$
crawsnesthotel.co.uk - Craw's Nest Hotel, Anstruther $$
crusoehotel.co.uk - Crusoe Hotel, Lower Largo $$
discoverstandrews.com - St. Andrews University housing $$
dunvegan-hotel.com - Dunvegan Hotel, St. Andrews $$$
fairmont.com/standrews - Fairmont St Andrews $$$$
5pilmourplace.com - 5 Pilmour Place, St. Andrews $$$
hampton-house.co.uk - Hampton House GH, Lundin Links $$
hazelbank.com - Hazelbank Hotel, St. Andrews $$$
kinburnguesthouse.co.uk - Kinburn GH, St. Andrews $$
lundin-links-hotel.co.uk - Lundin Links Hotel, Largo $$
macdonaldhotels.co.uk - Rusacks Hotel, St. Andrews $$$$
mansedalehouse.co.uk - Mansedale House B & B, nr St. Andrews $$
ogstonsonnorthstreet.com - Ogston's on North Street, St. Andrews $$$
oldcoursehotel.co.uk - Old Course Hotel, St. Andrews $$$$
rufflets.co.uk - Rufflets, nr St. Andrews $$$$
russellhotelstandrews.co.uk - Russell Hotel, St. Andrews $$$
scoreshotel.co.uk - Scores Hotel, St. Andrews $$$
standrewsbandbs.com - private association of B & Bs
standrews-golf.co.uk - St. Andrews Golf Hotel, St. Andrews $$$
stayinstandrews.co.uk - St. Andrews Hotel and Guest House Association
thealbanystandrews.co.uk - Albany Hotel, St. Andrews $$$
thegolfhotelcrail.com - Golf Hotel, Crail $$
thehazelton.co.uk - Hazelton B & B, Crail $$
theinn.co.uk - Inn at Lathones, nr St. Andrews $$$
theoldmanorhotel.co.uk - Old Manor Hotel, Lundin Links $$$
thespindrift.co.uk - Spindrift Hotel, Anstruther $$

Lodging - Region #2 (Ayrshire)

anchoragehoteltroon.co.uk - Anchorage Hotel, Troon $$
barceló-hotels.co.uk - Barceló Marine Hotel, Troon $$$
chestnutshotel.com - The Chestnuts Hotel, Ayr $$$
copperbeechfreeservers.com - Copper Beech B & B $$
costley-hotels.co.uk - Lochgreen House, Highgrove House, Troon $$$
enterkine.com - Enterkine Country House Hotel, nr Troon $$$$
fairfieldhotel.co.uk - Fairfield House Hotel, Ayr $$$
fairways-turnberry.co.uk - Fairways B & B, Turnberry $$
golfviewhotel.com - Golf View Guest House, Prestwick $$
greenanlodge.com - Greenan Lodge, Ayr $$
lochwoodfarm.co.uk - Lochwood Farm B & B, Saltcoats $$
parkstonehotel.co.uk - Parkstone Hotel, Prestwick $$
piersland.co.uk - Piersland House Hotel, Troon $$$
sandhillhouse.com - Sandhill House B & B, Troon $$
southbeach.co.uk - South Beach Hotel, Troon $$$
turnberry.co.uk - Turnberry Hotel $$$$
wildingshotel.com – Wildings Hotel & Restaurant, Maidens $$$

Lodging - Region #3 (E. Lothian)

castleinndirleton.com - Castle Inn, Dirleton $$
glebehouse-nb.co.uk - Glebe House B & B, North Berwick $$$
golfinn.co.uk - Golf Inn, Gullane $$
kaimend.com - Kaimend B & B $$$
kilspindie.co.uk - Kilspindie House Hotel, Aberlady $$$
macdonaldhotels.co.uk - Marine Hotel, North Berwick $$$
netherabbey.co.uk - Nether Abbey, North Berwick $$$
northberwickgolflodge.co.uk - N Berwick Golf Lodge $$$$
northberwickgolflodge.co.uk - Golf Lodge B & B, North Berwick $$
openarmshotel.com - Open Arms Hotel, Dirleton $$$

Lodging - Region #4 (Inverness/Dornoch)

braevalhotel.co.uk - Braeval Hotel, Nairn $$
carnegiehotel.co.uk - Carnegie Lodge Hotel, Tain $$
clubhousenairn.co.uk - Clubhouse Hotel, Nairn $$$
cullodenhouse.co.uk - nr Inverness $$$
dornochbankhouse.com - Bank House, Dornoch $$
dornochcastlehotel.com - Dornoch Castle Hotel, Dornoch $$
dunainparkhotel.co.uk - nr Inverness $$$
highfieldhouse.co.uk - Highfield House, Dornoch B & B $$
glebe-end.co.uk - Glebe End B & B, Nairn $$
golf-view.co.uk - Golf View B & B, Tain $$
golfviewhotelnairn.co.uk - Golf View Hotel, Nairn $$$
greenlawns.uk.com - Greenlawns Guest House, Nairn $$
hotels-of-distinction.com/hotels/royal-marine - Royal Marine, Brora $$$
inveranlodge.co.uk - Inveran Lodge, Nairn $$
invernessbedandbreakfast.co.uk - Inverness Assoc. of B & Bs
mansfieldcastle.co.uk - Mansfield Castle Hotel, Tain $$$
morangiehotel.com - Morangie House Hotel, Tain $$$

moyness.co.uk - Moyness House B & B, Inverness $$
oxfordhotelsandinns.com - Newton Hotel, Nairn $$$
royalgolfhoteldornoch.co.uk - Royal Golf Hotel, Dornoch $$$
sunnybraehotel.co.uk - Sunny Brae Hotel, Nairn $$
sandownhouse.com - Sandown Guest House, Nairn $$$

Lodging - Region #5 (North/Northeast)
aboutscotland.com/aberdeen/savock.html - Savock B & B, Foveran $$
atholl-aberdeen.com - Atholl Hotel, Aberdeen $$
kilmarnockarms.com - Kilmarnock Arms, Cruden Bay $$
marcliffe.com - Marcliffe at Pitfodels, Aberdeen $$$$
mercure.com - Mercure Ardoe House, Aberdeen $$$
redhouse-hotel.com - Red House Hotel, Cruden Bay $$
stolafhotel.co.uk - St. Olaf Hotel, Cruden Bay $$
udny.co.uk - Udny Arms, Newburgh $$$

Lodging - Region #6 (Angus)
aboukirhotel.com - Aboukir Hotel, Carnoustie $$
bbcarnoustie.fsnet.co.uk - Park House, Carnoustie $$
linksviewcarnoustie.com - Linksview GH, Carnoustie $$
morvenhouse.com - Morven House, Carnoustie $$
oldmanorcarnoustie.com - Old Manor B & B, Carnoustie $$
oxfordhotelsandinns.com/ourhotels/carnoustie - Carnoustie Golf Course Hotel $$$
stationhotel.uk.com - Station Hotel, Carnoustie $$
(see also internet listings for lodgings in Dundee, Arbroath, and Montrose)

Lodging - Region #7 (Perthshire/Central)
beinnbhracaigh.com - Beinn Bhracaigh B & B, Pitlochry $$
dunmurray.co.uk - Dunmurray B & B, Pitlochry $$
gleneagles.com - Gleneagles Resort Hotel $$$$
moulinhotel.co.uk - Moulin Hotel, Pitlochry $$
See pitlochry.org for more information

Lodging - Region #8 (Arran/Kintyre/Islay)
bridgend-hotel.com - Bridgend Hotel, Islay $$
craigard-house.co.uk - Campbeltown $$
glenmachrie.com - Glenmachrie B & B, Islay $$
kilmichael.com - Kilmichael Country House Hotel, Arran $$$$
lilybank-arran.co.uk – Lilybank GH, Lamlash, Arran $$
machrie.net - Machrie Hotel & Golf Links nr Port Ellen, Islay $$$
machrihanishdunes.com - Royal Hotel, Ugadale Hotel and Cottages $$$
oatfield.org - Oatfield House nr Campbeltown $$
theislayhotel.com - Islay Hotel, Port Ellen $$
theoldexcisehouse.com - The Old Excise House B & B, Laphroig $$
(for more lodgings on Kintyre see machgolf.com)

APPENDIX D

Daylight Hours, April - October

(Glasgow - Central Scotland - daylight-saving time throughout; times will vary slightly)

Date	Sunrise	Sunset
April 1	6:49 a.m.	7:54 p.m.
April 15	6:13 a.m.	8:22 p.m.
May 1	5:35 a.m.	8:55 p.m.
May 15	5:06 a.m.	9:22 p.m.
June 1	4:41 a.m.	9:50 p.m.
June 15	4:31 a.m.	10:04 p.m.
July 1	4:36 a.m.	10:05 p.m.
July 15	4:52 a.m.	9:53 p.m.
August 1	5:21 a.m.	9:25 p.m.
August 15	5:47 a.m.	8:54 p.m.
September 1	6:20 a.m.	8:12 p.m.
September 15	6:48 a.m.	7:36 p.m.
October 1	7:19 a.m.	6:54 p.m.
October 15	7:47 a.m.	6:18 p.m.

Daylight Saving Time - "British Summer Time" (BST) begins the last Sunday in March and ends on the last Sunday in October

APPENDIX E

Bibliography

General

Blundell, Nigel. *Scotland.* London: PRC Publishing, Ltd., 1998.

Fisher, Andrew. *A Traveller's History of Scotland.* Gloucestershire UK: The Windrush Press, 1990.

Fraser, Elisabeth. *An Illustrated History of Scotland.* Norwich UK: Jarrold Publishing, 1997

Herman, Arthur. *How the Scots Invented the Modern World.* New York: Crown Publishers, 2001.

Sawyer, June Skinner (ed). *The Road North: 300 Years of Classic Scottish Travel Writing*. Glasgow: Neil Wilson Publishing, 2000.

Taylor, Nicola. *Live and Work in Scotland.* Oxford: Vacation Work, 2001.

Tranter, Nigel. *The Story of Scotland.* Moffat, Scotland: Lochar Publishing, 1987.

Fiction: Catherine Coulter, Antonia Fraser, Diana Gabaldon, Margaret George, Neil Gunn, Margot Livesey, Jenifer Roberson, Sir Walter Scott, Jessica Stirling, Nigel Tranter.

Guidebooks

Baxter, John, et. al. *Scotland: Highlands and Islands.* Lincolnwood, IL: Passport Books, 1997

McNeeley, Scott, ed. *Fodor's Scotland.* NY: Random House (Fodor's Travel Publications), revised periodically.

Ramsay, Alex. *Scotland.* London: HarperCollins, 1996.

Wilson, Neil, and Murphy, Alan. Graeme. *Scotland.* Melbourne, Australia: Lonely Planet Publications, 2008.

Williams, David. *Scotland's Best-Loved Driving Tours.* NY: Macmillan Travel, 2007.

Golf

Bamberger, Michael. *To the Linksland: a Golfing Adventure.* NY: Penguin Books, 1992.

Browning, Robert. *A History of Golf: The Royal and Ancient Game.* NY: E.P. Dutton & Company, Inc., 1955.

Campbell, Malcolm. *The Scottish Golf Book.* Edinburgh: Lomond Books, 1999.

Cook, Kevin. *Tommy's Honor: The Story of Old Tom Morris and Young Tom Morris, Golf's Founding Father and Son.* NY: Gotham Books, 2007.

Dodson, James. *Final Rounds: A Father, a Son, the Golf Journey of a Lifetime.* New York: Bantam Books, 1996.

Finegan, James W. *Blasted Heaths and Blessed Greens: A Golfer's Pilgrimage to the Courses of Scotland.* New York: Simon & Schuster, 1996.

________. *Where Golf is Great: The Finest Courses of Scotland and Ireland.* Photography by Laurence Lambrecht and Tim Thompson. NY: Workman Publishing, Inc., 2006.

Gillespie, Curtis. *Playing Through: A Year of Life and Links Along the Scottish Coast.* NY: Scribner, 2003.

Greig, Andrew. *Preferred Lies: A Journey to the Heart of Scottish Golf.* London: Weidenfield & Nicolson, 2006.

Hamilton, David. *Golf: Scotland's Game.* Kilmacolm, Scotland: The Partick Press, 1998.

________. *The Scottish Golf Guide.* Edinburgh: Canongate Books, Ltd., 2009.

Konik, Michael. *In Search of Burningbush: a Story of Golf, Friendship, and the Meaning of Irons.* New York: McGraw-Hill, 2004.

Lowe, Iain Macfarlane with Joy, David, and Phillips, Kyle. *Scottish Golf Links: A Photographer's Journey.* Chelsea, MI: Clock Tower Press, 2004.

McGuire, Brenda and John. *Golf at the Water's Edge: Scotland's Seaside Links.* NY: Abbeville Press, 1997.

Murphy, Michael. *Golf in the Kingdom.* New York: Viking, 1972.

________. *The Kingdom of Shivas Irons.* NY: Broadway Books, 1997.

Peper, George. *Two Years in St. Andrews: At Home on the 18th Hole.* New York: Simon & Schuster, 2006.

__________ and Campbell, Malcolm. *True Links.* NY: Artisan Books, 2010.

Rubenstein, Lorne. *A Season in Dornoch: Golf and Life in the Scottish Highlands.* NY: Simon & Schuster, 2001.

Stewart, Tanner. *Hallowed Ground: A Golf Trip to Scotland.* Baltimore: PublishAmerica, 2004.

Tobert, Michael. *Pilgrims in the Rough: St. Andrews Beyond the 19th Hole.* Edinburgh: Luath Press Ltd., 2000.

Whyte, David J. *Golfer's Guide: Scotland - 150 Courses and Facilities.* London: New Holland Publishers, 2001.

INDEX

Note: Bold page numbers indicate the course profiles in Part III, "The Directory of Courses."

D

G

H

L

M

N

O

P

T

Golf in Scotland can be purchased either in whole or in part in electronic format from Ferguson Golf (1-800-835-6692) or at ***www.fergusongolf.com.***

Updates and corrections to critical information in *Golf in Scotland* will be posted on the Ferguson Golf website.

Wholesale buyers: contact Baker & Taylor or Ferguson Golf.

The Author

Allan McAllister Ferguson was born in Decatur, Illinois, in 1944. As president, chief cook, and bottlewasher of Ferguson Golf since 1999, he personally works with golfers to create memorable trips to Scotland. He typically makes two trips annually to refresh contacts and conduct research. Mr. Ferguson is retired from other businesses. During the 1980s, he and his wife, Ruth Wimmer, changed the look of commercial baby toys with their line of black and white developmental products still sold under the trade name, "Wimmer-Ferguson Child Products." Mr. Ferguson lives in Denver, Colorado.

NOTES

NOTES

NOTES